The Editor

MARGARET HOMANS is Professor of English and Women's, Gender, and Sexuality Studies at Yale University. She is the author of *Bearing the Word: Language and Female Experience in Nineteenth-Century Women's Writing; Royal Representations: Queen Victoria and British Culture, 1837–1876; Women Writers and Poetic Identity: Dorothy Wordsworth, Emily Bronte, and Emily Dickinson; The Imprint of Another Life: Adoption Narratives and Human Possibility;* and editor of *Virginia Woolf: A Collection of Critical Essays.*

For a complete list of Norton Critical Editions, visit
wwnorton.com/nortoncriticals

A NORTON CRITICAL EDITION

Virginia Woolf

TO THE LIGHTHOUSE

AUTHORITATIVE TEXT

CONTEXTS

CRITICISM

Edited by

MARGARET HOMANS

YALE UNIVERSITY

W. W. NORTON & COMPANY

Celebrating a Century of Independent Publishing

W. W. Norton & Company has been independent since its founding in 1923, when William Warder Norton and Mary D. Herter Norton first published lectures delivered at the People's Institute, publishing books by celebrated academics from America and abroad. By midcentury, the two major pillars of Norton's publishing program—trade books and college texts—were firmly established. In the 1950s, the Norton family transferred control of the company to its employees, and today—with a staff of five hundred and hundreds of trade, college, and professional titles published each year—W. W. Norton & Company stands as the largest and oldest publishing house owned wholly by its employees.

Library of Congress Cataloging-in-Publication Data

Names: Woolf, Virginia, 1882–1941, author. | Homans, Margaret, 1952– editor.
Title: To the lighthouse: authoritative text, contexts, criticism / Virginia Woolf; edited by Margaret Homans.
Description: A Norton critical edition. | New York: W.W. Norton and Company, Inc., [2023] |
Series: Norton critical edition | Includes bibliographical references.
Identifiers: LCCN 2022051926 | ISBN 9780393422597 (paperback) | ISBN 9781324045526 (ebook)
Subjects: LCSH: English—Scotland—Fiction. | Skye, Island of (Scotland)—Fiction. | Loss (Psychology)—Fiction. | Summer resorts—Fiction. | Married people—Fiction. | Lighthouses—Fiction. Widowers—Fiction. | Woolf, Virginia, 1882–1941—Criticism and interpretation.
Classification: LCC PR6045.O72 T6 2023c | DDC 823/.912–dc23/eng/20221216
LC record available at https://lccn.loc.gov/2022051926

ISBN: 978-0-393-42259-7 (pbk)

W. W. Norton & Company, Inc., 500 Fifth Avenue, New York, NY 10110
wwnorton.com
W. W. Norton & Company Ltd., 15 Carlisle Street, London W1D 3BS

1 2 3 4 5 6 7 8 9 0

Contents

v

Criticism

Introduction

To the Lighthouse is a book about Virginia Woolf's childhood and her ambivalence about her late parents, represented in the novel by Mr. and Mrs. Ramsay; it is an autobiographical and psychological novel.

To the Lighthouse is a work of social commentary about the end of the Victorian era and the changes in class and gender brought about by the Great War and other political upheavals of the early twentieth century, as measured through changes in the lives of the Ramsay family and their guests.

To the Lighthouse is an intellectual history tracing the dissolution of Victorian certainties and their replacement by early twentieth-century relativisms.

To the Lighthouse is an experiment in reimagining reality on the basis of early twentieth-century scientific discoveries in physics and astronomy.

To the Lighthouse is a political novel about the "Celtic fringe"—Cornwall and/or Scotland—and the dissolving edge between Britain and its internal and global empires; *To the Lighthouse* is about the collapse of the British Empire.

To the Lighthouse is a *künstlerroman* about the development of an artist, Lily Briscoe, that reflects the development of its author.

To the Lighthouse is part of an early twentieth-century conversation about art, the relation of visual to literary art, and the relation of both to life; it is an exercise in turning life into art that is also *about* turning life into art.

To the Lighthouse is a philosophical novel about a conundrum—"think of a table . . . when you're not there"—that is solved when the artist-heroine finally captures her "vision" on canvas.

To the Lighthouse embodies the emergence of modernist literary form: it is a formal experiment in making prose poetic; in multiplying points of view, including some that aren't human; and in representing consciousness and, at times, the unconscious.

To the Lighthouse is an endearingly human book, full of relatable characters; it is also a posthuman one.

To the Lighthouse is a book about memory and the passage of time.

To the Lighthouse is a feminist book; a queer and nonbinary book; an elitist book; an anti-elitist book; it can inspire love, identification, alienation, and anger.

To the Lighthouse is a book about weather.

To the Lighthouse is a ghost story.

The contexts and criticism assembled in this Norton Critical Edition of *To the Lighthouse* are intended to help you, the reader, discover that *To the Lighthouse* is all of these books, and more. What the novel means—what it *is*—has changed for readers over the years since it was first published in 1927, and it continues to change, depending on the contexts in which a reader encounters it and the knowledge and the questions they bring to it. *To the Lighthouse* is a novel that unfolds new meanings when read next to works of art, literature, and intellectual inquiry from Woolf's day to our own. This Introduction outlines some of the major ways the novel has been read and points to the relevant contexts and critical works provided in this edition that will help readers appreciate the novel's many sides.

The Writer, Her Life, and Her Novel

Virginia Woolf left an extraordinarily rich record of her work on *To the Lighthouse*. Her handwritten manuscript can be consulted both in print transcription and online (see A Note on the Text, xliii, and Note on Woolf Online, 151). The Contexts section includes Woolf's Undated Notes and an Outline (161–62) and, in The Composition, Revision, Publication, and Reception of *To the Lighthouse*—A Virginia Woolf Chronology, 1924–28 (163–84), selections from Woolf's notes, her diaries, and her correspondence with friends and family commenting on the entire process of creating the novel. Woolf's starting point was her reflections on her family, especially her father and mother, yet soon other concerns made their way in, whether deliberately or not: her conversations with her sister and with friends about art and writing; her responses to historical events such as the aftereffects of the Great War and the General Strike of May 1926; her thoughts on politics, especially feminist and queer or anti-homophobic politics and the anti-imperial and Labour politics advocated by her husband; her curiosity about developments in philosophy and the sciences, including physics and the new science of psychoanalysis; challenges she set herself as a writer; her complex new relationship with Vita Sackville-West; and her observations on her own sometimes rapidly shifting moods. While working on the novel, Woolf wrote in her diary, "I'm the only woman in England free to write what I like."[1] Some of these concerns are easily visible in the novel and in her other writings at the time, such as the essays she produced while working on the novel and the private documents collected in this edition's Composition Chronology; others remain more implicit and are teased out by studies included in the Criticism section of this book. Even when Woolf was working most intensely on the novel, she continued to produce book reviews and essays for periodicals in Britain and the United States, and some of these are excerpted here, in Essays by Virginia Woolf (247–65), as they illuminate the artistic and philosophical concerns that she simultaneously addressed in *To the Lighthouse*. Because she occasionally dated her manuscript, the Composition Chronology also aligns Woolf's life and thoughts about her work with the progress she was making in writing the novel.

Studies of *To the Lighthouse* often assume that the principal characters and the setting are based on members of her family and their long summer vacations in rural, seaside Cornwall in the 1880s and '90s. The novel is generally seen as the most autobiographical of Woolf's novels, and critics sometimes move back and forth between Leslie Stephen (her father) and Mr. Ramsay, or Julia Stephen (her mother) and Mrs. Ramsay, or Talland House (their summer home) and the Ramsays' house, as if there were little difference between history and fiction. This assumption was fostered by Woolf herself in correspondence and conversation with friends and family, and many of the selections in Contexts refer to and emerge from Woolf's multifaceted life. The Autobiographical Writings (185–202) excerpted here reveal the life experiences and some of the life-writing on which Woolf drew, from her earliest scene-shaping in the handwritten newspaper she produced as a child, to her journal on revisiting Cornwall as a young adult, to memoirs—"Reminiscences" (191–94) and

---

1. September 22, 1925. Virginia Woolf, *The Diary of Virginia Woolf*, ed. Anne Olivier Bell, vol. 3: 1925–30 (San Diego: Harcourt, Brace, 1980), p. 43. Hereafter cited as *Diary* with volume and page numbers. Hogarth Press, the publishing house she and Leonard founded in 1917, published all of her novels after *The Voyage Out* (1915) and *Night and Day* (1919). "The others," she continued, "must be thinking of series & editors."

"A Sketch of the Past" (195–202)—that she wrote later on. Readers of these sources will find strong, even uncanny, resonances between her life and the novel. The same may be true if you read the excerpt from Leslie Stephen's memoir about Julia Stephen, *The Mausoleum Book* (210–15), accompanied by the idealizing visual images of her by Edward Burne-Jones and Julia Margaret Cameron that the memoir refers to.

Among the Criticism selections chosen for this Norton Critical Edition and discussed in this Introduction are also critical approaches that make use of these biographical sources, emphasizing to varying degrees Woolf's personal connection with issues the novel raises. For example, Woolf's family history on both sides linked her to Britain's empire: her mother was born in India and her father's family included men who worked in the Indian Civil Service (as did her husband Leonard before becoming a dedicated critic of empire). These connections both grounded her mockery of empire and made it difficult for her to see the racial and class hierarchies from which she benefited. In the Criticism section, Urmila Seshagiri (312–26) reads the novel's themes of imperialism and racial differentiation in part on the basis of those personal connections. Also drawing on biographical sources are feminist approaches such as those included here by Adrienne Rich (290–92) and Rachel Bowlby (293–305) that focus on what Freud called the "family romance."[2] Although Woolf's tone was irreverent when the Hogarth Press began publishing Freud—she reported that "all the psycho-analyst books have been dumped in a fortress the size of Windsor castle in ruins upon the floor"[3]—she later said that in writing the novel she did for herself "what psycho-analysts do for their patients" (198).

The novel's investigation of fraught family relationships—fathers and sons, mothers and daughters—and of the relation between the private family and public life may draw on biographical sources, but the investigation is more than personal. As Woolf's biographer Hermione Lee points out, the novel is no "simple transcription of Virginia Stephen's family life."[4] No one character stands in for Woolf, whose experiences can be seen refracted in several characters: not only daughter figures such as Lily Briscoe and Cam Ramsay but also the questing intellectual Mr. Ramsay. More importantly,

2. Freud's 1909 coinage in the essay "Family Romances" refers to the intense, conflicted, and often eroticized relationships among nuclear family members: mothers and sons, fathers and daughters, mothers and daughters, and the triangle of mother, son, and father.
3. July 20, 1924, to Marjorie Joad, an employee of the press. Virginia Woolf, *The Letters of Virginia Woolf*, ed. Nigel Nicolson and Joanne Trautmann, vol. 3: 1923–28 (New York: Harcourt, Brace, 1977), p. 119. Hereafter cited as *Letters* with volume and page numbers. In 1924 Hogarth Press, at the instigation of James Strachey (1887–1967), took over the publication of Freud's multivolume *Collected Papers*. James was the brother of Virginia and Leonard's friend Lytton Strachey and had studied with Freud and translated his writings.
4. Hermione Lee, *Virginia Woolf: A Biography* (New York: Knopf, 1997), p. 474.

one of the novel's central themes is the difficult process through which artists transform life into art. That complex transformation is the subject of "Life and the Novelist" (255–57), a review Woolf wrote while working on *To the Lighthouse*. In an essay written as she finished her revisions, "Poetry, Fiction and the Future" (257–65), Woolf said that she wanted literature to become impersonal, to step back from life, and long after publishing the novel she wrote: "I don't like being exposed as a novelist and told my people are my mother and father, when, being in a novel, they're not."[5] Biographical sources are provided in this edition, but it is up to the reader to decide what these connections may mean for reading the novel.

Kabe Wilson's essay (243–46) linking Vanessa Bell's 1927 cover for the novel with his 2020 painting of two lighthouses on the south coast of Britain, close to the Sussex homes of Woolf and Bell, shows how limiting it can be when readers assume a one-to-one correspondence between the novel and the Stephen family summer home in Cornwall. Once the novel's lighthouse comes unstuck from the lighthouse on Godrevy Island in Carbis Bay, Cornwall, that it has long been thought to portray, it becomes possible to observe a complex, multimedia exchange among Woolf, Bell, and other Sussex painters about British lighthouses, the locations they mark and guard, and the changing historical meaning of Britain's coastal defenses. "Nothing was simply one thing. The other Lighthouse was true too," thinks James, as the sailboat draws near (135).

Works of art and writings by Woolf's family members and friends appear in the Contexts section following the selection of Autobiographical Writings. These materials are included for more than biographical reasons: they shed light on the intellectual and social crosscurrents in which Woolf wrote *To the Lighthouse*. Both her mother and her father were writers: Leslie Stephen (210–15 and 219–23) was a historian of ideas, a philosopher, and a memoirist; Julia Stephen (206–10) wrote stories for children and nonfiction on nursing and household management; and *To the Lighthouse* engages with them as authors, as parents, and as Victorian ideologues of gender, class, and empire. (Woolf was able to be quite impartial in her judgment: looking back, she wrote of her father's books, "I find not a subtle mind; not an imaginative mind; not a suggestive mind. But a strong mind; a healthy out of door, moor striding mind; an impatient, limited mind; a conventional mind . . . It was a black and white world compared with ours."[6]) Woolf's sister, the painter Vanessa Bell (233–34), not only provided a striking model of the woman artist and, in her paintings, examples of the problems artists

---

5. *Letters* 6: 464, January 25, 1941.
6. "A Sketch of the Past," in *Moments of Being*, ed. Jeanne Schulkind, 2nd ed. (San Diego: Harcourt Brace Jovanovich, 1985), p. 115.

set themselves, problems of design and of representation; she also connected Woolf with major art theorists of their day: her husband, Clive Bell (235–39), and her friend and (for a brief period) her lover Roger Fry (239–43). Woolf's father, her sister, her brother-in-law, and her close friend Roger Fry all reflected on the relation of art to life, and this Norton Critical Edition's selections of their art and writing on art add yet another dimension to the question of *To the Lighthouse*'s relation to the author's life—and to "life" more generally.

Capturing Reality: Philosophy, Science, and Visual Art

In her early essay "Modern Fiction," often considered Woolf's manifesto for the modernist art she was just beginning to write, she argues that then fashionable novels detailing the material circumstances of their characters may appear lifelike but actually fail to capture "life or spirit, truth or reality," and that—because "life is a luminous halo, a semi-transparent envelope surrounding us from the beginning of consciousness to the end"—new literary methods are required to "convey this varying, this unknown and uncircumscribed spirit."[7] Beginning in 1917 Woolf had been publishing short stories that tried out new ways of capturing "life," and prior to *To the Lighthouse*, her novels *Jacob's Room* (1922) and *Mrs. Dalloway* (1925) had experimented at greater length with representing the immaterial reality Woolf believed should be a novel's subject. *To the Lighthouse* not only continues this methodological and stylistic experimentation; it also addresses questions about "reality"—what it is, and how to represent it—as subject matter. In the vibrant early twentieth-century intellectual and artistic milieu in which Woolf lived and wrote, revolutionary investigations into the nature and representation of reality were ongoing in the realms of science, philosophy, and art; *To the Lighthouse* reflects Woolf's engagement with these discourses as they helped to shape her own unique approach to conveying "life or spirit, truth or reality."

To the Lighthouse is constructed in three parts: "The Window," which takes place over the course of a day in 1908 or 1909; "Time Passes," which rapidly covers the passage of ten years; and "The Lighthouse," which covers another single day. Early in "The Window," in a flashback within a conversation with Mr. Bankes, the painter Lily Briscoe thinks about Andrew Ramsay's explanation of his father's philosophical work: "'Subject and object and the nature of reality,'

---

7. Virginia Woolf, *The Essays of Virginia Woolf*, vol. 4: *1925–28*, ed. Andrew McNeillie (Orlando: Harcourt, 1994), pp. 157–65, quotations 160. Hereafter cited as *Essays* with volume and page number. The first version of "Modern Fiction" was published as "Modern Novels" in 1919. Woolf revised it for publication in her essay collection *The Common Reader* in 1925.

Andrew had said." These terms prove too abstract for Lily. "'Think of a kitchen table then,' he told her, 'when you're not there'" (20). As a result, Lily always sees a "phantom kitchen table," like the one "lodged now in the fork of a pear tree," as she walks in the orchard while reminding Mr. Bankes to "think of his work." Using an imaginary table to concretize Mr. Ramsay's philosophical work turns out to be a sly joke, because across the long history of debates about this problem, one philosopher after another has used the example of a table to investigate whether or not objects can be proven to exist independently of human perceptions of them. Mr. Ramsay will have solved this knotty problem if he can prove that the table exists without a human perceiver ("when you're not there").

Idealist philosophers such as Bishop George Berkeley (1685–1753) believed that God's perception of the world could be relied on to prove the existence of objects apart from human perceptions of them. The problem became more difficult for those who refused to believe in God or in any innate ideas, a tradition of skeptical empiricists such as David Hume (1711–1776) whose philosophical systems were constructed to depend only on the evidence of the senses. The Contexts section includes a series of meditations on tables that lie behind Lily's amusing vision: excerpts from Leslie Stephen's *History of English Thought in the Eighteenth Century* (220–21) centering on Hume, from Stephen's own philosophical work (his essay "What Is Materialism?" [221–23]), and from Woolf's contemporary the philosopher Bertrand Russell (223–26), all of them using a table to discuss what an object is and how it may be known. Russell contrasts a table seen by one individual to a dinner table surrounded by ten guests, each of them seeing it differently, an image anticipating the disparate points of view around Mrs. Ramsay's dinner table.[8]

Contemporary developments in physics and astronomy, too, raised questions about the reality of the table. The popular science writer Arthur Eddington, introducing a lecture series he gave as Woolf was finishing *To the Lighthouse*, drew a contrast between two tables—the illusory one produced by human perceptions of its appearance and the real one made of atoms—to describe how new understandings of particle physics, particularly the perpetual motion of electrons, destabilize the taken-for-granted solidity of objects. The essay by Paul Tolliver Brown (226–31) provides background on the theory of

8. On philosophy and *To the Lighthouse* see Ann Banfield, *The Phantom Table: Woolf, Fry, Russell and the Epistemology of Modernism* (Cambridge: Cambridge UP, 2000); and Gillian Beer, "Hume, Stephen, and Elegy in *To the Lighthouse*," in *Virginia Woolf: The Common Ground* (Ann Arbor: U of Michigan P, 1996), pp. 29–47; on Woolf and Russell, see also Timothy Mackin, "Private Worlds, Public Minds: Woolf, Russell, and Photographic Vision," *Journal of Modern Literature* 33.3 (2010): 112–30; and Emily Dalgarno, "Reality and Perception: Philosophical Approaches to *To the Lighthouse*," in *The Cambridge Companion to* To the Lighthouse, ed. Alison Pease (Cambridge: Cambridge UP, 2015), pp. 69–79.

relativity and quantum physics and suggests how they are reflected in the two tables in *To the Lighthouse*: the spare, stark table of Mr. Ramsay's philosophical speculations and the amply laden dining table where Mrs. Ramsay seats her guests. Despite Mr. Ramsay's logic-driven endeavor to imagine the table with no one there, an object divided from any perceiving subject, the world of the novel is a relativistic one, with shifts in reality that occur with shifts of perspective, and with permeable boundaries between subjects and objects.[9]

The questions raised by the "table . . . when you're not there" pervade the novel. In "Time Passes," the house, left empty soon after the events of "The Window," is abandoned because of Mrs. Ramsay's death and the onset of the Great War, the "downpouring of immense darkness" that arrives once "the lamps were all extinguished" (94). "Time Passes" tests out the existence of objects without perceivers. Ann Banfield shows that Woolf's "eyeless" vision matches Bertrand Russell's assertion that the world of objects does exist and can be known apart from human perception. The ordinary hierarchy between human subjects and objects is reversed: the weather, the house, and the garden have agency and no concern for human needs, while events in the Ramsay family are reported briefly and matter-of-factly, as if they were of little interest. No distinction is made between destruction wrought by nature and the violence of the war; the weeds are already tapping at the window-panes, the shawl has already loosened a fold or two, when "ominous sounds like the measured blows of hammers dulled on felt . . . further loosened the shawl and cracked the tea-cups" (99): At this point, Andrew is killed by a bomb exploding in France, but his death, like others, is minimized by being placed in brackets. With no human eye to observe, there's no difference between the lovely fertility and the terrible chaos of the decaying house.

This demotion of the human subject can seem to reach a cruel dead end (and see below on the debate about Mrs. McNab's humanity), yet Maurizia Boscagli finds that "Time Passes" optimistically asks: "what endures in the absence of the subject?"[1] She argues that, precisely because of the novel's permeable boundaries between objects and perceiving subjects (Mrs. Ramsay "became the thing she looked at," 50), the material remnants in the house preserve the imprint of the humans, the memory of Mrs. Ramsay still held by her empty cloak and shawl. This decentering of the human subject anticipates an environmental ethics. Elsa Högberg points out that Russell's philosophy and "Time Passes" together provide rich resources for a twenty-first century anti-anthropocentric ethics of

9. On Woolf and physics and astronomy, see also Holly Henry, *Virginia Woolf and the Discourse of Science* (Cambridge: Cambridge UP, 2003).
1. Maurizia Boscagli, *Stuff Theory: Everyday Objects, Radical Materialism* (New York: Bloomsbury, 2014), p. 200.

humility, an ethics urgently needed in our time of ecological collapse.[2] A closely related environmental ethics is also visible in Woolf's 1924 essay "Thunder at Wembley" (247–49).

When the human subjects return in "The Lighthouse," their relation to the world of objects has changed. Nothing has meaning after so much death and destruction; for Lily, "words fluttered sideways and struck the object inches too low" (129). But the novel's ending affirms as a positive value the independent reality of objects, an affirmation made possible by the terrible losses and the painful, necessary rebalancing of subject and object in "Time Passes." Annoyed by his failure to solve his philosophical problem in "The Window," Mr. Ramsay thinks, echoing Dr. Johnson's famous saying, "the very stone one kicks with one's boot will outlast Shakespeare" (29). But when the sailboat arrives at the lighthouse, this self-centered lament becomes the positive answer to his own philosophical query. From the bow of the boat "he sprang, lightly like a young man, holding his parcel, on to the rock." To James, he looks "as if he were saying, 'There is no God,' and Cam thought, as if he were leaping into space" (149). To leap onto the rock in this way is to affirm the reality of objects in a modern, secular world: that he knows the rock is "there" proves that the table (in his old philosophical puzzle) remains "when you're not there." Mr. Ramsay's losses ironically enable this conclusion to his intellectual quest.

Lily, too, has been working out her own version of "subject and object and the nature of reality." As a painter, she is deeply concerned with the relation between the mind and external reality, and her focus on the look and feel of the kitchen table she sees when she thinks of Mr. Ramsay's work—"one of those scrubbed board tables, grained and knotted" (20)—is another instance of the novel's permeable boundary between mind and world. Her vision of the table renders in comical form her endeavor, both in "The Window" and in "The Lighthouse," to capture with paint her "vision which she had seen clearly once." In order to paint it, she must find her internal vision outside of herself "among hedges and houses and mothers and children" (43), and "this passage from conception to work [is] as dreadful as any down a dark passage for a child" (17).[3]

2. Elsa Högberg, "Virginia Woolf's Object-Oriented Ecology," in *Virginia Woolf: Writing the World*, ed. Pamela L. Caughie and Diana L. Swanson (Clemson U Digital P, 2015); for more on objects in *To the Lighthouse* see Graham Fraser, "Solid Objects/Ghosts of Chairs: Virginia Woolf and the Afterlife of Things," *Journal of Modern Literature* 43.2 (2020): 80–97; and for an environmentalist treatment of weather in *To the Lighthouse* see Bonnie Kime Scott, "Ecocritical Woolf," in *A Companion to Virginia Woolf*, ed. Jessica Berman (Oxford: Wiley Blackwell, 2016), pp. 319–31.

3. Painter and critic Suzanne Bellamy not only wrote about Lily's painting but also attempted to paint it, as a triptych: see "'Painting the Words:' A Version of Lily Briscoe's Paintings from *To the Lighthouse*," in *Virginia Woolf: Turning the Centuries*, ed. Ann Ardis and Bonnie Kime Scott (New York: Pace UP, 2000), pp. 244–51.

Lily's struggle with her painting is the reverse of the problem Mr. Ramsay works on, since he—like Hume and Russell—is trying to establish not the power of the mind but rather the independent existence of objects. Nonetheless the problem of the mind's relation to the world, posed as the relation between the artist's abstract design and the observable appearances of life, is the central problem explored and debated, both in paint and in words, by the modernist artists and art theorists who surrounded Woolf: her sister Vanessa Bell, her brother-in-law Clive Bell, and their friend Roger Fry. Woolf's essay "Pictures" (250–53) indicates some of the ways she responded to these influences. Clive insisted that "representation" should always be subordinate to "significant form," or form for its own sake. Fry's views evolved from an equally firm advocacy for abstract design, as in Post-Impressionist painting—he thought that writers should follow the Post-Impressionists and "fling representation to the winds"—to a more nuanced view that acknowledged the emotional value of references to life.[4] Vanessa's paintings—such as the one reproduced here—almost always refer to recognizable objects, scenes, and people (she made only a few purely abstract paintings) while also presenting their colorful shapes as an arrangement of abstract forms. Woolf admired the "silence" of her paintings and her levelling of the distinction between human and object. In the forward to a 1930 Vanessa Bell exhibition catalogue, Woolf praises the "emotion" the pictures give the viewer without recourse to "stories," "psychology," or "morality": in a phrasing that recalls the posthumanism of "Time Passes," what may appear to be "portraits . . . are pictures of flesh which happens from its texture or its modelling to be aesthetically on an equality with the China pot or the chrysanthemum."[5]

Lily's explanation to Mr. Bankes of her painting in "The Window" places her squarely within this modernist art discourse. Mr. Bankes has a traditionalist's liking for representational art; his favorite picture is "of the cherry trees in blossom on the banks of the Kennet" where "he had spent his honeymoon" (42); the painting is meaningful for its reminder of a lived experience in a real place. Looking at Lily's painting, he asks her what is meant by a "triangular purple shape, 'just there'?"

> It was Mrs. Ramsay reading to James, she said. She knew his objection—that no one could tell it for a human shape. But she had made no attempt at likeness, she said. For what reason had

4. Virginia Woolf, *Roger Fry: A Biography* (New York: Harcourt, Brace, 1940), 172. For more of Roger Fry's writings, see *A Roger Fry Reader*, ed. Christopher Reed (Chicago: U of Chicago P, 1966) and Roger Fry, *Vision and Design* (London: Chatto & Windus, 1920).
5. Virginia Woolf, *The Essays of Virginia Woolf*, vol. 5: 1929–32, ed. Stuart N. Clarke (Orlando: Harcourt, 2009), pp. 139–40.

she introduced them then? he asked. Why indeed?—except that
if there, in that corner, it was bright, here, in this, she felt the
need of darkness. . . . Mother and child then—objects of universal veneration, and in this case the mother was famous for
her beauty—might be reduced, he pondered, to a purple shadow
without irreverence. (42)

Despite the prominence of the abstract "purple triangle," the painting
doesn't simply privilege design over representation. Lily is definitely
painting Mrs. Ramsay, for she has set up her canvas in just this spot
and has asked Mrs. Ramsay not to move. Moreover, Mrs. Ramsay's
private self-representation is a "wedge-shaped core of darkness" (49),
as if Lily's triangle were after all not an abstract shape but an uncannily apt description; and the triangle shape may refer, as well, to the
prehistoric, archetypal figure for the mother. Lily finds it difficult
to explain what Roger Fry would later call "the double nature of
painting:"[6] "the picture was not of them, she said. Or not in his sense.
There were other senses too in which one might reverence them. By a
shadow here and a light there, for instance. Her tribute took that form
if, as she vaguely supposed, a picture must be a tribute" (42). Were she
to paint the figures as recognizable individuals, she would fall into
the "materialist" novelists' error of mistaking description for "life
or spirit, truth or reality," and yet she cannot altogether discard
Mrs. Ramsay's appearance, as when Vanessa Bell painted family and
friends as at once a pattern of colorful shapes and as human figures
in *Studland Beach* (234).[7] Nor can she altogether escape the iconic
resonance of "mother and child." These questions about the relation
between art and life, design and representation, Woolf also directly
addresses in the essay "Life and the Novelist" (255–57), written just
as she completed the manuscript of *To the Lighthouse*.

Lily's attention now turns to her second painterly problem, the
"question . . . how to connect this mass on the right hand with that
on the left" (43), and it is this compositional problem that she continues to work on for the rest of the novel, although it will turn out
that these two problems (of representation and of connection) are
the same. At dinner, she moves a salt cellar to a sprig in the table-
cloth to remind herself to "put the tree further in the middle" so as
to "avoid that awkward space" (65), and when Lily starts her painting again ten years later, with a fresh canvas propped in the old location, she recalls her plan to "move the tree to the middle" (108).
This problem of bridging a central space is a problem posed also in

---

6. Roger Fry, "The Double Nature of Painting," in *A Roger Fry Reader*, pp. 380–92.
7. Lisa Tickner reads Bell's *Studland Beach* as "Vanessa's *To the Lighthouse*," as a painting
   that, like Lily's, connects abstract forms with "life:" "Vanessa Bell: *Studland Beach*,
   Domesticity, and 'Significant Form,'" *Representations* 65 (Winter 1999): 63–92. Vanessa's portraits, including those of her sister, tend to have featureless faces.

Vanessa Bell's *Studland Beach*, in which "masses" to left and right surround a blank, open space in the middle; Woolf hinted in a letter that Vanessa still had not solved the problem (Composition Chronology, 170). At the dinner, Lily had connected this design solution with the solution to a problem in her own life: seeing the salt cellar on the tablecloth reminds her "she need not marry . . . she need not undergo that degradation" (77). Moving the tree to the middle affirms her cherished independence as an artist, in defiance of Mrs. Ramsay's insistence. Later when recalling her friendship with Mr. Bankes and the vicissitudes of the Rayleys' marriage, Lily again links the solution to her design to the solution to her life: "she had been looking at the table-cloth, and it had flashed upon her that she would move the tree to the middle, and need never marry anybody, and she had felt an enormous exultation" (128). She then recalls her conversation with Mr. Bankes: the painting is both of Mrs. Ramsay and not of her, it might or might not be reverent, and thus its form expresses her ambivalent feelings for Mrs. Ramsay.

The formal problem of connecting two masses thus becomes a representational one, and when Lily draws her line in the center at the very end, she captures two realities at once: the representational or objective reality of the scene she describes, and the subjective reality of her "vision," or, in the terms used by Clive Bell and by Roger Fry, both the representation of "life" and abstract or "significant form." Like Mr. Ramsay, Lily too resolves the problem of "subject and object and the nature of reality." And when Woolf has both her philosopher and her artist work out "the nature of reality"—what it is, how to know it, how to capture it—she is at the same time reflecting on, and working through, her own questions about writing fiction: how can a novel both represent life and create meaning through abstract form?

Modernist Form: Design, Consciousness, and Poetry

Woolf's notes for *To the Lighthouse* begin with a diagram that looks like an abstract design, as if she were thinking like a modern painter. It has an architectural look, and the words above it read: "Two blocks joined by a corridor" (see Woolf's Undated Notes and an Outline, 161). The "blocks"—rooms, spaces, or just shapes—are roughly square, and the "corridor" looks like a narrow passage connecting them. The block on the left, the corridor, and the block on the right correspond to the three parts of the novel: "The Window," "Time Passes," and "The Lighthouse." Looking back later, Woolf wrote that in *To the Lighthouse*, she "made shapes square up."[8] The two symmetrical blocks are mirror images of one another, and everything

8. *Diary* 3: 203.

that occurs in the left-hand block occurs again on the right, but differently (the journey to the lighthouse that doesn't happen, and then does; Lily's painting; a shared meal—and much else). The diagram also calls attention to the novel's inversion of large and small, which in "Modern Fiction" Woolf claimed would characterize the novel that conveys "reality."[9] Nothing much happens in the large blocks of "The Window" and "The Lighthouse": privileged people share a summer evening and a dinner party, children go to bed, a couple reads after dinner; then, a sailboat crosses a peaceful bay and a woman paints at an easel on the lawn. The big events, by contrast, many of them terrifying, are squeezed into the corridor, so compressed it's easy to miss some of them, especially those that happen in brackets, as if they were almost irrelevant.[1]

That the word "corridor," with its analog "passage," is important thematically shows the interdependence of the novel's abstract design and its content. As we have seen, Lily's early struggle with her painting is "as dreadful as any down a dark passage for a child" (17). In a disconcerting echo, "passage" recurs in "Time Passes" when Mr. Ramsay reacts to Mrs. Ramsay's sudden death, his arms stretched out yet empty, "stumbling along a passage one dark morning" (96).[2] The loss of Mrs. Ramsay is thus verbally linked to the struggle to paint one's "vision." And ten years later, registering how everything Mrs. Ramsay stood for has "faded and gone," Lily can "see her there at the end of the corridor of years" (127). The corridor or passage is at once a key feature of Woolf's design and her image for the transformations brought by the passing of time—both for her characters and for her own practice as novelist. The novel, Pamela L. Caughie (306–11) points out, is the story of its own composition, just as it both represents and constructs the relationship between life and art.

The compellingly simple structure that Woolf maintained throughout the composition of the novel upholds any amount of detail and elaboration, just as Lily sees her painting as "colour burning on a framework of steel; the light of a butterfly's wing lying upon the arches of a cathedral" (39). As we have seen, this novel about the growth and development of an artist puts into practice the artist's questions about capturing reality, and her final "line there, in the centre" (150) completes both Lily's painting and the novel itself.

---

9. "Let us not take it for granted that life exists more fully in what is commonly thought big than in what is commonly thought small," *Essays* 4: 161.
1. On Woolf's use of brackets, see Kate McGloughlin, "Woolf's Crochets: Textual Cryogenics in *To the Lighthouse*," *Textual Practice* 28.6 (2014): 949–67.
2. Woolf kept rewriting this shocking passage: it is phrased and punctuated differently in the uncorrected proofs and in the separate corrections she made for the UK and US editions; see Selected Textual Variants (154). Another variation: in "A Sketch of the Past," Woolf describes herself (not her father) stretching out her arms in a corridor following her mother's death, *Moments of Being*, p. 91.

As Woolf wrote her way into the novel's final section, its shape changed from the simple "block" of the diagram: with Mrs. Ramsay no longer present to hold the narrative together, the structure of "The Lighthouse" zigzags between Lily painting onshore and the sailboat crossing the bay. The intercutting between the two simultaneous narratives can be jarring, yet its modernist angularity accomplishes something not less than but different from the reassuring Victorian cohesion that characterized Mrs. Ramsay's domestic art (and Woolf's art) in "The Window." Decentered, Mr. Ramsay making his leap onto the island is just one of two conclusions; there need be no center, or only the merest "line . . . in the centre," which, like the "corridor," may divide as well as join. (You can see Woolf thinking about this design problem in the Composition Chronology, 173.) The practitioner of modernist art—Lily, and Woolf herself—brings into existence a daring new design.

Woolf considered dedicating *To the Lighthouse* to Roger Fry, who had urged her to write like an abstract painter. Woolf valued his delight in extending art theory to literature and wrote that "many of his theories held good for both arts. Design, rhythm, texture—there they were again—in Flaubert as in Cézanne."[3] The novel's three-part design—its "framework of steel"—echoes Fry's emphasis on abstract design, and her depiction of Lily painting to a rhythm (and her contemporaneous discussion of rhythm in a letter to Vita Sackville-West, 169) may owe something to Fry's view that rhythm is one of the key formal elements of any work of art.[4] Fry was an early admirer of Woolf's style, praising her story "Mark on the Wall" for "us[ing] language as a medium of art [and] mak[ing] the very texture of the words have a meaning and quality really almost apart from what you are talking about."[5] Yet as a novelist, she was bound as well to the novelist's task of conveying life objectively—"what you are talking about"—as well as subjectively via "texture" or "art": prose as well as poetry.

Woolf's conversation with Fry about art sometimes turned to the differing affordances of poetry and prose. Fry thought poetry more compatible than prose with his kind of formalism (he was a devotee of French poet Stéphane Mallarmé), and when he wanted to pay a compliment, he described *Mrs. Dalloway* to his friend Charles Mauron as "a very beautiful book . . . a novel poem."[6] He hoped Mauron might translate it into French, and he later arranged for Mauron to translate "Time Passes," the most lyrical of the novel's sections, rendered all the more so by Woolf's detaching it from the novel's plot and characters.

3. *Roger Fry*, p. 240.
4. Roger Fry, "An Essay on Aesthetics," *Vision and Design*, pp. 11–26.
5. Letter of October 18, 1918, to Woolf, quoted in Frances Spalding, *Roger Fry: Art and Life* (Berkeley: U of California P, 1980), p. 212.
6. *Letters of Roger Fry*, ed. Denys Sutton, 2 vols. (London: Chatto & Windus, 1972), vol. 2, p. 562.

During the period when she was writing *To the Lighthouse*, Woolf discussed the relative claims of prose and poetry with Vita Sackville-West (see Composition Chronology, 170) and wrote essays that find value in saturating prose with poetry: "Impassioned Prose" (253–55) and "Poetry, Fiction and the Future" (257–65), later retitled "The Narrow Bridge of Art." Could the form of the novel become more poetic; could it focus less on the "appalling narrative business of the realist: getting on from lunch to dinner,"[7] and more on states of mind? In "Modern Fiction," in which Woolf described the novelist's task as conveying "life or spirit, truth or reality," she also wrote that the novel must avoid narrative conventions—"no plot, no comedy, no tragedy, no love interest or catastrophe in the accepted style"—if it is to portray "life," or "an ordinary mind on an ordinary day."[8] She had long disliked the label "novel," tried out the term "elegy" for *To the Lighthouse* (165), and in a short, funny essay, "What Is a Novel?" listed a long string of alternative labels and proclaimed "there is no such thing as 'a novel.'"[9] Perhaps when Woolf wrote in *A Room of One's Own* that some of the great nineteenth-century women novelists should have written histories or operas, so awkwardly do their creative impulses fit the only form that was open to them, she was thinking of herself as well. She stretched the boundaries of the novel in prose.

Carrying out her purpose to portray "an ordinary mind on an ordinary day," *To the Lighthouse* represents its characters' minds from the inside: initially, James Ramsay's followed by his mother's. The narrative perspective touches down in many character's minds, sometimes for pages at a time, sometimes just for part of a sentence; at the dinner party, as David Bradshaw puts it, the "point of view is passed around the dining-table like a bottle of wine."[1] The varying point of view echoes Woolf's interest in Russell's claim that reality shifts depending on the angle of vision, a situation he explains with the image of a dinner table. As many readers have observed, Woolf provides not so much a continuous "stream of consciousness" (the term generally used for the modernist innovation of giving extended representation to the inner thoughts of a single mind) as a continuously varying account that reveals a character's conscious or unconscious thoughts sometimes in language that can be attributed to them (Mrs. Ramsay or Lily, often though not always), sometimes in language that could only be provided by a narrator at a remove (James, or the interior snapshots that mock Mr. Ramsay's vanity).

---

7. *Diary* 3: 209, November 28, 1928.
8. *Essays* 4: 160.
9. *Essays* 4: 415–16, written while Woolf corrected the proofs of *To the Lighthouse*.
1. David Bradshaw, Introduction, *To the Lighthouse*, Oxford World's Classics (Oxford: Oxford UP, 2006), p. xlv.

Erich Auerbach's influential 1946 book chapter "The Brown Stocking" (287–90) singled out *To the Lighthouse* to typify the revolution in modernist fiction associated with stream of consciousness; he emphasizes the departure of the authoritative narrator, whether first or third person. Michael Levenson, however, has recently revisited Auerbach's reading to show how complexly Woolf nuances the novel's angles of vision, not so much giving up on omniscience as blending it carefully with the characters' inner visions.[2]

Woolf had already practiced the narrative method of *To the Lighthouse* in *Mrs. Dalloway*, where the perspective shifts from character to character, occasionally lodging in an impersonal viewpoint. She further develops this method here, making the shifts often more rapid, subtle, and ambiguous and devoting a longer section—most of "Time Passes"—to an "eyeless" view from nowhere. She wondered if she had reached the final form of her method in *To the Lighthouse*, worrying that thereafter she would start to repeat herself (see Composition Chronology, 174).

The stylistic innovation of *To the Lighthouse*, then, as suggested above, is not so much its narration of subjective states as something else rising to prominence in Woolf's conversations of the time: its poetry. In "Impassioned Prose," some of which she drafted in the manuscript of *To the Lighthouse*, she praises De Quincey's innovative prose in autobiographical writings where the "scenes have something of the soundlessness and the lustre of dreams" while "facts" are few, only those "chosen for the sake of some adventitious quality—that it fitted in here, or was the right colour to go there" (255). Note the echo of Lily's explanation to Mr. Bankes as to why she placed the purple triangle "just there." Both formulations in turn echo the belief that the forms in a painting should be arranged for their own sakes, not for the sake of reference outside the work. De Quincey's prose makes us ask whether the novelist might capture poetry in prose. The Early Reviews (281–86) of the novel repeatedly call it "lyrical."

"Poetry, Fiction and the Future," based on a lecture Woolf gave the same month *To the Lighthouse* was published, speculates even more broadly about infusing prose with poetry.[3] For an age of conflict and contradiction in which "the mind is full of monstrous, hybrid, unmanageable emotions" and "life is infinitely beautiful yet repulsive" (258), lyric poetry is too frail and too "aloof." Since prose is habituated to "dirty work . . . it may be possible that prose is going to take over— has indeed, already taken over—some of the duties which were once discharged by poetry" (261–62). The capacious new literary form

---

2. Michael Levenson, "Narrative Perspective in *To the Lighthouse*," in *The Cambridge Companion to* To the Lighthouse, pp. 19–29.
3. Emily Kopley explores Woolf's ambivalence about verse and her interest in "poetry" more broadly defined in *Virginia Woolf and Poetry* (Oxford: Oxford UP, 2021).

Woolf imagines, suited to "the modern mind" (261), will transcend individual characters and their personal dramas, especially the courtship plot, to give the reader "some more impersonal relationship. We long for ideas, for dreams, for imaginations, for poetry" (263). Although the essay's interest in blending drama into the generic mix along with prose and poetry has led readers to call it a forerunner of *The Waves* (which Woolf called a "playpoem" and which adapts the form of the dramatic monologue), "Poetry, Fiction and the Future" also reflects the just-completed *To the Lighthouse*, which brims over with "poetry" and "imaginations" that transform ugliness or grief into beauty, that pause the forward progress of the narrative, and that are more beautiful than they need to be, such as these lines in "Time Passes:"

> Let the wind blow; let the poppy seed itself and the carnation mate with the cabbage. Let the swallow build in the drawing-room, and the thistle thrust aside the tiles, and the butterfly sun itself on the faded chintz of the arm-chairs. Let the broken glass and the china lie out on the lawn and be tangled over with grass and wild berries. (103)

Although Woolf wrote equivocally in her diary that "the lyric portions . . . are collected in the 10 year lapse, & don't interfere with the text so much as usual,"[4] poetry saturates "The Window" and "The Lighthouse" as well. Words have poetic, incantatory power near the end of "The Window," when Mrs. Ramsay talks Cam to sleep: "she could see the words echoing as she spoke them rhythmically in Cam's mind" as she tells her daughter to "dream of mountains and valleys and stars falling and parrots and antelopes and gardens, and everything lovely" (87). And in "The Lighthouse," when Cam looks back at the island from the boat, words form rhythmically in her mind, as if she were echoing her mother's poetic style as it blends with her father's habitual chant:

> She was thinking how all those paths and the lawn, thick and knotted with the lives they had lived there, were gone: were rubbed out; were past; were unreal, and now this was real; the boat and the sail with its patch; Macalister with his earrings; the noise of the waves—all this was real. Thinking this, she was murmuring to herself, "We perished, each alone," for her father's words broke and broke again in her mind. (121)

A few pages later, Lily's vision of Mrs. Ramsay's death takes form in rhythmic phrasing: "It was strange how clearly she saw her, stepping with her usual quickness across fields among whose folds, purplish

4. *Diary* 3: 106–7, September 5, 1926.

and soft, among whose flowers, hyacinths or lilies, she vanished. . . .
The sight, the phrase, had its power to console" (131). Readers
will be able to supply their own instances of the "poetry" in *To the
Lighthouse*.[5]

Gender, Sexuality, Class, the Great War, and Social Change

To the Lighthouse opens with an iconic tableau: "mother and child . . .
objects of universal veneration, and in this case the mother was
famous for her beauty" (42). The mother—Mrs. Ramsay—is knitting, which makes her not only an avatar of the Madonna but also
one of the Fates of classical mythology, and indeed she aspires to
preside over the destinies of many of the characters we are about to
meet. She sees her six-year-old son James as "the image of stark and
uncompromising severity," as a future judge on a high court "or
directing a stern and momentous enterprise in some crisis of public
affairs"(5).[6] Mr. Ramsay soon intrudes, to his son's dismay: "Had
there been an axe handy, or a poker, any weapon that would have
gashed a hole in his father's breast and killed him, there and then,
James would have seized it" (5). But although father and son are at
odds—Mr. Ramsay with his "caustic" and "uncompromising" commitment to facts insists there will be no sailing to the lighthouse
the next day—they are alike. While the son pictures himself wield-
ing an axe, the father is "lean as a knife, narrow as the blade of one"
(5), an "arid scimitar" (31), and he entertains fantasies of himself as
the leader of a grand yet doomed expedition—perhaps to the South
Pole, perhaps in battle, as he chants Tennyson's "Charge of the
Light Brigade" (267) as he paces. This tableau looks a lot like
Freud's Oedipal triangle, and according to Freud, the son eventually tolerates giving up the exclusive love of his mother in exchange
for access to the father's privileges and powers; this scene forecasts
that very result, as Rachel Bowlby shows (see Criticism, 293). Meanwhile Mrs. Ramsay does her best to soothe her son, assuring him
that "perhaps it will be fine tomorrow" (14). While Mr. Ramsay
enjoys saying "no" and demanding his wife's attention, a "beak of
brass" that "plunge[s]" into Mrs. Ramsay's "delicious fecundity, this
fountain and spray of life" (31), Mrs. Ramsay—embodying

---

5. Susan Stanford Friedman found that lyric is linked to female characters, narrative to
men (e.g. after dinner in "The Window" Mrs. Ramsay reads poetry while Mr. Ramsay
reads a densely plotted novel): "Lyric Subversion of Narrative in Women's Writing:
Virginia Woolf and the Tyranny of Plot," in *Reading Narrative: Form, Ethics, Ideology*,
ed. James Phelan (Columbus: Ohio State UP, 1989), pp. 162–85.
6. Sadly and ironically, a British reader in 1927 would have known that a child such as
James—a ruling class boy of six—was about to be sent away to a boys' boarding school, to
sever his intimacy with his mother and socialize him into a world ruled by men.

Coventry Patmore's "Angel in the House" (203–4) and one of John Ruskin's "queens" (204–5)—is a domestic artist of "yes": "flashing her needles, confident, upright, she created drawing-room and kitchen, set them all aglow" (31). The Victorian gender binarism of this scene is captured in the title of another book Woolf was working on while writing *To the Lighthouse: Victorian Photographs of Famous Men and Fair Women*, a collection of her aunt Julia Margaret Cameron's artwork that included three portraits of Julia Stephen, images that had helped perpetuate the family myth of Julia's beauty (see Leslie Stephen, *The Mausoleum Book*, 210–15).[7]

The almost cartoonish gender binary and heteronormativity of this scene initiates the novel's diagnosis of Victorian patriarchal excess (what we might now call toxic masculinity).[8] Gender hierarchy is reinforced in a darker tone by Mrs. Ramsay herself, in the choice of a Grimm's "household tale" to read to James while attempting to justify to herself her matchmaking project of "making Minta marry Paul Rayley" (47). In Mrs. Ramsay's view, "people must marry," and the fairy tale gives insight into her understanding of the power dynamics of marriage. "The Fisherman and His Wife" (269–72) tells of a woman whose excessive desire to achieve wealth and power by dominating her husband is finally contained and punished. Although James's sister Cam has been invited to listen, she is seen "dashing past" on her own adventures (43), chasing her own "vision," briefly "attracted" back "only by the word 'Flounder'" (44). Mrs. Ramsay reads the story to James alone: its lesson supports his journey towards empowered masculinity, so it's no wonder Cam runs away or attends only to the sound of the words (a hint that she may have a future as a poet), not their meanings.

Woolf carefully chose this story. In the manuscript, Mrs. Ramsay reads to Cam and James together, and the story was at first going to be "3 Dwarfs" or, next, "the story of the Woodman's daughter . . . about the little girl who had tea with the bears."[9] Again in the manuscript, by the time Mrs. Ramsay is finishing the story, it is "The Three Bears," and as she reads the last words, boy and girl together imagine a girl protagonist who seems to be both happy and

---

7. *Victorian Photographs of Famous Men and Fair Women* was published by Hogarth Press in October 1926, with introductions by Woolf and Roger Fry.
8. Reading Woolf as a feminist writer began with American literary scholars in the 1970s; Jane Marcus reviews the conflicts her early feminist scholarship aroused, in "Wrapped in The Stars and Stripes: Virginia Woolf in the U.S.A.," *South Carolina Review* 29.1 (Fall 1996): 17–23. *The Cambridge Companion to* To the Lighthouse includes two essays on gender in the novel: Gabrielle McIntire, "Feminism and Gender in *To the Lighthouse*" (80–91) and Ana Parejo Vadillo, "Generational Difference in *To the Lighthouse*" (122–35). See also Maggie Humm, "Beauty and Woolf," *Feminist Theory* 7.2 (2006): 237–54.
9. Virginia Woolf, *To the Lighthouse: The Original Holograph Draft*, transcribed and ed., with Woolf's notes and outlines for the novel, by Susan Dick (Toronto: U of Toronto P, 1982), pp. 73, 96. Hereafter abbreviated *Original Holograph*.

adventurous: "one could almost see them both pondering those last words about the little girl dreaming of the bears."[1] "The Fisherman and His Wife," by contrast, delivers a cruelly doctrinaire message to any girl who might hear it. Read aloud by a wife and mother who favors her son and husband over her daughter, it clarifies the restricted terms of a woman's power. Men's chivalrous, "reverential" (7) attitude toward her depends on her deference to them. As in Coventry Patmore and John Ruskin's influential Victorian idealizations of married women as queens, she is (twice) compared to a queen whose powers are ceremonial but not political. Woolf chooses to expose, not soften, the rigidly gendered message of Mrs. Ramsay's choices. Adrienne Rich (in Criticism, 290–92) explores the loss to Mrs. Ramsay's daughters: for them, she is adored yet unavailable.[2]

"The Window," while exhibiting the rigid reinforcement of Victorian norms of gender and sexuality, also entertains questions and alternatives. Does Cam avoid absorbing the message of the Grimms' tale? What does it mean that Mrs. Ramsay harbors questions about her matchmaking scheme? Her daughters, after all, quietly imagine a different life, "not always taking care of some man or other" (7), and Cam, "wild and fierce . . . would not 'give a flower to the gentleman' as the nursemaid told her. No! no! no!" (19). What of Minta, Mrs. Ramsay's latest victim, and "independent" Lily Briscoe, who is "in love with this all" and yearns not for marriage but for "unity . . . like waters poured into one jar" (41) with Mrs. Ramsay? When she paints Mrs. Ramsay and James as a "purple triangle," as we have seen, she rejects simultaneously two representational models of visual art: accurate portraiture, on the one hand, and, on the other, paintings that "venerate" male-serving maternity (Lily later specifies that Mr. Bankes was thinking of Raphael Madonnas).[3] Lily rejects the belief held by the men in the book that Mrs. Ramsay's value resides in her "incomparable beauty" (24); rejects, that is, the belief that women exist to serve the male gaze; and later reflects that to appreciate Mrs. Ramsay, one needed "fifty pairs of eyes" including "one that

---

1. *Original Holograph*, p. 104.
2. On the bonds between female figures in the novel and their losses, see also Jane Lilienfeld, "'The Deceptiveness of Beauty': Mother Love and Mother Hate in *To the Lighthouse*," *Twentieth-Century Literature* 23.3 (1977): 345–76; Elizabeth Abel, *Virginia Woolf and the Fictions of Psychoanalysis* (Chicago: U of Chicago P, 1989); Ruth Vanita, "Bringing Buried Things to Light: Homoerotic Alliances in *To the Lighthouse*," in *Virginia Woolf: Lesbian Readings*, ed. Eileen Barrett and Patricia Kramer (New York: New York UP, 1997), pp. 165–79.
3. See p. 212 for the Raphael Madonna Leslie Stephen had in mind when he looked at Julia, and *The Mausoleum Book* (210–15) for his worship of her beauty. Vanessa Bell's monumental, lost painting *Women and Baby* (1912, also titled *A Nativity*) pictures maternity in a way that radically differs from Raphael's Madonnas, decentering and de-idealizing mother and child. A black-and-white photograph of this painting when it hung in Roger Fry's house, published in *Vogue* in 1926, can be seen in Christopher Reed, *Bloomsbury Rooms: Modernism, Subculture, and Domesticity* (New Haven: Yale UP, 2004), p. 44.

was stone blind to her beauty" (143). Painting the purple triangle, Lily unpaints the beauty myth that locks women into marriage as their only career. She is a marriage resister, rejecting Mrs. Ramsay's "absurd" demand that she marry Mr. Bankes, her "independence" marking the opening up of possibilities for middle-class women in the early twentieth century. Similarly, Minta Doyle failed to finish reading *Middlemarch*, a virtual guidebook to Victorian rules about gender and sexuality, and wears knickerbockers (instead of the expected long skirt) to hike on the beach with a man she's not yet engaged to.

As long as Mrs. Ramsay presides, the Victorian rules hold. The dinner party epitomizes her domestic art of knitting people together and becomes a tacit celebration of Minta and Paul's engagement. Under pressure of Mrs. Ramsay's silent demand, Lily abandons her "experiment—what happens if one is not nice to that young man there" (70). Prue, destined to become "a beauty" like her mother, begins, in the reflected "glow of Minta," to feel "some anticipation of happiness . . . as if the sun of the love of men and women rose over the rim of the table-cloth, and without knowing what it was she bent towards it and greeted it" (83). Yet when the dinner ends, the party "had become . . . already the past" (84), and with Mrs. Ramsay's departure, "a sort of disintegration set in" (85). This "disintegration" may sound like a loss, but it is a societal transition Woolf continued to describe and to call for in her other writings. In "Professions for Women," based on a 1931 lecture, she explained how her writing used to be hampered by the hovering shadow of a Victorian Angel who told her not to criticize men, until she killed her by throwing an inkpot at her.[4] Woolf's *Three Guineas* (1938) connects the social, legal, and economic oppression of women to the global rise of nationalism that was leading to tyranny and war, and it imagines a female Society of Outsiders that conducts "experiments" like Lily's, such as refusing to attend church, which was then an entirely male-dominated institution.

The "disintegration" at the end of the dinner party anticipates the sweeping away, in "Time Passes," not only of Mrs. Ramsay but also of the rigid Victorian social order maintained by her presence. Mrs. Ramsay dies; Prue marries and almost immediately dies; Andrew, too, who was to follow in Mr. Ramsay's footsteps, goes off to the Great War—defining manliness through militarism, like so many of his gender, class, and generation—and is killed.[5] These

---

4. "Professions for Women," *Essays* 6: 479–84.
5. Much has been written on the social and cultural changes brought about by World War I, and scholars argue about whether modernism as an aesthetic movement was caused by the war, or only accelerated by it, or even served as one of its contributing causes. See Samuel Hynes, *A War Imagined: The First World War and English Culture* (1990); Paul Fussell, *The Great War and Modern Memory* (1977); and Modris Eksteins, *Rites of Spring: The Great War and the Birth of the Modern Age* (1989).

three characters represent the strictest adherence to Victorian social codes, and their abruptly narrated deaths, though shocking, are necessary for a new way of life to begin, just as Woolf would later write that the Angel must be killed in order for a woman to write what she thinks. In "The Lighthouse" Lily thinks, "one would have to say to her, It has all gone against your wishes. . . . Life has changed completely" (127). What comes next? Lily has remained single; she has continued painting and, as we have seen, associates her art with her defiance of Mrs. Ramsay. She and Mr. Bankes have enjoyed a long friendship, while Minta's marriage neutralizes Mrs. Ramsay's "mania for marriage" by evolving into a distinctly modern one: initially "things were horribly strained," but then Paul's affair with "a serious woman" who shares his leftist political commitments "far from breaking up the marriage . . . had righted it," so that they are now "excellent friends" (126). Minta's boldness, the younger Ramsay girls' resistance, and Lily's "independence" and her unpainting of a loved woman's beauty in "The Window" anticipate the enormous social changes that have occurred by the time of "The Lighthouse," ten years later, where an entire value system for organizing human life has disintegrated. Only with the radical decentering of the human, which as we have seen was Woolf's great challenge in writing "Time Passes," can the solidities of Victorian social formation be dislodged.

The certainties that "Time Passes" sweeps away include not only norms of gender and sexuality, but also a rigid class system that was unquestioned in "The Window." Woolf wrote "Time Passes" during the General Strike of May 1926, which made visible the needs of working people at the same time that it emptied the streets of London (see Composition Chronology, 170).[6] Although Mrs. Ramsay worries about money, it's the repair of the greenhouse (a luxury) that bothers her, and the Ramsays are wealthy enough to employ several servants and a gardener. Mildred, the cook, makes the magnificent *boeuf en daube* (216–18) for which her employer gets the credit, and she puts the younger children to bed before the adults' dinner; other servants include Ellen and Marie, who weeps in her attic room because her father is dying back home in Switzerland. Cam reports on "an old woman in the kitchen with very red cheeks, drinking soup out of a basin" (44): a domestic worker (red cheeks mean hard labor; soup in the kitchen means working class) who has done the laundry in the town and carried it uphill to the house.[7] But then

6. On the General Strike and "Time Passes" see Kate Flint, "Virginia Woolf and the General Strike," *Essays in Criticism* 36.4 (1986): 319–34.

7. Elizabeth Abel sees Cam's vision of the "old woman" in terms of gender, in "'Cam the Wicked': Woolf's Portrait of the Artist as Her Father's Daughter," in *Virginia Woolf and Bloomsbury: A Centenary Celebration*, ed. Jane Marcus (Basingstoke: Macmillan, 1987), pp. 170–89.

"Time Passes" flips the class hierarchy that is naturalized in "The Window." With all traces of upper-middle-class family life giving way to the impersonal forces of nature, two working women—first Mrs. McNab, probably an Irishwoman, who recalls bringing laundry to the house and drinking soup, later joined by Mrs. Bast—are central to "Time Passes." Their labor is depicted as hardly human—"as she lurched (she rolled like a ship at sea) and leered . . . she was witless, she knew it" (97–98)—and yet it is their persistent, skilled work that rescues the house and readies it for the family's return. Mrs. McNab preserves the family itself in memories that seem to have an objective existence, like an old home movie: "She could see her now, stooping over her flowers; and faint and flickering, like a yellow beam or the circle at the end of a telescope, a lady in a grey cloak . . . went wandering over the bedroom wall" (102). The work of memory is part of her creative labor of saving what time and war have destroyed.

Readers have been divided over Woolf's representation of these working-class figures: on the one hand, they are subhuman caricatures who disappear from the novel once their work is done, yet on the other, they are granted creative powers and their own points of view, their own humanity and subjectivity. Maurizia Boscagli, exploring the reversal of the usual subject-object hierarchy in "Time Passes," finds that Mrs. McNab, as a servant, is a non-subject, part of the object world; Susan Stanford Friedman, by contrast, finds "the interiority of Mrs. McNab's consciousness sympathetically rendered in the same free indirect discourse used to represent English characters of a different class."[8] In the manuscript and the version of "Time Passes" published as a separate story, Woolf detailed Mrs. McNab's life and her place in class hierarchy more fully and more bitterly (see Selected Textual Variants, 154–55). Either she and Mrs. Bast are the heroic human exceptions to the disintegration that occurs in "Time Passes," or, as nonhuman beings, they underscore the absence of the human from the chaos and inertia of a world made only of things.

Either way, enormous social changes have occurred across the ten years of "Time Passes," the "corridor" (in Woolf's diagram) that both links and divides the two longer parts of the novel. When the family and guests reassemble at the house, it feels to Lily as if "the link that usually bound things together had been cut" (107); it was Mrs. Ramsay, knitting, who gave domestic life its cohesion, value,

---

8. Boscagli, *Stuff Theory*, 204–5; Susan Stanford Friedman, *Mappings: Feminism and the Cultural Geographies of Encounter* (Princeton: Princeton UP, 1998), p. 121. See also Alison Light, *Mrs. Woolf and the Servants: An Intimate History of Domestic Life in Bloomsbury* (New York: Bloomsbury, 2010), and Katherine Simpson, "Social Class in To the Lighthouse," in *The Cambridge Companion to* To the Lighthouse, pp. 110–21, for other treatments of this question.

and meaning, but now the characters find their way to new forms, new designs. In contrast to accepting Mrs. Ramsay's demand that she "be nice" to Mr. Tansley at the dinner party, Lily now refuses to play the Victorian Angel and indulge the self-pitying Mr. Ramsay, whose need for sympathy "spread itself in pools at her feet" (112); instead, by speaking of a neutral topic, she aids their arrival together at "the blessed island of good boots" (113). Gender has become less rigidly binarized, and class hierarchy has softened, too. There's still a cook—Nancy forgot to "order the sandwiches" for the trip to the lighthouse—but otherwise family members appear to look after themselves. On the sailboat, although Mr. Macalister and his son are distinctly rural, working-class characters (Mr. Ramsay orders the boy to row during a calm), Mr. Ramsay accords Mr. Macalister a degree of respect and even cross-class identification that would have been unimaginable in "The Window." The elaborate dinner of "The Window" is replaced by sandwiches in a fishing boat: "he was happy, eating bread and cheese with these fishermen" (147).

In "The Window," Mr. Tansley's pro-Labour socialist politics—his advocacy for working people, especially the downtrodden fishermen of Scotland—is both cautiously supported by male characters such as Mr. Bankes and Mr. Ramsay and denigrated by association with his class resentment, his misogyny, and his rude self-assertion. "I—I—I," he says (80), an ideogram Woolf will reuse in *A Room of One's Own* and *The Years* to mock other egotistical men. Proud of refusing to dress for dinner, he asserts his poverty too aggressively, and his remark, "women can't paint, women can't write" (39), echoes in Lily's mind all day and blocks her progress on her painting. "The Window" thus sets up a conflict between the questioning of gender rules and the questioning of social class; Lily's nascent feminism is at odds with Mr. Tansley's left politics, and the violence of their conflict makes both look ungracious. In the manuscript, Woolf staged this as a conflict in Lily's mind: "Lily Briscoe remembered that every man has Shakespeare behind him, & women have not," yet two pages later Lily "had no militancy in her" and "could not bear to be called a feminist."[9] In "The Lighthouse," however, this conflict has dissipated, for "the war had drawn the sting" of her feminist anger; "poor devils," she thinks, "of both sexes" (117). Lily now recalls Mr. Tansley in a completely different way: he becomes harmless and likable in a remembered scene at the beach, the two of them skipping rocks ("ducks and drakes") while Mrs. Ramsay, who for once isn't trying to make anyone marry, writes letters. Lily can now "re-fashion her memory of him" (117). This scene from the past could only be narrated in the changed

---

9. *Original Holograph*, pp. 136, 138.

world of "The Lighthouse." Lily has other challenges to meet before she can complete her painting, but the "sting" of "women can't paint"—his attack and her angry, paralyzing response—has been neutralized.

What enables Lily finally to complete her painting? As she paints, her painful process of remembering and yearning for Mrs. Ramsay alternates with the sailboat's journey to the island. Both halves of this bifurcated narrative return to the gender narrative of the novel's opening. At first it seems as though nothing has changed between father and son: James at seventeen relives his childhood fury at his father, he and Cam are "united by their compact to fight tyranny to the death" (120), and he bitterly recalls his mother's superiority: "she alone spoke the truth" (136). And yet as the boat draws near the lighthouse James notices his father's old age, his vulnerability, and the "loneliness" (146) they share, and when Mr. Ramsay praises James's skill handling the sailboat, Cam thinks, "you've got it now" (149), the approval that finally reconciles James to his father and allows him to complete the trajectory of masculine development (from competition to identification) that Freud described.

Similarly, Cam begins the journey alienated from her father; she too recollects her mother's beloved presence, drowsily repeating the incantatory words her mother spoke when soothing her to sleep in "The Window" and mimicking the symbolic description of her mother as a "fountain" for her "arid" husband (31) when, holding her hand beneath the rushing water, "there spurted up a fountain of joy" (137). But Woolf transforms this image of self-sacrificing feminine abundance, a potentially disabling inheritance, into a powerful claim for Cam's future as an artist. "Drops" from this fountain fall "on the dark, the slumberous shapes in her mind; shapes of a world not realised but turning in their darkness, catching here and there, a spark of light" (137). This depiction ambitiously identifies Cam's emergent imaginative powers with those of the Romantic poet William Wordsworth, as he retrospectively described them in "Ode: Intimations of Immortality from Recollections of Early Childhood" (see note 3 p. 116). Cam also recalls the pleasure of visiting her father in his booklined study: to be sure, not as his (male) inheritor—that was Andrew's role—but positioned, advantageously for her as an artist, at the edge of his attention, so that "one could let whatever one thought expand here like a leaf in water" (137). By the end of the journey, she too can feel love for her father; both children are reconciled to their positioning between their lost, mourned mother and their diminished yet valiant father.

Meanwhile onshore, Lily, painting, weeps for Mrs. Ramsay. "To want and want—how that wrung the heart, and wrung it again and again" (129). At first, all she can see is Mrs. Ramsay's absence: the empty steps where she had posed for Lily's picture is now "a centre of complete emptiness" (130). But gradually the pain and anger "lessened;" she feels "a sense of some one there" (131) as she conjures an image of Mrs. Ramsay crossing the classical Elysian fields; and she finds herself looking for Mr. Ramsay and the sailboat "in the middle of the bay" (132). Sometime later, this dynamic recurs: someone sits on a chair inside the window, throwing "a triangular shadow over the step" (145) and summoning for Lily Mrs. Ramsay's ghostly presence, after which—perhaps because this vision has helped Lily with her picture—she no longer needs Mrs. Ramsay; instead, "she wanted him" (146). Lily is positioned as a daughter to Mr. and Mrs. Ramsay, and like Cam she finds a way to balance deep mourning for the lost mother—now transformed into an inspiration for art—with appreciation for the father who, with all his faults, survives. Pamela L. Caughie (306–11) argues that the scenes in the boat are actually happening in Lily's mind, making the children's resolutions into projections or doublings of Lily's own artistic conclusion.

Once she sees that Mr. Ramsay has landed, Lily can place the final stroke on her painting, saying both of it and of Mr. Ramsay's journey, "it is finished" (150). Some readers believe that Lily shifts her allegiance from Mrs. to Mr. Ramsay—moving on, as Freud said daughters must, from early, pre-Oedipal love of the mother to the love of the father that leads eventually to heterosexual marriage. But Lily is a resistant daughter, and she needn't choose, as the bifurcated narrative of "The Lighthouse" was organized from the start to show. As Marianne Hirsch points out, Lily's "line there, in the centre" (150) is left uncertain: neither horizontal nor vertical, neither clearly dividing nor clearly joining the two sides of her painting, or the two parents; it might even be a diagonal ray. Open to multiple interpretations, it represents a "both/and" vision that conveys her "acceptance of contradiction" and with it, the novel's too.[1] That Lily, expecting her painting not to last, values the experience of having her "vision" over the resulting work of art further emphasizes that what she achieves is not a final resolution but a step in a process. Gender remains an ongoing negotiation.

Scotland, Cornwall, Empire, and Race

Gender difference also helps to organize the novel's global politics, through the connections drawn between family life and Britain's imperial projects. When Mr. Ramsay chants Tennyson's "The Charge of the Light Brigade" as he paces the lawn, he doesn't just entertain

---

1. Marianne Hirsch, *The Mother/Daughter Plot: Narrative, Psychoanalysis, Feminism* (Bloomington: Indiana UP, 1989), p. 115, and see Caughie's view of the ending, in conversation with Hirsch's, this edition, p. 311.

a fantasy identification with heroic, violent masculinity; he also, in Susan Stanford Friedman's view, "discloses the interpenetration of the domestic, the national, and the transnational. Patriarchal folly at home is both a cause and a reflection of militarist and nationalist folly abroad."[2] Mrs. Ramsay's enabling of Mr. Ramsay's excesses has broader implications than the merely personal or familial. As Friedman points out, the perpetuation of empire depends on its normalization and domestication by women, tasks Mrs. Ramsay willingly, reflexively performs. When, early in the novel, Nancy complains about Mr. Tansley, whom the children all dislike, their mother turns severely on the girls: as an Angel in the House and a Ruskinian "queen," she advocates for firm gender identities organized around the structures in place for ruling the British Empire: "she had the whole of the other sex under her protection; for reasons she could not explain, for their chivalry and valour, for the fact that they negotiated treaties, ruled India, controlled finance" (7). As we have seen, men's chivalrous reverence for her—which we soon see in action when Mr. Tansley, walking with her, deeply desires to carry her bag—is symmetrically matched by her reverence for men. Reprimanded, her daughters can rebel "only in silence" (7), but their rebellion, like her reverence, is represented through the discourse of empire: they "sport with infidel ideas," fantasizing an exotic Other to the Christian value system of Europe and the West. The daughters imagine "a life different from hers; in Paris, perhaps; a wilder life; not always taking care of some man or other; for there was in all their minds a mute questioning of deference and chivalry, of the Bank of England and the Indian Empire, of ringed fingers and lace" (7–8). In this early scene, control of the empire (specifically, ruling India) is aligned with and supported by traditional gender: to question "the Bank of England and the Indian Empire" is also to question male dominance.

Mrs. Ramsay's life is intertwined with India's economic and political domination by Britain: close relatives apparently work in the Indian Civil Service. Yet she isn't conscious of either the violence or the profit motive subtending her investment in empire and in the male dominance it runs on: "she could not explain" the connections the narrator draws on her behalf between India, banking, and her reverence for men. The opening mockery of Mrs. Ramsay's deference to men and to empire is broadly drawn, and it hints at a different future for her daughters, but as the novel proceeds, the economic benefits of empire that Mrs. Ramsay unthinkingly accepts are casually integrated into the texture of the narrative in the form of imported domestic luxuries. The named plants in the garden (the

2. Friedman, *Mappings*, p. 125.

red-hot pokers and the pampas grass) along with the bananas and
the conch shell in Rose's beautiful centerpiece at dinner are all from
remote parts of the empire. In the British edition Mrs. Ramsay's
green shawl is cashmere, from Kashmir, and among the jewels she
invites her children to choose before dinner is an opal necklace (the
opals almost certainly mined in Australia) brought by the children's
Uncle James from India (62). The boar's skull, a gift from Edward
(perhaps another of their uncles), "shot in foreign parts" (105), is the
kind of hunting trophy that affirms imperial conquest. It shores up
James's nascent identification with male rule (he can't go to sleep
without it) at the same time that it rightly terrifies Cam, the young
girl named for Virgil's woman warrior Camilla, who fights on the
losing side against what will become the Roman Empire.

That Mrs. Ramsay satisfies both children by wrapping her Indian
shawl around the skull, so that it is both there and not there, suggests how empire can be domesticated and rendered acceptable. But
in "Time Passes" the shawl slides off the skull, exposing the violence
it once concealed. At first, "one fold of the shawl loosened and swung
to and fro" (97), and then another, owing merely to the house's emptiness and gradual decay; then, during the war, come "ominous
sounds like the measured blows of hammers dulled on felt, which,
with their repeated shocks still further loosened the shawl and
cracked the tea-cups" (99). (The description echoes "Thunder at
Wembley," 247–49, which envisions nature bringing an apocalyptic
end to a miniature version of the British Empire.) Once, the domestic practices of a Victorian Angel served to endorse an expansive
empire; now, allied with natural entropy, the empire's inevitable
sequel—the Great War, launched by Europe's imperial powers in
part over their conflicting global ambitions—enters and despoils the
home. When Mrs. McNab comes still later to clean, the "beast's
skull" has become visible (102); though the shawl still hangs from it,
swaying, Mrs. Ramsay's concealment of imperial violence has proved
short lived. By the time of the family's return in "The Lighthouse,"
both the beauty of Britain's far-flung empire (the shawl, the opals)
and its dangers have ebbed: the war has consumed the domestic
regime that produced it.

In these ways, the novel consistently and visibly critiques Britain's
empire, yet in other ways it undermines this critique. Readers of
Woolf generally—not just of *To the Lighthouse*—have disagreed on
whether she should be seen more as a deliberate critic or as an unwitting supporter of imperialism and of the racial attitudes that often
accompany advocacy for empire.[3] As Urmila Seshagiri outlines the

---

3. See for example Kathy Phillips, *Virginia Woolf Against Empire* (Knoxville: U of Tennessee P, 1994); Jane Marcus, *Hearts of Darkness: White Women Write Race* (New

problem, the novel "opposes imperialism, insists on racial hierarchies, *and* valorizes nonwhite otherness" (316). The facial type shared by James and Mrs. Ramsay is emphatically Aryan: he has a "high forehead" and "fierce blue eyes" that suit Mrs. Ramsay's fantasy of him as a powerful judge (5), while Mr. Bankes pictures her at the other end of the telephone line "very clearly Greek, straight, blue-eyed" (24), with a beauty that is so often insisted upon as to make it clear she embodies the prevalent beauty ideals of her class and time. By contrast, Lily Briscoe's "Chinese eyes" are equally insisted upon, not only from Mrs. Ramsay's point of view (15, 79) but by the omniscient narrator (115). Not of Chinese descent but simply looking different, Lily's social gender deviance—her refusal to marry, her unfeminine insistence on continuing to paint—is expressed by her nonconformity to the dominant racial type. While the novel values Lily's accomplishments in "The Lighthouse," her racial alterity remains, leaving in place the Orientalism that the war, having levelled other differences, has not undone.

Britain's empire and the attitudes and practices of "othering" that accompanied it didn't derive only from its conquests on other continents. Why did Woolf set *To the Lighthouse* on the Isle of Skye, a place she'd never visited, in the Hebrides Islands off the west coast of Scotland? Nels Pearson points out that by 1925 Cornwall was a familiar holiday destination for Londoners and no longer the exotic, isolated place it had seemed in her childhood; instead, in order to conjure a feeling of remoteness, she needed a setting further off.[4] And yet Skye is no random choice; Woolf mobilizes the Scottish features of her setting in ways that both support and undercut her critique of empire.[5]

When Woolf set the novel on Skye, no one was fooled. The reviewer for the *Glasgow Herald* praised the novel for its "beautiful lyrical imagery" but issued a "protest" over its "describing a place which is very obviously Cornwall and calling it Skye."[6] Readers informed Woolf that her flora and fauna were all wrong (there are no rooks, elm trees, or dahlias in the Hebrides; Composition Chronology, 180). Her friends and family as well as readers guided by

Brunswick: Rutgers UP, 2004); and Gretchen Gerzina, "Virginia Woolf, Performing Race," in *The Edinburgh Companion to Virginia Woolf and The Arts*, ed. Maggie Humm (Edinburgh: Edinburgh UP, 2010), pp. 74–87.

4. Nels Pearson, "Recovering Islands: Scotland, Ocean, and Archipelago in *To the Lighthouse*," *Twentieth-Century Literature* 64.3 (Sept. 2018): 347–70.

5. For more on the significance of the Scottish setting, see Jane Goldman, "'With You in the Hebrides': Virginia Woolf and Scotland* (London: Cecil Woolf, 2013); and on Scotland and the theme of empire more generally, see Janet Winston, "'Something Out of Harmony': *To the Lighthouse* and the Subject(s) of Empire," *Woolf Studies Annual* 2 (1996): 39–70.

6. "Lyrical Fiction," *Glasgow Herald*, May 26, 1927, p. 4. Accessed from Woolf Online; ed. Pamela L. Caughie, Nick Hayward, Mark Hussey, Peter Shillingsburg, and George K. Thiruvathakal.

her biography have understood that the novel takes place in the Cornwall of Woolf's childhood summers. No town on Skye resembles the one described in the novel, with its clusters of ancient stone houses, fishing fleet, sandy beaches and lighthouse on an island across the bay—all of which adds up to an accurate depiction of St. Ives, Carbis Bay, and Godrevy Island. No one in the novel mentions travel by boat, necessary then to reach Skye; instead, when Mr. Bankes recalls telephoning about his journey, it's the train schedule he discusses with Mrs. Ramsay.[7] Woolf's knowledge of Skye came from romanticizing sources such as Sir Walter Scott's early nineteenth-century Waverley novels and Samuel Johnson's and James Boswell's books about their eighteenth-century travels in the Hebrides. She wasn't even sure whether to call it "the Isle" or "the Isles" of Skye; she introduced the wrong term as a correction in her manuscript. When Woolf finally visited Skye, she wrote that "it feels like the South Seas—completely remote, surrounded by sea," and again, "remote as Samoa; deserted; prehistoric,"[8] echoing Dr. Johnson, who wrote that to the rest of Scotland, "the state of the mountains and the islands is equally unknown with that of *Borneo* or *Sumatra*."[9]

Great Britain had formed through a centuries-long process of internal colonization, and both Cornwall and the Hebrides (along with the Scottish Highlands, Wales, and—until the creation of the Irish Free State in 1921—Ireland) were culturally, linguistically, and politically distinct places that had been colonized by England and that remain part of Britain's internal empire, both inside and outside the political center. Today, post-imperial Britain can be seen as an archipelago, its constituent parts such as the Hebrides or Cornwall not (in Pearson's words) as "peripheral sites of archaic, romanticized or inherently distinct subcultures within a centripetal Anglocentric Britishness and more as examples of an interactive history of diverse cultures played out across a shared island ecology and maritime economy."[1] But in Woolf's novel, the remote coastal location with its threatening high tides, its house-destroying "clammy sea airs" (97) and its many shipwrecks can suggest anxiety about the fragility of Great Britain's cohesion, at least at its outer edges.[2]

---

7. It was the 1881 opening of the spur train line from St. Erth to St. Ives that sparked Leslie Stephen's decision to lease Talland House; the station was a short walk from the house.

8. *Letters* 6: 243, 248.

9. Samuel Johnson and James Boswell, *A Journey to the Western Islands of Scotland* and *The Journal of a Tour to the Hebrides*, ed. Celia Barnes and Jack Lynch, Oxford World Classics (Oxford: Oxford UP, 2020), p. 71.

1. Pearson, "Recovering Islands," pp. 347–48.

2. John Brannigan's archipelagic, post-imperial reading of the novel focuses on its unruly weather: *Archipelagic Modernism: Literature in the Irish and British Isles, 1890–1970* (Edinburgh: Edinburgh UP, 2015), pp. 109–26. Janet Winston discusses the novel's watery threats to empire, in "'Something Out of Harmony,'" pp. 39–70.

Although Scotland formed a Union with England when James VI of Scotland became James I of England in 1603, the Scottish Highlands and the Hebrides had resisted incorporation into Great Britain, partly because Catholicism remained prevalent long after Britain became a Protestant country, and they were conquered in 1715, with a military occupation left in place. But Jacobite (that is, seeking to restore King James) resistance remained until 1745–46, when Bonnie Prince Charlie—the grandson of King James VII of Scotland and II of England and heir to the British throne had it not been given in 1688 to Protestant Mary Stuart and her husband William—failed in his attempt to liberate Scotland. He made a last stand at the battle of Culloden in 1746 and escaped to the Isle of Skye in a boat rowed by the intrepid Flora Macdonald. This famous escape (memorialized by the song "Speed, bonnie boat, like a bird on the wing, over the sea to Skye . . .") made Skye synonymous with Jacobite political resistance. As David Bradshaw points out, Woolf's choice of this setting aligns her novel with resistance to the imperial center.[3] In Boswell's and Johnson's narratives, Skye is both a locus of nostalgia for a romanticized, heroic past—they met Flora Macdonald in 1773 and Boswell recorded her narrative—and of political injustice and economic oppression. Johnson and Boswell had gone to the Hebrides seeking a timeless past and were disappointed to find that the population had been forced to accept the Union, complying with laws designed to erase cultural identity such as the outlawing of Gaelic language and wearing "the plaid." They witnessed boatloads of emigrating islanders.

As Pearson points out, both Mr. Ramsay and Mr. Tansley are given Scottish connections, Mr. Ramsay through his Scottish surname, his sentimental identification with Macalister's tragic fishing stories, and even the "little tinge of Scottish accent which came into his voice" when "he brought his voice into tune with Macalister's voice" (120); Mr. Tansley through the uncle who "kept the light on some rock or other off the Scottish coast" (70) and his outrage on behalf of the local fishermen oppressed by "one of the most scandalous acts of the present government" (71).[4] These sympathies and identifications align Mr. Tansley's Labour politics and Mr. Ramsay's anti-elitist advocacy for the "liftman in the tube" (35) with Scotland's status as an internal colony and activate the Scottish setting as part of the novel's anti-imperialism. Yet the novel's representations of Scotland, like the continued Orientalizing of Lily, also leave imperial attitudes and investments in place. The Indian shawl may

---

3. Bradshaw, Introduction, pp. xxvii–xxxii.
4. For more on the plight of the fishermen, see Brannigan, *Archipelagic Modernism*, pp. 123–26.

be beyond rescuing from the ruins of the house, but an entire set of Scott's Waverley novels survives: exposing them to the sunshine, Mrs. Bast and Mrs. McNab "triumph over long rows of books, black as ravens once, now white-stained, breeding pale mushrooms and secreting furtive spiders" (104). These are the books from which Mr. Ramsay selected *The Antiquary* to read after dinner to prove to himself that his works, too, would "last," books that shore up, as well, old-school constructions of gender and sexuality. Sir Walter Scott hailed not from the resistant Highlands or Islands but from the conciliatory Border country in the south of Scotland adjoining England, and his Waverley novels romanticize Jacobite rebellion but usually end by reconciling Scotland's subjection to England, often through a cross-border marriage. The survival of the Waverley novels signals, then, both the novel's resistant political allegiances and its acceptance of the internal imperialism embodied in the term Great Britain.

Reception and Afterlife of To the Lighthouse

As Woolf was completing revisions and correcting two sets of proofs—one for Harcourt Brace in the United States, one for her own Hogarth Press (see A Note on the Text and Selected Textual Variants)—Woolf's view of her novel alternated between pleasure and boredom. When *To the Lighthouse* was published, on May 5, 1927, it was widely praised, with the exception of a few reviews that found the book too cerebral (see the Early Reviews, 281–86). She was relieved to have it out of her hands and warmly received by friends and family; especially moving is Vanessa's letter (see Composition Chronology, 177–82, for Vanessa's and other responses).

To the Lighthouse sold better than any of Woolf's previous books. She recorded the mounting numbers in her diary: 2,555 copies by June 23; 3,000 by July 13; and her expectation ten days later that it would "sell 3,500 before it dies, & thus far exceeds any other of mine" (183).[5] "Fame increases," she noted in November (183). Even more than success and the praise of her loved ones, she was excited about what came with the profits. She had often equated her writings with what they would buy: a new stove, a hot water range, an added room for the house in Sussex. In July 1927, with the

---

5. Of course, the novel didn't "die" but has become a classic: beloved, studied, and quarreled with by students and "common readers" (Woolf's favorite kind of reader) around the world. By 1965, Leonard could report that *To the Lighthouse* had sold 253,362 copies in Britain and the United States, and in 1969 he said the novel was selling around 50,000 copies a year (cited in Susan Dick, "Introduction," *To the Lighthouse*, ed. Susan Dick, Shakespeare Head Edition [Oxford: Blackwell, 1992], p. xxx). When the novel came out of copyright in Britain in 1992, a flurry of new editions both popular and scholarly led to increased sales, and by now the novel has sold in the millions.

proceeds from *To the Lighthouse*, she and Leonard purchased their first car, a dark blue Singer that promised to make "a great opening up in our lives" (183). That summer, she learned to drive, and she predicted accurately that the car would both "demolish loneliness" and "imperil complete privacy" (183). Although she earned money by her journalism as well as her fiction (she had begun writing for American media because they paid so well), Woolf had long been anxious about depending financially on a family inheritance. That she could now "make her living by her wits" was a source of enormous pride to her.[6] And the car would "expand . . . the map of the world in one's mind" (183).

At the same time, she recorded a private benchmark: in September 1927 she recalled from a year earlier the "vision of a fin rising on a wide blank sea" (183) that came to her as she was struggling to finish "The Lighthouse." This "fin passing far out" (174) she would continue to pursue in her writing: on finishing *The Waves* (1931), she wrote, looking back five years, "I have netted that fin in the waste of waters which appeared to me over the marshes out of my window at Rodmell."[7] What is this "fin"? Woolf doesn't explain in these diary entries, but in her essay "Modern Fiction" a decade earlier she had used a metaphorical net to explain that the novelist's task is to capture "life or spirit, truth or reality."[8] *To the Lighthouse* was an extraordinary achievement, yet the "fin" had remained far out on the horizon, as if her completion of the novel had only posed fresh challenges, leading her on as she continued her pursuit of "this varying, this unknown and uncircumscribed spirit"—reality itself.[9]

---

6. Virginia Woolf, *A Room of One's Own* (1929; San Diego: Harcourt Brace Jovanovich, 1981), p. 64: Woolf says that seventeenth-century poet and playwright Aphra Behn was the first British woman to show this could be done.
7. *Diary* 4: 10, February 7, 1931.
8. *Essays* 4: 160. The metaphorical net is wielded by a materialist novelist who "has come down with his magnificent apparatus for catching life just an inch or two on the wrong side," *Essays* 4: 159.
9. *Essays* 4: 160.

Acknowledgments

My first thanks go to the undergraduate students at Yale University who, over the last two decades, have enrolled in my senior seminar on Virginia Woolf. From their conversations with each other and with me, as well as from their often brilliant writing on Woolf, I have learned much of what I know about Woolf's novels. On *To the Lighthouse*, they have written on all kinds of subjects, from Mrs. Ramsay and her daughters as artists to the significance of the brackets and the novel's "corridor" structure; from the minute shifts of perspective that can occur in a single sentence to the intrusive presence of the Great War. Some have linked the novel to Vanessa Bell's art, and many have found new meanings in Lily's final line. I wish to thank in particular the crew who volunteered, in the fall of 2021, to help select the Contexts and Criticism in this Norton Critical Edition by telling me which of my proposed choices were relevant to reading *To the Lighthouse* and which, decidedly, were not: Ella Cox, Shayna Elliot, Mauricio Gonzalez Sanchez, Gianna Meloni, Eli Mennerick, Audrey Steinkamp, Curtis Sun, Katia Vanlandingham, and Christie Yu. I followed almost all of their advice.

But I would have no students to thank (and no edition of *To the Lighthouse* to need help with) if it weren't for the generosity of my friend and former colleague, the Woolf scholar Patricia Klindienst, who used to teach a course on Woolf and who gave me—a Victorianist who had taught only *A Room of One's Own* and *Three Guineas* in feminist theory classes—her notes on Woolf and, just as important, her encouragement to teach Woolf's fiction at full length. I cannot thank her enough for this gift, as well as for our long friendship and for her fierce advocacy for Woolf as a radical thinker.

Susan Stanford Friedman, a great Woolf scholar and a dear friend, passed away while this book was in production. I treasure the memory of our friendship as I also treasure her adventurous scholarship on Woolf and on modernism. She introduced me to Kabe Wilson, whose painting appears on the cover of this Norton Critical Edition; generously shared ideas for this volume in a series of Covid-era Zoom calls; and read and commented on a draft of the Introduction. I miss, and mourn, her joyful vision.

I thank my friend Julie Rivkin, too, for her careful reading of the Introduction and for our many rich conversations over the years about literature, teaching, and—more recently—editing. I am grateful likewise to Rachel Bowlby, innovative scholar of modernism and of Woolf, whose long-distance friendship has been sustaining and who drove me to see the beautiful Woolf-Bell landscape when I visited Sussex. Special thanks as well to my colleague Jill Campbell for our enduring friendship and our many non-Woolf collaborations; and to my sister Katy, who visited St. Ives and hiked the Cornish coast with me, and who indulged my longing to see Godrevy Island lighthouse by boat on a sparkling day in June.

I wish also to thank those who have helped me in particular ways as I worked on this project. Kabe Wilson not only contributed his haunting artwork and provocative essay to this volume but also kindly joined the (fruitless, as it turned out) search to learn which photograph of Julia Stephen by Julia Margaret Cameron was given to Vanessa by her father Leslie Stephen. Maggie Humm joined this effort as well—thank you both for your expertise and your deep knowledge of Woolf as a visual thinker.

To Mert Dilek, an alum of my Woolf seminar, I owe a great debt of thanks for his rapid, expert, and comprehensive research in secondary sources on Woolf and for drafting many of the footnotes to the text of the novel. I thank Emily Kopley, another alum of my course (author of the "corridor" essay just mentioned), whose book on Woolf and poetry appeared just in time for me to learn from it. I am grateful to Alec Pollak, also a student from long ago, for sharing incisive research on copyrights and Woolf's literary estate.

Thank you to Mark Hussey for advice on my selections, and to him and to Pamela Caughie for help with matters relating to Woolf Online, an extraordinary resource for which all readers of *To the Lighthouse* must be enduringly grateful. I thank Anne Fernald, whose Norton Critical Edition of *Mrs. Dalloway* was then in press, for an early consultation about editing, as well as for her example as a Woolf scholar and editor.

Jacob Hobson cooked up a gorgeous batch of *boeuf en daube* over the requisite three days to help me refine the recipe that appears in this edition; thank you to him and my daughter Marian, who recreated Rose's centerpiece when we shared the *boeuf* with friends, and to my daughter Sylvia for your good company when, for far too long, I kept the dining table covered with Woolf books.

Thank you finally to Carol Bemis and Rachel Goodman, the editors at W. W. Norton who have patiently worked with me to realize almost all my ambitious plans for this edition. I have always loved teaching from Norton Critical Editions, and it made me enormously happy to be invited to edit this one.

A Note on the Text

The text of this Norton Critical Edition of *To the Lighthouse* is the American edition, first published by Harcourt Brace in New York on May 5, 1927. In 2005 Harcourt published an annotated edition, edited by Mark Hussey, with minor corrections and emendations. Until January 1, 2023, when the novel came out of US copyright, Harcourt's editions were the only ones readily available for purchase in the United States since 1927.

Harcourt Brace's *To the Lighthouse* was not the only first edition of the novel, however. On the same day in May 1927, Leonard and Virginia Woolf's Hogarth Press published the first British edition, and this has been the base text for almost all subsequent British editions. As Hogarth reprinted and reissued the novel, Woolf continued to make minor corrections to the British edition; she didn't make further changes to the American edition, and possibly never even saw a copy of it. One British edition, the Shakespeare Head (1992), edited by Susan Dick, follows the only surviving proof that Woolf herself corrected, the proof for the American edition (which differs in mostly minor ways from the first American edition), while following the British edition's punctuation.

There are many differences between the two first editions, and neither can be conclusively shown to be closer to Woolf's intentions than the other, or to represent her final thoughts about the text—her ultimate vision of the novel.[1] When she had finished revising the novel, she sent a clean typescript (now lost) to her printers in Edinburgh, R. & R. Clark, Limited, who set the type and made several sets of page proofs. In February and March 1927, she made changes separately to the proofs going to Harcourt Brace in the United States (two sets, eventually, now held in the Smith College Library) and to the set (now lost) going back to Edinburgh for production of the British edition. It is unknown in what order she made these changes.

---

1. For fuller explanation of the reasons for finding the British or the US edition (or neither) to represent Woolf's intentions, see Susan Dick, "Introduction," in *To the Lighthouse*, ed. Susan Dick, Shakespeare Head Edition (Oxford: Blackwell, 1992), xxx–xxxiii; and Mark Hussey and Peter Shillingsburg, "The Composition, Revision, Printing and Publication of *To the Lighthouse*," in Pamela L. Caughie, Nick Hayward, Mark Hussey, Peter Shillingsburg, and George K. Thiruvathukal, eds., Woolf Online.

Sometimes she made identical changes, but there are significant differences that have meant different experiences of the novel for those reading Harcourt Brace's editions and for those reading the first and subsequent British editions, which are the ones distributed in the rest of the world. (There are as well many minor differences owing to printer's errors on both sides of the Atlantic.)

Shortly after completing her draft of the novel in the fall of 1926, Woolf also prepared a typescript of the middle section of the novel, "Time Passes," for translation and publication as a free-standing "story" in the French literary journal *Commerce*: the first of her works to appear in translation. The English typescript of this version of "Time Passes," first published in an American scholarly journal in 1983, differs both from the holograph (the heavily amended handwritten draft from which Woolf made the clean typescript for the printers) and from both first editions, both because it represents an intermediate stage of the novel and because it was to be published on its own. She removed almost all mention of the named characters, the Ramsay family and their guests, and there are many other substantive differences.

Readers can now access multiple versions of the novel, in published book form and through the website Woolf Online (see Note on Woolf Online, 151):

—the holograph (in Woolf Online and as *To the Lighthouse: The Original Holograph Draft*, transcribed and edited, with Woolf's notes and outlines for the novel, by Susan Dick, Toronto: University of Toronto Press, 1982);

—the typescript of "Time Passes" prepared for translation and separate publication (Woolf Online and published as James M. Haule, Virginia Woolf, and Charles Mauron, "'Le Temps Passe' and the Original Typescript: An Early Version of the 'Time Passes' Section of *To the Lighthouse*, *Twentieth Century Literature* 29:3 [Autumn 1983]: 267–311);

—the corrected US page proofs (Woolf Online and in *To the Lighthouse*, ed. Susan Dick, Shakespeare Head Edition (Oxford: Blackwell, 1992); the uncorrected proofs can be seen under the violet ink of Woolf's corrections in Woolf Online);

—the original British edition (in Woolf Online) and subsequent British editions with changes and corrections by Woolf and later editors (see Selected Bibliography; some of these are in Woolf Online as well);

—and the American edition, in this Norton Critical Edition and (the first US edition) in Woolf Online.

The Text of
TO THE LIGHTHOUSE

Contents

The Window

I

"Yes, of course, if it's fine tomorrow," said Mrs. Ramsay. "But you'll have to be up with the lark," she added.

To her son these words conveyed an extraordinary joy, as if it were settled, the expedition were bound to take place, and the wonder to which he had looked forward, for years and years it seemed, was, after a night's darkness and a day's sail, within touch. Since he belonged, even at the age of six, to that great clan which cannot keep this feeling separate from that, but must let future prospects, with their joys and sorrows, cloud what is actually at hand, since to such people even in earliest childhood any turn in the wheel of sensation has the power to crystallise and transfix the moment upon which its gloom or radiance rests, James Ramsay, sitting on the floor cutting out pictures from the illustrated catalogue of the Army and Navy Stores,[1] endowed the picture of a refrigerator, as his mother spoke, with heavenly bliss. It was fringed with joy. The wheelbarrow, the lawnmower, the sound of poplar trees, leaves whitening before rain, rooks cawing, brooms knocking, dresses rustling—all these were so coloured and distinguished in his mind that he had already his private code, his secret language, though he appeared the image of stark and uncompromising severity, with his high forehead and his fierce blue eyes, impeccably candid and pure, frowning slightly at the sight of human frailty, so that his mother, watching him guide his scissors neatly round the refrigerator, imagined him all red and ermine on the Bench[2] or directing a stern and momentous enterprise in some crisis of public affairs.

"But," said his father, stopping in front of the drawing-room window, "it won't be fine."

Had there been an axe handy, or a poker, any weapon that would have gashed a hole in his father's breast and killed him, there and then, James would have seized it. Such were the extremes of emotion that Mr. Ramsay[3] excited in his children's breasts by his mere presence; standing, as now, lean as a knife, narrow as the blade of one, grinning sarcastically, not only with the pleasure of disillusioning his son and casting ridicule upon his wife, who was ten thousand times better in every way than he was (James thought), but also with some

---

1. A department store on Victoria St. in London that originated as a cooperative store for officers' families and opened to the public in 1918; there were branches in India as well.
2. The King's or Queen's Bench, the highest division of the High Court of Justice in Britain, founded in 1215 when it was presided over by the monarch, hence the royal imagery of red and ermine.
3. Ramsay is a Scottish surname.

secret conceit at his own accuracy of judgement. What he said was true. It was always true. He was incapable of untruth; never tampered with a fact; never altered a disagreeable word to suit the pleasure or convenience of any mortal being, least of all of his own children, who, sprung from his loins, should be aware from childhood that life is difficult; facts uncompromising; and the passage to that fabled land where our brightest hopes are extinguished, our frail barks founder in darkness (here Mr. Ramsay would straighten his back and narrow his little blue eyes upon the horizon), one that needs, above all, courage, truth, and the power to endure.

"But it may be fine—I expect it will be fine," said Mrs. Ramsay, making some little twist of the reddish brown stocking[4] she was knitting, impatiently. If she finished it tonight, if they did go to the Lighthouse after all, it was to be given to the Lighthouse keeper for his little boy, who was threatened with a tuberculous hip;[5] together with a pile of old magazines, and some tobacco, indeed, whatever she could find lying about, not really wanted, but only littering the room, to give those poor fellows, who must be bored to death sitting all day with nothing to do but polish the lamp and trim the wick and rake about on their scrap of garden, something to amuse them. For how would you like to be shut up for a whole month at a time, and possibly more in stormy weather, upon a rock the size of a tennis lawn? she would ask; and to have no letters or newspapers, and to see nobody; if you were married, not to see your wife, not to know how your children were,—if they were ill, if they had fallen down and broken their legs or arms; to see the same dreary waves breaking week after week, and then a dreadful storm coming, and the windows covered with spray, and birds dashed against the lamp, and the whole place rocking, and not be able to put your nose out of doors for fear of being swept into the sea? How would you like that? she asked, addressing herself particularly to her daughters. So she added, rather differently, one must take them whatever comforts one can.

"It's due west," said the atheist Tansley, holding his bony fingers spread so that the wind blew through them, for he was sharing Mr. Ramsay's evening walk up and down, up and down the terrace. That is to say, the wind blew from the worst possible direction for landing at the Lighthouse. Yes, he did say disagreeable things, Mrs. Ramsay admitted; it was odious of him to rub this in, and make James still more disappointed; but at the same time, she would not let them laugh at him. "The atheist," they called him; "the little atheist."

4. A long sock, worn by girls and small boys (not what would now in the United States be called a stocking).
5. Tuberculosis could be caught from drinking unpasteurized cows' milk; the disease could affect bones and joints, most often the spine and the hip.

Rose mocked him; Prue mocked him; Andrew, Jasper, Roger mocked him; even old Badger without a tooth in his head had bit him, for being (as Nancy put it) the hundred and tenth young man to chase them all the way up to the Hebrides[6] when it was ever so much nicer to be alone.

"Nonsense," said Mrs. Ramsay, with great severity. Apart from the habit of exaggeration which they had from her, and from the implication (which was true) that she asked too many people to stay, and had to lodge some in the town, she could not bear incivility to her guests, to young men in particular, who were poor as church mice, "exceptionally able," her husband said, his great admirers, and come there for a holiday. Indeed, she had the whole of the other sex under her protection; for reasons she could not explain, for their chivalry and valour, for the fact that they negotiated treaties, ruled India,[7] controlled finance; finally for an attitude towards herself which no woman could fail to feel or to find agreeable, something trustful, childlike, reverential; which an old woman could take from a young man without loss of dignity, and woe betide the girl—pray Heaven it was none of her daughters!—who did not feel the worth of it, and all that it implied, to the marrow of her bones!

She turned with severity upon Nancy. He had not chased them, she said. He had been asked.

They must find a way out of it all. There might be some simpler way, some less laborious way, she sighed. When she looked in the glass and saw her hair grey, her cheek sunk, at fifty, she thought, possibly she might have managed things better—her husband; money; his books. But for her own part she would never for a single second regret her decision, evade difficulties, or slur over duties. She was now formidable to behold, and it was only in silence, looking up from their plates, after she had spoken so severely about Charles Tansley, that her daughters, Prue, Nancy, Rose—could sport with infidel ideas which they had brewed for themselves of a life different from hers; in Paris, perhaps; a wilder life; not always taking care of some man or other; for there was in all their minds a mute questioning of deference and chivalry, of the Bank of England and the

6. The novel's setting is the Isle of Skye, one of the Hebrides islands off the west coast of Scotland, although Woolf drew many features of the setting from the Cornwall of her childhood summer home near the town of St. Ives, transposing it to Scotland with little alteration to local flora and fauna, geography, or architecture. She didn't visit Skye until 1938.
7. British rule in India began in the 1600s with the East India Company's domination of international trade, enforced by a private army; in 1857 following the so-called "Indian Mutiny" the British government itself took control of what is now India and Pakistan, until Independence and Partition in 1947. Queen Victoria (1819–1901) was crowned Empress of India in 1877. Relatives on both sides of Woolf's family had worked for the Indian Civil Service, including her husband Leonard, who was a colonial administrator in Ceylon until 1911 and thereafter became a vocal critic of British imperial rule.

Indian Empire,[8] of ringed fingers and lace; though to them all there was something in this of the essence of beauty, which called out the manliness in their girlish hearts, and made them, as they sat at table beneath their mother's eyes, honour her strange severity, her extreme courtesy, like a Queen's raising from the mud to wash a beggar's dirty foot,[9] when she thus admonished them so very severely about that wretched atheist who had chased them—or, speaking accurately, been invited to stay with them—in the Isles of Skye.

"There'll be no landing at the Lighthouse tomorrow," said Charles Tansley, clapping his hands together as he stood at the window with her husband. Surely, he had said enough. She wished they would both leave her and James alone and go on talking. She looked at him. He was such a miserable specimen, the children said, all humps and hollows. He couldn't play cricket; he poked; he shuffled. He was a sarcastic brute, Andrew said. They knew what he liked best—to be for ever walking up and down, up and down, with Mr. Ramsay, and saying who had won this, who had won that, who was a "first-rate man" at Latin verses, who was "brilliant but I think fundamentally unsound," who was undoubtedly the "ablest fellow in Balliol,"[1] who had buried his light temporarily at Bristol or Bedford,[2] but was bound to be heard of later when his Prolegomena,[3] of which Mr. Tansley had the first pages in proof with him if Mr. Ramsay would like to see them, to some branch of mathematics or philosophy saw the light of day. That was what they talked about.

She could not help laughing herself sometimes. She said, the other day, something about "waves mountains high." Yes, said Charles Tansley, it was a little rough. "Aren't you drenched to the skin?" she had said. "Damp, not wet through," said Mr. Tansley, pinching his sleeve, feeling his socks.

But it was not that they minded, the children said. It was not his face; it was not his manners. It was him—his point of view. When they talked about something interesting, people, music, history, anything, even said it was a fine evening so why not sit out of doors, then what they complained of about Charles Tansley was that until he had turned the whole thing round and made it somehow reflect himself and disparage them—he was not satisfied. And he would go

8. The Bank of England is the British government's central bank, which controls the nation's supply of money. It was founded in 1694 and underwrote the Union with Scotland in 1707 and enabled subsequent imperial ventures including in India.
9. Aligns Mrs. Ramsay with Homer's Penelope, queen of Ithaka in the *Odyssey* who washes the feet of Odysseus, disguised as a beggar, on his return from twenty years absence.
1. One of the oldest constituent colleges of the University of Oxford; a fellow is a teacher and researcher ranking anywhere from postdoctoral fellow to senior member of the faculty.
2. University College, Bristol (a city in the west of England), and (probably) Bedford College, London: schools founded in the nineteenth century, open to women, and thus of lower prestige than the ancient foundations of Oxford or Cambridge.
3. Preliminary discourse preceding the main text of a book or chapter.

to picture galleries they said and he would ask one, did one like his tie? God knows, said Rose, one did not.

Disappearing as stealthily as stags from the dinner-table directly the meal was over, the eight sons and daughters of Mr. and Mrs. Ramsay sought their bedrooms, their fastnesses in a house where there was no other privacy to debate anything, everything; Tansley's tie; the passing of the Reform Bill;[4] sea birds and butterflies; people; while the sun poured into those attics, which a plank alone separated from each other so that every footstep could be plainly heard and the Swiss girl sobbing for her father who was dying of cancer in a valley of the Grisons,[5] and lit up bats, flannels, straw hats, ink-pots, paint-pots, beetles, and the skulls of small birds, while it drew from the long frilled strips of seaweed pinned to the wall a smell of salt and weeds, which was in the towels too, gritty with sand from bathing.

Strife, divisions, difference of opinion, prejudices twisted into the very fibre of being, oh, that they should begin so early, Mrs. Ramsay deplored. They were so critical, her children. They talked such nonsense. She went from the dining-room, holding James by the hand, since he would not go with the others. It seemed to her such nonsense—inventing differences, when people, heaven knows, were different enough without that. The real differences, she thought, standing by the drawing-room window, are enough, quite enough. She had in mind at the moment, rich and poor, high and low; the great in birth receiving from her, some half grudgingly, half respect, for had she not in her veins the blood of that very noble, if slightly mythical, Italian house, whose daughters, scattered about English drawing-rooms in the nineteenth century, had lisped so charmingly, had stormed so wildly, and all her wit and her bearing and her temper came from them, and not from the sluggish English, or the cold Scotch; but more profoundly, she ruminated the other problem, of rich and poor, and the things she saw with her own eyes, weekly, daily, here or in London, when she visited this widow, or that struggling wife in person with a bag on her arm, and a note-book and pencil with which she wrote down in columns carefully ruled for the purpose wages and spendings, employment and unemployment, in the hope that thus she would cease to be a private woman whose

4. The children may be discussing any of three nineteenth-century Reform Bills that successively expanded the franchise (male-only and based on property), the last being the 1884 Representation of the People Act, which allowed about half of all men in Britain to vote. Or they could be talking about bills under discussion when this part of the novel is set: a bill that would become the Parliament Act of 1911, which reduced the aristocratic, conservative power of the House of Lords; or even the People's Budget, introduced April 1909, which proposed to tax wealth in the form of land or other privately owned assets (as distinct from taxing income), to reduce poverty and strengthen the social safety net.
5. The largest and easternmost canton of Switzerland.

charity was half a sop to her own indignation, half a relief to her own curiosity, and become what with her untrained mind she greatly admired, an investigator, elucidating the social problem.[6]

Insoluble questions they were, it seemed to her, standing there, holding James by the hand. He had followed her into the drawing-room, that young man they laughed at; he was standing by the table, fidgeting with something, awkwardly, feeling himself out of things, as she knew without looking round. They had all gone—the children; Minta Doyle and Paul Rayley; Augustus Carmichael; her husband— they had all gone. So she turned with a sigh and said, "Would it bore you to come with me, Mr. Tansley?"

She had a dull errand in the town; she had a letter or two to write; she would be ten minutes perhaps; she would put on her hat. And, with her basket and her parasol, there she was again, ten minutes later, giving out a sense of being ready, of being equipped for a jaunt, which, however, she must interrupt for a moment, as they passed the tennis lawn, to ask Mr. Carmichael, who was basking with his yellow cat's eyes ajar, so that like a cat's they seemed to reflect the branches moving or the clouds passing, but to give no inkling of any inner thoughts or emotion whatsoever, if he wanted anything.

For they were making the great expedition, she said, laughing. They were going to the town. "Stamps, writing-paper, tobacco?" she suggested, stopping by his side. But no, he wanted nothing. His hands clasped themselves over his capacious paunch, his eyes blinked, as if he would have liked to reply kindly to these blandishments (she was seductive but a little nervous) but could not, sunk as he was in a grey-green somnolence which embraced them all, without need of words, in a vast and benevolent lethargy of well-wishing; all the house; all the world; all the people in it, for he had slipped into his glass at lunch a few drops of something,[7] which accounted, the children thought, for the vivid streak of canary-yellow in moustache and beard that were otherwise milk white. No, nothing, he murmured.

He should have been a great philosopher, said Mrs. Ramsay, as they went down the road to the fishing village, but he had made an unfortunate marriage. Holding her black parasol very erect, and moving with an indescribable air of expectation, as if she were going to meet some one round the corner, she told the story; an affair at Oxford with some girl; an early marriage; poverty; going to India;

---

6. This ambition (with her later thoughts about "hospitals and drains and the dairy," 46) provides a basis for linking Mrs. Ramsay to Julia Stephen. See in this edition Woolf, "Reminiscences" (191–94); Julia Stephen, *Notes from Sick Rooms* (206–10); and Leslie Stephen, *The Mausoleum Book* (210–15).
7. Mr. Carmichael apparently uses laudanum, made from opium, which was imported from India and was not yet a legally controlled substance.

translating a little poetry "very beautifully, I believe," being willing to teach the boys Persian or Hindustanee,[8] but what really was the use of that?—and then lying, as they saw him, on the lawn.

It flattered him; snubbed as he had been, it soothed him that Mrs. Ramsay should tell him this. Charles Tansley revived. Insinuating, too, as she did the greatness of man's intellect, even in its decay, the subjection of all wives—not that she blamed the girl, and the marriage had been happy enough, she believed—to their husband's labours, she made him feel better pleased with himself than he had done yet, and he would have liked, had they taken a cab, for example, to have paid for it. As for her little bag, might he not carry that? No, no, she said, she always carried *that* herself. She did too. Yes, he felt that in her. He felt many things, something in particular that excited him and disturbed him for reasons which he could not give. He would like her to see him, gowned and hooded, walking in a procession. A fellowship, a professorship, he felt capable of anything and saw himself—but what was she looking at? At a man pasting a bill. The vast flapping sheet flattened itself out, and each shove of the brush revealed fresh legs, hoops, horses, glistening reds and blues, beautifully smooth, until half the wall was covered with the advertisement of a circus; a hundred horsemen, twenty performing seals, lions, tigers . . . Craning forwards, for she was short-sighted, she read it out . . . "will visit this town," she read. It was terribly dangerous work for a one-armed man, she exclaimed, to stand on top of a ladder like that—his left arm had been cut off in a reaping machine two years ago.

"Let us all go!" she cried, moving on, as if all those riders and horses had filled her with childlike exultation and made her forget her pity.

"Let's go," he said, repeating her words, clicking them out, however, with a self-consciousness that made her wince. "Let us go to the circus." No. He could not say it right. He could not feel it right. But why not? she wondered. What was wrong with him then? She liked him warmly, at the moment. Had they not been taken, she asked, to circuses when they were children? Never, he answered, as if she asked the very thing he wanted; had been longing all these days to say, how they did not go to circuses. It was a large family, nine brothers and sisters, and his father was a working man. "My

---

8. Hindustani is the dominant language of northern India and modern Pakistan; Persian (Farsi) is spoken in modern Iran and Afghanistan; to offer to teach these languages to the boys suggests the expectation that they would grow up to work in the imperial civil service. Woolf initially elaborated on Mr. Carmichael's life in India by including, for example, a story of his "meeting a bear on a pass in the Himalayas": see the holograph in Woolf Online or *Original Holograph*, p. 155.

father is a chemist,[9] Mrs. Ramsay. He keeps a shop." He himself had
paid his own way since he was thirteen. Often he went without a
greatcoat in winter. He could never "return hospitality" (those were
his parched stiff words) at college. He had to make things last twice
the time other people did; he smoked the cheapest tobacco; shag;
the same the old men did in the quays. He worked hard—seven
hours a day; his subject was now the influence of something upon
somebody—they were walking on and Mrs. Ramsay did not quite
catch the meaning, only the words, here and there . . . dissertation . . . fellowship . . . readership . . . lectureship. She could not
follow the ugly academic jargon, that rattled itself off so glibly, but
said to herself that she saw now why going to the circus had knocked
him off his perch, poor little man, and why he came out, instantly,
with all that about his father and mother and brothers and sisters,
and she would see to it that they didn't laugh at him any more; she
would tell Prue about it. What he would have liked, she supposed,
would have been to say how he had gone not to the circus but to
Ibsen[1] with the Ramsays. He was an awful prig—oh yes, an insuf-
ferable bore. For, though they had reached the town now and were
in the main street, with carts grinding past on the cobbles, still he
went on talking, about settlements, and teaching, and working men,
and helping our own class, and lectures, till she gathered that he
had got back entire self-confidence, had recovered from the circus,
and was about (and now again she liked him warmly) to tell her—
but here, the houses falling away on both sides, they came out on
the quay, and the whole bay spread before them and Mrs. Ramsay
could not help exclaiming, "Oh, how beautiful!" For the great
plateful of blue water was before her; the hoary Lighthouse, distant,
austere, in the midst; and on the right, as far as the eye could see,
fading and falling, in soft low pleats, the green sand dunes with the
wild flowing grasses on them, which always seemed to be running
away into some moon country, uninhabited of men.

That was the view, she said, stopping, growing greyer-eyed, that
her husband loved.

She paused a moment. But now, she said, artists had come here.
There indeed, only a few paces off, stood one of them, in Panama
hat and yellow boots, seriously, softly, absorbedly, for all that he was
watched by ten little boys, with an air of profound contentment on
his round red face gazing, and then, when he had gazed, dipping;
imbuing the tip of his brush in some soft mound of green or pink.
Since Mr. Paunceforte[2] had been there, three years before, all the

9. A pharmacist.
1. Henrik Ibsen (1828–1906), Norwegian author of modernist plays including *A Doll's House*.
2. A fictional character, a typical producer of decorative works of *plein air* impressionism;
   in summer St. Ives attracted visiting amateur painters.

pictures were like that, she said, green and grey, with lemon-coloured sailing-boats, and pink women on the beach.

But her grandmother's friends, she said, glancing discreetly as they passed, took the greatest pains; first they mixed their own colours, and then they ground them, and then they put damp cloths to keep them moist.

So Mr. Tansley supposed she meant him to see that that man's picture was skimpy, was that what one said? The colours weren't solid? Was that what one said? Under the influence of that extraordinary emotion which had been growing all the walk, had begun in the garden when he had wanted to take her bag, had increased in the town when he had wanted to tell her everything about himself, he was coming to see himself, and everything he had ever known gone crooked a little. It was awfully strange.

There he stood in the parlour of the poky little house where she had taken him, waiting for her, while she went upstairs a moment to see a woman. He heard her quick step above; heard her voice cheerful, then low; looked at the mats, tea-caddies, glass shades; waited quite impatiently; looked forward eagerly to the walk home; determined to carry her bag; then heard her come out; shut a door; say they must keep the windows open and the doors shut, ask at the house for anything they wanted (she must be talking to a child) when, suddenly, in she came, stood for a moment silent (as if she had been pretending up there, and for a moment let herself be now), stood quite motionless for a moment against a picture of Queen Victoria wearing the blue ribbon of the Garter;[3] when all at once he realised that it was this: it was this:—she was the most beautiful person he had ever seen.

With stars in her eyes and veils in her hair, with cyclamen and wild violets[4]—what nonsense was he thinking? She was fifty at least; she had eight children. Stepping through fields of flowers and taking to her breast buds that had broken and lambs that had fallen; with the stars in her eyes and the wind in her hair— He took her bag.

"Good-bye, Elsie," she said, and they walked up the street, she holding her parasol erect and walking as if she expected to meet some one round the corner, while for the first time in his life Charles Tansley felt an extraordinary pride; a man digging in a drain stopped

3. Its blue silk insignia worn diagonally across the chest, The Order of the Garter is the most senior order of British knighthood founded by King Edward III (1312–1377) in 1348. Such a portrait would represent the queen in a formal pose, typically seated on a throne, crowned and bejewelled. Especially following her golden and diamond jubilees in 1887 and 1897, engravings of the queen in her widow's black dress and enthroned as empress were widely available and often hung in middle- and working-class homes.
4. This imagery evokes the world of classical mythology: cyclamen flowers are native to Greece and other parts of the Mediterranean. See also "[Mother-Daughter Loss in *To the Lighthouse*]," in which Adrienne Rich connects Mrs. Ramsay to the Greek goddess Demeter, this edition, pp. 290–92.

digging and looked at her, let his arm fall down and looked at her; for the first time in his life Charles Tansley felt an extraordinary pride; felt the wind and the cyclamen and the violets for he was walking with a beautiful woman. He had hold of her bag.

II

"No going to the Lighthouse, James," he said, as he stood by the window, speaking awkwardly, but trying in deference to Mrs. Ramsay to soften his voice into some semblance of geniality at least.

Odious little man, thought Mrs. Ramsay, why go on saying that?

III

"Perhaps you will wake up and find the sun shining and the birds singing," she said compassionately, smoothing the little boy's hair, for her husband, with his caustic saying that it would not be fine, had dashed his spirits she could see. This going to the Lighthouse was a passion of his, she saw, and then, as if her husband had not said enough, with his caustic saying that it would not be fine tomorrow, this odious little man went and rubbed it in all over again.

"Perhaps it will be fine tomorrow," she said, smoothing his hair.

All she could do now was to admire the refrigerator, and turn the pages of the Stores list in the hope that she might come upon something like a rake, or a mowing-machine, which, with its prongs and its handles, would need the greatest skill and care in cutting out. All these young men parodied her husband, she reflected; he said it would rain; they said it would be a positive tornado.

But here, as she turned the page, suddenly her search for the picture of a rake or a mowing-machine was interrupted. The gruff murmur, irregularly broken by the taking out of pipes and the putting in of pipes which had kept on assuring her, though she could not hear what was said (as she sat in the window which opened on the terrace), that the men were happily talking; this sound, which had lasted now half an hour and had taken its place soothingly in the scale of sounds pressing on top of her, such as the tap of balls upon bats, the sharp, sudden bark now and then, "How's that?[1] How's that?" of the children playing cricket, had ceased; so that the monotonous fall of the waves on the beach, which for the most part beat a measured and soothing tattoo to her thoughts and seemed consolingly to repeat over and over again as she sat with the children the words of some old cradle song, murmured by nature, "I am guarding you—I am your support," but at other times suddenly and

---

1. In the game of cricket, the bowling side must shout an appeal of "how's that?" for the umpire to dismiss a batsman. See also Undated Notes and an Outline, this edition, p. 161.

unexpectedly, especially when her mind raised itself slightly from the task actually in hand, had no such kindly meaning, but like a ghostly roll of drums remorselessly beat the measure of life, made one think of the destruction of the island and its engulfment in the sea, and warned her whose day had slipped past in one quick doing after another that it was all ephemeral as a rainbow—this sound which had been obscured and concealed under the other sounds suddenly thundered hollow in her ears and made her look up with an impulse of terror.

They had ceased to talk; that was the explanation. Falling in one second from the tension which had gripped her to the other extreme which, as if to recoup her for her unnecessary expense of emotion, was cool, amused, and even faintly malicious, she concluded that poor Charles Tansley had been shed. That was of little account to her. If her husband required sacrifices (and indeed he did) she cheerfully offered up to him Charles Tansley, who had snubbed her little boy.

One moment more, with her head raised, she listened, as if she waited for some habitual sound, some regular mechanical sound; and then, hearing something rhythmical, half said, half chanted, beginning in the garden, as her husband beat up and down the terrace, something between a croak and a song, she was soothed once more, assured again that all was well, and looking down at the book on her knee found the picture of a pocket knife with six blades which could only be cut out if James was very careful.

Suddenly a loud cry, as of a sleep-walker, half roused, something about

Stormed at with shot and shell[2]

sung out with the utmost intensity in her ear, made her turn apprehensively to see if any one heard him. Only Lily Briscoe, she was glad to find; and that did not matter. But the sight of the girl standing on the edge of the lawn painting reminded her; she was supposed to be keeping her head as much in the same position as possible for Lily's picture. Lily's picture! Mrs. Ramsay smiled. With her little Chinese eyes[3] and her puckered-up face, she would never marry; one could not take her painting very seriously; she was an independent

2. This and further lines that Mr. Ramsay recites are from Tennyson's poem "The Charge of the Light Brigade," a tribute to the Battle of Balaclava, fought on October 25, 1854, in the Crimean War. When he shouts "Boldly we rode and well" at the beginning of the next section, Mr. Ramsay has changed "they rode" in the original to "we rode." Alfred Tennyson (1809–1892) was Britain's Poet Laureate from 1850 until his death. See the text of the poem, this edition, pp. 267–68.
3. It is unlikely that Woolf intends the reader to envision Lily as being of Chinese or partly Chinese descent; Elizabeth Dalloway, the daughter of the central family in *Mrs. Dalloway*, also has "Chinese eyes." In this context, "Chinese" refers to the modernist fascination with Asian arts; it suggests a distinctive and unfamiliar point of view. See Urmila Seshagiri's discussion of the novel's Orientalism, this edition, pp. 312–26.

little creature, and Mrs. Ramsay liked her for it; so, remembering
her promise, she bent her head.

IV

Indeed, he almost knocked her easel over, coming down upon her
with his hands waving shouting out, "Boldly we rode and well," but,
mercifully, he turned sharp, and rode off, to die gloriously she supposed upon the heights of Balaclava. Never was anybody at once so
ridiculous and so alarming. But so long as he kept like that, waving,
shouting, she was safe; he would not stand still and look at her picture. And that was what Lily Briscoe could not have endured. Even
while she looked at the mass, at the line, at the colour, at Mrs. Ramsay sitting in the window with James, she kept a feeler on her surroundings lest some one should creep up, and suddenly she should
find her picture looked at. But now, with all her senses quickened
as they were, looking, straining, till the colour of the wall and the
jacmanna[1] beyond burnt into her eyes, she was aware of some one
coming out of the house, coming towards her; but somehow divined,
from the footfall, William Bankes, so that though her brush quivered, she did not, as she would have done had it been Mr. Tansley,
Paul Rayley, Minta Doyle, or practically anybody else, turn her canvas
upon the grass, but let it stand. William Bankes stood beside her.

They had rooms in the village, and so, walking in, walking out,
parting late on door-mats, had said little things about the soup, about
the children, about one thing and another which made them allies;
so that when he stood beside her now in his judicial way (he was old
enough to be her father too, a botanist, a widower, smelling of soap,
very scrupulous and clean) she just stood there. He just stood there.
Her shoes were excellent, he observed. They allowed the toes their
natural expansion. Lodging in the same house with her, he had
noticed too, how orderly she was, up before breakfast and off to
paint, he believed, alone: poor, presumably, and without the com-
plexion or the allurement of Miss Doyle certainly, but with a good
sense which made her in his eyes superior to that young lady. Now,
for instance, when Ramsay bore down on them, shouting, gesticu-
lating, Miss Briscoe, he felt certain, understood.

"Some one had blundered."

Mr. Ramsay glared at them. He glared at them without seeming
to see them. That did make them both vaguely uncomfortable.
Together they had seen a thing they had not been meant to see. They

---

1. *Clematis jackmannii* or purple clematis, a popular ornamental vine with large, brilliant
   purple flowers that blooms in summer and autumn.

had encroached upon a privacy. So, Lily thought, it was probably an excuse of his for moving, for getting out of earshot, that made Mr. Bankes almost immediately say something about its being chilly and suggest taking a stroll. She would come, yes. But it was with difficulty that she took her eyes off her picture.

The jacmanna was bright violet; the wall staring white. She would not have considered it honest to tamper with the bright violet and the staring white, since she saw them like that, fashionable though it was, since Mr. Paunceforte's visit, to see everything pale, elegant, semitransparent. Then beneath the colour there was the shape. She could see it all so clearly, so commandingly, when she looked: it was when she took her brush in hand that the whole thing changed. It was in that moment's flight between the picture and her canvas that the demons set on her who often brought her to the verge of tears and made this passage from conception to work as dreadful as any down a dark passage for a child. Such she often felt herself— struggling against terrific odds to maintain her courage; to say: "But this is what I see; this is what I see," and so to clasp some miserable remnant of her vision to her breast, which a thousand forces did their best to pluck from her. And it was then too, in that chill and windy way, as she began to paint, that there forced themselves upon her other things, her own inadequacy, her insignificance, keeping house for her father off the Brompton Road,[2] and had much ado to control her impulse to fling herself (thank Heaven she had always resisted so far) at Mrs. Ramsay's knee and say to her—but what could one say to her? "I'm in love with you?" No, that was not true. "I'm in love with this all," waving her hand at the hedge, at the house, at the children. It was absurd, it was impossible. So now she laid her brushes neatly in the box, side by side, and said to William Bankes:

"It suddenly gets cold. The sun seems to give less heat," she said, looking about her, for it was bright enough, the grass still a soft deep green, the house starred in its greenery with purple passion flowers, and rooks[3] dropping cool cries from the high blue. But something moved, flashed, turned a silver wing in the air. It was September after all, the middle of September, and past six in the evening. So off they strolled down the garden in the usual direction, past the tennis lawn, past the pampas grass,[4] to that break in the thick hedge, guarded by

2. A main street in the then suburban district of Knightsbridge, London; originally Woolf had Lily think of her neighborhood as "familiar" and "dull," weighed down by "the florid solidity of Harrods," a large department store (*Original Holograph*, p. 34).
3. *Corvus frugilegus*, a large and gregarious black bird, similar to a crow, known for forming rookeries (roosting) in or near the rooftops of English castles and country houses. Woolf was told, after the novel came out, that there are no rooks in the Hebrides.
4. *Cortaderia selloana*, a tall, stiff-stalked grass that flowers with a feathery plume, native to South America and named for a German botanist who collected in Brazil.

red-hot pokers[5] like brasiers of clear burning coal, between which the blue waters of the bay looked bluer than ever.

They came there regularly every evening drawn by some need. It was as if the water floated off and set sailing thoughts which had grown stagnant on dry land, and gave to their bodies even some sort of physical relief. First, the pulse of colour flooded the bay with blue, and the heart expanded with it and the body swam, only the next instant to be checked and chilled by the prickly blackness on the ruffled waves. Then, up behind the great black rock, almost every evening spurted irregularly, so that one had to watch for it and it was a delight when it came, a fountain of white water; and then, while one waited for that, one watched, on the pale semicircular beach, wave after wave shedding again and again smoothly, a film of mother of pearl.

They both smiled, standing there. They both felt a common hilarity, excited by the moving waves; and then by the swift cutting race of a sailing boat, which, having sliced a curve in the bay, stopped; shivered; let its sails drop down; and then, with a natural instinct to complete the picture, after this swift movement, both of them looked at the dunes far away, and instead of merriment felt come over them some sadness—because the thing was completed partly, and partly because distant views seem to outlast by a million years (Lily thought) the gazer and to be communing already with a sky which beholds an earth entirely at rest.

Looking at the far sand hills, William Bankes thought of Ramsay: thought of a road in Westmorland,[6] thought of Ramsay striding along a road by himself hung round with that solitude which seemed to be his natural air. But this was suddenly interrupted, William Bankes remembered (and this must refer to some actual incident), by a hen, straddling her wings out in protection of a covey of little chicks, upon which Ramsay, stopping, pointed his stick and said "Pretty—pretty," an odd illumination in to his heart, Bankes had thought it, which showed his simplicity, his sympathy with humble things; but it seemed to him as if their friendship had ceased, there, on that stretch of road. After that, Ramsay had married. After that, what with one thing and another, the pulp had gone out of their friendship. Whose fault it was he could not say, only, after a time, repetition had taken the place of newness. It was to repeat that they met. But in this dumb colloquy with the sand dunes he maintained that his affection for Ramsay had in no way diminished; but there,

---

5. *Kniphofia*, a genus of flowering plants with spikes of upright, brightly colored flowers above grasslike foliage, in shades of red, orange, and yellow; brought to Britain from Africa in the eighteenth century and named for a German botanist.
6. A historic county in northwest England. It formed an administrative county between 1889 and 1974 and is now part of Cumbria. *Sand hills*: Sand dunes.

like the body of a young man laid up in peat for a century,[7] with the red fresh on his lips, was his friendship, in its acuteness and reality, laid up across the bay among the sandhills.

He was anxious for the sake of this friendship and perhaps too in order to clear himself in his own mind from the imputation of having dried and shrunk—for Ramsay lived in a welter of children, whereas Bankes was childless and a widower—he was anxious that Lily Briscoe should not disparage Ramsay (a great man in his own way) yet should understand how things stood between them. Begun long years ago, their friendship had petered out on a Westmorland road, where the hen spread her wings before her chicks; after which Ramsay had married, and their paths lying different ways, there had been, certainly for no one's fault, some tendency, when they met, to repeat.

Yes. That was it. He finished. He turned from the view. And, turning to walk back the other way, up the drive, Mr. Bankes was alive to things which would not have struck him had not those sandhills revealed to him the body of his friendship lying with the red on its lips laid up in peat—for instance, Cam, the little girl, Ramsay's youngest daughter.[8] She was picking Sweet Alice[9] on the bank. She was wild and fierce. She would not "give a flower to the gentleman" as the nursemaid told her. No! no! no! she would not! She clenched her fist. She stamped. And Mr. Bankes felt aged and saddened and somehow put into the wrong by her about his friendship. He must have dried and shrunk.

The Ramsays were not rich, and it was a wonder how they managed to contrive it all. Eight children! To feed eight children on philosophy! Here was another of them, Jasper this time, strolling past, to have a shot at a bird, he said, nonchalantly, swinging Lily's hand like a pump-handle as he passed, which caused Mr. Bankes to say, bitterly, how *she* was a favourite. There was education now to be considered (true, Mrs. Ramsay had something of her own perhaps) let alone the daily wear and tear of shoes and stockings which those "great fellows," all well grown, angular, ruthless youngsters, must require. As for being sure which was which, or in what order they came, that was beyond him. He called them privately after the Kings

7. "Bog bodies," as they are now called, are cadavers—some of them hundreds or thousands of years old—that have been naturally preserved by the extreme acid conditions of a peat bog (a wetland made of dead plant material, found mostly in colder climates). Many such cadavers have been found in the British Isles and northern Europe.
8. The name of the youngest Ramsay daughter (apparently named for Mrs. Ramsay's Aunt Camilla, 52) evokes the Volscian warrior Camilla in the *Aeneid* (epic poem by Virgil, 70–19 B.C.E.), who as a child was tied to a spear and shot across a river by her father; she fights fiercely and runs so fast her feet don't bend the wheat when she races across a field. The *Aeneid* recounts the Trojans' invasion of Italy and their founding of Rome following the fall of Troy; Camilla fought on the losing side.
9. *Lobularia maritima* or "sweet alyssum" is a low-growing flowering plant. That she is a young girl out picking flowers and resisting male appropriation aligns Cam with Persephone, the daughter of the Greek goddess Demeter.

and Queens of England; Cam the Wicked, James the Ruthless, Andrew the Just, Prue the Fair[1]—for Prue would have beauty, he thought, how could she help it?—and Andrew brains. While he walked up the drive and Lily Briscoe said yes and no and capped his comments (for she was in love with them all, in love with this world) he weighed Ramsay's case, commiserated him, envied him, as if he had seen him divest himself of all those glories of isolation and austerity which crowned him in youth to cumber himself definitely with fluttering wings and clucking domesticities. They gave him something—William Bankes acknowledged that; it would have been pleasant if Cam had stuck a flower in his coat or clambered over his shoulder, to look at a picture of Vesuvius in eruption; but they had also, his old friends could not but feel, destroyed something. What would a stranger think now? What did this Lily Briscoe think? Could one help noticing that habits grew on him? eccentricities, weaknesses perhaps? It was astonishing that a man of his intellect could stoop so low as he did—but that was too harsh a phrase—could depend so much as he did upon people's praise.

"Oh, but," said Lily, "think of his work!"

Whenever she "thought of his work" she always saw clearly before her a large kitchen table. It was Andrew's doing. She asked him what his father's books were about. "Subject and object and the nature of reality," Andrew had said. And when she said Heavens, she had no notion what that meant. "Think of a kitchen table then," he told her, "when you're not there."[2]

So now she always saw, when she thought of Mr. Ramsay's work, a scrubbed kitchen table. It lodged now in the fork of a pear tree, for they had reached the orchard. And with a painful effort of concentration, she focused her mind, not upon the silver-bossed bark of the tree, or upon its fish-shaped leaves, but upon a phantom kitchen table, one of those scrubbed board tables, grained and knotted, whose virtue seems to have been laid bare by years of muscular integrity, which stuck there, its four legs in air. Naturally, if one's days were passed in this seeing of angular essences, this reducing of lovely evenings, with all their flamingo clouds and blue and silver to a white deal four-legged table (and it was a mark of the finest minds so to do), naturally one could not be judged like an ordinary person.

1. Mr. Bankes humorously imitates the nicknames of early English monarchs such as Alfred the Great (849–899), Ethelred the Unready (968–1016), and Edward the Confessor (1003–1066).
2. David Hume (1711–1776) and other empiricist philosophers (see also note 9 p. 36) asked whether the existence of objects depended on human perception or whether they could be shown to exist independently of their being perceived. Leslie Stephen wrote about the development of this central problem in the history of philosophy, an account focusing on Hume and using a table to exemplify the problem; so did Woolf's contemporary Bertrand Russell; see the selections in "Reality, Philosophy, and Science," this edition, pp. 219–31.

Mr. Bankes liked her for bidding him "think of his work." He had thought of it, often and often. Times without number, he had said, "Ramsay is one of those men who do their best work before they are forty." He had made a definite contribution to philosophy in one little book when he was only five and twenty; what came after was more or less amplification, repetition. But the number of men who make a definite contribution to anything whatsoever is very small, he said, pausing by the pear tree, well brushed, scrupulously exact, exquisitely judicial. Suddenly, as if the movement of his hand had released it, the load of her accumulated impressions of him tilted up, and down poured in a ponderous avalanche all she felt about him. That was one sensation. Then up rose in a fume the essence of his being. That was another. She felt herself transfixed by the intensity of her perception; it was his severity; his goodness. I respect you (she addressed silently him in person) in every atom; you are not vain; you are entirely impersonal; you are finer than Mr. Ramsay; you are the finest human being that I know; you have neither wife nor child (without any sexual feeling, she longed to cherish that loneliness), you live for science (involuntarily, sections of potatoes rose before her eyes); praise would be an insult to you; generous, pure-hearted, heroic man! But simultaneously, she remembered how he had brought a valet all the way up here; objected to dogs on chairs; would prose for hours (until Mr. Ramsay slammed out of the room) about salt in vegetables and the iniquity of English cooks.

How then did it work out, all this? How did one judge people, think of them? How did one add up this and that and conclude that it was liking one felt, or disliking? And to those words, what meaning attached, after all? Standing now, apparently transfixed, by the pear tree, impressions poured in upon her of those two men, and to follow her thought was like following a voice which speaks too quickly to be taken down by one's pencil, and the voice was her own voice saying without prompting undeniable, everlasting, contradictory things, so that even the fissures and humps on the bark of the pear tree were irrevocably fixed there for eternity. You have greatness, she continued, but Mr. Ramsay has none of it. He is petty, selfish, vain, egotistical; he is spoilt; he is a tyrant; he wears Mrs. Ramsay to death; but he has what you (she addressed Mr. Bankes) have not; a fiery unworldliness; he knows nothing about trifles; he loves dogs and his children. He has eight. Mr. Bankes has none. Did he not come down in two coats the other night and let Mrs. Ramsay trim his hair into a pudding basin? All of this danced up and down, like a company of gnats, each separate, but all marvellously controlled in an invisible elastic net—danced up and down in Lily's mind, in and about the branches of the pear tree, where still hung in effigy the scrubbed kitchen table, symbol of her profound respect for Mr. Ramsay's mind, until her thought which had spun quicker and quicker exploded of its own intensity; she felt released; a shot went off close at hand, and there came, flying from its fragments, frightened, effusive, tumultuous, a flock of starlings.

"Jasper!" said Mr. Bankes. They turned the way the starlings flew, over the terrace. Following the scatter of swift-flying birds in the sky they stepped through the gap in the high hedge straight into Mr. Ramsay, who boomed tragically at them, "Some one had blundered!"

His eyes, glazed with emotion, defiant with tragic intensity, met theirs for a second, and trembled on the verge of recognition; but then, raising his hand, half-way to his face as if to avert, to brush off, in an agony of peevish shame, their normal gaze, as if he begged them to withhold for a moment what he knew to be inevitable, as if he impressed upon them his own child-like resentment of interruption, yet even in the moment of discovery was not to be routed utterly, but was determined to hold fast to something of this delicious emotion, this impure rhapsody of which he was ashamed, but in which he revelled—he turned abruptly, slammed his private door on them; and, Lily Briscoe and Mr. Bankes, looking uneasily up into the sky, observed that the flock of starlings which Jasper had routed with his gun had settled on the tops of the elm trees.

V

"And even if it isn't fine tomorrow," said Mrs. Ramsay, raising her eyes to glance at William Bankes and Lily Briscoe as they passed, "it will be another day. And now," she said, thinking that Lily's charm was her Chinese eyes, aslant in her white, puckered little face, but it would take a clever man to see it, "and now stand up, and let me measure your leg," for they might go to the Lighthouse after all, and she must see if the stocking did not need to be an inch or two longer in the leg.

Smiling, for it was an admirable idea, that had flashed upon her this very second—William and Lily should marry—she took the heather-mixture stocking, with its criss-cross of steel needles at the mouth of it, and measured it against James's leg.

"My dear, stand still," she said, for in his jealousy, not liking to serve as measuring block for the Lighthouse keeper's little boy, James fidgeted purposely; and if he did that, how could she see, was it too long, was it too short? she asked.

She looked up—what demon possessed him, her youngest, her cherished?—and saw the room, saw the chairs, thought them fearfully shabby. Their entrails, as Andrew said the other day, were all over the floor; but then what was the point, she asked, of buying good chairs to let them spoil up here all through the winter when the house, with only one old woman to see to it, positively dripped with wet? Never mind, the rent was precisely twopence halfpenny;[1] the children loved it; it did her husband good to be three thousand, or if she must be accurate, three hundred miles from his libraries and his lectures and his disciples; and there was room for visitors. Mats, camp beds, crazy ghosts of chairs and tables whose London life of service was done—they did well enough here; and a photograph or two, and books. Books, she thought, grew of themselves. She never had time to read them. Alas! even the books that had been given her and inscribed by the hand of the poet himself: "For her whose wishes must be obeyed" . . . "The happier Helen of our days"[2] . . . disgraceful to say, she had never read them. And Croom on the Mind and Bates on the Savage Customs of Polynesia[3] ("My dear, stand still," she said)—neither of those could one send to the Lighthouse. At a certain moment, she supposed, the house would become so shabby that something must be done. If they could be taught to wipe their feet and not bring the beach in with them—that would be something. Crabs, she had to allow, if Andrew really wished to dissect them, or if Jasper believed that one could make soup from seaweed, one could not prevent it; or Rose's objects—shells, reeds, stones; for they were gifted, her children, but all in quite different ways. And the result of it was, she sighed, taking in the whole room from floor to ceiling, as she held the stocking against James's leg, that things got shabbier and got shabbier summer after summer. The mat was fading; the wall-paper was flapping. You couldn't tell any more that those were roses on it. Still, if every door in a house is left perpetually open, and no lockmaker in the whole of Scotland can mend a bolt, things must spoil. Every door was left open. She listened. The drawing-room door was open; the hall door was open; it sounded as if the bedroom doors were open; and certainly the window on the landing was open, for that she had opened herself. That windows should be open, and doors shut—simple as it was, could none of them remember it? She would go into the maids' bedrooms at night and find them sealed like ovens, except for Marie's, the Swiss girl, who would rather go without a bath than without

1. Mrs. Ramsay's "habit of exaggeration" (7), like "three thousand, or if she must be accurate, three hundred miles from his libraries." In the currency of the time, there were twelve pence (pennies) in a shilling, and twenty shillings in a pound; twopence halfpenny would have been about the price of a loaf of bread.
2. These two gift inscriptions link Mrs. Ramsay to the terrifyingly beautiful and immortal queen Ayesha, "she-who-must-be-obeyed," in the novel *She* (1887) by H. Rider Haggard (1856–1925); and to Helen of Troy, the woman so beautiful the Trojan War was said to have been started in a dispute over her.
3. References to the Scottish philosopher George Croom Robertson (1842–1892), who was editor of the journal *Mind*, and to the British naturalist and explorer Henry Walter Bates (1825–1892).

fresh air, but then at home, she had said, "the mountains are so beautiful." She had said that last night looking out of the window with tears in her eyes. "The mountains are so beautiful." Her father was dying there, Mrs. Ramsay knew. He was leaving them fatherless. Scolding and demonstrating (how to make a bed, how to open a window, with hands that shut and spread like a Frenchwoman's) all had folded itself quietly about her, when the girl spoke, as, after a flight through the sunshine the wings of a bird fold themselves quietly and the blue of its plumage changes from bright steel to soft purple. She had stood there silent for there was nothing to be said. He had cancer of the throat. At the recollection—how she had stood there, how the girl had said, "At home the mountains are so beautiful," and there was no hope, no hope whatever, she had a spasm of irritation, and speaking sharply, said to James:

"Stand still. Don't be tiresome," so that he knew instantly that her severity was real, and straightened his leg and she measured it.

The stocking was too short by half an inch at least, making allowance for the fact that Sorley's little boy would be less well grown than James.

"It's too short," she said, "ever so much too short."

Never did anybody look so sad. Bitter and black, half-way down, in the darkness, in the shaft which ran from the sunlight to the depths, perhaps a tear formed; a tear fell; the waters swayed this way and that, received it, and were at rest. Never did anybody look so sad.

But was it nothing but looks, people said? What was there behind it—her beauty and splendour? Had he blown his brains out, they asked, had he died the week before they were married—some other, earlier lover, of whom rumours reached one? Or was there nothing? nothing but an incomparable beauty which she lived behind, and could do nothing to disturb? For easily though she might have said at some moment of intimacy when stories of great passion, of love foiled, of ambition thwarted came her way how she too had known or felt or been through it herself, she never spoke. She was silent always. She knew then—she knew without having learnt. Her simplicity fathomed what clever people falsified. Her singleness of mind made her drop plumb like a stone, alight exact as a bird, gave her, naturally, this swoop and fall of the spirit upon truth which delighted, eased, sustained—falsely perhaps.

("Nature has but little clay," said Mr. Bankes once, much moved by her voice on the telephone, though she was only telling him a fact about a train, "like that of which she moulded you." He saw her at the end of the line very clearly Greek, straight, blue-eyed. How incongruous it seemed to be telephoning to a woman like that. The

Graces assembling seemed to have joined hands in meadows of asphodel[4] to compose that face. He would catch the 10:30 at Euston.[5]

"Yet she's no more aware of her beauty than a child," said Mr. Bankes, replacing the receiver and crossing the room to see what progress the workmen were making with an hotel which they were building at the back of his house. And he thought of Mrs. Ramsay as he looked at that stir among the unfinished walls. For always, he thought, there was something incongruous to be worked into the harmony of her face. She clapped a deer-stalker's hat[6] on her head; she ran across the lawn in goloshes to snatch a child from mischief. So that if it was her beauty merely that one thought of, one must remember the quivering thing, the living thing (they were carrying bricks up a little plank as he watched them), and work it into the picture; or if one thought of her simply as a woman, one must endow her with some freak of idiosyncrasy—she did not like admiration— or suppose some latent desire to doff her royalty of form as if her beauty bored her and all that men say of beauty, and she wanted only to be like other people, insignificant. He did not know. He did not know. He must go to his work.)

Knitting her reddish-brown hairy stocking, with her head outlined absurdly by the gilt frame, the green shawl which she had tossed over the edge of the frame, and the authenticated masterpiece by Michael Angelo,[7] Mrs. Ramsay smoothed out what had been harsh in her manner a moment before, raised his head, and kissed her little boy on the forehead. "Let us find another picture to cut out," she said.

VI

But what had happened?

Some one had blundered.

Starting from her musing she gave meaning to words which she had held meaningless in her mind for a long stretch of time. "Some one had blundered—" Fixing her short-sighted eyes upon her husband, who was now bearing down upon her, she gazed steadily until his closeness revealed to her (the jingle mated itself in her head) that

4. A lily-like flowering plant bearing stalks of white blooms, native to Europe, said to grow in the Elysian fields of the classical underworld. *The Graces*: Aglaia, Thalia, and Euphrosyne in Greek mythology, beautiful sister goddesses and attendants of Aphrodite, regarded as the givers of beauty and charm.
5. A railway station in central London.
6. A round cloth cap with visors on the front and back and ear flaps that tie on top, typically worn for hunting (and now popularly associated with Sherlock Holmes).
7. Michelangelo Buonarotti (1475–1564). In the holograph the description is ampler: "one of those large brown photographs of authenticated masterpieces (Michael Angelo, Titian) which, rigged in a cheap frame stood upon an easel" (*Original Holograph*, p. 54). In the holograph and in the British edition the green shawl is cashmerc, an import from India's Kashmir region (*Original Holograph*, p. 55).

something had happened, some one had blundered. But she could not for the life of her think what.

He shivered; he quivered. All his vanity, all his satisfaction in his own splendour, riding fell as a thunderbolt, fierce as a hawk at the head of his men through the valley of death, had been shattered, destroyed. Stormed at by shot and shell, boldly we rode and well, flashed through the valley of death, volleyed and thundered[1]—straight into Lily Briscoe and William Bankes. He quivered; he shivered.

Not for the world would she have spoken to him, realising, from the familiar signs, his eyes averted, and some curious gathering together of his person, as if he wrapped himself about and needed privacy into which to regain his equilibrium, that he was outraged and anguished. She stroked James's head; she transferred to him what she felt for her husband, and, as she watched him chalk yellow the white dress shirt of a gentleman in the Army and Navy Stores catalogue, thought what a delight it would be to her should he turn out a great artist; and why should he not? He had a splendid fore-head. Then, looking up, as her husband passed her once more, she was relieved to find that the ruin was veiled; domesticity triumphed; custom crooned its soothing rhythm, so that when stopping deliberately, as his turn came round again, at the window he bent quizzically and whimsically to tickle James's bare calf with a sprig of something, she twitted him for having dispatched "that poor young man," Charles Tansley. Tansley had had to go in and write his dissertation, he said.

"James will have to write *his* dissertation one of these days," he added ironically, flicking his sprig.

Hating his father, James brushed away the tickling spray with which in a manner peculiar to him, compound of severity and humour, he teased his youngest son's bare leg.

She was trying to get these tiresome stockings finished to send to Sorley's little boy tomorrow, said Mrs. Ramsay.

There wasn't the slightest possible chance that they could go to the Lighthouse tomorrow, Mr. Ramsay snapped out irascibly.

How did he know? she asked. The wind often changed.

The extraordinary irrationality of her remark, the folly of women's minds enraged him. He had ridden through the valley of death, been shattered and shivered; and now, she flew in the face of facts, made his children hope what was utterly out of the question, in effect, told lies. He stamped his foot on the stone step. "Damn you," he said. But what had she said? Simply that it might be fine tomorrow. So it might.

Not with the barometer falling and the wind due west.

---

1. Mr. Ramsay chanting "The Charge of the Light Brigade" when he ran into Lily and William, pp. 16, 22. See note 2 p. 15 and the text of the poem, this edition, pp. 267–68.

To pursue truth with such astonishing lack of consideration for other people's feelings, to rend the thin veils of civilisation so wantonly, so brutally, was to her so horrible an outrage of human decency that, without replying, dazed and blinded, she bent her head as if to let the pelt of jagged hail, the drench of dirty water, bespatter her unrebuked. There was nothing to be said.

He stood by her in silence. Very humbly, at length, he said that he would step over and ask the Coastguards if she liked.

There was nobody whom she reverenced as she reverenced him.

She was quite ready to take his word for it, she said. Only then they need not cut sandwiches—that was all. They came to her, naturally, since she was a woman, all day long with this and that; one wanting this, another that; the children were growing up; she often felt she was nothing but a sponge sopped full of human emotions. Then he said, Damn you. He said, It must rain. He said, It won't rain; and instantly a Heaven of security opened before her. There was nobody she reverenced more.[2] She was not good enough to tie his shoe strings, she felt.

Already ashamed of that petulance, of that gesticulation of the hands when charging at the head of his troops, Mr. Ramsay rather sheepishly prodded his son's bare legs once more, and then, as if he had her leave for it, with a movement which oddly reminded his wife of the great sea lion at the Zoo tumbling backwards after swallowing his fish and walloping off so that the water in the tank washes from side to side, he dived into the evening air which, already thinner, was taking the substance from leaves and hedges but, as if in return, restoring to roses and pinks a lustre which they had not had by day.

"Some one had blundered," he said again, striding off, up and down the terrace.

But how extraordinarily his note had changed! It was like the cuckoo; "in June he gets out of tune;"[3] as if he were trying over, tentatively seeking, some phrase for a new mood, and having only this at hand, used it, cracked though it was. But it sounded ridiculous—"Some one had blundered"—said like that, almost as a question, without any conviction, melodiously. Mrs. Ramsay could not help smiling, and soon, sure enough, walking up and down, he hummed it, dropped it, fell silent.

He was safe, he was restored to his privacy. He stopped to light his pipe, looked once at his wife and son in the window, and as one

2. In *The Mausoleum Book* Leslie Stephen quotes poet and novelist George Meredith saying of Julia Stephen that he never "reverenced a woman more." Leslie Stephen, *The Mausoleum Book* (Oxford: Oxford UP, 1977), p. 74.
3. Altered from the traditional English nursery rhyme "To the Cuckoo": "In April he shows his bill / In May he sings all day / In June he'll change his tune . . ."

raises one's eyes from a page in an express train and sees a farm, a tree, a cluster of cottages as an illustration, a confirmation of something on the printed page to which one returns, fortified, and satisfied, so without his distinguishing either his son or his wife, the sight of them fortified him and satisfied him and consecrated his effort to arrive at a perfectly clear understanding of the problem which now engaged the energies of his splendid mind.

It was a splendid mind. For if thought is like the keyboard of a piano, divided into so many notes, or like the alphabet is ranged in twenty-six letters all in order, then his splendid mind had no sort of difficulty in running over those letters one by one, firmly and accurately, until it had reached, say, the letter Q.[4] He reached Q. Very few people in the whole of England ever reach Q. Here, stopping for one moment by the stone urn which held the geraniums, he saw, but now far, far away, like children picking up shells, divinely innocent and occupied with little trifles at their feet and somehow entirely defenceless against a doom which he perceived, his wife and son, together, in the window. They needed his protection; he gave it them. But after Q? What comes next? After Q there are a number of letters the last of which is scarcely visible to mortal eyes, but glimmers red in the distance. Z is only reached once by one man in a generation. Still, if he could reach R it would be something. Here at least was Q. He dug his heels in at Q. Q he was sure of. Q he could demonstrate. If Q then is Q—R— Here he knocked his pipe out, with two or three resonant taps on the handle of the urn, and proceeded. "Then R . . ." He braced himself. He clenched himself.

Qualities that would have saved a ship's company exposed on a broiling sea with six biscuits and a flask of water—endurance and justice, foresight, devotion, skill, came to his help. R is then—what is R?

A shutter, like the leathern eyelid of a lizard, flickered over the intensity of his gaze and obscured the letter R. In that flash of darkness he heard people saying—he was a failure—that R was beyond him. He would never reach R. On to R, once more. R——

Qualities that in a desolate expedition across the icy solitudes of the Polar region[5] would have made him the leader, the guide, the

---

4. Suggests at once Leslie Stephen's editorship of the multivolume *Dictionary of National Biography*—no matter how hard he worked, he was never to complete the alphabetical sequence of biographies of eminent British men—and the conventional form in which philosophers explain syllogism, as Rachel Bowlby points out (see this edition, p. 293). Mark Hussey explains: "All P are Q / R is P / Therefore R is Q" is the example used in Alfred N. Whitehead and Bertrand Russell's *Principia Mathematica* (1910–13); Virginia Woolf, *To the Lighthouse*, annotated and with an introduction by Mark Hussey (Orlando: Harcourt, 2005), p. 220.
5. Narratives of polar exploration were popular in the early twentieth century: Robert F. Scott (1868–1912) became a hero on his return to Britain after his exploration of Antarctica in 1901–4; American Robert A. Peary (1856–1920) reached the North Pole in

counsellor, whose temper, neither sanguine nor despondent, surveys with equanimity what is to be and faces it, came to his help again. R——

The lizard's eye flickered once more. The veins on his forehead bulged. The geranium in the urn became startlingly visible and, displayed among its leaves, he could see, without wishing it, that old, that obvious distinction between the two classes of men; on the one hand the steady goers of superhuman strength who, plodding and persevering, repeat the whole alphabet in order, twenty-six letters in all, from start to finish; on the other the gifted, the inspired who, miraculously, lump all the letters together in one flash—the way of genius. He had not genius; he laid no claim to that: but he had, or might have had, the power to repeat every letter of the alphabet from A to Z accurately in order. Meanwhile, he stuck at Q. On, then, on to R.

Feelings that would not have disgraced a leader who, now that the snow has begun to fall and the mountain top is covered in mist, knows that he must lay himself down and die before morning comes, stole upon him, paling the colour of his eyes, giving him, even in the two minutes of his turn on the terrace, the bleached look of withered old age. Yet he would not die lying down; he would find some crag of rock, and there, his eyes fixed on the storm, trying to the end to pierce the darkness, he would die standing. He would never reach R.

He stood stock-still, by the urn, with the geranium flowing over it. How many men in a thousand million, he asked himself, reach Z after all? Surely the leader of a forlorn hope may ask himself that, and answer, without treachery to the expedition behind him, "One perhaps." One in a generation. Is he to be blamed then if he is not that one? provided he has toiled honestly, given to the best of his power, and till he has no more left to give? And his fame lasts how long? It is permissible even for a dying hero to think before he dies how men will speak of him hereafter. His fame lasts perhaps two thousand years. And what are two thousand years? (asked Mr. Ramsay ironically, staring at the hedge). What, indeed, if you look from a mountain top down the long wastes of the ages? The very stone one kicks with one's boot will outlast Shakespeare.[6] His own little light would shine, not very brightly, for a year or two, and would then be merged in some bigger light, and that in a bigger still. (He looked into the hedge, into the intricacy of the twigs.) Who then could

---

1909; Roald Amundsen (1872–1928) reached the South Pole in December 1911, just ahead of Scott, who arrived there in January 1912 but whose expedition ended with the entire team's starving and freezing to death on the way back.

6. Alludes to a famous anecdote about Samuel Johnson (1709–1784): according to his biographer James Boswell (1740–1795), while discussing Berkeley's idealist philosophy (proving "the nonexistence of matter"), Johnson struck his foot against a stone and said, "I refute it *thus*."

blame the leader of that forlorn party which after all has climbed high enough to see the waste of the years and the perishing of stars, if before death stiffens his limbs beyond the power of movement he does a little consciously raise his numbed fingers to his brow, and square his shoulders, so that when the search party comes they will find him dead at his post, the fine figure of a soldier? Mr. Ramsay squared his shoulders and stood very upright by the urn.

Who shall blame him, if, so standing for a moment, he dwells upon fame, upon search parties, upon cairns raised by grateful followers over his bones? Finally, who shall blame the leader of the doomed expedition, if, having adventured to the uttermost, and used his strength wholly to the last ounce and fallen asleep not much caring if he wakes or not, he now perceives by some pricking in his toes that he lives, and does not on the whole object to live, but requires sympathy, and whisky, and some one to tell the story of his suffering to at once? Who shall blame him? Who will not secretly rejoice when the hero puts his armour off, and halts by the window and gazes at his wife and son, who, very distant at first, gradually come closer and closer, till lips and book and head are clearly before him, though still lovely and unfamiliar from the intensity of his isolation and the waste of ages and the perishing of the stars, and finally putting his pipe in his pocket and bending his magnificent head before her—who will blame him if he does homage to the beauty of the world?

VII

But his son hated him. He hated him for coming up to them, for stopping and looking down on them; he hated him for interrupting them; he hated him for the exaltation and sublimity of his gestures; for the magnificence of his head; for his exactingness and egotism (for there he stood, commanding them to attend to him); but most of all he hated the twang and twitter of his father's emotion which, vibrating round them, disturbed the perfect simplicity and good sense of his relations with his mother. By looking fixedly at the page, he hoped to make him move on; by pointing his finger at a word, he hoped to recall his mother's attention, which, he knew angrily, wavered instantly his father stopped. But, no. Nothing would make Mr. Ramsay move on. There he stood, demanding sympathy.

Mrs. Ramsay, who had been sitting loosely, folding her son in her arm, braced herself, and, half turning, seemed to raise herself with an effort, and at once to pour erect into the air a rain of energy, a column of spray, looking at the same time animated and alive as if all her energies were being fused into force, burning and illuminating (quietly though she sat, taking up her stocking again), and into

this delicious fecundity, this fountain and spray of life, the fatal sterility of the male plunged itself, like a beak of brass, barren and
bare. He wanted sympathy. He was a failure, he said. Mrs. Ramsay
flashed her needles. Mr. Ramsay repeated, never taking his eyes
from her face, that he was a failure. She blew the words back at him.
"Charles Tansley . . ." she said. But he must have more than that. It
was sympathy he wanted, to be assured of his genius, first of all, and
then to be taken within the circle of life, warmed and soothed, to
have his senses restored to him, his barrenness made fertile, and all
the rooms of the house made full of life—the drawing-room; behind
the drawing-room the kitchen; above the kitchen the bedrooms; and
beyond them the nurseries; they must be furnished, they must be
filled with life.

Charles Tansley thought him the greatest metaphysician of the
time, she said. But he must have more than that. He must have sympathy. He must be assured that he too lived in the heart of life; was
needed; not here only, but all over the world. Flashing her needles,
confident, upright, she created drawing-room and kitchen, set them
all aglow; bade him take his ease there, go in and out, enjoy himself. She laughed, she knitted. Standing between her knees, very
stiff, James felt all her strength flaring up to be drunk and quenched
by the beak of brass, the arid scimitar[1] of the male, which smote mer-
cilessly, again and again, demanding sympathy.

He was a failure, he repeated. Well, look then, feel then. Flashing
her needles, glancing round about her, out of the window, into the
room, at James himself, she assured him, beyond a shadow of a
doubt, by her laugh, her poise, her competence (as a nurse carrying
a light across a dark room assures a fractious child), that it was real;
the house was full; the garden blowing. If he put implicit faith in
her, nothing should hurt him; however deep he buried himself or
climbed high, not for a second should he find himself without her.
So boasting of her capacity to surround and protect, there was
scarcely a shell of herself left for her to know herself by; all was so
lavished and spent; and James, as he stood stiff between her knees,
felt her rise in a rosy-flowered fruit tree laid with leaves and
dancing boughs into which the beak of brass, the arid scimitar of
his father, the egotistical man, plunged and smote, demanding
sympathy.

Filled with her words, like a child who drops off satisfied, he said,
at last, looking at her with humble gratitude, restored, renewed, that
he would take a turn; he would watch the children playing cricket.
He went.

---

1. A sword with a curved blade, widening toward the tip; evokes Middle Eastern and
   South Asian cultures.

Immediately, Mrs. Ramsay seemed to fold herself together, one petal closed in another, and the whole fabric fell in exhaustion upon itself, so that she had only strength enough to move her finger, in exquisite abandonment to exhaustion, across the page of Grimm's fairy story, while there throbbed through her, like the pulse in a spring which has expanded to its full width and now gently ceases to beat, the rapture of successful creation.

Every throb of this pulse seemed, as he walked away, to enclose her and her husband, and to give to each that solace which two different notes, one high, one low, struck together, seem to give each other as they combine. Yet, as the resonance died, and she turned to the Fairy Tale again, Mrs. Ramsay felt not only exhausted in body (afterwards, not at the time, she always felt this) but also there tinged her physical fatigue some faintly disagreeable sensation with another origin. Not that, as she read aloud the story of the Fisherman's Wife,[2] she knew precisely what it came from; nor did she let herself put into words her dissatisfaction when she realised, at the turn of the page when she stopped and heard dully, ominously, a wave fall, how it came from this: she did not like, even for a second, to feel finer than her husband; and further, could not bear not being entirely sure, when she spoke to him, of the truth of what she said. Universities and people wanting him, lectures and books and their being of the highest importance—all that she did not doubt for a moment; but it was their relation, and his coming to her like that, openly, so that any one could see, that discomposed her; for then people said he depended on her, when they must know that of the two he was infinitely the more important, and what she gave the world, in comparison with what he gave, negligible. But then again, it was the other thing too—not being able to tell him the truth, being afraid, for instance, about the greenhouse roof and the expense it would be, fifty pounds perhaps, to mend it;[3] and then about his books, to be afraid that he might guess, what she a little suspected, that his last book was not quite his best book (she gathered that from William Bankes); and then to hide small daily things, and the children seeing it, and the burden it laid on them—all this diminished the entire joy, the pure joy, of the two notes sounding together, and let the sound die on her ear now with a dismal flatness.

A shadow was on the page; she looked up. It was Augustus Carmichael shuffling past, precisely now, at the very moment when it

2. One of the German fairy tales collected by the Brothers Grimm in the early nineteenth century. For the tale, see this edition, pp. 269–72. Before settling on "The Fisherman and His Wife," Woolf considered other stories for Mrs. Ramsay to read aloud: "the three dwarfs" and "the story of the Woodman's daughter . . . about the little girl who had tea with the bears" appear at different points in the holograph (Original Holograph, pp. 73 and 96).
3. A serious expense, equivalent now to about £6,000, or about $8,000; although the Ramsays rent or hold a lease on the house, they are apparently responsible for maintenance.

was painful to be reminded of the inadequacy of human relationships, that the most perfect was flawed, and could not bear the
examination which, loving her husband, with her instinct for truth,
she turned upon it; when it was painful to feel herself convicted of
unworthiness, and impeded in her proper function by these lies,
these exaggerations—it was at this moment when she was fretted
thus ignobly in the wake of her exaltation, that Mr. Carmichael shuffled past, in his yellow slippers, and some demon in her made it
necessary for her to call out, as he passed,

"Going indoors, Mr. Carmichael?"

VIII

He said nothing. He took opium. The children said he had stained
his beard yellow with it. Perhaps. What was obvious to her was that
the poor man was unhappy, came to them every year as an escape;
and yet every year, she felt the same thing; he did not trust her. She
said, "I am going to the town. Shall I get you stamps, paper, tobacco?"
and she felt him wince. He did not trust her. It was his wife's doing.
She remembered that iniquity of his wife's towards him, which had
made her turn to steel and adamant there, in the horrid little room
in St. John's Wood,[1] when with her own eyes she had seen that odious woman turn him out of the house. He was unkempt; he dropped
things on his coat; he had the tiresomeness of an old man with nothing in the world to do; and she turned him out of the room. She
said, in her odious way, "Now, Mrs. Ramsay and I want to have a
little talk together," and Mrs. Ramsay could see, as if before her eyes,
the innumerable miseries of his life. Had he money enough to buy
tobacco? Did he have to ask her for it? half-a-crown? eighteenpence?[2]
Oh, she could not bear to think of the little indignities she made
him suffer. And always now (why, she could not guess, except that
it came probably from that woman somehow) he shrank from her.
He never told her anything. But what more could she have done?
There was a sunny room given up to him. The children were good
to him. Never did she show a sign of not wanting him. She went out
of her way indeed to be friendly. Do you want stamps, do you want
tobacco? Here's a book you might like and so on. And after all—after
all (here insensibly she drew herself together, physically, the sense
of her own beauty becoming, as it did so seldom, present to her)—
after all, she had not generally any difficulty in making people like
her; for instance, George Manning; Mr. Wallace; famous as they
were, they would come to her of an evening, quietly, and talk alone

1. A residential district in west London.
2. Half a crown is two shillings and six pence, or two and a half shillings (see note 1 p. 23).

over her fire. She bore about with her, she could not help knowing it, the torch of her beauty; she carried it erect into any room that she entered; and after all, veil it as she might, and shrink from the monotony of bearing that it imposed on her, her beauty was apparent. She had been admired. She had been loved. She had entered rooms where mourners sat. Tears had flown in her presence. Men, and women too, letting go the multiplicity of things, had allowed themselves with her the relief of simplicity. It injured her that he should shrink. It hurt her. And yet not cleanly, not rightly. That was what she minded, coming as it did on top of her discontent with her husband; the sense she had now when Mr. Carmichael shuffled past, just nodding to her question, with a book beneath his arm, in his yellow slippers, that she was suspected; and that all this desire of hers to give, to help, was vanity. For her own self-satisfaction was it that she wished so instinctively to help, to give, that people might say of her, "O Mrs. Ramsay! dear Mrs. Ramsay . . . Mrs. Ramsay, of course!" and need her and send for her and admire her? Was it not secretly this that she wanted, and therefore when Mr. Carmichael shrank away from her, as he did at this moment, making off to some corner where he did acrostics[3] endlessly, she did not feel merely snubbed back in her instinct, but made aware of the pettiness of some part of her, and of human relations, how flawed they are, how despicable, how self-seeking, at their best. Shabby and worn out, and not presumably (her cheeks were hollow, her hair was white) any longer a sight that filled the eyes with joy, she had better devote her mind to the story of the Fisherman and his Wife and so pacify that bundle of sensitiveness (none of her children was as sensitive as he was), her son James.

"The man's heart grew heavy," she read aloud, "and he would not go. He said to himself, 'It is not right,' and yet he went. And when he came to the sea the water was quite purple and dark blue, and grey and thick, and no longer so green and yellow, but it was still quiet. And he stood there and said——"

Mrs. Ramsay could have wished that her husband had not chosen that moment to stop. Why had he not gone as he said to watch the children playing cricket? But he did not speak; he looked; he nodded; he approved; he went on. He slipped, seeing before him that hedge which had over and over again rounded some pause, signified some conclusion, seeing his wife and child, seeing again the urns with the trailing red geraniums which had so often decorated processes of thought, and bore, written up among their leaves, as if they were scraps of paper on which one scribbles notes in the rush of

---

3. Word puzzles, often in verse form, in which the first letters of the lines spell out a word or words that solve the puzzle; an ancient form—there are acrostics in the Hebrew Bible.

reading—he slipped, seeing all this, smoothly into speculation suggested by an article in *The Times*[4] about the number of Americans who visit Shakespeare's house every year. If Shakespeare had never existed, he asked, would the world have differed much from what it is today? Does the progress of civilisation depend upon great men?[5] Is the lot of the average human being better now than in the time of the Pharaohs? Is the lot of the average human being, however, he asked himself, the criterion by which we judge the measure of civilisation? Possibly not. Possibly the greatest good requires the existence of a slave class.[6] The liftman in the Tube[7] is an eternal necessity. The thought was distasteful to him. He tossed his head. To avoid it, he would find some way of snubbing the predominance of the arts. He would argue that the world exists for the average human being; that the arts are merely a decoration imposed on the top of human life; they do not express it. Nor is Shakespeare necessary to it. Not knowing precisely why it was that he wanted to disparage Shakespeare and come to the rescue of the man who stands eternally in the door of the lift, he picked a leaf sharply from the hedge. All this would have to be dished up for the young men at Cardiff[8] next month, he thought; here, on his terrace, he was merely foraging and picnicking (he threw away the leaf that he had picked so peevishly) like a man who reaches from his horse to pick a bunch of roses, or stuffs his pockets with nuts as he ambles at his ease through the lanes and fields of a country known to him from boyhood. It was all familiar; this turning, that stile, that cut across the fields. Hours he would spend thus, with his pipe, of an evening, thinking up and down and in and out of the old familiar lanes and commons, which were all stuck about with the history of that campaign there, the life of this statesman here, with poems and with anecdotes, with figures too, this thinker, that soldier; all very brisk and clear; but at length the lane, the field, the common, the fruitful nut-tree and the flowering hedge led him on to that further turn of the road where he dismounted always, tied his horse to a tree, and proceeded on foot alone. He reached the edge of the lawn and looked out on the bay beneath.

4. London's leading newspaper.
5. Mr. Ramsay's train of thought about "great men," Shakespeare, and ordinary people recalls Leslie Stephen's criticism of the theory articulated by Thomas Carlyle (1795–1881) that "everything was due to the hero," in Leslie Stephen, *English Literature and Society in the Eighteenth Century* (London: Duckworth, 1904), p. 14. See also note 1 p. 37.
6. Clive Bell argued in his book *Civilization: An Essay* (New York: Harcourt Brace, 1928) that what he calls civilization—modeled on classical Athens—has historically depended on social inequality, un-democratic governance, and the existence of an elite "leisured class" that in turn "requires the existence of slaves" (210); he dedicated the book to Woolf, but Leonard wrote a negative review in *Nation & Athenaeum*.
7. The elevator operator in a London underground railway station; here, a prototypical workingman.
8. Undergraduates at what is now Cardiff University in Wales, founded in 1893.

It was his fate, his peculiarity, whether he wished it or not, to come out thus on a spit of land which the sea is slowly eating away, and there to stand, like a desolate sea-bird, alone. It was his power, his gift, suddenly to shed all superfluities, to shrink and diminish so that he looked barer and felt sparer, even physically, yet lost none of his intensity of mind, and so to stand on his little ledge facing the dark of human ignorance, how we know nothing and the sea eats away the ground we stand on—that was his fate, his gift. But having thrown away, when he dismounted, all gestures and fripperies, all trophies of nuts and roses, and shrunk so that not only fame but even his own name was forgotten by him, he kept even in that desolation a vigilance which spared no phantom and luxuriated in no vision, and it was in this guise that he inspired in William Bankes (intermittently) and in Charles Tansley (obsequiously) and in his wife now, when she looked up and saw him standing at the edge of the lawn, profoundly, reverence, and pity, and gratitude too, as a stake driven into the bed of a channel upon which the gulls perch and the waves beat inspires in merry boat-loads a feeling of gratitude for the duty it is taking upon itself of marking the channel out there in the floods alone.

"But the father of eight children has no choice." Muttering half aloud, so he broke off, turned, sighed, raised his eyes, sought the figure of his wife reading stories to his little boy, filled his pipe. He turned from the sight of human ignorance and human fate and the sea eating the ground we stand on, which, had he been able to contemplate it fixedly might have led to something; and found consolation in trifles so slight compared with the august theme just now before him that he was disposed to slur that comfort over, to deprecate it, as if to be caught happy in a world of misery was for an honest man the most despicable of crimes. It was true; he was for the most part happy; he had his wife; he had his children; he had promised in six weeks' time to talk "some nonsense" to the young men of Cardiff about Locke, Hume, Berkeley,[9] and the causes of the French Revolution. But this and his pleasure in it, his glory in the phrases he made, in the ardour of youth, in his wife's beauty, in the tributes that reached him from Swansea, Cardiff, Exeter, Southampton, Kidderminster, Oxford, Cambridge[1]—all had to be deprecated and concealed under the phrase "talking nonsense," because, in effect, he

9. John Locke (1632–1704) and Bishop George Berkeley (1685–1753) preceded Hume in exploring questions akin to Mr. Ramsay's study of "subject and object and the nature of reality." Leslie Stephen treats Locke and Berkeley as predecessors to Hume in his *History of English Thought in the Eighteenth Century*: Locke provided the basis for Hume's skepticism about the existence of God by claiming that there are no "innate ideas" and that we can know only through the senses. See note 2 p. 20.

1. University colleges were founded at the first five of these regional cities in England and Wales in the 1890s and early 1900s. See also notes 1 and 2 p. 8.

had not done the thing he might have done. It was a disguise; it was the refuge of a man afraid to own his own feelings, who could not say, This is what I like—this is what I am; and rather pitiable and distasteful to William Bankes and Lily Briscoe, who wondered why such concealments should be necessary; why he needed always praise; why so brave a man in thought should be so timid in life; how strangely he was venerable and laughable at one and the same time.

Teaching and preaching is beyond human power, Lily suspected. (She was putting away her things.) If you are exalted you must somehow come a cropper. Mrs. Ramsay gave him what he asked too easily. Then the change must be so upsetting, Lily said. He comes in from his books and finds us all playing games and talking nonsense. Imagine what a change from the things he thinks about, she said.

He was bearing down upon them. Now he stopped dead and stood looking in silence at the sea. Now he had turned away again.

IX

Yes, Mr. Bankes said, watching him go. It was a thousand pities. (Lily had said something about his frightening her—he changed from one mood to another so suddenly.) Yes, said Mr. Bankes, it was a thousand pities that Ramsay could not behave a little more like other people. (For he liked Lily Briscoe; he could discuss Ramsay with her quite openly.) It was for that reason, he said, that the young don't read Carlyle.[1] A crusty old grumbler who lost his temper if the porridge was cold, why should he preach to us? was what Mr. Bankes understood that young people said nowadays. It was a thousand pities if you thought, as he did, that Carlyle was one of the great teachers of mankind. Lily was ashamed to say that she had not read Carlyle since she was at school. But in her opinion one liked Mr. Ramsay all the better for thinking that if his little finger ached the whole world must come to an end. It was not *that* she minded. For who could be deceived by him? He asked you quite openly to flatter him, to admire him, his little dodges deceived nobody. What she disliked was his narrowness, his blindness, she said, looking after him.

"A bit of a hypocrite?" Mr. Bankes suggested, looking too at Mr. Ramsay's back, for was he not thinking of his friendship, and of Cam refusing to give him a flower, and of all those boys and girls, and his own house, full of comfort, but, since his wife's death, quiet

---

1. Thomas Carlyle (1795–1881), Scottish historian and essayist whose major works include *The French Revolution* (1837), *On Heroes, Hero-Worship, and the Heroic in History* (1841), and *The History of Friedrich II of Prussia* (1858–65). His reputation for bad temper was well known, as was his faith in what Mr. Ramsay calls "great men" (see note 5 p. 35). He is one of the "famous men" in Woolf's edition of Julia Margaret Cameron's *Victorian Photographs of Famous Men and Fair Women.*

rather? Of course, he had his work. . . . All the same, he rather wished Lily to agree that Ramsay was, as he said, "a bit of a hypocrite."

Lily Briscoe went on putting away her brushes, looking up, looking down. Looking up, there he was—Mr. Ramsay—advancing towards them, swinging, careless, oblivious, remote. A bit of a hypocrite? she repeated. Oh, no—the most sincere of men, the truest (here he was), the best; but, looking down, she thought, he is absorbed in himself, he is tyrannical, he is unjust; and kept looking down, purposely, for only so could she keep steady, staying with the Ramsays. Directly one looked up and saw them, what she called "being in love" flooded them. They became part of that unreal but penetrating and exciting universe which is the world seen through the eyes of love. The sky stuck to them; the birds sang through them. And, what was even more exciting, she felt, too, as she saw Mr. Ramsay bearing down and retreating, and Mrs. Ramsay sitting with James in the window and the cloud moving and the tree bending, how life, from being made up of little separate incidents which one lived one by one, became curled and whole like a wave which bore one up with it and threw one down with it, there, with a dash on the beach.

Mr. Bankes expected her to answer. And she was about to say something criticising Mrs. Ramsay, how she was alarming, too, in her way, high-handed, or words to that effect, when Mr. Bankes made it entirely unnecessary for her to speak by his rapture. For such it was considering his age, turned sixty, and his cleanliness and his impersonality, and the white scientific coat which seemed to clothe him. For him to gaze as Lily saw him gazing at Mrs. Ramsay was a rapture, equivalent, Lily felt, to the loves of dozens of young men (and perhaps Mrs. Ramsay had never excited the loves of dozens of young men). It was love, she thought, pretending to move her canvas, distilled and filtered; love that never attempted to clutch its object; but, like the love which mathematicians bear their symbols, or poets their phrases, was meant to be spread over the world and become part of the human gain. So it was indeed. The world by all means should have shared it, could Mr. Bankes have said why that woman pleased him so; why the sight of her reading a fairy tale to her boy had upon him precisely the same effect as the solution of a scientific problem, so that he rested in contemplation of it, and felt, as he felt when he had proved something absolute about the digestive system of plants, that barbarity was tamed, the reign of chaos subdued.

Such a rapture—for by what other name could one call it?—made Lily Briscoe forget entirely what she had been about to say. It was nothing of importance; something about Mrs. Ramsay. It paled beside this "rapture," this silent stare, for which she felt intense gratitude;

for nothing so solaced her, eased her of the perplexity of life, and miraculously raised its burdens, as this sublime power, this heavenly gift, and one would no more disturb it, while it lasted, than break up the shaft of sunlight, lying level across the floor.

That people should love like this, that Mr. Bankes should feel this for Mrs. Ramsay (she glanced at him musing) was helpful, was exalting. She wiped one brush after another upon a piece of old rag, menially, on purpose. She took shelter from the reverence which covered all women; she felt herself praised. Let him gaze; she would steal a look at her picture.

She could have wept. It was bad, it was bad, it was infinitely bad! She could have done it differently of course; the colour could have been thinned and faded; the shapes etherealised; that was how Paunceforte would have seen it. But then she did not see it like that. She saw the colour burning on a framework of steel; the light of a butterfly's wing lying upon the arches of a cathedral.[2] Of all that only a few random marks scrawled upon the canvas remained. And it would never be seen; never be hung even, and there was Mr. Tansley whispering in her ear, "Women can't paint, women can't write . . ."

She now remembered what she had been going to say about Mrs. Ramsay. She did not know how she would have put it; but it would have been something critical. She had been annoyed the other night by some highhandedness. Looking along the level of Mr. Bankes's glance at her, she thought that no woman could worship another woman in the way he worshipped; they could only seek shelter under the shade which Mr. Bankes extended over them both. Looking along his beam she added to it her different ray, thinking that she was unquestionably the loveliest of people (bowed over her book); the best perhaps; but also, different too from the perfect shape which one saw there. But why different, and how different? she asked herself, scraping her palette of all those mounds of blue and green which seemed to her like clods with no life in them now, yet she vowed, she would inspire them, force them to move, flow, do her bidding tomorrow. How did she differ? What was the spirit in her, the essential thing, by which, had you found a crumpled glove in the corner of a sofa, you would have known it, from its twisted finger, hers indisputably? She was like a bird for speed, an arrow for directness. She was wilful; she was commanding (of course, Lily reminded herself, I am thinking of her relations with women, and I am much younger, an insignificant person, living off the Brompton Road). She

2. While reading French novelist Marcel Proust (1871–1922) in April 1925 for her essay "Pictures," this edition, pp. 250–53, Woolf wrote admiringly in her diary, "[h]e searches out these butterfly shades to the last grain. He is as tough as catgut & as evanescent as a butterfly's bloom" (*Diary* 3: 7, April 8, 1925).

opened bedroom windows. She shut doors. (So she tried to start the tune of Mrs. Ramsay in her head.) Arriving late at night, with a light tap on one's bedroom door, wrapped in an old fur coat (for the setting of her beauty was always that—hasty, but apt), she would enact again whatever it might be—Charles Tansley losing his umbrella; Mr. Carmichael snuffling and sniffing; Mr. Bankes saying, "The vegetable salts are lost." All this she would adroitly shape; even maliciously twist; and, moving over to the window, in pretence that she must go,—it was dawn, she could see the sun rising,—half turn back, more intimately, but still always laughing, insist that she must, Minta must, they all must marry, since in the whole world whatever laurels might be tossed to her (but Mrs. Ramsay cared not a fig for her painting), or triumphs won by her (probably Mrs. Ramsay had had her share of those), and here she saddened, darkened, and came back to her chair, there could be no disputing this: an unmarried woman (she lightly took her hand for a moment), an unmarried woman has missed the best of life. The house seemed full of children sleeping and Mrs. Ramsay listening; shaded lights and regular breathing.

Oh, but, Lily would say, there was her father; her home; even, had she dared to say it, her painting. But all this seemed so little, so virginal, against the other. Yet, as the night wore on, and white lights parted the curtains, and even now and then some bird chirped in the garden, gathering a desperate courage she would urge her own exemption from the universal law; plead for it; she liked to be alone; she liked to be herself; she was not made for that; and so have to meet a serious stare from eyes of unparalleled depth, and confront Mrs. Ramsay's simple certainty (and she was childlike now) that her dear Lily, her little Brisk, was a fool. Then, she remembered, she had laid her head on Mrs. Ramsay's lap and laughed and laughed and laughed, laughed almost hysterically at the thought of Mrs. Ramsay presiding with immutable calm over destinies which she completely failed to understand. There she sat, simple, serious. She had recovered her sense of her now—this was the glove's twisted finger. But into what sanctuary had one penetrated? Lily Briscoe had looked up at last, and there was Mrs. Ramsay, unwitting entirely what had caused her laughter, still presiding, but now with every trace of wilfulness abolished, and in its stead, something clear as the space which the clouds at last uncover—the little space of sky which sleeps beside the moon.

Was it wisdom? Was it knowledge? Was it, once more, the deceptiveness of beauty, so that all one's perceptions, half way to truth, were tangled in a golden mesh? or did she lock up within her some secret which certainly Lily Briscoe believed people must have for the world to go on at all? Every one could not be as helter skelter, hand to mouth as she was. But if they knew, could they tell one what they knew? Sitting on the floor with her arms round Mrs. Ramsay's knees, close as she could get, smiling to think that Mrs. Ramsay would never know the reason of that pressure, she imagined how in the chambers of the mind and heart of the woman who was, physically, touching her, were stood, like the treasures in the tombs of kings,[3] tablets bearing sacred inscriptions, which if one could spell them out, would teach one everything, but they would never be offered openly, never made public. What art was there, known to love or cunning, by which one pressed through into those secret chambers? What device for becoming, like waters poured into one jar, inextricably the same, one with the object one adored? Could the body achieve, or the mind, subtly mingling in the intricate passages of the brain? or the heart? Could loving, as people called it, make her and Mrs. Ramsay one? for it was not knowledge but unity that she desired, not inscriptions on tablets, nothing that could be written in any language known to men, but intimacy itself, which is knowledge, she had thought, leaning her head on Mrs. Ramsay's knee.

Nothing happened. Nothing! Nothing! as she leant her head against Mrs. Ramsay's knee. And yet, she knew knowledge and wisdom were stored up in Mrs. Ramsay's heart. How then, she had asked herself, did one know one thing or another thing about people, sealed as they were? Only like a bee, drawn by some sweetness or sharpness in the air intangible to touch or taste, one haunted the dome-shaped hive, ranged the wastes of the air over the countries of the world alone, and then haunted the hives with their murmurs and their stirrings; the hives, which were people. Mrs. Ramsay rose. Lily rose. Mrs. Ramsay went. For days there hung about her, as after a dream some subtle change is felt in the person one has dreamt of, more vividly than anything she said, the sound of murmuring and, as she sat in the wicker arm-chair in the drawing-room window she wore, to Lily's eyes, an august shape; the shape of a dome.

This ray passed level with Mr. Bankes's ray straight to Mrs. Ramsay sitting reading there with James at her knee. But now while she still looked, Mr. Bankes had done. He had put on his spectacles. He had stepped back. He had raised his hand. He had slightly narrowed his clear blue eyes, when Lily, rousing herself, saw what he was at, and winced like a dog who sees a hand raised to strike it. She would have snatched her picture off the easel, but she said to herself, One must. She braced herself to stand the awful trial of some one looking at her picture. One must, she said, one must. And if it must be seen, Mr. Bankes was less alarming than another. But that any other

3. The tomb of King Tutankhamen (d. 1323 B.C.E.) was not found and opened until 1922, but European archaeologists had been excavating Egyptian remains since Napoleon invaded Egypt at the end of the eighteenth century.

eyes should see the residue of her thirty-three years,[4] the deposit of each day's living mixed with something more secret than she had ever spoken or shown in the course of all those days was an agony. At the same time it was immensely exciting.

Nothing could be cooler and quieter. Taking out a pen-knife, Mr. Bankes tapped the canvas with the bone handle. What did she wish to indicate by the triangular purple shape, "just there"? he asked.

It was Mrs. Ramsay reading to James, she said. She knew his objection—that no one could tell it for a human shape. But she had made no attempt at likeness, she said. For what reason had she introduced them then? he asked. Why indeed?—except that if there, in that corner, it was bright, here, in this, she felt the need of darkness.[5] Simple, obvious, commonplace, as it was, Mr. Bankes was interested. Mother and child then—objects of universal veneration,[6] and in this case the mother was famous for her beauty—might be reduced, he pondered, to a purple shadow without irreverence.

But the picture was not of them, she said. Or, not in his sense. There were other senses too in which one might reverence them. By a shadow here and a light there, for instance. Her tribute took that form if, as she vaguely supposed, a picture must be a tribute. A mother and child might be reduced to a shadow without irreverence. A light here required a shadow there. He considered. He was interested. He took it scientifically in complete good faith. The truth was that all his prejudices were on the other side, he explained. The largest picture in his drawing-room, which painters had praised, and valued at a higher price than he had given for it, was of the cherry trees in blossom on the banks of the Kennet.[7] He had spent his honeymoon on the banks of the Kennet, he said. Lily must come and see that picture, he said. But now—he turned, with his glasses raised to the scientific examination of her canvas. The question being one of the relations of masses, of lights and shadows, which, to be honest, he had never considered before, he would like to have it explained—what then did she wish to make of it? And he indicated the scene before them. She looked. She could not show him what she wished to make of it, could not see it even herself, without a brush in her hand. She took up once more her old painting position with the dim eyes and the

---

4. Because Lily is forty-four on p. 110, ten or eleven years pass between the beginning and the end of the novel and thus, because "The Lighthouse" is set in September 1919 after the end of World War I, "The Window" must be set in 1909 or 1908.

5. Lily's explanation of her painting reflects the postimpressionist theories of visual art of Clive Bell and of Roger Fry, who claimed that painting doesn't represent but rather creates its own reality through "significant form." See the selections from Bell, Fry, and Vanessa Bell in this edition, pp. 233–43.

6. Mr. Bankes refers to the traditional Christian iconography of Mary (the Madonna) holding the baby Jesus; Julia Stephen had served as the model for Mary in Edward Burne-Jones's *Annunciation* (1879), and Leslie Stephen compared Julia to the *Sistine Madonna* of Raphael (1483–1520). See *The Mausoleum Book*, this edition, pp. 210–15.

7. A river in the south of England, a tributary of the River Thames.

absent-minded manner, subduing all her impressions as a woman to
something much more general; becoming once more under the power
of that vision which she had seen clearly once and must now grope for
among hedges and houses and mothers and children—her picture. It
was a question, she remembered, how to connect this mass on the
right hand with that on the left.[8] She might do it by bringing the line
of the branch across so; or break the vacancy in the foreground by
an object (James perhaps) so. But the danger was that by doing that
the unity of the whole might be broken. She stopped; she did not
want to bore him; she took the canvas lightly off the easel.

But it had been seen; it had been taken from her. This man had
shared with her something profoundly intimate. And, thanking
Mr. Ramsay for it and Mrs. Ramsay for it and the hour and the place,
crediting the world with a power which she had not suspected—that
one could walk away down that long gallery not alone any more but
arm in arm with somebody—the strangest feeling in the world, and
the most exhilarating—she nicked the catch of her paint-box to,
more firmly than was necessary, and the nick seemed to surround
in a circle forever the paint-box, the lawn, Mr. Bankes, and that wild
villain, Cam, dashing past.

X

For Cam grazed the easel by an inch; she would not stop for
Mr. Bankes and Lily Briscoe; though Mr. Bankes, who would have
liked a daughter of his own, held out his hand; she would not stop
for her father, whom she grazed also by an inch; nor for her mother,
who called "Cam! I want you a moment!" as she dashed past. She
was off like a bird, bullet, or arrow, impelled by what desire, shot by
whom, at what directed, who could say? What, what? Mrs. Ramsay
pondered, watching her. It might be a vision—of a shell, of a wheelbarrow, of a fairy kingdom on the far side of the hedge; or it might
be the glory of speed; no one knew. But when Mrs. Ramsay called
"Cam!" a second time, the projectile dropped in mid career, and Cam
came lagging back, pulling a leaf by the way, to her mother.

What was she dreaming about, Mrs. Ramsay wondered, seeing her
engrossed, as she stood there, with some thought of her own, so that
she had to repeat the message twice—ask Mildred if Andrew, Miss
Doyle, and Mr. Rayley have come back?— The words seemed to be
dropped into a well, where, if the waters were clear, they were also
so extraordinarily distorting that, even as they descended, one saw
them twisting about to make Heaven knows what pattern on the

---

8. In the holograph Lily thinks of her compositional challenge about "the relations of
masses" in terms that recall Woolf's diagram of the novel: "two chief blocks of matter
must somehow be joined together" (*Original Holograph*, p. 93). See Woolf's Undated
Notes and an Outline, this edition, p. 161.

floor of the child's mind. What message would Cam give the cook? Mrs. Ramsay wondered. And indeed it was only by waiting patiently, and hearing that there was an old woman in the kitchen with very red cheeks, drinking soup out of a basin,[1] that Mrs. Ramsay at last prompted that parrot-like instinct which had picked up Mildred's words quite accurately and could now produce them, if one waited, in a colourless singsong. Shifting from foot to foot, Cam repeated the words, "No, they haven't, and I've told Ellen to clear away tea."

Minta Doyle and Paul Rayley had not come back then. That could only mean, Mrs. Ramsay thought, one thing.[2] She must accept him, or she must refuse him. This going off after luncheon for a walk, even though Andrew was with them—what could it mean? except that she had decided, rightly, Mrs. Ramsay thought (and she was very, very fond of Minta), to accept that good fellow, who might not be brilliant, but then, thought Mrs. Ramsay, realising that James was tugging at her, to make her go on reading aloud the Fisherman and his Wife, she did in her own heart infinitely prefer boobies to clever men who wrote dissertations; Charles Tansley, for instance. It must have happened, one way or the other, by now.

But she read, "Next morning the wife awoke first, and it was just daybreak, and from her bed she saw the beautiful country lying before her. Her husband was still stretching himself. . . ."

But how could Minta say now that she would not have him? Not if she agreed to spend whole afternoons trapesing about the country alone—for Andrew would be off after his crabs—but possibly Nancy was with them. She tried to recall the sight of them standing at the hall door after lunch. There they stood, looking at the sky, wondering about the weather, and she had said, thinking partly to cover their shyness, partly to encourage them to be off (for her sympathies were with Paul),

"There isn't a cloud anywhere within miles," at which she could feel little Charles Tansley, who had followed them out, snigger. But she did it on purpose. Whether Nancy was there or not, she could not be certain, looking from one to the other in her mind's eye.

She read on: "Ah, wife," said the man, "why should we be King? I do not want to be King." "Well," said the wife, "if you won't be King, I will; go to the Flounder, for I will be King."

"Come in or go out, Cam," she said, knowing that Cam was attracted only by the word "Flounder" and that in a moment she would fidget and fight with James as usual. Cam shot off. Mrs. Ramsay went on

---

1. Mrs. McNab recalls this scene when she revisits the house years later in "Time Passes."
2. Victorian middle- and upper-class social rules prohibited an unmarried woman from spending time alone with an unmarried man unless they were engaged to be married. The penalty for breaking this rule could be severe for the woman: a scandal that could prevent her from ever marrying within her social class. But the Victorian Age had been over for eight years.

reading, relieved, for she and James shared the same tastes and were comfortable together.

"And when he came to the sea, it was quite dark grey, and the water heaved up from below, and smelt putrid. Then he went and stood by it and said,

'Flounder, flounder, in the sea,
Come, I pray thee, here to me;
For my wife, good Ilsabil,
Wills not as I'd have her will.'

'Well, what does she want then?' said the Flounder." And where were they now? Mrs. Ramsay wondered, reading and thinking, quite easily, both at the same time; for the story of the Fisherman and his Wife was like the bass gently accompanying a tune, which now and then ran up unexpectedly into the melody. And when should she be told? If nothing happened, she would have to speak seriously to Minta. For she could not go trapesing about all over the country, even if Nancy were with them (she tried again, unsuccessfully, to visualise their backs going down the path, and to count them). She was responsible to Minta's parents—the Owl and the Poker.[3] Her nicknames for them shot into her mind as she read. The Owl and the Poker—yes, they would be annoyed if they heard—and they were certain to hear—that Minta, staying with the Ramsays, had been seen etcetera, etcetera, etcetera. "He wore a wig in the House of Commons and she ably assisted him at the head of the stairs," she repeated, fishing them up out of her mind by a phrase which, coming back from some party, she had made to amuse her husband. Dear, dear, Mrs. Ramsay said to herself, how did they produce this incongruous daughter? this tomboy Minta, with a hole in her stocking? How did she exist in that portentous atmosphere where the maid was always removing in a dust-pan the sand that the parrot had scattered, and conversation was almost entirely reduced to the exploits—interesting perhaps, but limited after all—of that bird? Naturally, one had asked her to lunch, tea, dinner, finally to stay with them up at Finlay,[4] which had resulted in some friction with the Owl, her mother, and more calling, and more conversation, and more sand, and really at the end of it, she had told enough lies about parrots to last her a lifetime (so she had said to her husband that night, coming back from the party). However, Minta came. . . . Yes, she came, Mrs. Ramsay thought, suspecting some thorn in the tangle of this thought; and disengaging it found it to be this: a woman had once accused her of "robbing her of her daughter's affections";

3. These nicknames that privately ridicule Minta's parents obliquely echo Edward Lear's nonsense poem "The Owl and the Pussy-cat" (1871).
4. The name of the Ramsays' summer house, not of the town.

something Mrs. Doyle had said made her remember that charge again. Wishing to dominate, wishing to interfere, making people do what she wished—that was the charge against her, and she thought it most unjust. How could she help being "like that" to look at? No one could accuse her of taking pains to impress. She was often ashamed of her own shabbiness. Nor was she domineering, nor was she tyrannical. It was more true about hospitals and drains and the dairy.[5] About things like that she did feel passionately, and would, if she had had the chance, have liked to take people by the scruff of their necks and make them see. No hospital on the whole island. It was a disgrace. Milk delivered at your door in London positively brown with dirt. It should be made illegal. A model dairy and a hospital up here—those two things she would have liked to do, herself. But how? With all these children? When they were older, then perhaps she would have time; when they were all at school.

Oh, but she never wanted James to grow a day older! or Cam either. These two she would have liked to keep for ever just as they were, demons of wickedness, angels of delight, never to see them grow up into long-legged monsters. Nothing made up for the loss. When she read just now to James, "and there were numbers of soldiers with kettledrums and trumpets," and his eyes darkened, she thought, why should they grow up, and lose all that? He was the most gifted, the most sensitive of her children. But all, she thought, were full of promise. Prue, a perfect angel with the others, and sometimes now, at night especially, she took one's breath away with her beauty. Andrew—even her husband admitted that his gift for mathematics was extraordinary. And Nancy and Roger, they were both wild creatures now, scampering about over the country all day long. As for Rose, her mouth was too big, but she had a wonderful gift with her hands. If they had charades, Rose made the dresses; made everything; liked best arranging tables, flowers, anything. She did not like it that Jasper should shoot birds; but it was only a stage; they all went through stages. Why, she asked, pressing her chin on James's head, should they grow up so fast? Why should they go to school? She would have liked always to have had a baby. She was happiest carrying one in her arms. Then people might say she was tyrannical, domineering, masterful, if they chose; she did not mind. And, touching his hair with her lips, she thought, he will never be so happy again, but stopped herself, remembering how it angered her husband that she should say that. Still, it was true. They were happier now than

---

5. The holograph makes Mrs. Ramsay's commitments even more explicit, both "to get a small hospital built up in these islands; that was a matter she had set on foot" and "to found a model dairy near London" (*Original Holograph*, p. 98). Mrs. Ramsay's views about dairies and public health services recall those of Julia Stephen in *Notes from Sick Rooms*, this edition, pp. 206–10.

they would ever be again. A tenpenny tea set made Cam happy for
days. She heard them stamping and crowing on the floor above her
head the moment they woke. They came bustling along the passage.
Then the door sprang open and in they came, fresh as roses, staring, wide awake, as if this coming into the dining-room after breakfast, which they did every day of their lives, was a positive event to
them, and so on, with one thing after another, all day long, until
she went up to say good-night to them, and found them netted in
their cots like birds among cherries and raspberries, still making up
stories about some little bit of rubbish—something they had heard,
something they had picked up in the garden. They had all their little
treasures. . . . And so she went down and said to her husband, Why
must they grow up and lose it all? Never will they be so happy again.
And he was angry. Why take such a gloomy view of life? he said. It
is not sensible. For it was odd; and she believed it to be true; that
with all his gloom and desperation he was happier, more hopeful on
the whole, than she was. Less exposed to human worries—perhaps
that was it. He had always his work to fall back on. Not that she herself was "pessimistic," as he accused her of being. Only she thought
life—and a little strip of time presented itself to her eyes—her fifty
years. There it was before her—life. Life, she thought—but she did
not finish her thought. She took a look at life, for she had a clear
sense of it there, something real, something private, which she
shared neither with her children nor with her husband. A sort of
transaction went on between them, in which she was on one side,
and life was on another, and she was always trying to get the better
of it, as it was of her; and sometimes they parleyed (when she sat
alone); there were, she remembered, great reconciliation scenes; but
for the most part, oddly enough, she must admit that she felt this
thing that she called life terrible, hostile, and quick to pounce on
you if you gave it a chance. There were the eternal problems: suffering; death; the poor. There was always a woman dying of cancer
even here. And yet she had said to all these children, You shall go
through it all. To eight people she had said relentlessly that (and the
bill for the greenhouse would be fifty pounds). For that reason,
knowing what was before them—love and ambition and being
wretched alone in dreary places—she had often the feeling, Why
must they grow up and lose it all? And then she said to herself, brandishing her sword at life, Nonsense. They will be perfectly happy.
And here she was, she reflected, feeling life rather sinister again,
making Minta marry Paul Rayley; because whatever she might feel
about her own transaction, she had had experiences which need not
happen to every one (she did not name them to herself); she was
driven on, too quickly she knew, almost as if it were an escape for
her too, to say that people must marry; people must have children.

Was she wrong in this, she asked herself, reviewing her conduct for the past week or two, and wondering if she had indeed put any pressure upon Minta, who was only twenty-four, to make up her mind. She was uneasy. Had she not laughed about it? Was she not forgetting again how strongly she influenced people? Marriage needed—oh, all sorts of qualities (the bill for the greenhouse would be fifty pounds); one—she need not name it—that was essential; the thing she had with her husband. Had they that?

"Then he put on his trousers and ran away like a madman," she read. "But outside a great storm was raging and blowing so hard that he could scarcely keep his feet; houses and trees toppled over, the mountains trembled, rocks rolled into the sea, the sky was pitch black, and it thundered and lightened, and the sea came in with black waves as high as church towers and mountains, and all with white foam at the top."

She turned the page; there were only a few lines more, so that she would finish the story, though it was past bed-time. It was getting late. The light in the garden told her that; and the whitening of the flowers and something grey in the leaves conspired together, to rouse in her a feeling of anxiety. What it was about she could not think at first. Then she remembered; Paul and Minta and Andrew had not come back. She summoned before her again the little group on the terrace in front of the hall door, standing looking up into the sky. Andrew had his net and basket. That meant he was going to catch crabs and things. That meant he would climb out on to a rock; he would be cut off. Or coming back single file on one of those little paths above the cliff one of them might slip. He would roll and then crash. It was growing quite dark.

But she did not let her voice change in the least as she finished the story, and added, shutting the book, and speaking the last words as if she had made them up herself, looking into James's eyes: "And there they are living still at this very time."[6]

"And that's the end," she said, and she saw in his eyes, as the interest of the story died away in them, something else take its place; something wondering, pale, like the reflection of a light, which at once made him gaze and marvel. Turning, she looked across the bay, and there, sure enough, coming regularly across the waves first two quick strokes and then one long steady stroke, was the light of the Lighthouse. It had been lit.

In a moment he would ask her, "Are we going to the Lighthouse?" And she would have to say, "No: not tomorrow; your father says not."

6. In the holograph, Mrs. Ramsay is reading "The story of the Woodman's daughter" to both children, and the moment when she finishes the story includes Cam: "one could almost see them both pondering those last words about the little girl dreaming of the bears" (*Original Holograph*, p. 104).

Happily, Mildred came in to fetch them, and the bustle distracted them. But he kept looking back over his shoulder as Mildred carried him out, and she was certain that he was thinking, we are not going to the Lighthouse tomorrow; and she thought, he will remember that all his life.

XI

No, she thought, putting together some of the pictures he had cut out—a refrigerator, a mowing machine, a gentleman in evening dress—children never forget. For this reason, it was so important what one said, and what one did, and it was a relief when they went to bed. For now she need not think about anybody. She could be herself, by herself. And that was what now she often felt the need of—to think; well, not even to think. To be silent; to be alone. All the being and the doing, expansive, glittering, vocal, evaporated; and one shrunk, with a sense of solemnity, to being oneself, a wedge-shaped core of darkness, something invisible to others. Although she continued to knit, and sat upright, it was thus that she felt herself; and this self having shed its attachments was free for the strangest adventures. When life sank down for a moment, the range of experience seemed limitless. And to everybody there was always this sense of unlimited resources, she supposed; one after another, she, Lily, Augustus Carmichael, must feel, our apparitions, the things you know us by, are simply childish. Beneath it is all dark, it is all spreading, it is unfathomably deep; but now and again we rise to the surface and that is what you see us by. Her horizon seemed to her limitless. There were all the places she had not seen; the Indian plains;[1] she felt herself pushing aside the thick leather curtain of a church in Rome. This core of darkness could go anywhere, for no one saw it. They could not stop it, she thought, exulting. There was freedom, there was peace, there was, most welcome of all, a summoning together, a resting on a platform of stability. Not as oneself did one find rest ever, in her experience (she accomplished here something dexterous with her needles) but as a wedge of darkness. Losing personality, one lost the fret, the hurry, the stir; and there rose to her lips always some exclamation of triumph over life when things came together in this peace, this rest, this eternity; and pausing there she looked out to meet that stroke of the Lighthouse, the long steady stroke, the last of the three, which was her stroke, for watching them in this mood always at this hour one could not help attaching oneself to one thing especially of the things one saw; and

---

1. Could refer to the Deccan plateau of central and southern India, or to the Indo-Gangetic plain, south of the Himalayas, which stretches across northern and eastern India and what is now Bangladesh.

this thing, the long steady stroke, was her stroke. Often she found herself sitting and looking, sitting and looking, with her work in her hands until she became the thing she looked at—that light, for example. And it would lift up on it some little phrase or other which had been lying in her mind like that—"Children don't forget, children don't forget"—which she would repeat and begin adding to it, It will end, it will end, she said. It will come, it will come, when suddenly she added, We are in the hands of the Lord.[2]

But instantly she was annoyed with herself for saying that. Who had said it? Not she; she had been trapped into saying something she did not mean. She looked up over her knitting and met the third stroke and it seemed to her like her own eyes meeting her own eyes, searching as she alone could search into her mind and her heart, purifying out of existence that lie, any lie. She praised herself in praising the light, without vanity, for she was stern, she was searching, she was beautiful like that light. It was odd, she thought, how if one was alone, one leant to inanimate things; trees, streams, flowers; felt they expressed one; felt they became one; felt they knew one, in a sense were one; felt an irrational tenderness thus (she looked at that long steady light) as for oneself. There rose, and she looked and looked with her needles suspended, there curled up off the floor of the mind, rose from the lake of one's being, a mist, a bride to meet her lover.

What brought her to say that: "We are in the hands of the Lord?" she wondered. The insincerity slipping in among the truths roused her, annoyed her. She returned to her knitting again. How could any Lord have made this world? she asked. With her mind she had always seized the fact that there is no reason, order, justice: but suffering, death, the poor. There was no treachery too base for the world to commit; she knew that. No happiness lasted; she knew that. She knitted with firm composure, slightly pursing her lips and, without being aware of it, so stiffened and composed the lines of her face in a habit of sternness that when her husband passed, though he was chuckling at the thought that Hume, the philosopher, grown enormously fat, had stuck in a bog,[3] he could not help noting, as he passed, the sternness at the heart of her beauty. It saddened him, and her remoteness pained him, and he felt, as he passed, that he could not protect her, and, when he reached the hedge, he was sad.

---

2. Mrs. Ramsay's involuntary quotation could come from various places in the Bible, such as Ecclesiastes 2:18: "We will fall into the hands of the Lord, not into the hands of men;" or from the Anglican prayer book: "Father, into thy hands I commend my spirit." All references to the Bible are to the King James Version.
3. Mr. Ramsay doesn't finish telling himself this famous anecdote until the end of section 13 (57); the story pokes gentle fun at Hume's skepticism about the existence of God, which is related to his view that objects cannot be shown to exist independent of human perceptions of them. Leslie Stephen recounted this anecdote in his entry on Hume in the *Dictionary of National Biography*.

He could do nothing to help her. He must stand by and watch her. Indeed, the infernal truth was, he made things worse for her. He was irritable—he was touchy. He had lost his temper over the Lighthouse. He looked into the hedge, into its intricacy, its darkness.

Always, Mrs. Ramsay felt, one helped oneself out of solitude reluctantly by laying hold of some little odd or end, some sound, some sight. She listened, but it was all very still; cricket was over; the children were in their baths; there was only the sound of the sea. She stopped knitting; she held the long reddish-brown stocking dangling in her hands a moment. She saw the light again. With some irony in her interrogation, for when one woke at all, one's relations changed, she looked at the steady light, the pitiless, the remorseless, which was so much her, yet so little her, which had her at its beck and call (she woke in the night and saw it bent across their bed, stroking the floor), but for all that she thought, watching it with fascination, hypnotised, as if it were stroking with its silver fingers some sealed vessel in her brain whose bursting would flood her with delight, she had known happiness, exquisite happiness, intense happiness, and it silvered the rough waves a little more brightly, as daylight faded, and the blue went out of the sea and it rolled in waves of pure lemon which curved and swelled and broke upon the beach and the ecstasy burst in her eyes and waves of pure delight raced over the floor of her mind and she felt, It is enough! It is enough!

He turned and saw her. Ah! She was lovely, lovelier now than ever he thought. But he could not speak to her. He could not interrupt her. He wanted urgently to speak to her now that James was gone and she was alone at last. But he resolved, no; he would not interrupt her. She was aloof from him now in her beauty, in her sadness. He would let her be, and he passed her without a word, though it hurt him that she should look so distant, and he could not reach her, he could do nothing to help her. And again he would have passed her without a word had she not, at that very moment, given him of her own free will what she knew he would never ask, and called to him and taken the green shawl off the picture frame, and gone to him. For he wished, she knew, to protect her.

XII

She folded the green shawl about her shoulders. She took his arm. His beauty was so great, she said, beginning to speak of Kennedy the gardener, at once he was so awfully handsome, that she couldn't dismiss him. There was a ladder against the greenhouse, and little lumps of putty stuck about, for they were beginning to mend the greenhouse. Yes, but as she strolled along with her husband, she felt that that particular source of worry had been placed. She had it on the tip of her tongue to say, as they strolled, "It'll cost fifty pounds," but instead, for her heart failed her about money, she talked about Jasper shooting birds, and he said, at once, soothing her instantly, that it was natural in a boy, and he trusted he would find better ways of amusing himself before long. Her husband was so sensible, so just. And so she said, "Yes; all children go through stages," and began considering the dahlias in the big bed, and wondering what about next year's flowers, and had he heard the children's nickname for Charles Tansley, she asked. The atheist, they called him, the little atheist. "He's not a polished specimen," said Mr. Ramsay. "Far from it," said Mrs. Ramsay.

She supposed it was all right leaving him to his own devices, Mrs. Ramsay said, wondering whether it was any use sending down bulbs; did they plant them? "Oh, he has his dissertation to write," said Mr. Ramsay. She knew all about *that*, said Mrs. Ramsay. He talked of nothing else. It was about the influence of somebody upon something. "Well, it's all he has to count on," said Mr. Ramsay. "Pray Heaven he won't fall in love with Prue," said Mrs. Ramsay. He'd disinherit her if she married him, said Mr. Ramsay. He did not look at the flowers, which his wife was considering, but at a spot about a foot or so above them. There was no harm in him, he added, and was just about to say that anyhow he was the only young man in England who admired his—— when he choked it back. He would not bother her again about his books. These flowers seemed creditable, Mr. Ramsay said, lowering his gaze and noticing something red, something brown. Yes, but then these she had put in with her own hands, said Mrs. Ramsay. The question was, what happened if she sent bulbs down; did Kennedy plant them? It was his incurable laziness; she added, moving on. If she stood over him all day long with a spade in her hand, he did sometimes do a stroke of work. So they strolled along, towards the red-hot pokers. "You're teaching your daughters to exaggerate," said Mr. Ramsay, reproving her. Her Aunt Camilla was far worse than she was, Mrs. Ramsay remarked. "Nobody ever held up your Aunt Camilla as a model of virtue that I'm aware of," said Mr. Ramsay. "She was the most beautiful woman I ever saw," said Mrs. Ramsay. "Somebody else was that," said Mr. Ramsay. Prue was going to be far more beautiful than she was, said Mrs. Ramsay. He saw no trace of it, said Mr. Ramsay. "Well, then, look tonight," said Mrs. Ramsay. They paused. He wished Andrew could be induced to work harder. He would lose every chance of a scholarship if he didn't. "Oh, scholarships!" she said. Mr. Ramsay thought her foolish for saying that about a serious thing like a scholarship. He should be very proud of Andrew if he got a scholarship, he said. She would be just as proud of him if he didn't, she answered. They disagreed always about this, but it did not matter. She liked him to believe in scholarships, and he liked her to be proud of Andrew whatever he did. Suddenly she remembered those little paths on the edge of the cliffs.

Wasn't it late? she asked. They hadn't come home yet. He flicked his watch carelessly open. But it was only just past seven. He held his watch open for a moment, deciding that he would tell her what he had felt on the terrace. To begin with, it was not reasonable to be so nervous. Andrew could look after himself. Then, he wanted to tell her that when he was walking on the terrace just now—here he became uncomfortable, as if he were breaking into that solitude, that aloofness, that remoteness of hers. . . . But she pressed him. What had he wanted to tell her, she asked, thinking it was about going to the Lighthouse; that he was sorry he had said "Damn you." But no. He did not like to see her look so sad, he said. Only wool gathering, she protested, flushing a little. They both felt uncomfortable, as if they did not know whether to go on or go back. She had been reading fairy tales to James, she said. No, they could not share that; they could not say that.

They had reached the gap between the two clumps of red-hot pokers, and there was the Lighthouse again, but she would not let herself look at it. Had she known that he was looking at her, she thought, she would not have let herself sit there, thinking. She disliked anything that reminded her that she had been seen sitting thinking. So she looked over her shoulder, at the town. The lights were rippling and running as if they were drops of silver water held firm in a wind. And all the poverty, all the suffering had turned to that, Mrs. Ramsay thought. The lights of the town and of the harbour and of the boats seemed like a phantom net floating there to mark something which had sunk. Well, if he could not share her thoughts, Mr. Ramsay said to himself, he would be off, then, on his own. He wanted to go on thinking, telling himself the story how Hume was stuck in a bog; he wanted to laugh. But first it was nonsense to be anxious about Andrew. When he was Andrew's age he used to walk about the country all day long, with nothing but a biscuit in his pocket and nobody bothered about him, or thought that he had fallen over a cliff. He said aloud he thought he would be off for a day's walk if the weather held. He had had about enough of Bankes and of Carmichael. He would like a little solitude. Yes, she said. It annoyed him that she did not protest. She knew that he would never do it. He was too old now to walk all day long with a biscuit in his pocket. She worried about the boys, but not about him. Years ago, before he had married, he thought, looking across the bay, as they stood between the clumps of red-hot pokers, he had walked all day. He had made a meal off bread and cheese in a public house.[1] He had worked ten

---

1. Now familiarly referred to as a pub.

hours at a stretch; an old woman just popped her head in now and again and saw to the fire. That was the country he liked best, over there; those sandhills dwindling away into darkness. One could walk all day without meeting a soul. There was not a house scarcely, not a single village for miles on end. One could worry things out alone. There were little sandy beaches where no one had been since the beginning of time. The seals sat up and looked at you. It sometimes seemed to him that in a little house out there, alone—he broke off, sighing. He had no right. The father of eight children—he reminded himself. And he would have been a beast and a cur to wish a single thing altered. Andrew would be a better man than he had been. Prue would be a beauty, her mother said. They would stem the flood a bit. That was a good bit of work on the whole—his eight children. They showed he did not damn the poor little universe entirely, for on an evening like this, he thought, looking at the land dwindling away, the little island seemed pathetically small, half swallowed up in the sea.

"Poor little place," he murmured with a sigh.

She heard him. He said the most melancholy things, but she noticed that directly he had said them he always seemed more cheerful than usual. All this phrase-making was a game, she thought, for if she had said half what he said, she would have blown her brains out by now.

It annoyed her, this phrase-making, and she said to him, in a matter-of-fact way, that it was a perfectly lovely evening. And what was he groaning about, she asked, half laughing, half complaining, for she guessed what he was thinking—he would have written better books if he had not married.

He was not complaining, he said. She knew that he did not complain. She knew that he had nothing whatever to complain of. And he seized her hand and raised it to his lips and kissed it with an intensity that brought the tears to her eyes, and quickly he dropped it.

They turned away from the view and began to walk up the path where the silver-green spear-like plants[2] grew, arm in arm. His arm was almost like a young man's arm, Mrs. Ramsay thought, thin and hard, and she thought with delight how strong he still was, though he was over sixty, and how untamed and optimistic, and how strange it was that being convinced, as he was, of all sorts of horrors, seemed not to depress him, but to cheer him. Was it not odd, she reflected? Indeed he seemed to her sometimes made differently from other people, born blind, deaf, and dumb, to the ordinary things, but to the extraordinary things, with an eye like an eagle's. His understanding often astonished her. But did he notice the flowers? No. Did he

---

2. Probably yuccas, native to the hot and dry parts of the Americas and the Caribbean, members of the *Asparagaceae* family.

notice the view? No. Did he even notice his own daughter's beauty, or whether there was pudding on his plate or roast beef? He would sit at table with them like a person in a dream. And his habit of talking aloud, or saying poetry aloud, was growing on him, she was afraid; for sometimes it was awkward—

Best and brightest come away![3]

poor Miss Giddings, when he shouted that at her, almost jumped out of her skin. But then, Mrs. Ramsay, though instantly taking his side against all the silly Giddingses in the world, then, she thought, intimating by a little pressure on his arm that he walked up hill too fast for her, and she must stop for a moment to see whether those were fresh molehills on the bank, then, she thought, stooping down to look, a great mind like his must be different in every way from ours. All the great men she had ever known, she thought, deciding that a rabbit must have got in, were like that, and it was good for young men (though the atmosphere of lecture-rooms was stuffy and depressing to her beyond endurance almost) simply to hear him, simply to look at him. But without shooting rabbits, how was one to keep them down? she wondered. It might be a rabbit; it might be a mole. Some creature anyhow was ruining her Evening Primroses.[4] And looking up, she saw above the thin trees the first pulse of the full-throbbing star, and wanted to make her husband look at it; for the sight gave her such keen pleasure. But she stopped herself. He never looked at things. If he did, all he would say would be, Poor little world, with one of his sighs.

At that moment, he said, "Very fine," to please her, and pretended to admire the flowers. But she knew quite well that he did not admire them, or even realise that they were there. It was only to please her . . . Ah, but was that not Lily Briscoe strolling along with William Bankes? She focussed her short-sighted eyes upon the backs of a retreating couple. Yes, indeed it was. Did that not mean that they would marry? Yes, it must! What an admirable idea! They must marry!

XIII

He had been to Amsterdam, Mr. Bankes was saying as he strolled across the lawn with Lily Briscoe. He had seen the Rembrandts. He had been to Madrid. Unfortunately, it was Good Friday and the Prado was shut. He had been to Rome. Had Miss Briscoe never been to Rome? Oh, she should—— It would be a wonderful experience

---

3. The opening line of "To Jane: The Invitation," a love poem by Percy Bysshe Shelley (1792–1822).
4. *Oenothera biennis,* a yellow-flowering perennial plant native to North America.

for her—the Sistine Chapel; Michael Angelo; and Padua, with its Giottos.[1] His wife had been in bad health for many years, so that their sight-seeing had been on a modest scale.

She had been to Brussels; she had been to Paris, but only for a flying visit to see an aunt who was ill. She had been to Dresden; there were masses of pictures she had not seen; however, Lily Briscoe reflected, perhaps it was better not to see pictures: they only made one hopelessly discontented with one's own work. Mr. Bankes thought one could carry that point of view too far. We can't all be Titians and we can't all be Darwins, he said; at the same time he doubted whether you could have your Darwin and your Titian if it weren't for humble people like ourselves.[2] Lily would have liked to pay him a compliment; you're not humble, Mr. Bankes, she would have liked to have said. But he did not want compliments (most men do, she thought), and she was a little ashamed of her impulse and said nothing while he remarked that perhaps what he was saying did not apply to pictures. Anyhow, said Lily, tossing off her little insincerity, she would always go on painting, because it interested her. Yes, said Mr. Bankes, he was sure she would, and, as they reached the end of the lawn he was asking her whether she had difficulty in finding subjects in London when they turned and saw the Ramsays. So that is marriage, Lily thought, a man and a woman looking at a girl throwing a ball. That is what Mrs. Ramsay tried to tell me the other night, she thought. For Mrs. Ramsay was wearing a green shawl, and they were standing close together watching Prue and Jasper throwing catches. And suddenly the meaning which, for no reason at all, as perhaps they are stepping out of the Tube or ringing a doorbell, descends on people, making them symbolical, making them representative, came upon them, and made them in the dusk standing, looking, the symbols of marriage, husband and wife. Then, after an instant, the symbolical outline which transcended the real figures sank down again, and they became, as they met them, Mr. and Mrs. Ramsay watching the children throwing catches. But still for a moment, though Mrs. Ramsay greeted them with her usual smile (oh, she's thinking we're going to get married, Lily thought) and said, "I have triumphed tonight," meaning that for once Mr. Bankes had

1. The paintings by Rembrandt (1606–1669) at the Rijksmuseum in Amsterdam, Madrid's Prado Museum with its superlative collection of European and especially Spanish art, the Sistine Chapel in the Vatican City in Rome famed for its frescos by Michelangelo, and the Scrovegni (or Arena) Chapel in the Italian city of Padua with its fresco cycle by the Florentine painter Giotto (1267–1337): these are all typical stops on the British visitor's tour of European art masterpieces, especially those of the Middle Ages and the Renaissance, which include many images of Madonna and child.
2. Charles Darwin (1809–1882), author of *On the Origin of Species by Means of Natural Selection* (1859) and *The Descent of Man* (1871), is the nineteenth-century naturalist who verified the theory of evolution and who is credited both with revolutionizing natural history and with destabilizing religious belief. Titian or Tiziano Vecellio (1488–1576), the great Italian Renaissance painter from Venice.

agreed to dine with them and not run off to his own lodging where his man cooked vegetables properly; still, for one moment, there was a sense of things having been blown apart, of space, of irresponsibility as the ball soared high, and they followed it and lost it and saw the one star and the draped branches. In the failing light they all looked sharp-edged and ethereal and divided by great distances. Then, darting backwards over the vast space (for it seemed as if solidity had vanished altogether), Prue ran full tilt into them and caught the ball brilliantly high up in her left hand, and her mother said, "Haven't they come back yet?" whereupon the spell was broken. Mr. Ramsay felt free now to laugh out loud at the thought that Hume had stuck in a bog and an old woman rescued him on condition he said the Lord's prayer, and chuckling to himself he strolled off to his study. Mrs. Ramsay, bringing Prue back into throwing catches again, from which she had escaped, asked,

"Did Nancy go with them?"

XIV

(Certainly, Nancy had gone with them, since Minta Doyle had asked it with her dumb look, holding out her hand, as Nancy made off, after lunch, to her attic, to escape the horror of family life. She supposed she must go then. She did not want to go. She did not want to be drawn into it all. For as they walked along the road to the cliff Minta kept on taking her hand. Then she would let it go. Then she would take it again. What was it she wanted? Nancy asked herself. There was something, of course, that people wanted; for when Minta took her hand and held it, Nancy, reluctantly, saw the whole world spread out beneath her, as if it were Constantinople seen through a mist, and then, however heavy-eyed one might be, one must needs ask, "Is that Santa Sofia?" "Is that the Golden Horn?"[1] So Nancy asked, when Minta took her hand. "What is it that she wants? Is it that?" And what was that? Here and there emerged from the mist (as Nancy looked down upon life spread beneath her) a pinnacle, a dome; prominent things, without names. But when Minta dropped her hand, as she did when they ran down the hillside, all that, the dome, the pinnacle, whatever it was that had protruded through the mist, sank down into it and disappeared. Minta, Andrew observed, was rather a good walker. She wore more sensible clothes than most

---

1. Constantinople, the modern-day city of Istanbul, Turkey, was Byzantium, the capital of the Byzantine Empire, until 1453, when it was conquered by the Turks; it became the capital city of the Ottoman Empire until its dissolution in 1923. Hagia Sofia, built as a cathedral in the sixth century c.e., became a mosque after the Turkish conquest of Constantinople; it was a museum from 1935 to 2020, but was then reclassified as a mosque. The Golden Horn is Istanbul's harbor, an inlet of the Bosporus, the strait that connects the Mediterranean to the Black Sea and thus Europe to Asia. Woolf and her siblings visited and admired Constantinople in 1906.

women. She wore very short skirts and black knickerbockers.[2] She would jump straight into a stream and flounder across. He liked her rashness, but he saw that it would not do—she would kill herself in some idiotic way one of these days. She seemed to be afraid of nothing—except bulls. At the mere sight of a bull in a field she would throw up her arms and fly screaming, which was the very thing to enrage a bull of course. But she did not mind owning up to it in the least; one must admit that. She knew she was an awful coward about bulls, she said. She thought she must have been tossed in her perambulator when she was a baby. She didn't seem to mind what she said or did. Suddenly now she pitched down on the edge of the cliff and began to sing some song about

Damn your eyes, damn your eyes.[3]

They all had to join in and sing the chorus, and shout out together:

Damn your eyes, damn your eyes,

but it would be fatal to let the tide come in and cover up all the good hunting-grounds before they got on to the beach.

"Fatal," Paul agreed, springing up, and as they went slithering down, he kept quoting the guidebook about "these islands being justly celebrated for their park-like prospects and the extent and variety of their marine curiosities."[4] But it would not do altogether, this shouting and damning your eyes, Andrew felt, picking his way down the cliff, this clapping him on the back, and calling him "old fellow" and all that; it would not altogether do. It was the worst of taking women on walks. Once on the beach they separated, he going out on to the Pope's Nose,[5] taking his shoes off, and rolling his socks in them and letting that couple look after themselves; Nancy waded out to her own rocks and searched her own pools and let that couple look after themselves. She crouched low down and touched the smooth rubber-like sea anemones, who were stuck like lumps of jelly to the side of the rock. Brooding, she changed the pool into the sea, and made the minnows into sharks and whales, and cast vast clouds over this tiny

2. Baggy-kneed trousers that end and are cinched in just below the knee, worn with long socks or stockings; in this period, worn by boys, also by girls and women for playing sports or hiking; *very short skirts*: Prior to World War I, women in Britain still wore skirts to their ankles, so a "very short skirt" would still have been well below the knee.
3. Minta sings "Sam Hall," a popular ballad about an unrepentant Robin Hood–like criminal, condemned to death. For the text of the ballad, see this edition, pp. 272–73.
4. It's unlikely that Woolf is quoting from an actual guidebook here; in the holograph she tries different phrasings to get the stilted tone just right (*Original Holograph*, pp. 123–24).
5. A slang term for the rump of a chicken or turkey; here apparently a local name for a rocky outcropping; possibly also evokes a World War I German outpost near Thiepval on the Western Front that the British attacked (with many casualties) in the Battle of the Somme; see Jane Goldman, "Who is Mr. Ramsay? Where Is the Lighthouse?: The Politics and Pragmatics of Scholarly Annotation," in *Woolf Editing / Editing Woolf*, ed. Eleanor McNees and Sara Veglahn (Clemson: Clemson U Digital P, 2009), pp. 189–95.

world by holding her hand against the sun, and so brought darkness and desolation, like God himself, to millions of ignorant and innocent creatures, and then took her hand away suddenly and let the sun stream down. Out on the pale criss-crossed sand, high-stepping, fringed, gauntleted, stalked some fantastic leviathan (she was still enlarging the pool), and slipped into the vast fissures of the mountain side. And then, letting her eyes slide imperceptibly above the pool and rest on that wavering line of sea and sky, on the tree trunks which the smoke of steamers made waver upon the horizon, she became with all that power sweeping savagely in and inevitably withdrawing, hypnotised, and the two senses of that vastness and this tininess (the pool had diminished again) flowering within it made her feel that she was bound hand and foot and unable to move by the intensity of feelings which reduced her own body, her own life, and the lives of all the people in the world, for ever, to nothingness. So listening to the waves, crouching over the pool, she brooded.

And Andrew shouted that the sea was coming in, so she leapt splashing through the shallow waves on to the shore and ran up the beach and was carried by her own impetuosity and her desire for rapid movement right behind a rock and there—oh, heavens! in each other's arms, were Paul and Minta kissing probably. She was outraged, indignant. She and Andrew put on their shoes and stockings in dead silence without saying a thing about it. Indeed they were rather sharp with each other. She might have called him when she saw the crayfish or whatever it was, Andrew grumbled. However, they both felt, it's not our fault. They had not wanted this horrid nuisance to happen. All the same it irritated Andrew that Nancy should be a woman, and Nancy that Andrew should be a man, and they tied their shoes very neatly and drew the bows rather tight.

It was not until they had climbed right up on to the top of the cliff again that Minta cried out that she had lost her grandmother's brooch—her grandmother's brooch, the sole ornament she possessed—a weeping willow, it was (they must remember it) set in pearls.[6] They must have seen it, she said, with the tears running down her cheeks, the brooch which her grandmother had fastened her cap with till the last day of her life. Now she had lost it. She would rather have lost anything than that! She would go back and look for it. They all went back. They poked and peered and looked. They kept their heads very low, and said things shortly and gruffly. Paul Rayley searched like a madman all about the rock where they had been sitting. All this pother about a brooch really didn't do at all, Andrew thought, as Paul told him to make a "thorough search between this point and that." The tide was coming in fast. The sea

---

6. A Victorian mourning brooch, since willows were an emblem of grieving.

would cover the place where they had sat in a minute. There was
not a ghost of a chance of their finding it now. "We shall be cut off!"
Minta shrieked, suddenly terrified. As if there were any danger of
that! It was the same as the bulls all over again—she had no control
over her emotions, Andrew thought. Women hadn't. The wretched
Paul had to pacify her. The men (Andrew and Paul at once became
manly, and different from usual) took counsel briefly and decided
that they would plant Rayley's stick where they had sat and come
back at low tide again. There was nothing more that could be done
now. If the brooch was there, it would still be there in the morning,
they assured her, but Minta still sobbed, all the way up to the top of
the cliff. It was her grandmother's brooch; she would rather have
lost anything but that, and yet Nancy felt, it might be true that she
minded losing her brooch, but she wasn't crying only for that. She was
crying for something else. We might all sit down and cry, she felt. But
she did not know what for.

They drew ahead together, Paul and Minta, and he comforted her,
and said how famous he was for finding things. Once when he was a
little boy he had found a gold watch. He would get up at daybreak and
he was positive he would find it. It seemed to him that it would be
almost dark, and he would be alone on the beach, and somehow it
would be rather dangerous. He began telling her, however, that he
would certainly find it, and she said that she would not hear of his
getting up at dawn: it was lost: she knew that: she had had a presenti-
ment when she put it on that afternoon. And secretly he resolved that
he would not tell her, but he would slip out of the house at dawn when
they were all asleep and if he could not find it he would go to Edinburgh and buy her another,[7] just like it but more beautiful. He would
prove what he could do. And as they came out on the hill and saw the
lights of the town beneath them, the lights coming out suddenly one
by one seemed like things that were going to happen to him—his
marriage, his children, his house; and again he thought, as they came
out on to the high road, which was shaded with high bushes, how
they would retreat into solitude together, and walk on and on, he
always leading her, and she pressing close to his side (as she did now).
As they turned by the cross roads he thought what an appalling experience he had been through, and he must tell someone—Mrs. Ramsay of course, for it took his breath away to think what he had been
and done. It had been far and away the worst moment of his life when
he asked Minta to marry him. He would go straight to Mrs. Ramsay,
because he felt somehow that she was the person who had made him
do it. She had made him think he could do anything. Nobody else

---

7. Edinburgh is the capital of Scotland and would require a complicated and lengthy
journey from a house on the Isle of Skye: Paul would have to get to a ferry crossing,
then travel about 200 miles on the mainland.

took him seriously. But she made him believe that he could do whatever he wanted. He had felt her eyes on him all day today, following him about (though she never said a word) as if she were saying, "Yes, you can do it. I believe in you. I expect it of you." She had made him feel all that, and directly they got back (he looked for the lights of the house above the bay) he would go to her and say, "I've done it, Mrs. Ramsay; thanks to you." And so turning into the lane that led to the house he could see lights moving about in the upper windows. They must be awfully late then. People were getting ready for dinner. The house was all lit up, and the lights after the darkness made his eyes feel full, and he said to himself, childishly, as he walked up the drive, Lights, lights, lights, and repeated in a dazed way, Lights, lights, lights, as they came into the house staring about him with his face quite stiff. But, good heavens, he said to himself, putting his hand to his tie, I must not make a fool of myself.)

XV

"Yes," said Prue, in her considering way, answering her mother's question, "I think Nancy did go with them."

XVI

Well then, Nancy had gone with them, Mrs. Ramsay supposed, wondering, as she put down a brush, took up a comb, and said "Come in" to a tap at the door (Jasper and Rose came in), whether the fact that Nancy was with them made it less likely or more likely that anything would happen; it made it less likely, somehow, Mrs. Ramsay felt, very irrationally, except that after all holocaust on such a scale was not probable. They could not all be drowned. And again she felt alone in the presence of her old antagonist, life.

Jasper and Rose said that Mildred wanted to know whether she should wait dinner.

"Not for the Queen of England," said Mrs. Ramsay emphatically.

"Not for the Empress of Mexico,"[1] she added, laughing at Jasper; for he shared his mother's vice: he, too, exaggerated.

And if Rose liked, she said, while Jasper took the message, she might choose which jewels she was to wear. When there are fifteen people sitting down to dinner, one cannot keep things waiting for ever.[2] She was now beginning to feel annoyed with them for being so

1. When Napoleon III (1808–1873), emperor of France, invaded Mexico in 1864 he installed Archduke Maximilian of Austria (1832–1867) as ruler; his wife, the Belgian Princess Charlotte (1840–1927) held the title of Empress Carlota until 1867, when Mexican resistance ended their rule and her husband was executed.
2. The fourteen (not fifteen) people who will sit down to this dinner include all the guests and family members mentioned in the novel except for Cam and James, who have been taken by Mildred, the cook, to eat their supper in the nursery.

late; it was inconsiderate of them, and it annoyed her on top of her anxiety about them, that they should choose this very night to be out late, when, in fact, she wished the dinner to be particularly nice, since William Bankes had at last consented to dine with them; and they were having Mildred's masterpiece—Bœuf en Daube.[3] Everything depended upon things being served up to the precise moment they were ready. The beef, the bayleaf, and the wine—all must be done to a turn. To keep it waiting was out of the question. Yet of course tonight, of all nights, out they went, and they came in late, and things had to be sent out, things had to be kept hot; the Bœuf en Daube would be entirely spoilt.

Jasper offered her an opal necklace; Rose a gold necklace. Which looked best against her black dress? Which did indeed, said Mrs. Ramsay absentmindedly, looking at her neck and shoulders (but avoiding her face) in the glass. And then, while the children rummaged among her things, she looked out of the window at a sight which always amused her—the rooks trying to decide which tree to settle on. Every time, they seemed to change their minds and rose up into the air again, because, she thought, the old rook, the father rook, old Joseph was her name for him, was a bird of a very trying and difficult disposition. He was a disreputable old bird, with half his wing feathers missing. He was like some seedy old gentleman in a top hat she had seen playing the horn in front of a public house.

"Look!" she said, laughing. They were actually fighting. Joseph and Mary were fighting. Anyhow they all went up again, and the air was shoved aside by their black wings and cut into exquisite scimitar shapes. The movement of the wings beating out, out, out—she could never describe it accurately enough to please herself—was one of the loveliest of all to her. Look at that, she said to Rose, hoping that Rose would see it more clearly than she could. For one's children so often gave one's own perceptions a little thrust forwards.

But which was it to be? They had all the trays of her jewel-case open. The gold necklace, which was Italian, or the opal necklace, which Uncle James had brought her from India; or should she wear her amethysts?[4]

"Choose, dearest, choose," she said, hoping that they would make haste.

---

3. A dish of beef, olives, and wine cooked slowly in a tall, thick-walled earthenware pot (the *daube* or *daubière*); part of the traditional cuisine of the South of France and a specialty of Roger Fry's; see *Bœuf en Daube* for Fourteen, this edition, pp. 216–18.
4. That Mrs. Ramsay changes her clothes in the evening for dinner, adding jewelry from an ample collection, indicates the family's adherence to the Victorian upper-class custom of changing into formal dress clothes for dinner; *Opal necklace*: opals are chiefly mined in Australia, at that time still a British colony; an opal necklace from Uncle James in India (apparently Mrs. Ramsay's brother) is a reminder both that the men of the family "ruled India" (7) and that the British Empire at this time extended around the globe.

But she let them take their time to choose: she let Rose, particularly, take up this and then that, and hold her jewels against the black dress, for this little ceremony of choosing jewels, which was gone through every night, was what Rose liked best, she knew. She had some hidden reason of her own for attaching great importance to this choosing what her mother was to wear. What was the reason, Mrs. Ramsay wondered, standing still to let her clasp the necklace she had chosen, divining, through her own past, some deep, some buried, some quite speechless feeling that one had for one's mother at Rose's age. Like all feelings felt for oneself, Mrs. Ramsay thought, it made one sad. It was so inadequate, what one could give in return; and what Rose felt was quite out of proportion to anything she actually was. And Rose would grow up; and Rose would suffer, she supposed, with these deep feelings, and she said she was ready now, and they would go down, and Jasper, because he was the gentleman, should give her his arm, and Rose, as she was the lady, should carry her handkerchief (she gave her the handkerchief), and what else? oh, yes, it might be cold: a shawl. Choose me a shawl, she said, for that would please Rose, who was bound to suffer so. "There," she said, stopping by the window on the landing, "there they are again." Joseph had settled on another tree-top. "Don't you think they mind," she said to Jasper, "having their wings broken?" Why did he want to shoot poor old Joseph and Mary? He shuffled a little on the stairs, and felt rebuked, but not seriously, for she did not understand the fun of shooting birds; and they did not feel; and being his mother she lived away in another division of the world, but he rather liked her stories about Mary and Joseph. She made him laugh. But how did she know that those were Mary and Joseph? Did she think the same birds came to the same trees every night? he asked. But here, suddenly, like all grown-up people, she ceased to pay him the least attention. She was listening to a clatter in the hall.

"They've come back!" she exclaimed, and at once she felt much more annoyed with them than relieved. Then she wondered, had it happened? She would go down and they would tell her—but no. They could not tell her anything, with all these people about. So she must go down and begin dinner and wait. And, like some queen who, finding her people gathered in the hall, looks down upon them, and descends among them, and acknowledges their tributes silently, and accepts their devotion and their prostration before her (Paul did not move a muscle but looked straight before him as she passed) she went down, and crossed the hall and bowed her head very slightly, as if she accepted what they could not say: their tribute to her beauty.

But she stopped. There was a smell of burning. Could they have let the Bœuf en Daube overboil? she wondered, pray heaven not! when the great clangour of the gong announced solemnly, authoritatively, that all those scattered about, in attics, in bedrooms, on little perches of their own, reading, writing, putting the last smooth to their hair, or fastening dresses, must leave all that, and the little odds and ends on their washing-tables and dressing-tables, and the novels on the bed-tables, and the diaries which were so private, and assemble in the dining-room for dinner.

XVII

But what have I done with my life? thought Mrs. Ramsay, taking her place at the head of the table, and looking at all the plates making white circles on it. "William, sit by me," she said. "Lily," she said, wearily, "over there." They had that—Paul Rayley and Minta Doyle— she, only this—an infinitely long table and plates and knives. At the far end, was her husband, sitting down, all in a heap, frowning. What at? She did not know. She did not mind. She could not understand how she had ever felt any emotion or affection for him. She had a sense of being past everything, through everything, out of everything, as she helped the soup, as if there was an eddy—there—and one could be in it, or one could be out of it, and she was out of it. It's all come to an end, she thought, while they came in one after another, Charles Tansley—"Sit there, please," she said—Augustus Carmichael—and sat down. And meanwhile she waited, passively, for some one to answer her, for something to happen. But this is not a thing, she thought, ladling out soup, that one says.

Raising her eyebrows at the discrepancy—that was what she was thinking, this was what she was doing—ladling out soup—she felt, more and more strongly, outside that eddy; or as if a shade had fallen, and, robbed of colour, she saw things truly. The room (she looked round it) was very shabby. There was no beauty anywhere. She forebore to look at Mr. Tansley. Nothing seemed to have merged. They all sat separate. And the whole of the effort of merging and flowing and creating rested on her. Again she felt, as a fact without hostility, the sterility of men, for if she did not do it nobody would do it, and so, giving herself the little shake that one gives a watch that has stopped, the old familiar pulse began beating, as the watch begins ticking—one, two, three, one, two, three. And so on and so on, she repeated, listening to it, sheltering and fostering the still feeble pulse as one might guard a weak flame with a newspaper. And so then, she concluded, addressing herself by bending silently in his direction to William Bankes—poor man! who had no wife, and no children and dined alone in lodgings except for tonight; and in pity for him, life being now strong enough to bear her on again, she began all this business, as a sailor not without weariness sees the wind fill his sail and yet hardly wants to be off again and thinks how, had the ship sunk, he would have whirled round and round and found rest on the floor of the sea.

"Did you find your letters? I told them to put them in the hall for you," she said to William Bankes.

Lily Briscoe watched her drifting into that strange no-man's land where to follow people is impossible and yet their going inflicts such a chill on those who watch them that they always try at least to follow them with their eyes as one follows a fading ship until the sails have sunk beneath the horizon.

How old she looks, how worn she looks, Lily thought, and how remote. Then when she turned to William Bankes, smiling, it was as if the ship had turned and the sun had struck its sails again, and Lily thought with some amusement because she was relieved, Why does she pity him? For that was the impression she gave, when she told him that his letters were in the hall. Poor William Bankes, she seemed to be saying, as if her own weariness had been partly pitying people, and the life in her, her resolve to live again, had been stirred by pity. And it was not true, Lily thought; it was one of those misjudgments of hers that seemed to be instinctive and to arise from some need of her own rather than of other people's. He is not in the least pitiable. He has his work, Lily said to herself. She remembered, all of a sudden as if she had found a treasure, that she had her work. In a flash she saw her picture, and thought, Yes, I shall put the tree further in the middle; then I shall avoid that awkward space. That's what I shall do. That's what has been puzzling me. She took up the salt cellar and put it down again on a flower in pattern in the table-cloth, so as to remind herself to move the tree.

"It's odd that one scarcely gets anything worth having by post, yet one always wants one's letters," said Mr. Bankes.

What damned rot they talk, thought Charles Tansley, laying down his spoon precisely in the middle of his plate, which he had swept clean, as if, Lily thought (he sat opposite to her with his back to the window precisely in the middle of view), he were determined to make sure of his meals. Everything about him had that meagre fixity, that bare unloveliness. But nevertheless, the fact remained, it was almost impossible to dislike any one if one looked at them. She liked his eyes; they were blue, deep set, frightening.

"Do you write many letters, Mr. Tansley?" asked Mrs. Ramsay, pitying him too, Lily supposed; for that was true of Mrs. Ramsay—she pitied men always as if they lacked something—women never, as if they had something. He wrote to his mother; otherwise he did not suppose he wrote one letter a month, said Mr. Tansley, shortly.

For he was not going to talk the sort of rot these people wanted him to talk. He was not going to be condescended to by these silly women. He had been reading in his room, and now he came down and it all seemed to him silly, superficial, flimsy. Why did they dress? He had come down in his ordinary clothes. He had not got any dress clothes. "One never gets anything worth having by post"—that was the sort of thing they were always saying. They made men say that sort of thing. Yes, it was pretty well true, he thought. They never got anything worth having from one year's end to another. They did nothing but talk, talk, talk, eat, eat, eat. It was the women's fault. Women made civilisation impossible with all their "charm," all their silliness.

"No going to the Lighthouse tomorrow, Mrs. Ramsay," he said, asserting himself. He liked her; he admired her; he still thought of the man in the drain-pipe looking up at her; but he felt it necessary to assert himself.

He was really, Lily Briscoe thought, in spite of his eyes, but then look at his nose, look at his hands, the most uncharming human being she had ever met. Then why did she mind what he said? Women can't write, women can't paint—what did that matter coming from him, since clearly it was not true to him but for some reason helpful to him, and that was why he said it? Why did her whole being bow, like corn under a wind, and erect itself again from this abasement only with a great and rather painful effort? She must make it once more. There's the sprig on the table-cloth; there's my painting; I must move the tree to the middle; that matters—nothing else. Could she not hold fast to that, she asked herself, and not lose her temper, and not argue; and if she wanted revenge take it by laughing at him?

"Oh, Mr. Tansley," she said, "do take me to the Lighthouse with you. I should so love it."

She was telling lies he could see. She was saying what she did not mean to annoy him, for some reason. She was laughing at him. He was in his old flannel trousers. He had no others. He felt very rough and isolated and lonely. He knew that she was trying to tease him for some reason; she didn't want to go to the Lighthouse with him; she despised him: so did Prue Ramsay; so did they all. But he was not going to be made a fool of by women, so he turned deliberately in his chair and looked out of the window and said, all in a jerk, very rudely, it would be too rough for her tomorrow. She would be sick.

It annoyed him that she should have made him speak like that, with Mrs. Ramsay listening. If only he could be alone in his room working, he thought, among his books. That was where he felt at his ease. And he had never run a penny into debt; he had never cost his father a penny since he was fifteen; he had helped them at home out of his savings; he was educating his sister. Still, he wished he had known how to answer Miss Briscoe properly; he wished it had not come out all in a jerk like that. "You'd be sick." He wished he could think of something to say to Mrs. Ramsay, something which would show her he was not just a dry prig. That was what they all thought him. He turned to her. But Mrs. Ramsay was talking about people he had never heard of to William Bankes.

"Yes, take it away," she said briefly, interrupting what she was saying to Mr. Bankes to speak to the maid. "It must have been fifteen—no, twenty years ago—that I last saw her," she was saying, turning back to him again as if she could not lose a moment of their talk, for she was absorbed by what they were saying. So he had actually heard from her this evening! And was Carrie still living at Marlow, and was everything still the same? Oh, she could remember as if it were yesterday—going on the river, feeling very cold. But if the Mannings made a plan they stuck to it. Never should she forget Herbert killing a wasp with a teaspoon on the bank! And it was still going on, Mrs. Ramsay mused, gliding like a ghost among the chairs and tables of that drawing-room on the banks of the Thames where she had been so very, very cold twenty years ago; but now she went among them like a ghost; and it fascinated her, as if, while she had changed, that particular day, now become very still and beautiful, had remained there, all these years. Had Carrie written to him herself? she asked.

"Yes. She says they're building a new billiard room," he said. No! No! That was out of the question! Building a billiard room! It seemed to her impossible.

Mr. Bankes could not see that there was anything very odd about it. They were very well off now. Should he give her love to Carrie?

"Oh," said Mrs. Ramsay with a little start, "No," she added, reflecting that she did not know this Carrie who built a new billiard room. But how strange, she repeated, to Mr. Bankes's amusement, that they should be going on there still. For it was extraordinary to think that they had been capable of going on living all these years when she had not thought of them more than once all that time. How eventful her own life had been, during those same years. Yet perhaps Carrie Manning had not thought about her either. The thought was strange and distasteful.

"People soon drift apart," said Mr. Bankes, feeling, however, some satisfaction when he thought that after all he knew both the Mannings and the Ramsays. He had not drifted apart he thought, laying down his spoon and wiping his clean-shaven lips punctiliously. But perhaps he was rather unusual, he thought, in this; he never let himself get into a groove. He had friends in all circles. . . . Mrs. Ramsay had to break off here to tell the maid something about keeping food hot. That was why he preferred dining alone. All those interruptions annoyed him. Well, thought William Bankes, preserving a demeanour of exquisite courtesy and merely spreading the fingers of his left hand on the table-cloth as a mechanic examines a tool beautifully polished and ready for use in an interval of leisure, such are the sacrifices one's friends ask of one. It would have hurt her if he had refused to come. But it was not worth it for him. Looking at his hand he thought that if he had been alone dinner would have been almost over now; he would have been free to work. Yes, he thought, it is a terrible waste of time. The children were dropping in still. "I wish one of you would run up to Roger's room," Mrs. Ramsay was saying. How trifling it all is, how boring it all is, he thought, compared with the other thing—work. Here he sat drumming his fingers on the table-cloth when he might have been—he took a flashing bird's-eye view of his work. What a waste of time it all was to be sure! Yet, he thought, she is one of my oldest friends. I am by way of being devoted to her. Yet now, at this moment her presence meant absolutely nothing to him: her beauty meant nothing to him; her sitting with her little boy at the window—nothing, nothing. He wished only to be alone and to take up that book. He felt uncomfortable; he felt treacherous, that he could sit by her side and feel nothing for her. The truth was that he did not enjoy family life. It was in this sort of state that one asked oneself, What does one live for? Why, one asked oneself, does one take all these pains for the human race to go on? Is it so very desirable? Are we attractive as a species? Not so very, he thought, looking at those rather untidy boys. His favourite, Cam, was in bed, he supposed. Foolish questions, vain questions, questions one never asked if one was occupied. Is human life this? Is human life that? One never had time to think about it. But here he was asking himself that sort of question, because Mrs. Ramsay was giving orders to servants, and also because it had struck him, thinking how surprised Mrs. Ramsay was that Carrie Manning should still exist, that friendships, even the best of them, are frail things. One drifts apart. He reproached himself again. He was sitting beside Mrs. Ramsay and he had nothing in the world to say to her.

"I'm so sorry," said Mrs. Ramsay, turning to him at last. He felt rigid and barren, like a pair of boots that have been soaked and gone dry so that you can hardly force your feet into them. Yet he must force his feet into them. He must make himself talk. Unless he were very careful, she would find out this treachery of his; that he did not care a straw for her, and that would not be at all pleasant, he thought. So he bent his head courteously in her direction.

"How you must detest dining in this bear garden," she said, making use, as she did when she was distracted, of her social manner. So, when there is a strife of tongues, at some meeting, the chairman, to obtain unity, suggests that every one shall speak in French. Perhaps it is bad French; French may not contain the words that express the speaker's thoughts; nevertheless speaking French imposes some order, some uniformity. Replying to her in the same language, Mr. Bankes said, "No, not at all," and Mr. Tansley, who had no knowledge of this language, even spoke thus in words of one syllable, at once suspected its insincerity. They did talk nonsense, he thought, the Ramsays; and he pounced on this fresh instance with joy, making a note which, one of these days, he would read aloud, to one or two friends. There, in a society where one could say what one liked he would sarcastically describe "staying with the Ramsays" and what nonsense they talked. It was worth while doing it once, he would say; but not again. The women bored one so, he would say. Of course Ramsay had dished himself by marrying a beautiful woman and having eight children. It would shape itself something like that, but now, at this moment, sitting stuck there with an empty seat beside him, nothing had shaped itself at all. It was all in scraps and fragments. He felt extremely, even physically, uncomfortable. He wanted somebody to give him a chance of asserting himself. He wanted it so urgently that he fidgeted in his chair, looked at this person, then at that person, tried to break into their talk, opened his mouth and shut it again. They were talking about the fishing industry. Why did no one ask him his opinion? What did they know about the fishing industry?

Lily Briscoe knew all that. Sitting opposite him, could she not see, as in an X-ray photograph,[1] the ribs and thigh bones of the young man's desire to impress himself, lying dark in the mist of his flesh— that thin mist which convention had laid over his burning desire to break into the conversation? But, she thought, screwing up her Chinese eyes, and remembering how he sneered at women, "can't paint, can't write," why should I help him to relieve himself?

There is a code of behaviour, she knew, whose seventh article (it may be) says that on occasions of this sort it behoves the woman, whatever her own occupation may be, to go to the help of the young man opposite so that he may expose and relieve the thigh bones, the ribs, of his vanity, of his urgent desire to assert himself; as indeed it is their duty, she reflected, in her old maidenly fairness, to help us, suppose the Tube were to burst into flames. Then, she thought, I should certainly expect Mr. Tansley to get me out. But how would it be, she thought, if neither of us did either of these things? So she sat there smiling.

"You're not planning to go to the Lighthouse, are you, Lily," said Mrs. Ramsay. "Remember poor Mr. Langley; he had been round the

---

1. A new, seemingly miraculous technology in the early twentieth century that appealed especially to artists seeking to portray more than surface visual appearances; see Rachel Crossland, "Exposing the Bones of Desire: Virginia Woolf's X-Ray Vision," *Virginia Woolf Miscellany* 85 (2014): 18–20. Woolf attended a lecture and demonstration on X-rays in January 1897. The dangers of radiation were not yet understood.

world dozens of times, but he told me he never suffered as he did when my husband took him there. Are you a good sailor, Mr. Tansley?" she asked.

Mr. Tansley raised a hammer: swung it high in air; but realising, as it descended, that he could not smite that butterfly with such an instrument as this, said only that he had never been sick in his life. But in that one sentence lay compact, like gunpowder, that his grandfather was a fisherman; his father a chemist; that he had worked his way up entirely himself; that he was proud of it; that he was Charles Tansley—a fact that nobody there seemed to realise; but one of these days every single person would know it. He scowled ahead of him. He could almost pity these mild cultivated people, who would be blown sky high, like bales of wool and barrels of apples, one of these days by the gunpowder that was in him.

"Will you take me, Mr. Tansley?" said Lily, quickly, kindly, for, of course, if Mrs. Ramsay said to her, as in effect she did, "I am drowning, my dear, in seas of fire. Unless you apply some balm to the anguish of this hour and say something nice to that young man there, life will run upon the rocks—indeed I hear the grating and the growling at this minute. My nerves are taut as fiddle strings. Another touch and they will snap"—when Mrs. Ramsay said all this, as the glance in her eyes said it, of course for the hundred and fiftieth time Lily Briscoe had to renounce the experiment—what happens if one is not nice to that young man there—and be nice.

Judging the turn in her mood correctly—that she was friendly to him now—he was relieved of his egotism, and told her how he had been thrown out of a boat when he was a baby; how his father used to fish him out with a boat-hook; that was how he had learnt to swim. One of his uncles kept the light on some rock or other off the Scottish coast, he said. He had been there with him in a storm. This was said loudly in a pause. They had to listen to him when he said that he had been with his uncle in a lighthouse in a storm. Ah, thought Lily Briscoe, as the conversation took this auspicious turn, and she felt Mrs. Ramsay's gratitude (for Mrs. Ramsay was free now to talk for a moment herself), ah, she thought, but what haven't I paid to get it for you? She had not been sincere.

She had done the usual trick—been nice. She would never know him. He would never know her. Human relations were all like that, she thought, and the worst (if it had not been for Mr. Bankes) were between men and women. Inevitably these were extremely insincere she thought. Then her eye caught the salt cellar, which she had placed there to remind her, and she remembered that next morning she would move the tree further towards the middle, and her spirits rose so high at the thought of painting tomorrow that she laughed out loud at what Mr. Tansley was saying. Let him talk all night if he liked it.

"But how long do they leave men on a Lighthouse?" she asked. He told her. He was amazingly well informed. And as he was grateful, and as he liked her, and as he was beginning to enjoy himself, so now, Mrs. Ramsay thought, she could return to that dream land, that unreal but fascinating place, the Mannings' drawing-room at Marlow twenty years ago; where one moved about without haste or anxiety, for there was no future to worry about. She knew what had happened to them, what to her. It was like reading a good book again, for she knew the end of that story, since it had happened twenty years ago, and life, which shot down even from this dining-room table in cascades, heaven knows where, was sealed up there, and lay, like a lake, placidly between its banks. He said they had built a billiard room—was it possible? Would William go on talking about the Mannings? She wanted him to. But, no—for some reason he was no longer in the mood. She tried. He did not respond. She could not force him. She was disappointed.

"The children are disgraceful," she said, sighing. He said something about punctuality being one of the minor virtues which we do not acquire until later in life.

"If at all," said Mrs. Ramsay merely to fill up space, thinking what an old maid William was becoming. Conscious of his treachery, conscious of her wish to talk about something more intimate, yet out of mood for it at present, he felt come over him the disagreeableness of life, sitting there, waiting. Perhaps the others were saying something interesting? What were they saying?

That the fishing season was bad; that the men were emigrating. They were talking about wages and unemployment. The young man was abusing the government. William Bankes, thinking what a relief it was to catch on to something of this sort when private life was disagreeable, heard him say something about "one of the most scandalous acts of the present government."[2] Lily was listening; Mrs. Ramsay was listening; they were all listening. But already bored, Lily felt that something was lacking; Mr. Bankes felt that something was lacking. Pulling her shawl round her Mrs. Ramsay felt that something was lacking. All of them bending themselves to listen thought, "Pray heaven that the inside of my mind may not be exposed," for each thought, "The others are feeling this. They are outraged and indignant with the government about the fishermen. Whereas, I feel nothing at all." But perhaps, thought Mr. Bankes, as he looked at

2. People had been emigrating from Scotland to North America since the Highland Clearances of the eighteenth century, when common agricultural lands were privatized by landowners from England, farmers were displaced, and poverty spread. In the late nineteenth century and the early 1900s, Parliament regulated the Scottish fishing industry; catches were limited and prices were kept artificially low; see Brannigan, *Archipelagic Modernisms*, p. 122.

Mr. Tansley, here is the man. One was always waiting for the man. There was always a chance. At any moment the leader might arise; the man of genius, in politics as in anything else. Probably he will be extremely disagreeable to us old fogies, thought Mr. Bankes, doing his best to make allowances, for he knew by some curious physical sensation, as of nerves erect in his spine, that he was jealous, for himself partly, partly more probably for his work, for his point of view, for his science; and therefore he was not entirely open-minded or altogether fair, for Mr. Tansley seemed to be saying, You have wasted your lives. You are all of you wrong. Poor old fogies, you're hopelessly behind the times. He seemed to be rather cocksure, this young man; and his manners were bad. But Mr. Bankes bade himself observe, he had courage; he had ability; he was extremely well up in the facts. Probably, Mr. Bankes thought, as Tansley abused the government, there is a good deal in what he says.

"Tell me now . . ." he said. So they argued about politics, and Lily looked at the leaf on the tablecloth; and Mrs. Ramsay, leaving the argument entirely in the hands of the two men, wondered why she was so bored by this talk, and wished, looking at her husband at the other end of the table, that he would say something. One word, she said to herself. For if he said a thing, it would make all the difference. He went to the heart of things. He cared about fishermen and their wages. He could not sleep for thinking of them. It was altogether different when he spoke; one did not feel then, pray heaven you don't see how little I care, because one did care. Then, realising that it was because she admired him so much that she was waiting for him to speak, she felt as if somebody had been praising her husband to her and their marriage, and she glowed all over without realising that it was she herself who had praised him. She looked at him thinking to find this in his face; he would be looking magnificent. . . . But not in the least! He was screwing his face up, he was scowling and frowning, and flushing with anger. What on earth was it about? she wondered. What could be the matter? Only that poor old Augustus had asked for another plate of soup—that was all. It was unthinkable, it was detestable (so he signalled to her across the table) that Augustus should be beginning his soup over again. He loathed people eating when he had finished. She saw his anger fly like a pack of hounds into his eyes, his brow, and she knew that in a moment something violent would explode, and then—thank goodness! she saw him clutch himself and clap a brake on the wheel, and the whole of his body seemed to emit sparks but not words. He sat there scowling. He had said nothing, he would have her observe. Let her give him the credit for that! But why after all should poor Augustus not ask for another plate of soup? He had merely touched Ellen's arm and said:

"Ellen, please, another plate of soup," and then Mr. Ramsay scowled like that.

And why not? Mrs. Ramsay demanded. Surely they could let Augustus have his soup if he wanted it. He hated people wallowing in food, Mr. Ramsay frowned at her. He hated everything dragging on for hours like this. But he had controlled himself, Mr. Ramsay would have her observe, disgusting though the sight was. But why show it so plainly, Mrs. Ramsay demanded (they looked at each other down the long table sending these questions and answers across, each knowing exactly what the other felt). Everybody could see, Mrs. Ramsay thought. There was Rose gazing at her father, there was Roger gazing at his father; both would be off in spasms of laughter in another second, she knew, and so she said promptly (indeed it was time):

"Light the candles,"[3] and they jumped up instantly and went and fumbled at the sideboard.

Why could he never conceal his feelings? Mrs. Ramsay wondered, and she wondered if Augustus Carmichael had noticed. Perhaps he had; perhaps he had not. She could not help respecting the composure with which he sat there, drinking his soup. If he wanted soup, he asked for soup. Whether people laughed at him or were angry with him he was the same. He did not like her, she knew that; but partly for that very reason she respected him, and looking at him, drinking soup, very large and calm in the failing light, and monumental, and contemplative, she wondered what he did feel then, and why he was always content and dignified; and she thought how devoted he was to Andrew, and would call him into his room, and Andrew said, "show him things." And there he would lie all day long on the lawn brooding presumably over his poetry, till he reminded one of a cat watching birds, and then he clapped his paws together when he had found the word, and her husband said, "Poor old Augustus—he's a true poet," which was high praise from her husband.

Now eight candles were stood down the table, and after the first stoop the flames stood upright and drew with them into visibility the long table entire, and in the middle a yellow and purple dish of fruit. What had she done with it, Mrs. Ramsay wondered, for Rose's arrangement of the grapes and pears, of the horny pink-lined shell, of the bananas, made her think of a trophy fetched from the bottom of the sea, of Neptune's banquet, of the bunch that hangs with vine leaves over the shoulder of Bacchus (in some picture), among the leopard skins and the torches lolloping red and gold.[4] . . . Thus

3. Echoes Genesis 1:3, "And God said, Let there be light: and there was light."
4. Neptune is the Roman name of Poseidon, the Greek god of the sea, often depicted holding a trident and accompanied by shells, fish, and other marine life; Bacchus (the Greek god Dionysus), the god of wine, fertility, and religious ecstasy, is typically represented with vines, grapes, and wild animals or animal skins. Both appear in Renaissance paintings.

brought up suddenly into the light it seemed possessed of great size
and depth, was like a world in which one could take one's staff and
climb hills, she thought, and go down into valleys, and to her pleasure (for it brought them into sympathy momentarily) she saw that
Augustus too feasted his eyes on the same plate of fruit, plunged in,
broke off a bloom there, a tassel here, and returned, after feasting,
to his hive. That was his way of looking, different from hers. But
looking together united them.

Now all the candles were lit up, and the faces on both sides of the
table were brought nearer by the candle light, and composed, as they
had not been in the twilight, into a party round a table, for the night
was now shut off by panes of glass, which, far from giving any accurate view of the outside world, rippled it so strangely that here, inside
the room, seemed to be order and dry land; there, outside, a reflection in which things wavered and vanished, waterily.

Some change at once went through them all, as if this had really
happened, and they were all conscious of making a party together
in a hollow, on an island; had their common cause against that fluidity out there. Mrs. Ramsay, who had been uneasy, waiting for Paul
and Minta to come in, and unable, she felt, to settle to things, now
felt her uneasiness changed to expectation. For now they must come,
and Lily Briscoe, trying to analyse the cause of the sudden exhilaration, compared it with that moment on the tennis lawn, when
solidity suddenly vanished, and such vast spaces lay between them;
and now the same effect was got by the many candles in the sparely
furnished room, and the uncurtained windows, and the bright masklike look of faces seen by candlelight. Some weight was taken off
them; anything might happen, she felt. They must come now,
Mrs. Ramsay thought, looking at the door, and at that instant, Minta
Doyle, Paul Rayley, and a maid carrying a great dish in her hands
came in together. They were awfully late; they were horribly late,
Minta said, as they found their way to different ends of the table.

"I lost my brooch—my grandmother's brooch," said Minta with a
sound of lamentation in her voice, and a suffusion in her large brown
eyes, looking down, looking up, as she sat by Mr. Ramsay, which
roused his chivalry so that he bantered her.

How could she be such a goose, he asked, as to scramble about
the rocks in jewels?

She was by way of being terrified of him—he was so fearfully
clever, and the first night when she had sat by him, and he talked
about George Eliot, she had been really frightened, for she had left
the third volume of *Middlemarch* in the train and she never knew

---

No particular picture has been identified as the one Mrs. Ramsay is thinking of. The
exotic "horny pink-lined shell" (a conch) and the bananas come from distant parts of
the empire, probably the Caribbean.

what happened in the end;[5] but afterwards she got on perfectly, and
made herself out even more ignorant than she was, because he liked
telling her she was a fool. And so tonight, directly he laughed at her,
she was not frightened. Besides, she knew, directly she came into
the room that the miracle had happened; she wore her golden haze.
Sometimes she had it; sometimes not. She never knew why it came
or why it went, or if she had it until she came into the room and
then she knew instantly by the way some man looked at her. Yes,
tonight she had it, tremendously; she knew that by the way Mr. Ramsay told her not to be a fool. She sat beside him, smiling.

It must have happened then, thought Mrs. Ramsay; they are
engaged. And for a moment she felt what she had never expected to
feel again—jealousy. For he, her husband, felt it too—Minta's glow;
he liked these girls, these golden-reddish girls, with something flying, something a little wild and harum-scarum about them, who
didn't "scrape their hair off," weren't, as he said about poor Lily Briscoe, ". . . skimpy." There was some quality which she herself had
not, some lustre, some richness, which attracted him, amused him,
led him to make favourites of girls like Minta. They might cut his
hair from him, plait him watch-chains, or interrupt him at his work,
hailing him (she heard them), "Come along, Mr. Ramsay; it's our
turn to beat them now," and out he came to play tennis.

But indeed she was not jealous, only, now and then, when she
made herself look in her glass a little resentful that she had grown
old, perhaps, by her own fault. (The bill for the greenhouse and all
the rest of it.) She was grateful to them for laughing at him. ("How
many pipes have you smoked today, Mr. Ramsay?" and so on), till
he seemed a young man; a man very attractive to women, not bur-
dened, not weighed down with the greatness of his labours and the
sorrows of the world and his fame or his failure, but again as she
had first known him, gaunt but gallant; helping her out of a boat,
she remembered; with delightful ways, like that (she looked at him,
and he looked astonishingly young, teasing Minta). For herself—
"Put it down there," she said, helping the Swiss girl to place gently
before her the huge brown pot in which was the Bœuf en Daube—
for her own part she liked her boobies. Paul must sit by her. She had
kept a place for him. Really, she sometimes thought she liked the

5. The novel *Middlemarch* (1871–72) by George Eliot (1819–1880) was so long it was published in four volumes rather than the usual (for Victorian novels) three, but Minta loses
the third and apparently final volume, missing (among other plot points) the wrapping up
of the novel's three love stories, which end in marriages—two of them happy, one of
them miserable. Woolf wrote three essays about George Eliot: in the first and longest, she
describes *Middlemarch* as a "magnificent book" that "is one of the few English novels
written for grown-up people" (*Times Literary Supplement*, Nov. 20, 1919); in the third, a
review of *The Letters of George Eliot* written during the composition of *To the Lighthouse*,
she wrote, "[t]he whole of the nineteenth century seems to be mirrored in the depths of
that sensitive and profound mind" (*Nation & Athenaeum*, Oct. 30, 1926).

boobies best. They did not bother one with their dissertations. How much they missed, after all, these very clever men! How dried up they did become, to be sure. There was something, she thought as he sat down, very charming about Paul. His manners were delightful to her, and his sharp-cut nose and his bright blue eyes. He was so considerate. Would he tell her—now that they were all talking again—what had happened?

"We went back to look for Minta's brooch," he said, sitting down by her. "We"—that was enough. She knew from the effort, the rise in his voice to surmount a difficult word that it was the first time he had said "we." "We did this, we did that." They'll say that all their lives, she thought, and an exquisite scent of olives and oil and juice rose from the great brown dish as Marthe, with a little flourish, took the cover off. The cook had spent three days over that dish. And she must take great care, Mrs. Ramsay thought, diving into the soft mass, to choose a specially tender piece for William Bankes. And she peered into the dish, with its shiny walls and its confusion of savoury brown and yellow meats and its bay leaves and its wine, and thought.[6] This will celebrate the occasion—a curious sense rising in her, at once freakish and tender, of celebrating a festival, as if two emotions were called up in her, one profound—for what could be more serious than the love of man for woman, what more commanding, more impressive, bearing in its bosom the seeds of death; at the same time these lovers, these people entering into illusion glittering eyed, must be danced round with mockery, decorated with garlands.

"It is a triumph," said Mr. Bankes, laying his knife down for a moment. He had eaten attentively. It was rich; it was tender. It was perfectly cooked. How did she manage these things in the depths of the country? he asked her. She was a wonderful woman. All his love, all his reverence, had returned; and she knew it.

"It is a French receipe[7] of my grandmother's," said Mrs. Ramsay, speaking with a ring of great pleasure in her voice. Of course it was French. What passes for cookery in England is an abomination (they agreed). It is putting cabbages in water. It is roasting meat till it is like leather. It is cutting off the delicious skins of vegetables. "In which," said Mr. Bankes, "all the virtue of the vegetable is contained." And the waste, said Mrs. Ramsay. A whole French family could live on what an English cook throws away. Spurred on by her sense that William's affection had come back to her, and that everything was all right again, and that her suspense was over, and that now she was free both to triumph and to mock, she laughed, she

---

6. A comma not a period should appear between "thought" and "This;" an American editor apparently introduced this error in the first edition; see *To the Lighthouse,* annotated and with an introduction by Mark Hussey, p. 226.
7. Woolf spelled "recipe" as "receipe" in the 1927 Harcourt edition.

gesticulated, till Lily thought, How childlike, how absurd she was, sitting up there with all her beauty opened again in her, talking about the skins of vegetables. There was something frightening about her. She was irresistible. Always she got her own way in the end, Lily thought. Now she had brought this off—Paul and Minta, one might suppose, were engaged. Mr. Bankes was dining here. She put a spell on them all, by wishing, so simply, so directly, and Lily contrasted that abundance with her own poverty of spirit, and supposed that it was partly that belief (for her face was all lit up—without looking young, she looked radiant) in this strange, this terrifying thing, which made Paul Rayley, sitting at her side, all of a tremor, yet abstract, absorbed, silent. Mrs. Ramsay, Lily felt, as she talked about the skins of vegetables, exalted that, worshipped that; held her hands over it to warm them, to protect it, and yet, having brought it all about, somehow laughed, led her victims, Lily felt, to the altar. It came over her too now—the emotion, the vibration, of love. How inconspicuous she felt herself by Paul's side! He, glowing, burning; she, aloof, satirical; he, bound for adventure; she, moored to the shore; he, launched, incautious; she, solitary, left out—and, ready to implore a share, if it were disaster, in his disaster, she said shyly:

"When did Minta lose her brooch?"

He smiled the most exquisite smile, veiled by memory, tinged by dreams. He shook his head. "On the beach," he said.

"I'm going to find it," he said, "I'm getting up early." This being kept secret from Minta, he lowered his voice, and turned his eyes to where she sat, laughing, beside Mr. Ramsay.

Lily wanted to protest violently and outrageously her desire to help him, envisaging how in the dawn on the beach she would be the one to pounce on the brooch half-hidden by some stone, and thus herself be included among the sailors and adventurers. But what did he reply to her offer? She actually said with an emotion that she seldom let appear, "Let me come with you," and he laughed. He meant yes or no—either perhaps. But it was not his meaning—it was the odd chuckle he gave, as if he had said, Throw yourself over the cliff if you like, I don't care. He turned on her cheek the heat of love, its horror, its cruelty, its unscrupulosity. It scorched her, and Lily, looking at Minta, being charming to Mr. Ramsay at the other end of the table, flinched for her exposed to these fangs, and was thankful. For at any rate, she said to herself, catching sight of the salt cellar on the pattern, she need not marry, thank Heaven: she need not undergo that degradation. She was saved from that dilution. She would move the tree rather more to the middle.

Such was the complexity of things. For what happened to her, especially staying with the Ramsays, was to be made to feel violently two opposite things at the same time; that's what you feel, was one; that's what I feel, was the other, and then they fought together in her mind, as now. It is so beautiful, so exciting, this love, that I tremble on the verge of it, and offer, quite out of my own habit, to look for a brooch on a beach; also it is the stupidest, the most barbaric of human passions, and turns a nice young man with a profile like a gem's (Paul's was exquisite) into a bully with a crowbar (he was swaggering, he was insolent) in the Mile End Road.[8] Yet, she said to herself, from the dawn of time odes have been sung to love; wreaths heaped and roses; and if you asked nine people out of ten they would say they wanted nothing but this—love; while the women, judging from her own experience, would all the time be feeling, This is not what we want; there is nothing more tedious, puerile, and inhumane than this; yet it is also beautiful and necessary. Well then, well then? she asked, somehow expecting the others to go on with the argument, as if in an argument like this one threw one's own little bolt which fell short obviously and left the others to carry it on. So she listened again to what they were saying in case they should throw any light upon the question of love.

"Then," said Mr. Bankes, "there is that liquid the English call coffee."

"Oh, coffee!" said Mrs. Ramsay. But it was much rather a question (she was thoroughly roused, Lily could see, and talked very emphatically) of real butter and clean milk. Speaking with warmth and eloquence, she described the iniquity of the English dairy system, and in what state milk was delivered at the door, and was about to prove her charges, for she had gone into the matter, when all round the table, beginning with Andrew in the middle, like a fire leaping from tuft to tuft of furze, her children laughed; her husband laughed; she was laughed at, fire-encircled, and forced to veil her crest, dismount her batteries,[9] and only retaliate by displaying the raillery and ridicule of the table to Mr. Bankes as an example of what one suffered if one attacked the prejudices of the British Public.

Purposely, however, for she had it on her mind that Lily, who had helped her with Mr. Tansley, was out of things, she exempted her from the rest; said "Lily anyhow agrees with me," and so drew her in, a little fluttered, a little startled. (For she was thinking about love.) They were both out of things, Mrs. Ramsay had been thinking, both Lily and Charles Tansley. Both suffered from the glow of

---

8. In London's East End, a part of the city that was notoriously rough and dangerous.
9. Guns or artillery mounted on a platform; *veil*: this misspelling was apparently introduced by an American editor, in error: as Mark Hussey points out, in all British editions and in the US proof that Woolf corrected, the word is "vail," which means to lower something as a sign of submission, here a crest or a plume of feathers. See *To the Lighthouse*, annotated and with an introduction by Mark Hussey, p. 226.

the other two. He, it was clear, felt himself utterly in the cold; no woman would look at him with Paul Rayley in the room. Poor fellow! Still, he had his dissertation, the influence of somebody upon something: he could take care of himself. With Lily it was different. She faded, under Minta's glow; became more inconspicuous than ever, in her little grey dress with her little puckered face and her little Chinese eyes. Everything about her was so small. Yet, thought Mrs. Ramsay, comparing her with Minta, as she claimed her help (for Lily should bear her out she talked no more about her dairies than her husband did about his boots—he would talk by the hour about his boots) of the two, Lily at forty will be the better. There was in Lily a thread of something; a flare of something; something of her own which Mrs. Ramsay liked very much indeed, but no man would, she feared. Obviously, not, unless it were a much older man, like William Bankes. But then he cared, well, Mrs. Ramsay sometimes thought that he cared, since his wife's death, perhaps for her. He was not "in love" of course; it was one of those unclassified affections of which there are so many. Oh, but nonsense, she thought; William must marry Lily. They have so many things in common. Lily is so fond of flowers. They are both cold and aloof and rather self-sufficing. She must arrange for them to take a long walk together.

Foolishly, she had set them opposite each other. That could be remedied tomorrow. If it were fine, they should go for a picnic. Everything seemed possible. Everything seemed right. Just now (but this cannot last, she thought, dissociating herself from the moment while they were all talking about boots) just now she had reached security; she hovered like a hawk suspended; like a flag floated in an element of joy which filled every nerve of her body fully and sweetly, not noisily, solemnly rather, for it arose, she thought, looking at them all eating there, from husband and children and friends; all of which rising in this profound stillness (she was helping William Bankes to one very small piece more, and peered into the depths of the earthenware pot) seemed now for no special reason to stay there like a smoke, like a fume rising upwards, holding them safe together. Nothing need be said; nothing could be said. There it was, all round them. It partook, she felt, carefully helping Mr. Bankes to a specially tender piece, of eternity; as she had already felt about something different once before that afternoon; there is a coherence in things, a stability; something, she meant, is immune from change, and shines out (she glanced at the window with its ripple of reflected lights) in the face of the flowing, the fleeting, the spectral, like a ruby; so that again tonight she had the feeling she had had once today, already, of peace, of rest. Of such moments, she thought, the thing is made that endures.

"Yes," she assured William Bankes, "there is plenty for everybody."

"Andrew," she said, "hold your plate lower, or I shall spill it." (The Bœuf en Daube was a perfect triumph.) Here, she felt, putting the spoon down, was the still space that lies about the heart of things, where one could move or rest; could wait now (they were all helped) listening; could then, like a hawk which lapses suddenly from its high station, flaunt and sink on laughter easily, resting her whole weight upon what at the other end of the table her husband was saying about the square root of one thousand two hundred and fifty-three. That was the number, it seemed, on his watch.

What did it all mean? To this day she had no notion. A square root? What was that? Her sons knew. She leant on them; on cubes and square roots; that was what they were talking about now; on Voltaire and Madame de Staël; on the character of Napoleon; on the French system of land tenure; on Lord Rosebery; on Creevey's Memoirs:[1] she let it uphold her and sustain her, this admirable fabric of the masculine intelligence, which ran up and down, crossed this way and that, like iron girders spanning the swaying fabric, upholding the world, so that she could trust herself to it utterly, even shut her eyes, or flicker them for a moment, as a child staring up from its pillow winks at the myriad layers of the leaves of a tree. Then she woke up. It was still being fabricated. William Bankes was praising the Waverley novels.[2]

He read one of them every six months, he said. And why should that make Charles Tansley angry? He rushed in (all, thought Mrs. Ramsay, because Prue will not be nice to him) and denounced the Waverley novels when he knew nothing about it, nothing about it whatsoever, Mrs. Ramsay thought, observing him rather than listening to what he said. She could see how it was from his manner—he wanted to assert himself, and so it would always be with him till he got his Professorship or married his wife, and so need not be always saying, "I—I—I." For that was what his criticism of poor Sir Walter, or perhaps it was Jane Austen,[3] amounted to. "I—I—I." He

1. Voltaire, pen name of François-Marie Arouet (1694–1778), was a philosopher, poet, dramatist, historian, and polemicist of the French Enlightenment who satirized authority and Christianity. Germaine de Staël (1766–1817) was a French-Swiss critic, letter writer, advocate for the French Revolution, and author of the protofeminist novel *Corinne* (1807). Napoleon Bonaparte (1769–1821), emperor of France following the French Revolution, redistributed land ownership to favor the middle class. Archibald Philip Primrose, 5th Earl of Rosebery (1847–1929), was a Whig prime minister from 1894 to 1895. The English politician Thomas Creevey's (1768–1838) memoirs and letters, published as *The Creevey Papers* in 1903, provide lively accounts of the Georgian era and of Brussels at the time of the Battle of Waterloo (1815).
2. The Scottish novelist, poet, historian, and biographer Sir Walter Scott (1771–1832) is often considered both the inventor and the greatest practitioner of the historical novel. The Waverley novels were a series of more than two dozen historical novels published by Scott between 1814 and 1832; they remained extremely popular throughout the nineteenth century, but Scott's popularity waned in the twentieth century. Both Leslie Stephen and Woolf wrote essays on Scott. See the excerpt from one of the series, *The Antiquary*, which Mr. Ramsay later reads, this edition, pp. 274–76.
3. English novelist (1775–1817), author of *Sense and Sensibility* (1811), *Emma* (1815), and four other celebrated novels.

was thinking of himself and the impression he was making, as she could tell by the sound of his voice, and his emphasis and his uneasiness. Success would be good for him. At any rate they were off again. Now she need not listen. It could not last, she knew, but at the moment her eyes were so clear that they seemed to go round the table unveiling each of these people, and their thoughts and their feelings, without effort like a light stealing under water so that its ripples and the reeds in it and the minnows balancing themselves, and the sudden silent trout are all lit up hanging, trembling. So she saw them; she heard them; but whatever they said had also this quality, as if what they said was like the movement of a trout when, at the same time, one can see the ripple and the gravel, something to the right, something to the left; and the whole is held together; for whereas in active life she would be netting and separating one thing from another; she would be saying she liked the Waverley novels or had not read them; she would be urging herself forward; now she said nothing. For the moment, she hung suspended.

"Ah, but how long do you think it'll last?" said somebody. It was as if she had antennæ trembling out from her, which, intercepting certain sentences, forced them upon her attention. This was one of them. She scented danger for her husband. A question like that would lead, almost certainly, to something being said which reminded him of his own failure. How long would he be read—he would think at once. William Bankes (who was entirely free from all such vanity) laughed, and said he attached no importance to changes in fashion. Who could tell what was going to last—in literature or indeed in anything else?

"Let us enjoy what we do enjoy," he said. His integrity seemed to Mrs. Ramsay quite admirable. He never seemed for a moment to think, But how does this affect me? But then if you had the other temperament, which must have praise, which must have encouragement, naturally you began (and she knew that Mr. Ramsay was beginning) to be uneasy; to want somebody to say, Oh, but your work will last, Mr. Ramsay, or something like that. He showed his uneasiness quite clearly now by saying, with some irritation, that, anyhow, Scott (or was it Shakespeare?) would last him his lifetime. He said it irritably. Everybody, she thought, felt a little uncomfortable, without knowing why. Then Minta Doyle, whose instinct was fine, said bluffly, absurdly, that she did not believe that any one really enjoyed reading Shakespeare. Mr. Ramsay said grimly (but his mind was turned away again) that very few people liked it as much as they said they did. But, he added, there is considerable merit in some of the plays nevertheless, and Mrs. Ramsay saw that it would be all right for the moment anyhow; he would laugh at Minta, and she, Mrs. Ramsay saw, realising his extreme anxiety about himself, would, in her own way, see that he was taken care of, and praise him, somehow or other. But she wished it was not necessary: perhaps it was her fault that it was necessary. Anyhow, she was free now to listen to what Paul Rayley was trying to say about books one had read as a boy. They lasted, he said. He had read some of Tolstoi at school.[4] There was one he always remembered, but he had forgotten the name. Russian names were impossible, said Mrs. Ramsay. "Vronsky," said Paul. He remembered that because he always thought it such a good name for a villain. "Vronsky," said Mrs. Ramsay; "Oh, *Anna Karenina*," but that did not take them very far; books were not in their line. No, Charles Tansley would put them both right in a second about books, but it was all so mixed up with, Am I saying the right thing? Am I making a good impression? that, after all, one knew more about him than about Tolstoi, whereas, what Paul said was about the thing, simply, not himself, nothing else. Like all stupid people, he had a kind of modesty too, a consideration for what you were feeling, which, once in a way at least, she found attractive. Now he was thinking, not about himself or about Tolstoi, but whether she was cold, whether she felt a draught, whether she would like a pear.

No, she said, she did not want a pear. Indeed she had been keeping guard over the dish of fruit (without realising it) jealously, hoping that nobody would touch it. Her eyes had been going in and out among the curves and shadows of the fruit, among the rich purples of the lowland grapes, then over the horny ridge of the shell, putting a yellow against a purple, a curved shape against a round shape, without knowing why she did it, or why, every time she did it, she felt more and more serene; until, oh, what a pity that they should do it—a hand reached out, took a pear, and spoilt the whole thing. In sympathy she looked at Rose. She looked at Rose sitting between Jasper and Prue. How odd that one's child should do that!

How odd to see them sitting there, in a row, her children, Jasper, Rose, Prue, Andrew, almost silent, but with some joke of their own going on, she guessed, from the twitching at their lips. It was something quite apart from everything else, something they were hoarding up to laugh over in their own room. It was not about their father, she hoped. No, she thought not. What was it, she wondered, sadly rather, for it seemed to her that they would laugh when she was not there. There was all that hoarded behind those rather set, still, masklike faces, for they did not join in easily; they were like watchers, surveyors, a little raised or set apart from the grown-up people. But when she looked at Prue tonight, she saw that this was not now quite

---

4. The Russian author Leo Tolstoy (1828–1910) is widely regarded as a master of realist fiction. Published in installments between 1875 and 1877, and considered one of the masterpieces of world literature, his novel *Anna Karenina* centers on an adulterous affair; Vronsky is the name of Anna's lover.

true of her. She was just beginning, just moving, just descending. The faintest light was on her face, as if the glow of Minta opposite, some excitement, some anticipation of happiness was reflected in her, as if the sun of the love of men and women rose over the rim of the table-cloth, and without knowing what it was she bent towards it and greeted it. She kept looking at Minta, shyly, yet curiously, so that Mrs. Ramsay looked from one to the other and said, speaking to Prue in her own mind, You will be as happy as she is one of these days. You will be much happier, she added, because you are my daughter, she meant; her own daughter must be happier than other people's daughters. But dinner was over. It was time to go. They were only playing with things on their plates. She would wait until they had done laughing at some story her husband was telling. He was having a joke with Minta about a bet. Then she would get up.

She liked Charles Tansley, she thought, suddenly; she liked his laugh. She liked him for being so angry with Paul and Minta. She liked his awkwardness. There was a lot in that young man after all. And Lily, she thought, putting her napkin beside her plate, she always has some joke of her own. One need never bother about Lily. She waited. She tucked her napkin under the edge of her plate. Well, were they done now? No. That story had led to another story. Her husband was in great spirits tonight, and wishing, she supposed, to make it all right with old Augustus after that scene about the soup, had drawn him in—they were telling stories about some one they had both known at college. She looked at the window in which the candle flames burnt brighter now that the panes were black, and looking at that outside the voices came to her very strangely, as if they were voices at a service in a cathedral, for she did not listen to the words. The sudden bursts of laughter and then one voice (Minta's) speaking alone, reminded her of men and boys crying out the Latin words of a service in some Roman Catholic cathedral. She waited. Her husband spoke. He was repeating something, and she knew it was poetry from the rhythm and the ring of exultation, and melancholy in his voice:

> Come out and climb the garden path,
>   Luriana Lurilee.
> The China rose is all abloom and buzzing with the
>   yellow bee.[5]

The words (she was looking at the window) sounded as if they were floating like flowers on water out there, cut off from them all, as if no one had said them, but they had come into existence of themselves.

5. The lines Mr. Ramsay and Mr. Carmichael recite are from Charles Elton's "Luriana Lurilee," in this edition, pp. 273–74.

"And all the lives we ever lived and all the lives to be are full of trees and changing leaves." She did not know what they meant, but, like music, the words seemed to be spoken by her own voice, outside her self, saying quite easily and naturally what had been in her mind the whole evening while she said different things. She knew, without looking round, that every one at the table was listening to the voice saying:

> I wonder if it seems to you,
> Luriana, Lurilee

with the same sort of relief and pleasure that she had, as if this were, at last, the natural thing to say, this were their own voice speaking.

But the voice stopped. She looked round. She made herself get up. Augustus Carmichael had risen and, holding his table napkin so that it looked like a long white robe he stood chanting:

> To see the Kings go riding by
> Over lawn and daisy lea
> With their palm leaves and cedar sheaves,
> Luriana, Lurilee,

and as she passed him, he turned slightly towards her repeating the last words:

> Luriana, Lurilee

and bowed to her as if he did her homage. Without knowing why, she felt that he liked her better than he had ever done before; and with a feeling of relief and gratitude she returned his bow and passed through the door which he held open for her.

It was necessary now to carry everything a step further. With her foot on the threshold she waited a moment longer in a scene which was vanishing even as she looked, and then, as she moved and took Minta's arm and left the room, it changed, it shaped itself differently; it had become, she knew, giving one last look at it over her shoulder, already the past.

XVIII

As usual, Lily thought. There was always something that had to be done at that precise moment, something that Mrs. Ramsay had decided for reasons of her own to do instantly, it might be with every one standing about making jokes, as now, not being able to decide whether they were going into the smoking-room, into the drawing-room, up to the attics. Then one saw Mrs. Ramsay in the midst of this hubbub standing there with Minta's arm in hers, bethink her, "Yes, it is time for that now," and so make off at once with an air of

secrecy to do something alone. And directly she went a sort of disintegration set in; they wavered about, went different ways,
Mr. Bankes took Charles Tansley by the arm and went off to finish
on the terrace the discussion they had begun at dinner about politics, thus giving a turn to the whole poise of the evening, making
the weight fall in a different direction, as if, Lily thought, seeing
them go, and hearing a word or two about the policy of the Labour
Party,[1] they had gone up on to the bridge of the ship and were taking their bearings; the change from poetry to politics struck her
like that; so Mr. Bankes and Charles Tansley went off, while the
others stood looking at Mrs. Ramsay going upstairs in the lamplight
alone. Where, Lily wondered, was she going so quickly?

Not that she did in fact run or hurry; she went indeed rather
slowly. She felt rather inclined just for a moment to stand still after
all that chatter, and pick out one particular thing; the thing that mattered; to detach it; separate it off; clean it of all the emotions and
odds and ends of things, and so hold it before her, and bring it to
the tribunal where, ranged about in conclave, sat the judges she had
set up to decide these things. Is it good, is it bad, is it right or wrong?
Where are we all going to? and so on. So she righted herself after
the shock of the event, and quite unconsciously and incongruously,
used the branches of the elm trees outside[2] to help her to stabilise
her position. Her world was changing: they were still. The event had
given her a sense of movement. All must be in order. She must get
that right and that right, she thought, insensibly approving of the
dignity of the trees' stillness, and now again of the superb upward
rise (like the beak of a ship up a wave) of the elm branches as the
wind raised them. For it was windy (she stood a moment to look out).
It was windy, so that the leaves now and then brushed open a star,
and the stars themselves seemed to be shaking and darting light and
trying to flash out between the edges of the leaves. Yes, that was
done then, accomplished; and as with all things done, became solemn. Now one thought of it, cleared of chatter and emotion, it
seemed always to have been, only was shown now and so being
shown, struck everything into stability. They would, she thought,
going on again, however long they lived, come back to this night;
this moon; this wind; this house: and to her too. It flattered her,
where she was most susceptible of flattery, to think how, wound
about in their hearts, however long they lived she would be woven;

---

1. The Labour Party, originating in nineteenth-century socialist and trade union movements, was founded in 1900 and attracted working-class voters away from the Liberal
   Party, which had sought to address working-class needs in the nineteenth century.
   Leonard Woolf was active in the Labour Party. The Liberal Party was in power during
   the time when this part of the novel is set.
2. Woolf was told after the novel was published that there are no elm trees in the Hebrides,
   along with other plants she mistakes. See Composition Chronology (180).

and this, and this, and this, she thought, going upstairs, laughing, but affectionately, at the sofa on the landing (her mother's); at the rocking-chair (her father's); at the map of the Hebrides. All that would be revived again in the lives of Paul and Minta; "the Rayleys"—she tried the new name over; and she felt, with her hand on the nursery door, that community of feeling with other people which emotion gives as if the walls of partition had become so thin that practically (the feeling was one of relief and happiness) it was all one stream, and chairs, tables, maps, were hers, were theirs, it did not matter whose, and Paul and Minta would carry it on when she was dead.

She turned the handle, firmly, lest it should squeak, and went in, pursing her lips slightly, as if to remind herself that she must not speak aloud. But directly she came in she saw, with annoyance, that the precaution was not needed. The children were not asleep. It was most annoying. Mildred should be more careful. There was James wide awake and Cam sitting bolt upright, and Mildred out of bed in her bare feet, and it was almost eleven and they were all talking. What was the matter? It was that horrid skull again.[3] She had told Mildred to move it, but Mildred, of course, had forgotten, and now there was Cam wide awake, and James wide awake quarrelling when they ought to have been asleep hours ago. What had possessed Edward to send them this horrid skull? She had been so foolish as to let them nail it up there. It was nailed fast, Mildred said, and Cam couldn't go to sleep with it in the room, and James screamed if she touched it.

Then Cam must go to sleep (it had great horns said Cam)—must go to sleep and dream of lovely palaces, said Mrs. Ramsay, sitting down on the bed by her side. She could see the horns, Cam said, all over the room. It was true. Wherever they put the light (and James could not sleep without a light) there was always a shadow somewhere.

"But think, Cam, it's only an old pig," said Mrs. Ramsay, "a nice black pig like the pigs at the farm." But Cam thought it was a horrid thing, branching at her all over the room.

"Well then," said Mrs. Ramsay, "we will cover it up," and they all watched her go to the chest of drawers, and open the little drawers quickly one after another, and not seeing anything that would do, she quickly took her own shawl off and wound it round the skull, round and round and round, and then she came back to Cam and

3. Edward, who sent the skull as a gift, is apparently another of Mrs. Ramsay's brothers; in the holograph, Edward shot the boar in India (*Original Holograph*, p. 188). In "A Sketch of the Past" Woolf describes a childhood memory of the "night nursery" that could have been the basis for this episode: "In winter I would slip in before bed to take a look at the fire. I was very anxious to see that the fire was low, because it frightened me if it burnt after we went to bed. I dreaded that little flickering flame on the walls; but Adrian liked it; and to make a compromise, Nurse folded a towel over the fender; but I could not help opening my eyes, and there often was the flickering flame; and I looked and looked and could not sleep" (*Moments of Being*, p. 78).

laid her head almost flat on the pillow beside Cam's and said how lovely it looked now; how the fairies would love it; it was like a bird's nest; it was like a beautiful mountain such as she had seen abroad, with valleys and flowers and bells ringing and birds singing and little goats and antelopes and . . . She could see the words echoing as she spoke them rhythmically in Cam's mind, and Cam was repeating after her how it was like a mountain, a bird's nest, a garden, and there were little antelopes, and her eyes were opening and shutting, and Mrs. Ramsay went on speaking still more monotonously, and more rhythmically and more nonsensically, how she must shut her eyes and go to sleep and dream of mountains and valleys and stars falling and parrots and antelopes and gardens, and everything lovely, she said, raising her head very slowly and speaking more and more mechanically, until she sat upright and saw that Cam was asleep.[4]

Now, she whispered, crossing over to his bed, James must go to sleep too, for see, she said, the boar's skull was still there; they had not touched it; they had done just what he wanted; it was there quite unhurt. He made sure that the skull was still there under the shawl. But he wanted to ask her something more. Would they go to the Lighthouse tomorrow?

No, not tomorrow, she said, but soon, she promised him; the next fine day. He was very good. He lay down. She covered him up. But he would never forget, she knew, and she felt angry with Charles Tansley, with her husband, and with herself, for she had raised his hopes. Then feeling for her shawl and remembering that she had wrapped it round the boar's skull, she got up, and pulled the window down another inch or two, and heard the wind, and got a breath of the perfectly indifferent chill night air and murmured good-night to Mildred and left the room and let the tongue of the door slowly lengthen in the lock and went out.

She hoped he would not bang his books on the floor above their heads, she thought, still thinking how annoying Charles Tansley was. For neither of them slept well; they were excitable children, and since he said things like that about the Lighthouse, it seemed to her likely that he would knock a pile of books over, just as they were going to sleep, clumsily sweeping them off the table with his elbow. For she supposed that he had gone upstairs to work. Yet he looked so desolate; yet she would feel relieved when he went; yet she would see that he was better treated tomorrow; yet he was admirable with her husband; yet his manners certainly wanted improving; yet she

---

4. In "A Sketch of the Past" Woolf recalls her mother helping her fall asleep as a young child: "like all children I lay awake sometimes and longed for her to come. Then she told me to think of all the lovely things I could imagine. Rainbows and bells" (this edition, p. 199).

liked his laugh—thinking this, as she came downstairs, she noticed that she could now see the moon itself through the staircase window—the yellow harvest moon—and turned, and they saw her, standing above them on the stairs.

"That's my mother," thought Prue. Yes; Minta should look at her; Paul Rayley should look at her. That is the thing itself, she felt, as if there were only one person like that in the world; her mother. And, from having been quite grown up, a moment before, talking with the others, she became a child again, and what they had been doing was a game, and would her mother sanction their game, or condemn it, she wondered. And thinking what a chance it was for Minta and Paul and Lily to see her, and feeling what an extraordinary stroke of fortune it was for her, to have her, and how she would never grow up and never leave home, she said, like a child, "We thought of going down to the beach to watch the waves."

Instantly, for no reason at all, Mrs. Ramsay became like a girl of twenty, full of gaiety. A mood of revelry suddenly took possession of her. Of course they must go; of course they must go, she cried, laughing; and running down the last three or four steps quickly, she began turning from one to the other and laughing and drawing Minta's wrap round her and saying she only wished she could come too, and would they be very late, and had any of them got a watch?

"Yes, Paul has," said Minta. Paul slipped a beautiful gold watch out of a little wash-leather[5] case to show her. And as he held it in the palm of his hand before her, he felt, "She knows all about it. I need not say anything." He was saying to her as he showed her the watch, "I've done it, Mrs. Ramsay. I owe it all to you." And seeing the gold watch lying in his hand, Mrs. Ramsay felt, How extraordinarily lucky Minta is! She is marrying a man who has a gold watch in a wash-leather bag!

"How I wish I could come with you!" she cried. But she was withheld by something so strong that she never even thought of asking herself what it was. Of course it was impossible for her to go with them. But she would have liked to go, had it not been for the other thing, and tickled by the absurdity of her thought (how lucky to marry a man with a wash-leather bag for his watch) she went with a smile on her lips into the other room, where her husband sat reading.

XIX

Of course, she said to herself, coming into the room, she had to come here to get something she wanted. First she wanted to sit down in a particular chair under a particular lamp. But she wanted something more, though she did not know, could not think what it

5. Thin, soft leather with a velvety surface, similar to chamois.

was that she wanted. She looked at her husband (taking up her stocking and beginning to knit), and saw that he did not want to be interrupted—that was clear. He was reading something that moved him very much. He was half smiling and then she knew he was controlling his emotion. He was tossing the pages over. He was acting it—perhaps he was thinking himself the person in the book. She wondered what book it was. Oh, it was one of old Sir Walter's she saw, adjusting the shade of her lamp so that the light fell on her knitting. For Charles Tansley had been saying (she looked up as if she expected to hear the crash of books on the floor above), had been saying that people don't read Scott any more. Then her husband thought, "That's what they'll say of me;" so he went and got one of those books.[1] And if he came to the conclusion "That's true" what Charles Tansley said, he would accept it about Scott. (She could see that he was weighing, considering, putting this with that as he read.) But not about himself. He was always uneasy about himself. That troubled her. He would always be worrying about his own books— will they be read, are they good, why aren't they better, what do people think of me? Not liking to think of him so, and wondering if they had guessed at dinner why he suddenly became irritable when they talked about fame and books lasting, wondering if the children were laughing at that, she twitched the stocking out, and all the fine gravings came drawn with steel instruments about her lips and forehead, and she grew still like a tree which has been tossing and quivering and now, when the breeze falls, settles, leaf by leaf, into quiet.

It didn't matter, any of it, she thought. A great man, a great book, fame—who could tell? She knew nothing about it. But it was his way with him, his truthfulness—for instance at dinner she had been thinking quite instinctively, If only he would speak! She had complete trust in him. And dismissing all this, as one passes in diving now a weed, now a straw, now a bubble, she felt again, sinking deeper, as she had felt in the hall when the others were talking, There is something I want—something I have come to get, and she fell deeper and deeper without knowing quite what it was, with her eyes closed. And she waited a little, knitting, wondering, and slowly those words they had said at dinner, "the China rose is all abloom and buzzing with the honey bee," began washing from side to side of her mind rhythmically, and as they washed, words, like little shaded lights, one red, one blue, one yellow, lit up in the dark of her mind, and seemed leaving their perches up there to fly across and across, or to cry out and to be echoed; so she turned and felt on the table beside her for a book.

1. Mr. Ramsay reads chapter XXXI of Sir Walter Scott's *The Antiquary* (1816); see this edition, pp. 274–76.

> And all the lives we ever lived
> And all the lives to be,
> Are full of trees and changing leaves,

she murmured, sticking her needles into the stocking. And she opened the book and began reading here and there at random, and as she did so she felt that she was climbing backwards, upwards, shoving her way up under petals that curved over her, so that she only knew this is white, or this is red. She did not know at first what the words meant at all.

> Steer, hither steer your winged pines, all beaten Mariners[2]

she read and turned the page, swinging herself, zigzagging this way and that, from one line to another as from one branch to another, from one red and white flower to another, until a little sound roused her—her husband slapping his thighs. Their eyes met for a second; but they did not want to speak to each other. They had nothing to say, but something seemed, nevertheless, to go from him to her. It was the life, it was the power of it, it was the tremendous humour, she knew, that made him slap his thighs. Don't interrupt me, he seemed to be saying, don't say anything; just sit there. And he went on reading. His lips twitched. It filled him. It fortified him. He clean forgot all the little rubs and digs of the evening, and how it bored him unutterably to sit still while people ate and drank interminably, and his being so irritable with his wife and so touchy and minding when they passed his books over as if they didn't exist at all. But now, he felt, it didn't matter a damn who reached Z (if thought ran like an alphabet from A to Z). Somebody would reach it—if not he, then another. This man's strength and sanity, his feeling for straight-forward simple things, these fishermen, the poor old crazed crea-ture in Mucklebackit's cottage[3] made him feel so vigorous, so relieved of something that he felt roused and triumphant and could not choke back his tears. Raising the book a little to hide his face, he let them fall and shook his head from side to side and forgot him-self completely (but not one or two reflections about morality and French novels and English novels and Scott's hands being tied but his view perhaps being as true as the other view), forgot his own bothers and failures completely in poor Steenie's drowning and Mucklebackit's sorrow (that was Scott at his best) and the astonish-ing delight and feeling of vigour that it gave him.

2. The opening lines of the first poem in "The Inner Temple Masque" (1614) by William Browne (1591–1643). Mrs. Ramsay appears to be reading an anthology (the holograph says so explicitly, *Original Holograph*, p. 194); this poem was anthologized as "The Sirens' Song" in Arthur Quiller-Couch's 1900 *Oxford Book of English Verse, 1250– 1900*, a copy of which Woolf owned.
3. Refers to characters in Scott's *The Antiquary*: the "crazed creature" is Elspeth, the grandmother; Steenie (who has just drowned) is Mucklebackit's son.

Well, let them improve upon that, he thought as he finished the chapter. He felt that he had been arguing with somebody, and had got the better of him. They could not improve upon that, whatever they might say; and his own position became more secure. The lovers were fiddlesticks, he thought, collecting it all in his mind again. That's fiddlesticks, that's first-rate, he thought, putting one thing beside another. But he must read it again. He could not remember the whole shape of the thing. He had to keep his judgement in suspense. So he returned to the other thought—if young men did not care for this, naturally they did not care for him either. One ought not to complain, thought Mr. Ramsay, trying to stifle his desire to complain to his wife that young men did not admire him. But he was determined; he would not bother her again. Here he looked at her reading. She looked very peaceful, reading. He liked to think that every one had taken themselves off and that he and she were alone. The whole of life did not consist in going to bed with a woman, he thought, returning to Scott and Balzac,[4] to the English novel and the French novel.

Mrs. Ramsay raised her head and like a person in a light sleep seemed to say that if he wanted her to wake she would, she really would, but otherwise, might she go on sleeping, just a little longer, just a little longer? She was climbing up those branches, this way and that, laying hands on one flower and then another.

"Nor praise the deep vermilion in the rose,"[5] she read, and so reading she was ascending, she felt, on to the top, on to the summit. How satisfying! How restful! All the odds and ends of the day stuck to this magnet; her mind felt swept, felt clean. And then there it was, suddenly entire; she held it in her hands, beautiful and reasonable, clear and complete, the essence sucked out of life and held rounded here—the sonnet.

But she was becoming conscious of her husband looking at her. He was smiling at her, quizzically, as if he were ridiculing her gently for being asleep in broad daylight, but at the same time he was thinking, Go on reading. You don't look sad now, he thought. And he wondered what she was reading, and exaggerated her ignorance, her simplicity, for he liked to think that she was not clever, not book-learned at all. He wondered if she understood what she was reading. Probably not, he thought. She was astonishingly beautiful. Her beauty seemed to him, if that were possible, to increase

Yet seem'd it winter still, and, you away,
As with your shadow I with these did play,

she finished.

4. Honoré de Balzac (1799–1850), prolific French author of socially realist historical novels.
5. From Shakespeare's Sonnet XCVIII; see this edition, p. 276.

"Well?" she said, echoing his smile dreamily, looking up from her book.

As with your shadow I with these did play,

she murmured, putting the book on the table.

What had happened, she wondered, as she took up her knitting, since she had seen him alone? She remembered dressing, and seeing the moon; Andrew holding his plate too high at dinner; being depressed by something William had said; the birds in the trees; the sofa on the landing; the children being awake; Charles Tansley waking them with his books falling—oh, no, that she had invented; and Paul having a wash-leather case for his watch. Which should she tell him about?

"They're engaged," she said, beginning to knit, "Paul and Minta."

"So I guessed," he said. There was nothing very much to be said about it. Her mind was still going up and down, up and down with the poetry; he was still feeling very vigorous, very forthright, after reading about Steenie's funeral. So they sat silent. Then she became aware that she wanted him to say something.

Anything, anything, she thought, going on with her knitting. Anything will do.

"How nice it would be to marry a man with a wash-leather bag for his watch," she said, for that was the sort of joke they had together.

He snorted. He felt about this engagement as he always felt about any engagement; the girl is much too good for that young man. Slowly it came into her head, why is it then that one wants people to marry? What was the value, the meaning of things? (Every word they said now would be true.) Do say something, she thought, wishing only to hear his voice. For the shadow, the thing folding them in was beginning, she felt, to close round her again. Say anything, she begged, looking at him, as if for help.

He was silent, swinging the compass on his watch-chain to and fro, and thinking of Scott's novels and Balzac's novels. But through the crepuscular walls of their intimacy, for they were drawing together, involuntarily, coming side by side, quite close, she could feel his mind like a raised hand shadowing her mind; and he was beginning, now that her thoughts took a turn he disliked—towards this "pessimism" as he called it—to fidget, though he said nothing, raising his hand to his forehead, twisting a lock of hair, letting it fall again.

"You won't finish that stocking tonight," he said, pointing to her stocking. That was what she wanted—the asperity in his voice reproving her. If he says it's wrong to be pessimistic probably it is wrong, she thought; the marriage will turn out all right.

"No," she said, flattening the stocking out upon her knee, "I shan't finish it."

And what then? For she felt that he was still looking at her, but that his look had changed. He wanted something—wanted the thing she always found it so difficult to give him; wanted her to tell him that she loved him. And that, no, she could not do. He found talking so much easier than she did. He could say things—she never could. So naturally it was always he that said the things, and then for some reason he would mind this suddenly, and would reproach her. A heartless woman he called her; she never told him that she loved him. But it was not so—it was not so. It was only that she never could say what she felt. Was there no crumb on his coat? Nothing she could do for him? Getting up, she stood at the window with the reddish-brown stocking in her hands, partly to turn away from him, partly because she remembered how beautiful it often is—the sea at night. But she knew that he had turned his head as she turned; he was watching her. She knew that he was thinking, You are more beautiful than ever. And she felt herself very beautiful. Will you not tell me just for once that you love me? He was thinking that, for he was roused, what with Minta and his book, and its being the end of the day and their having quarrelled about going to the Lighthouse. But she could not do it; she could not say it. Then, knowing that he was watching her, instead of saying anything she turned, holding her stocking, and looked at him. And as she looked at him she began to smile, for though she had not said a word, he knew, of course he knew, that she loved him. He could not deny it. And smiling she looked out of the window and said (thinking to herself, Nothing on earth can equal this happiness)—

"Yes, you were right. It's going to be wet tomorrow. You won't be able to go." And she looked at him smiling. For she had triumphed again. She had not said it: yet he knew.

Time Passes

I

"Well, we must wait for the future to show," said Mr. Bankes, coming in from the terrace.[1]

"It's almost too dark to see," said Andrew, coming up from the beach.

"One can hardly tell which is the sea and which is the land," said Prue.

"Do we leave that light burning?" said Lily as they took their coats off indoors.

"No," said Prue, "not if every one's in."

"Andrew," she called back, "just put out the light in the hall."

One by one the lamps were all extinguished, except that Mr. Carmichael, who liked to lie awake a little reading Virgil, kept his candle burning rather longer than the rest.

II

So with the lamps all put out,[1] the moon sunk, and a thin rain drumming on the roof a downpouring of immense darkness began. Nothing, it seemed, could survive the flood, the profusion of darkness which, creeping in at keyholes and crevices, stole round window blinds, came into bedrooms, swallowed up here a jug and basin, there a bowl of red and yellow dahlias, there the sharp edges and firm bulk of a chest of drawers. Not only was furniture confounded; there was scarcely anything left of body or mind by which one could say, "This is he" or "This is she." Sometimes a hand was raised as if to clutch something or ward off something, or somebody groaned, or somebody laughed aloud as if sharing a joke with nothingness.

Nothing stirred in the drawing-room or in the dining-room or on the staircase. Only through the rusty hinges and swollen sea-moistened

---

1. When published separately in a French translation four months before the novel's publication in English, "Time Passes" included no mention of the characters here; see Selected Textual Variants (152), and Composition Chronology (175). The typescript Woolf prepared for the translation can be read in Woolf Online and in James M. Haule, Virginia Woolf, and Charles Mauron, "'Le Temps Passe' and the Original Typescript: An Early Version of the 'Time Passes' Section of To the Lighthouse," Twentieth Century Literature 29:3 (Autumn 1983): 267–311. Haule examines in detail some of the many differences between the holograph, the typescript, and the final published version in "To the Lighthouse and the Great War: Evidence of Virginia Woolf's Revisions of 'Time Passes,'" in Virginia Woolf and War: Fiction, Reality, and Myth, ed. Mark Hussey (Syracuse: Syracuse UP, 1991), pp. 164–79.
1. Echoes a famous remark about the onset of World War I in August 1914 by Sir Edward Grey (1862–1933), the British foreign secretary (1905–16): "The lamps are going out all over Europe; we shall not see them lit again in our lifetime." From his 1925 memoir Twenty-Five Years, 1892–1916, a copy of which Woolf owned.

woodwork certain airs, detached from the body of the wind (the house was ramshackle after all) crept round corners and ventured indoors. Almost one might imagine them, as they entered the drawing-room questioning and wondering, toying with the flap of hanging wallpaper, asking, would it hang much longer, when would it fall? Then smoothly brushing the walls, they passed on musingly as if asking the red and yellow roses on the wall-paper whether they would fade, and questioning (gently, for there was time at their disposal) the torn letters in the waste-paper basket, the flowers, the books, all of which were now open to them and asking, Were they allies? Were they enemies? How long would they endure?

So some random light directing them with its pale footfall upon stair and mat, from some uncovered star, or wandering ship, or the Lighthouse even, the little airs mounted the staircase and nosed round bedroom doors. But here surely, they must cease. Whatever else may perish and disappear, what lies here is steadfast. Here one might say to those sliding lights, those fumbling airs that breathe and bend over the bed itself, here you can neither touch nor destroy. Upon which, wearily, ghostlily, as if they had feather-light fingers and the light persistency of feathers, they would look, once, on the shut eyes, and the loosely clasping fingers, and fold their garments wearily and disappear. And so, nosing, rubbing, they went to the window on the staircase, to the servants' bedrooms, to the boxes in the attics; descending, blanched the apples on the dining-room table, fumbled the petals of roses, tried the picture on the easel, brushed the mat and blew a little sand along the floor. At length, desisting, all ceased together, gathered together, all sighed together; all together gave off an aimless gust of lamentation to which some door in the kitchen replied; swung wide; admitted nothing; and slammed to.

[Here Mr. Carmichael, who was reading Virgil, blew out his candle. It was midnight.][2]

III

But what after all is one night? A short space, especially when the darkness dims so soon, and so soon a bird sings, a cock crows, or a faint green quickens, like a turning leaf, in the hollow of the wave. Night, however, succeeds to night. The winter holds a pack of them in store and deals them equally, evenly, with indefatigable fingers. They lengthen; they darken. Some of them hold aloft clear planets, plates of brightness. The autumn trees, ravaged as they are, take on the flash of tattered flags kindling in the gloom of cool cathedral

2. The bracketed passages in the "Time Passes" section are not present in the holograph, and they were enclosed in parentheses in the proofs; it was Woolf's last-minute decision to change them to brackets.

caves where gold letters on marble pages describe death in battle and how bones bleach and burn far away in Indian sands.[1] The autumn trees gleam in the yellow moonlight, in the light of harvest moons, the light which mellows the energy of labour, and smooths the stubble, and brings the wave lapping blue to the shore.

It seemed now as if, touched by human penitence and all its toil, divine goodness had parted the curtain and displayed behind it, single, distinct, the hare erect; the wave falling; the boat rocking, which, did we deserve them, should be ours always. But alas, divine goodness, twitching the cord, draws the curtain; it does not please him; he covers his treasures in a drench of hail, and so breaks them, so confuses them that it seems impossible that their calm should ever return or that we should ever compose from their fragments a perfect whole or read in the littered pieces the clear words of truth. For our penitence deserves a glimpse only; our toil respite only.

The nights now are full of wind and destruction; the trees plunge and bend and their leaves fly helter skelter until the lawn is plastered with them and they lie packed in gutters and choke rain pipes and scatter damp paths. Also the sea tosses itself and breaks itself, and should any sleeper fancying that he might find on the beach an answer to his doubts, a sharer of his solitude, throw off his bedclothes and go down by himself to walk on the sand, no image with semblance of serving and divine promptitude comes readily to hand bringing the night to order and making the world reflect the compass of the soul. The hand dwindles in his hand; the voice bellows in his ear. Almost it would appear that it is useless in such confusion to ask the night those questions as to what, and why, and wherefore, which tempt the sleeper from his bed to seek an answer.

[Mr. Ramsay, stumbling along a passage one dark morning, stretched his arms out, but Mrs. Ramsay having died rather suddenly the night before, his arms, though stretched out, remained empty.][2]

IV

So with the house empty and the doors locked and the mattresses rolled round, those stray airs, advance guards of great armies, blustered in, brushed bare boards, nibbled and fanned, met nothing in bedroom or drawing-room that wholly resisted them but only

1. The comparison of soldiers dying in battle to autumn leaves falling is a literary convention that goes back as far as Homer's *Iliad*. The bodies of British soldiers who died fighting to conquer India in the nineteenth century were not sent home for burial; instead, their names might be listed on stone tablets on the walls of local churches or cathedrals, while regimental battle flags might be hung there as memorials as well.
2. In "A Sketch of the Past," recalling her visit to her mother's deathbed early in the morning of May 5, 1895, Woolf wrote: "My father staggered from the bedroom as we came. I stretched out my arms to stop him, but he brushed past me, crying out something I could not catch; distraught" (*Moments of Being*, p. 91). See also Selected Textual Variants (154).

hangings that flapped, wood that creaked, the bare legs of tables, saucepans and china already furred, tarnished, cracked. What people had shed and left—a pair of shoes, a shooting cap, some faded skirts and coats in wardrobes—those alone kept the human shape and in the emptiness indicated how once they were filled and animated; how once hands were busy with hooks and buttons; how once the looking-glass had held a face; had held a world hollowed out in which a figure turned, a hand flashed, the door opened, in came children rushing and tumbling; and went out again. Now, day after day, light turned, like a flower reflected in water, its sharp image on the wall opposite. Only the shadows of the trees, flourishing in the wind, made obeisance on the wall, and for a moment darkened the pool in which light reflected itself; or birds, flying, made a soft spot flutter slowly across the bedroom floor.

So loveliness reigned and stillness, and together made the shape of loveliness itself, a form from which life had parted; solitary like a pool at evening, far distant, seen from a train window, vanishing so quickly that the pool, pale in the evening, is scarcely robbed of its solitude, though once seen. Loveliness and stillness clasped hands in the bedroom, and among the shrouded jugs and sheeted chairs even the prying of the wind, and the soft nose of the clammy sea airs, rubbing, snuffling, iterating, and reiterating their questions— "Will you fade? Will you perish?"—scarcely disturbed the peace, the indifference, the air of pure integrity, as if the question they asked scarcely needed that they should answer: we remain.

Nothing it seemed could break that image, corrupt that innocence, or disturb the swaying mantle of silence which, week after week, in the empty room, wove into itself the falling cries of birds, ships hooting, the drone and hum of the fields, a dog's bark, a man's shout, and folded them round the house in silence. Once only a board sprang on the landing; once in the middle of the night with a roar, with a rupture, as after centuries of quiescence, a rock rends itself from the mountain and hurtles crashing into the valley, one fold of the shawl loosened and swung to and fro. Then again peace descended; and the shadow wavered; light bent to its own image in adoration on the bedroom wall; and Mrs. McNab, tearing the veil of silence with hands that had stood in the wash-tub, grinding it with boots that had crunched the shingle, came as directed to open all windows, and dust the bedrooms.

V

As she lurched (for she rolled like a ship at sea) and leered (for her eyes fell on nothing directly, but with a sidelong glance that deprecated the scorn and anger of the world—she was witless, she knew it), as she clutched the banisters and hauled herself upstairs and rolled from room to room, she sang. Rubbing the glass of the long looking-glass and leering sideways at her swinging figure a sound issued from her lips—something that had been gay twenty years before on the stage perhaps, had been hummed and danced to, but now, coming from the toothless, bonneted, care-taking woman, was robbed of meaning, was like the voice of witlessness, humour, persistency itself, trodden down but springing up again, so that as she lurched, dusting, wiping, she seemed to say how it was one long sorrow and trouble, how it was getting up and going to bed again, and bringing things out and putting them away again. It was not easy or snug this world she had known for close on seventy years. Bowed down she was with weariness. How long, she asked, creaking and groaning on her knees under the bed, dusting the boards, how long shall it endure? but hobbled to her feet again, pulled herself up, and again with her sidelong leer which slipped and turned aside even from her own face, and her own sorrows, stood and gaped in the glass, aimlessly smiling, and began again the old amble and hobble, taking up mats, putting down china, looking sideways in the glass, as if, after all, she had her consolations, as if indeed there twined about her dirge some incorrigible hope. Visions of joy there must have been at the wash-tub, say with her children (yet two had been base-born[1] and one had deserted her), at the public-house, drinking; turning over scraps in her drawers. Some cleavage of the dark there must have been, some channel in the depths of obscurity through which light enough issued to twist her face grinning in the glass and make her, turning to her job again, mumble out the old music hall song. The mystic, the visionary, walking the beach on a fine night, stirring a puddle, looking at a stone, asking themselves "What am I," "What is this?" had suddenly an answer vouchsafed them: (they could not say what it was) so that they were warm in the frost and had comfort in the desert. But Mrs. McNab continued to drink and gossip as before.

VI

The spring without a leaf to toss, bare and bright like a virgin fierce in her chastity, scornful in her purity, was laid out on fields wide-eyed and watchful and entirely careless of what was done or thought by the beholders. [Prue Ramsay, leaning on her father's arm, was given in marriage. What, people said, could have been more fitting? And, they added, how beautiful she looked!]

As summer neared, as the evenings lengthened, there came to the wakeful, the hopeful, walking the beach, stirring the pool,

---

1. Born to an unmarried mother; see Selected Textual Variants (154–55) for the earlier, more extensive history of Mrs. McNab that was reduced for final publication.

imaginations of the strangest kind—of flesh turned to atoms which drove before the wind, of stars flashing in their hearts, of cliff, sea, cloud, and sky brought purposely together to assemble outwardly the scattered parts of the vision within. In those mirrors, the minds of men, in those pools of uneasy water, in which clouds for ever turn and shadows form, dreams persisted, and it was impossible to resist the strange intimation which every gull, flower, tree, man and woman, and the white earth itself seemed to declare (but if questioned at once to withdraw) that good triumphs, happiness prevails, order rules; or to resist the extraordinary stimulus to range hither and thither in search of some absolute good, some crystal of intensity, remote from the known pleasures and familiar virtues, something alien to the processes of domestic life, single, hard, bright, like a diamond in the sand, which would render the possessor secure. Moreover, softened and acquiescent, the spring with her bees humming and gnats dancing threw her cloak about her, veiled her eyes, averted her head, and among passing shadows and flights of small rain seemed to have taken upon her a knowledge of the sorrows of mankind.

[Prue Ramsay died that summer in some illness connected with childbirth, which was indeed a tragedy, people said, everything, they said, had promised so well.]

And now in the heat of summer the wind sent its spies about the house again. Flies wove a web in the sunny rooms; weeds that had grown close to the glass in the night tapped methodically at the window pane. When darkness fell, the stroke of the Lighthouse, which had laid itself with such authority upon the carpet in the darkness, tracing its pattern, came now in the softer light of spring mixed with moonlight gliding gently as if it laid its caress and lingered stealthily and looked and came lovingly again. But in the very lull of this loving caress, as the long stroke leant upon the bed, the rock was rent asunder; another fold of the shawl loosened; there it hung, and swayed. Through the short summer nights and the long summer days, when the empty rooms seemed to murmur with the echoes of the fields and the hum of flies, the long streamer waved gently, swayed aimlessly; while the sun so striped and barred the rooms and filled them with yellow haze that Mrs. McNab, when she broke in and lurched about, dusting, sweeping, looked like a tropical fish oaring its way through sun-lanced waters.

But slumber and sleep though it might there came later in the summer ominous sounds like the measured blows of hammers dulled on felt, which, with their repeated shocks still further loosened the shawl and cracked the tea-cups.[1] Now and again some glass tinkled

---

1. During World War I, then known as the Great War, the shock of bombs exploding on the Western Front in Belgium and France (especially the Battle of the Somme, July 1916) could be heard and felt in London and the south of England, though not in Scotland.

in the cupboard as if a giant voice had shrieked so loud in its agony that tumblers stood inside a cupboard vibrated too. Then again silence fell; and then, night after night, and sometimes in plain mid-day when the roses were bright and light turned on the wall its shape clearly there seemed to drop into this silence, this indifference, this integrity, the thud of something falling.

[A shell exploded. Twenty or thirty young men were blown up in France, among them Andrew Ramsay, whose death, mercifully, was instantaneous.]

At that season those who had gone down to pace the beach and ask of the sea and sky what message they reported or what vision they affirmed had to consider among the usual tokens of divine bounty—the sunset on the sea, the pallor of dawn, the moon rising, fishing-boats against the moon, and children making mud pies or pelting each other with handfuls of grass, something out of harmony with this jocundity and this serenity. There was the silent apparition of an ashen-coloured ship for instance, come, gone; there was à purplish stain upon the bland surface of the sea as if something had boiled and bled, invisibly, beneath.[2] This intrusion into a scene calculated to stir the most sublime reflections and lead to the most comfortable conclusions stayed their pacing. It was difficult blandly to overlook them; to abolish their significance in the landscape; to continue, as one walked by the sea, to marvel how beauty outside mirrored beauty within.

Did Nature supplement what man advanced? Did she complete what he began? With equal complacence she saw his misery, his meanness, and his torture. That dream, of sharing, completing, of finding in solitude on the beach an answer, was then but a reflection in a mirror, and the mirror itself was but the surface glassiness which forms in quiescence when the nobler powers sleep beneath? Impatient, despairing yet loth to go (for beauty offers her lures, has her consolations), to pace the beach was impossible; contemplation was unendurable; the mirror was broken.

[Mr. Carmichael brought out a volume of poems that spring, which had an unexpected success. The war, people said, had revived their interest in poetry.]

VII

Night after night, summer and winter, the torment of storms, the arrow-like stillness of fine weather, held their court without

2. In the holograph and in the typescript Woolf prepared for translation, the "ashen-coloured ship" and "purplish stain" even more explicitly refer to the Great War. In the holograph, the ship is "murderous looking" (*Original Holograph*, p. 221), and Woolf refers to a "snout thrusting itself up" that "meant death, & starvation, & pain" (*Original Holograph*, p. 222).

interference. Listening (had there been any one to listen) from the upper rooms of the empty house only gigantic chaos streaked with lightning could have been heard tumbling and tossing, as the winds and waves disported themselves like the amorphous bulks of leviathans[1] whose brows are pierced by no light of reason, and mounted one on top of another, and lunged and plunged in the darkness or the daylight (for night and day, month and year ran shapelessly together) in idiot games, until it seemed as if the universe were battling and tumbling, in brute confusion and wanton lust aimlessly by itself.

In spring the garden urns, casually filled with wind-blown plants, were gay as ever. Violets came and daffodils. But the stillness and the brightness of the day were as strange as the chaos and tumult of night, with the trees standing there, and the flowers standing there, looking before them, looking up, yet beholding nothing, eyeless, and so terrible.

VIII

Thinking no harm, for the family would not come, never again, some said, and the house would be sold at Michaelmas[1] perhaps, Mrs. McNab stooped and picked a bunch of flowers to take home with her. She laid them on the table while she dusted. She was fond of flowers. It was a pity to let them waste. Suppose the house were sold (she stood arms akimbo in front of the looking-glass) it would want seeing to—it would. There it had stood all these years without a soul in it. The books and things were mouldy, for, what with the war and help being hard to get,[2] the house had not been cleaned as she could have wished. It was beyond one person's strength to get it straight now. She was too old. Her legs pained her. All those books needed to be laid out on the grass in the sun; there was plaster fallen in the hall; the rain-pipe had blocked over the study window and let the water in; the carpet was ruined quite. But people should come themselves; they should have sent somebody down to see. For there were clothes in the cupboards; they had left clothes in all the bedrooms. What was she to do with them? They had the moth in them—Mrs. Ramsay's things. Poor lady! She would never want *them*

1. An archaic term for a huge sea creature, but also an allusion to *Leviathan* (1651) by political philosopher Thomas Hobbes (1588–1679), representing the Commonwealth or political society as vast, powerful, and potentially dangerous.
1. The period around September 29, the date of the feast of St. Michael; *house would be sold*: since the Ramsays pay rent, its sale would mean the sale of the lease.
2. Even before the war women had become less willing to work as domestic servants, as other job opportunities became available. During the war, men were subject to the draft, and women took up war-related work such as labor in munitions factories. See Alison Light, *Mrs. Woolf and the Servants* (New York: Bloomsbury Press, 2008) and Mary Wilson, *The Labors of Modernism: Domesticity, Servants, and Authorship in Modernist Fiction* (Farnham, Surrey, UK: Ashgate, 2013).

again. She was dead, they said; years ago, in London. There was the old grey cloak she wore gardening (Mrs. McNab fingered it). She could see her, as she came up the drive with the washing, stooping over her flowers (the garden was a pitiful sight now, all run to riot, and rabbits scuttling at you out of the beds)—she could see her with one of the children by her in that grey cloak. There were boots and shoes; and a brush and comb left on the dressing-table, for all the world as if she expected to come back tomorrow. (She had died very sudden at the end, they said.) And once they had been coming, but had put off coming, what with the war, and travel being so difficult these days; they had never come all these years; just sent her money; but never wrote, never came, and expected to find things as they had left them, ah, dear! Why the dressing-table drawers were full of things (she pulled them open), handkerchiefs, bits of ribbon. Yes, she could see Mrs. Ramsay as she came up the drive with the washing.

"Good-evening, Mrs. McNab," she would say.

She had a pleasant way with her. The girls all liked her. But, dear, many things had changed since then (she shut the drawer); many families had lost their dearest.[3] So she was dead; and Mr. Andrew killed; and Miss Prue dead too, they said, with her first baby; but every one had lost some one these years. Prices had gone up shamefully, and didn't come down again neither. She could well remember her in her grey cloak.

"Good-evening, Mrs. McNab," she said, and told cook to keep a plate of milk soup for her[4]—quite thought she wanted it, carrying that heavy basket all the way up from town. She could see her now, stooping over her flowers; and faint and flickering, like a yellow beam or the circle at the end of a telescope, a lady in a grey cloak, stooping over her flowers, went wandering over the bedroom wall, up the dressing-table, across the wash-stand, as Mrs. McNab hobbled and ambled, dusting, straightening. And cook's name now? Mildred? Marian?—some name like that. Ah, she had forgotten—she did forget things. Fiery, like all red-haired women. Many a laugh they had had. She was always welcome in the kitchen. She made them laugh, she did. Things were better then than now.

She sighed; there was too much work for one woman. She wagged her head this side and that. This had been the nursery. Why, it was all damp in here; the plaster was falling. Whatever did they want to hang a beast's skull there? gone mouldy too. And rats in all the attics. The rain came in. But they never sent; never came. Some of the locks had gone, so the doors banged. She didn't like to be up here at dusk

3. About a million British soldiers (including soldiers drafted from all parts of the empire) were killed in the conflict between 1914 and 1918.
4. Mrs. McNab recalls a scene narrated by Cam in "The Window" (44).

alone neither. It was too much for one woman, too much, too much. She creaked, she moaned. She banged the door. She turned the key in the lock, and left the house alone, shut up, locked.

IX

The house was left; the house was deserted. It was left like a shell on a sandhill to fill with dry salt grains now that life had left it. The long night seemed to have set in; the trifling airs, nibbling, the clammy breaths, fumbling, seemed to have triumphed. The saucepan had rusted and the mat decayed. Toads had nosed their way in. Idly, aimlessly, the swaying shawl swung to and fro. A thistle thrust itself between the tiles in the larder. The swallows nested in the drawing-room; the floor was strewn with straw; the plaster fell in shovelfuls; rafters were laid bare; rats carried off this and that to gnaw behind the wainscots. Tortoise-shell butterflies burst from the chrysalis and pattered their life out on the window-pane. Poppies sowed themselves among the dahlias; the lawn waved with long grass; giant artichokes towered among roses; a fringed carnation flowered among the cabbages; while the gentle tapping of a weed at the window had become, on winters' nights, a drumming from sturdy trees and thorned briars which made the whole room green in summer.

What power could now prevent the fertility, the insensibility of nature? Mrs. McNab's dream of a lady, of a child, of a plate of milk soup? It had wavered over the walls like a spot of sunlight and vanished. She had locked the door; she had gone. It was beyond the strength of one woman, she said. They never sent. They never wrote. There were things up there rotting in the drawers—it was a shame to leave them so, she said. The place was gone to rack and ruin. Only the Lighthouse beam entered the rooms for a moment, sent its sudden stare over bed and wall in the darkness of winter, looked with equanimity at the thistle and the swallow, the rat and the straw. Nothing now withstood them; nothing said no to them. Let the wind blow;[1] let the poppy seed itself and the carnation mate with the cabbage. Let the swallow build in the drawing-room, and the thistle thrust aside the tiles, and the butterfly sun itself on the faded chintz of the arm-chairs. Let the broken glass and the china lie out on the lawn and be tangled over with grass and wild berries.

For now had come that moment, that hesitation when dawn trembles and night pauses, when if a feather alight in the scale it will be weighed down. One feather, and the house, sinking, falling, would have turned and pitched downwards to the depths of darkness. In the ruined room, picnickers would have lit their kettles;

---

1. Like Mrs. Ramsay's "Light the candles" (73), this echoes Genesis 1:3, "And God said, Let there be light: and there was light."

lovers sought shelter there, lying on the bare boards; and the shepherd stored his dinner on the bricks, and the tramp slept with his coat round him to ward off the cold. Then the roof would have fallen; briars and hemlocks would have blotted out path, step, and window; would have grown, unequally but lustily over the mound, until some trespasser, losing his way, could have told only by a red-hot poker among the nettles, or a scrap of china in the hemlock that here once some one had lived; there had been a house.

If the feather had fallen, if it had tipped the scale downwards, the whole house would have plunged to the depths to lie upon the sands of oblivion. But there was a force working; something not highly conscious; something that leered, something that lurched; something not inspired to go about its work with dignified ritual or solemn chanting. Mrs. McNab groaned; Mrs. Bast creaked. They were old; they were stiff; their legs ached. They came with their brooms and pails at last; they got to work. All of a sudden, would Mrs. McNab see that the house was ready, one of the young ladies wrote: would she get this done; would she get that done; all in a hurry. They might be coming for the summer; had left everything to the last; expected to find things as they had left them. Slowly and painfully, with broom and pail, mopping, scouring, Mrs. McNab, Mrs. Bast, stayed the corruption and the rot;[2] rescued from the pool of Time that was fast closing over them now a basin, now a cupboard; fetched up from oblivion all the Waverley novels and a tea-set one morning; in the afternoon restored to sun and air a brass fender and a set of steel fire-irons. George, Mrs. Bast's son, caught the rats, and cut the grass. They had the builders. Attended with the creaking of hinges and the screeching of bolts, the slamming and banging of damp-swollen woodwork some rusty laborious birth seemed to be taking place, as the women, stooping, rising, groaning, singing, slapped and slammed, upstairs now, now down in the cellars. Oh, they said, the work!

They drank their tea in the bedroom sometimes, or in the study; breaking off work at mid-day with the smudge on their faces, and their old hands clasped and cramped with the broom handles. Flopped on chairs, they contemplated now the magnificent conquest over taps and bath; now the more arduous, more partial triumph over long rows of books, black as ravens once, now white-stained, breeding pale mushrooms and secreting furtive spiders. Once more, as she felt the tea warm in her, the telescope fitted itself to Mrs. McNab's eyes, and in a ring of light she saw the old gentleman, lean as a rake, wagging his head, as she came up with the washing, talking to himself, she supposed, on the lawn. He never noticed her. Some said he was dead; some said she was dead. Which was it? Mrs. Bast didn't

---

2. Echoes Matthew 6:19, "Lay not up for yourselves treasures upon earth, where moth and rust doth corrupt."

know for certain either. The young gentleman was dead. That she was sure. She had read his name in the papers.

There was the cook now, Mildred, Marian, some such name as that—a red-headed woman, quick-tempered like all her sort, but kind, too, if you knew the way with her. Many a laugh they had had together. She saved a plate of soup for Maggie; a bite of ham, sometimes; whatever was over. They lived well in those days. They had everything they wanted (glibly, jovially, with the tea hot in her, she unwound her ball of memories, sitting in the wicker arm-chair by the nursery fender). There was always plenty doing, people in the house, twenty staying sometimes, and washing up till long past midnight.

Mrs. Bast (she had never known them; had lived in Glasgow at that time) wondered, putting her cup down, whatever they hung that beast's skull there for? Shot in foreign parts no doubt.

It might well be, said Mrs. McNab, wantoning on with her memories; they had friends in eastern countries;[3] gentlemen staying there, ladies in evening dress; she had seen them once through the dining-room door all sitting at dinner. Twenty she dared say all in their jewellery, and she asked to stay help wash up, might be till after midnight.

Ah, said Mrs. Bast, they'd find it changed. She leant out of the window. She watched her son George scything the grass. They might well ask, what had been done to it? seeing how old Kennedy was supposed to have charge of it, and then his leg got so bad after he fell from the cart; and perhaps then no one for a year, or the better part of one; and then Davie Macdonald, and seeds might be sent, but who should say if they were ever planted? They'd find it changed.

She watched her son scything. He was a great one for work—one of those quiet ones. Well they must be getting along with the cupboards, she supposed. They hauled themselves up.

At last, after days of labour within, of cutting and digging without, dusters were flicked from the windows, the windows were shut to, keys were turned all over the house; the front door was banged; it was finished.

And now as if the cleaning and the scrubbing and the scything and the mowing had drowned it there rose that half-heard melody, that intermittent music which the ear half catches but lets fall; a bark, a bleat; irregular, intermittent, yet somehow related; the hum of an insect, the tremor of cut grass, dissevered yet somehow belonging; the jar of a dorbeetle, the squeak of a wheel, loud, low, but mysteriously related; which the ear strains to bring together and is always on the verge of harmonising, but they are never quite heard, never fully harmonised, and at last, in the evening, one after another the sounds die out, and the harmony falters, and silence falls. With the sunset

3. Like the skull "shot in foreign parts," this is a reminder that men in the family and its circle once "ruled India" (7).

sharpness was lost, and like mist rising, quiet rose, quiet spread, the wind settled; loosely the world shook itself down to sleep, darkly here without a light to it, save what came green suffused through leaves, or pale on the white flowers in the bed by the window.

(Lily Briscoe had her bag carried up to the house late one evening in September.)

X

Then indeed peace had come.[1] Messages of peace breathed from the sea to the shore. Never to break its sleep any more, to lull it rather more deeply to rest, and whatever the dreamers dreamt holily, dreamt wisely, to confirm—what else was it murmuring—as Lily Briscoe laid her head on the pillow in the clean still room and heard the sea. Through the open window the voice of the beauty of the world came murmuring, too softly to hear exactly what it said—but what mattered if the meaning were plain? entreating the sleepers (the house was full again; Mrs. Beckwith was staying there, also Mr. Carmichael), if they would not actually come down to the beach itself at least to lift the blind and look out. They would see then night flowing down in purple; his head crowned; his sceptre jewelled; and how in his eyes a child might look. And if they still faltered (Lily was tired out with travelling and slept almost at once; but Mr. Carmichael read a book by candlelight), if they still said no, that it was vapour, this splendour of his, and the dew had more power than he, and they preferred sleeping; gently then without complaint, or argument, the voice would sing its song. Gently the waves would break (Lily heard them in her sleep); tenderly the light fell (it seemed to come through her eyelids). And it all looked, Mr. Carmichael thought, shutting his book, falling asleep, much as it used to look.

Indeed the voice might resume, as the curtains of dark wrapped themselves over the house, over Mrs. Beckwith, Mr. Carmichael, and Lily Briscoe so that they lay with several folds of blackness on their eyes, why not accept this, be content with this, acquiesce and resign? The sigh of all the seas breaking in measure round the isles soothed them; the night wrapped them; nothing broke their sleep, until, the birds beginning and the dawn weaving their thin voices in to its whiteness, a cart grinding, a dog somewhere barking, the sun lifted the curtains, broke the veil on their eyes, and Lily Briscoe stirring in her sleep. She clutched at her blankets as a faller clutches at the turf on the edge of a cliff. Her eyes opened wide. Here she was again, she thought, sitting bolt upright in bed. Awake.

1. The Armistice that ended the fighting on the Western Front was signed on November 11, 1918, by representatives from Germany, France, and Britain, although the Great War did not officially end until the Treaty of Versailles, June 1919.

The Lighthouse

I

What does it mean then, what can it all mean? Lily Briscoe asked herself, wondering whether, since she had been left alone, it behoved her to go to the kitchen to fetch another cup of coffee or wait here. What does it mean?—a catchword that was, caught up from some book, fitting her thought loosely, for she could not, this first morning with the Ramsays, contract her feelings, could only make a phrase resound to cover the blankness of her mind until these vapours had shrunk. For really, what did she feel, come back after all these years and Mrs. Ramsay dead? Nothing, nothing—nothing that she could express at all.

She had come late last night when it was all mysterious, dark. Now she was awake, at her old place at the breakfast table, but alone. It was very early too, not yet eight. There was this expedition—they were going to the Lighthouse, Mr. Ramsay, Cam, and James. They should have gone already—they had to catch the tide or something. And Cam was not ready and James was not ready and Nancy had forgotten to order the sandwiches and Mr. Ramsay had lost his temper and banged out of the room.

"What's the use of going now?" he had stormed.

Nancy had vanished. There he was, marching up and down the terrace in a rage. One seemed to hear doors slamming and voices calling all over the house. Now Nancy burst in, and asked, looking round the room, in a queer half dazed, half desperate way, "What does one send to the Lighthouse?" as if she were forcing herself to do what she despaired of ever being able to do.

What does one send to the Lighthouse indeed! At any other time Lily could have suggested reasonably tea, tobacco, newspapers. But this morning everything seemed so extraordinarily queer that a question like Nancy's—What does one send to the Lighthouse?—opened doors in one's mind that went banging and swinging to and fro and made one keep asking, in a stupefied gape, What does one send? What does one do? Why is one sitting here, after all?

Sitting alone (for Nancy went out again) among the clean cups at the long table, she felt cut off from other people, and able only to go on watching, asking, wondering. The house, the place, the morning, all seemed strangers to her. She had no attachment here, she felt, no relations with it, anything might happen, and whatever did happen, a step outside, a voice calling ("It's not in the cupboard; it's on the landing," some one cried), was a question, as if the link that usually bound things together had been cut, and they floated up here, down there, off, anyhow. How aimless it was, how chaotic, how unreal it was, she thought, looking at her empty coffee cup. Mrs. Ramsay dead; Andrew killed; Prue dead too—repeat it as she might, it roused no feeling in her. And we all get together in a house like this on a morning like this, she said, looking out of the window. It was a beautiful still day.

Suddenly Mr. Ramsay raised his head as he passed and looked straight at her, with his distraught wild gaze which was yet so penetrating, as if he saw you, for one second, for the first time, for ever; and she pretended to drink out of her empty coffee cup so as to escape him—to escape his demand on her, to put aside a moment longer that imperious need. And he shook his head at her, and strode on ("Alone" she heard him say, "Perished" she heard him say)[1] and like everything else this strange morning the words became symbols, wrote themselves all over the grey-green walls. If only she could put them together, she felt, write them out in some sentence, then she would have got at the truth of things. Old Mr. Carmichael came padding softly in, fetched his coffee, took his cup and made off to sit in the sun. The extraordinary unreality was frightening; but it was also exciting. Going to the Lighthouse. But what does one send to the Lighthouse? Perished. Alone. The grey-green light on the wall opposite. The empty places. Such were some of the parts, but how bring them together? she asked. As if any interruption would break the frail shape she was building on the table she turned her back to the window lest Mr. Ramsay should see her. She must escape somewhere, be alone somewhere. Suddenly she remembered. When she had sat there last ten years ago there had been a little sprig or leaf pattern on the tablecloth, which she had looked at in a moment of revelation. There had been a problem about a foreground of a picture. Move the tree to the middle, she had said. She had never finished that picture. She would paint that picture now.[2] It had been knocking about in her mind all these years. Where were her paints, she wondered? Her paints, yes. She had left them in the hall last night. She would start at once. She got up quickly, before Mr. Ramsay turned.

She fetched herself a chair. She pitched her easel with her precise old-maidish movements on the edge of the lawn, not too close to Mr. Carmichael, but close enough for his protection. Yes, it must have been precisely here that she had stood ten years ago. There was the wall; the hedge; the tree. The question was of some relation between those masses. She had borne it in her mind all these years. It seemed as if the solution had come to her: she knew now what she wanted to do.

1. Mr. Ramsay is chanting William Cowper's poem "The Castaway," and he continues to do so throughout "The Lighthouse;" for the poem, see this edition, pp. 277–78.
2. Lily starts over with a fresh canvas, although she sets her materials up in the same location.

But with Mr. Ramsay bearing down on her, she could do nothing. Every time he approached—he was walking up and down the terrace—ruin approached, chaos approached. She could not paint. She stooped, she turned; she took up this rag; she squeezed that tube. But all she did was to ward him off a moment. He made it impossible for her to do anything. For if she gave him the least chance, if he saw her disengaged a moment, looking his way a moment, he would be on her, saying, as he had said last night, "You find us much changed." Last night he had got up and stopped before her, and said that. Dumb and staring though they had all sat, the six children whom they used to call after the Kings and Queens of England—the Red, the Fair, the Wicked, the Ruthless—she felt how they raged under it. Kind old Mrs. Beckwith said something sensible. But it was a house full of unrelated passions—she had felt that all the evening. And on top of this chaos Mr. Ramsay got up, pressed her hand, and said: "You will find us much changed" and none of them had moved or had spoken; but had sat there as if they were forced to let him say it. Only James (certainly the Sullen) scowled at the lamp; and Cam screwed her handkerchief round her finger. Then he reminded them that they were going to the Lighthouse tomorrow. They must be ready, in the hall, on the stroke of half-past seven. Then, with his hand on the door, he stopped; he turned upon them. Did they not want to go? he demanded. Had they dared say No (he had some reason for wanting it) he would have flung himself tragically backwards into the bitter waters of despair. Such a gift he had for gesture. He looked like a king in exile. Doggedly James said yes. Cam stumbled more wretchedly. Yes, oh, yes, they'd both be ready, they said. And it struck her, this was tragedy—not palls, dust, and the shroud; but children coerced, their spirits subdued. James was sixteen, Cam, seventeen, perhaps. She had looked round for some one who was not there, for Mrs. Ramsay, presumably. But there was only kind Mrs. Beckwith turning over her sketches under the lamp. Then, being tired, her mind still rising and falling with the sea, the taste and smell that places have after long absence possessing her, the candles wavering in her eyes, she had lost herself and gone under. It was a wonderful night, starlit; the waves sounded as they went upstairs; the moon surprised them, enormous, pale, as they passed the staircase window. She had slept at once.

She set her clean canvas firmly upon the easel, as a barrier, frail, but she hoped sufficiently substantial to ward off Mr. Ramsay and his exactingness. She did her best to look, when his back was turned, at her picture; that line there, that mass there. But it was out of the question. Let him be fifty feet away, let him not even speak to you, let him not even see you, he permeated, he prevailed, he imposed himself. He changed everything. She could not see the colour; she could not see the lines; even with his back turned to her, she could only think, But he'll be down on me in a moment, demanding—something she felt she could not give him. She rejected one brush; she chose another. When would those children come? When would they all be off? she fidgeted. That man, she thought, her anger rising in her, never gave; that man took. She, on the other hand, would be forced to give. Mrs. Ramsay had given. Giving, giving, giving, she had died—and had left all this. Really, she was angry with Mrs. Ramsay. With the brush slightly trembling in her fingers she looked at the hedge, the step, the wall. It was all Mrs. Ramsay's doing. She was dead. Here was Lily, at forty-four,[3] wasting her time, unable to do a thing, standing there, playing at painting, playing at the one thing one did not play at, and it was all Mrs. Ramsay's fault. She was dead. The step where she used to sit was empty. She was dead.

But why repeat this over and over again? Why be always trying to bring up some feeling she had not got? There was a kind of blasphemy in it. It was all dry: all withered: all spent. They ought not to have asked her; she ought not to have come. One can't waste one's time at forty-four, she thought. She hated playing at painting. A brush, the one dependable thing in a world of strife, ruin, chaos—that one should not play with, knowingly even: she detested it. But he made her. You shan't touch your canvas, he seemed to say, bearing down on her, till you've given me what I want of you. Here he was, close upon her again, greedy, distraught. Well, thought Lily in despair, letting her right hand fall at her side, it would be simpler then to have it over. Surely, she could imitate from recollection the glow, the rhapsody, the self-surrender, she had seen on so many women's faces (on Mrs. Ramsay's, for instance) when on some occasion like this they blazed up—she could remember the look on Mrs. Ramsay's face—into a rapture of sympathy, of delight in the reward they had, which, though the reason of it escaped her, evidently conferred on them the most supreme bliss of which human nature was capable. Here he was, stopped by her side. She would give him what she could.

II

She seemed to have shrivelled slightly, he thought. She looked a little skimpy, wispy; but not unattractive. He liked her. There had been some talk of her marrying William Bankes once, but nothing had come of it. His wife had been fond of her. He had been a little out of temper too at breakfast. And then, and then—this was one of those moments when an enormous need urged him, without being

---

3. Lily was thirty-three in "The Window;" that her age is given here gives the novel a clear timeline. See note 4 p. 42.

conscious what it was, to approach any woman, to force them, he did not care how, his need was so great, to give him what he wanted: sympathy.

Was anybody looking after her? he said. Had she everything she wanted?

"Oh, thanks, everything," said Lily Briscoe nervously. No; she could not do it. She ought to have floated off instantly upon some wave of sympathetic expansion: the pressure on her was tremendous. But she remained stuck. There was an awful pause. They both looked at the sea. Why, thought Mr. Ramsay, should she look at the sea when I am here? She hoped it would be calm enough for them to land at the Lighthouse, she said. The Lighthouse! The Lighthouse! What's that got to do with it? he thought impatiently. Instantly, with the force of some primeval gust (for really he could not restrain himself any longer), there issued from him such a groan that any other woman in the whole world would have done something, said something—all except myself, thought Lily, girding at herself bitterly, who am not a woman, but a peevish, ill-tempered, dried-up old maid, presumably.

Mr. Ramsay sighed to the full. He waited. Was she not going to say anything? Did she not see what he wanted from her? Then he said he had a particular reason for wanting to go to the Lighthouse. His wife used to send the men things. There was a poor boy with a tuberculous hip, the lightkeeper's son. He sighed profoundly. He sighed significantly. All Lily wished was that this enormous flood of grief, this insatiable hunger for sympathy, this demand that she should surrender herself up to him entirely, and even so he had sorrows enough to keep her supplied for ever, should leave her, should be diverted (she kept looking at the house, hoping for an interruption) before it swept her down in its flow.

"Such expeditions," said Mr. Ramsay, scraping the ground with his toe, "are very painful." Still Lily said nothing. (She is a stock, she is a stone, he said to himself.) "They are very exhausting," he said, looking, with a sickly look that nauseated her (he was acting, she felt, this great man was dramatising himself), at his beautiful hands. It was horrible, it was indecent. Would they never come, she asked, for she could not sustain this enormous weight of sorrow, support these heavy draperies of grief (he had assumed a pose of extreme decrepitude; he even tottered a little as he stood there) a moment longer.

Still she could say nothing; the whole horizon seemed swept bare of objects to talk about; could only feel, amazedly, as Mr. Ramsay stood there, how his gaze seemed to fall dolefully over the sunny grass and discolour it, and cast over the rubicund, drowsy, entirely contented figure of Mr. Carmichael, reading a French novel on a deck-chair, a veil of crape, as if such an existence, flaunting its prosperity in a world of woe, were enough to provoke the most dismal thoughts of all. Look at him, he seemed to be saying, look at me; and indeed, all the time he was feeling, Think of me, think of me. Ah, could that bulk only be wafted alongside of them, Lily wished; had she only pitched her easel a yard or two closer to him; a man, any man, would staunch this effusion, would stop these lamentations. A woman, she had provoked this horror; a woman, she should have known how to deal with it. It was immensely to her discredit, sexually, to stand there dumb. One said—what did one say?—Oh, Mr. Ramsay! Dear Mr. Ramsay! That was what that kind old lady who sketched, Mrs. Beckwith, would have said instantly, and rightly. But, no. They stood there, isolated from the rest of the world. His immense self-pity, his demand for sympathy poured and spread itself in pools at her feet, and all she did, miserable sinner that she was, was to draw her skirts a little closer round her ankles, lest she should get wet. In complete silence she stood there, grasping her paint brush.

Heaven could never be sufficiently praised! She heard sounds in the house. James and Cam must be coming. But Mr. Ramsay, as if he knew that his time ran short, exerted upon her solitary figure the immense pressure of his concentrated woe; his age; his frailty; his desolation; when suddenly, tossing his head impatiently, in his annoyance—for after all, what woman could resist him?—he noticed that his boot-laces were untied. Remarkable boots they were too, Lily thought, looking down at them: sculptured; colossal; like everything that Mr. Ramsay wore, from his frayed tie to his half-buttoned waistcoat, his own indisputably. She could see them walking to his room of their own accord, expressive in his absence of pathos, surliness, ill-temper, charm.

"What beautiful boots!" she exclaimed. She was ashamed of herself. To praise his boots when he asked her to solace his soul; when he had shown her his bleeding hands, his lacerated heart, and asked her to pity them, then to say, cheerfully, "Ah, but what beautiful boots you wear!" deserved, she knew, and she looked up expecting to get it, in one of his sudden roars of ill-temper, complete annihilation.

Instead, Mr. Ramsay smiled. His pall, his draperies, his infirmities fell from him. Ah, yes, he said, holding his foot up for her to look at, they were first-rate boots. There was only one man in England who could make boots like that. Boots are among the chief curses of mankind, he said. "Bootmakers make it their business," he exclaimed, "to cripple and torture the human foot." They are also the most obstinate and perverse of mankind. It had taken him the best part of his youth to get boots made as they should be made. He would have her observe (he lifted his right foot and then his left) that she had never seen boots made quite that shape before. They were made of the finest leather in the world, also. Most leather was mere brown paper and cardboard. He looked complacently at his foot, still held in the air. They had reached, she felt, a sunny island where peace dwelt, sanity reigned and the sun for ever shone, the blessed island of good boots. Her heart warmed to him. "Now let me see if you can tie a knot," he said. He poohpoohed her feeble system. He showed her his own invention. Once you tied it, it never came undone. Three times he knotted her shoe; three times he unknotted it.

Why, at this completely inappropriate moment, when he was stooping over her shoe, should she be so tormented with sympathy for him that, as she stooped too, the blood rushed to her face, and, thinking of her callousness (she had called him a play-actor) she felt her eyes swell and tingle with tears? Thus occupied he seemed to her a figure of infinite pathos. He tied knots. He bought boots. There was no helping Mr. Ramsay on the journey he was going. But now just as she wished to say something, could have said something, perhaps, here they were—Cam and James. They appeared on the terrace. They came, lagging, side by side, a serious, melancholy couple.

But why was it like *that* that they came? She could not help feeling annoyed with them; they might have come more cheerfully; they might have given him what, now that they were off, she would not have the chance of giving him. For she felt a sudden emptiness; a frustration. Her feeling had come too late; there it was ready; but he no longer needed it. He had become a very distinguished, elderly man, who had no need of her whatsoever. She felt snubbed. He slung a knapsack round his shoulders. He shared out the parcels—there were a number of them, ill tied in brown paper. He sent Cam for a cloak. He had all the appearance of a leader making ready for an expedition. Then, wheeling about, he led the way with his firm military tread, in those wonderful boots, carrying brown paper parcels, down the path, his children following him. They looked, she thought, as if fate had devoted them to some stern enterprise, and they went to it, still young enough to be drawn acquiescent in their father's wake, obediently, but with a pallor in their eyes which made her feel that they suffered something beyond their years in silence. So they passed the edge of the lawn, and it seemed to Lily that she watched a procession go, drawn on by some stress of common feeling which made it, faltering and flagging as it was, a little company bound together and strangely impressive to her. Politely, but very distantly, Mr. Ramsay raised his hand and saluted her as they passed.

But what a face, she thought, immediately finding the sympathy which she had not been asked to give troubling her for expression. What had made it like that? Thinking, night after night, she supposed—about the reality of kitchen tables, she added, remembering the symbol which in her vagueness as to what Mr. Ramsay did think about Andrew had given her. (He had been killed by the splinter of a shell instantly, she bethought her.) The kitchen table was something visionary, austere; something bare, hard, not ornamental. There was no colour to it; it was all edges and angles; it was uncompromisingly plain. But Mr. Ramsay kept always his eyes fixed upon it, never allowed himself to be distracted or deluded, until his face became worn too and ascetic and partook of this unornamented beauty which so deeply impressed her. Then, she recalled (standing where he had left her, holding her brush), worries had fretted it—not so nobly. He must have had his doubts about that table, she supposed; whether the table was a real table; whether it was worth the time he gave to it; whether he was able after all to find it. He had had doubts, she felt, or he would have asked less of people. That was what they talked about late at night sometimes, she suspected; and then next day Mrs. Ramsay looked tired, and Lily flew into a rage with him over some absurd little thing. But now he had nobody to talk to about that table, or his boots, or his knots; and he was like a lion seeking whom he could devour, and his face had that touch of desperation, of exaggeration in it which alarmed her, and made her pull her skirts about her. And then, she recalled, there was that sudden revivification, that sudden flare (when she praised his boots), that sudden recovery of vitality and interest in ordinary human things, which too passed and changed (for he was always changing, and hid nothing) into that other final phase which was new to her and had, she owned, made herself ashamed of her own irritability, when it seemed as if he had shed worries and ambitions, and the hope of sympathy and the desire for praise, had entered some other region, was drawn on, as if by curiosity, in dumb colloquy, whether with himself or another, at the head of that little procession out of one's range. An extraordinary face! The gate banged.

III

So they're gone, she thought, sighing with relief and disappointment. Her sympathy seemed to be cast back on her, like a bramble sprung across her face. She felt curiously divided, as if one part of her were drawn out there—it was a still day, hazy; the Lighthouse looked this morning at an immense distance; the other had fixed itself doggedly, solidly, here on the lawn. She saw her canvas as if it had floated up and placed itself white and uncompromising directly before her. It seemed to rebuke her with its cold stare for all this hurry and agitation; this folly and waste of emotion; it drastically recalled her and spread through her mind first a peace, as her disorderly sensations (he had gone and she had been so sorry for him and she had said nothing) trooped off the field; and then, emptiness.

She looked blankly at the canvas, with its uncompromising white stare; from the canvas to the garden. There was something (she stood screwing up her little Chinese eyes in her small puckered face), something she remembered in the relations of those lines cutting across, slicing down, and in the mass of the hedge with its green cave of blues and browns, which had stayed in her mind; which had tied a knot in her mind so that at odds and ends of time, involuntarily, as she walked along the Brompton Road, as she brushed her hair, she found herself painting that picture, passing her eye over it, and untying the knot in imagination. But there was all the difference in the world between this planning airily away from the canvas, and actually taking her brush and making the first mark.

She had taken the wrong brush in her agitation at Mr. Ramsay's presence, and her easel, rammed into the earth so nervously, was at the wrong angle. And now that she had put that right, and in so doing had subdued the impertinences and irrelevances that plucked her attention and made her remember how she was such and such a person, had such and such relations to people, she took her hand and raised her brush. For a moment it stayed trembling in a painful but exciting ecstasy in the air. Where to begin?—that was the question at what point to make the first mark?[1] One line placed on the canvas committed her to innumerable risks, to frequent and irrevocable decisions. All that in idea seemed simple became in practice immediately complex; as the waves shape themselves symmetrically from the cliff top, but to the swimmer among them are divided by steep gulfs, and foaming crests. Still the risk must be run; the mark made.

With a curious physical sensation, as if she were urged forward and at the same time must hold herself back, she made her first quick decisive stroke. The brush descended. It flickered brown over the white canvas; it left a running mark. A second time she did it—a third time. And so pausing and so flickering, she attained a dancing rhythmical movement, as if the pauses were one part of the rhythm and the strokes another, and all were related; and so, lightly and swiftly pausing, striking, she scored her canvas with brown running nervous lines which had no sooner settled there than they enclosed (she felt it looming out at her) a space. Down in the hollow of one wave she saw the next wave towering higher and higher above her. For what could be more formidable than that space? Here she was again, she thought, stepping back to look at it, drawn out of gossip, out of living, out of community with people into the presence of this formidable ancient enemy of hers—this other thing, this truth, this

1. This sentence would read better with a semicolon after "question," as in British editions. See *To the Lighthouse*, annotated and with an introduction by Mark Hussey, pp. 231–32.

reality, which suddenly laid hands on her, emerged stark at the back of appearances and commanded her attention. She was half unwilling, half reluctant. Why always be drawn out and haled away? Why not left in peace, to talk to Mr. Carmichael on the lawn? It was an exacting form of intercourse anyhow. Other worshipful objects were content with worship; men, women, God, all let one kneel prostrate; but this form, were it only the shape of a white lamp-shade looming on a wicker table, roused one to perpetual combat, challenged one to a fight in which one was bound to be worsted. Always (it was in her nature, or in her sex, she did not know which) before she exchanged the fluidity of life for the concentration of painting she had a few moments of nakedness when she seemed like an unborn soul, a soul reft of body,[2] hesitating on some windy pinnacle and exposed without protection to all the blasts of doubt. Why then did she do it? She looked at the canvas, lightly scored with running lines. It would be hung in the servants' bedrooms. It would be rolled up and stuffed under a sofa. What was the good of doing it then, and she heard some voice saying she couldn't paint, saying she couldn't create, as if she were caught up in one of those habitual currents in which after a certain time experience forms in the mind, so that one repeats words without being aware any longer who originally spoke them.

Can't paint, can't write, she murmured monotonously, anxiously considering what her plan of attack should be. For the mass loomed before her; it protruded; she felt it pressing on her eyeballs. Then, as if some juice necessary for the lubrication of her faculties were spontaneously squirted, she began precariously dipping among the blues and umbers, moving her brush hither and thither, but it was now heavier and went slower, as if it had fallen in with some rhythm which was dictated to her (she kept looking at the hedge, at the canvas) by what she saw, so that while her hand quivered with life, this rhythm was strong enough to bear her along with it on its current. Certainly she was losing consciousness of outer things.[3] And as she lost consciousness of outer things, and her name and her personality and her appearance, and whether Mr. Carmichael was there or not, her mind kept throwing up from its depths, scenes, and names, and

---

2. Alludes to "Ode: Intimations of Immortality from Recollections of Early Childhood" (1802–4) by William Wordsworth (1775–1850): "Our birth is but a sleep and a forgetting: / The Soul that rises with us, our life's Star, / Hath had elsewhere its setting, / And cometh from afar: / Not in entire forgetfulness, / And not in utter nakedness, / But trailing clouds of glory do we come" (stanza 5, lines 58–64). In *The Norton Anthology of English Literature,* ed. Stephen Greenblatt, 10th ed., 6 vols. (New York: Norton, 2018), vol. D, p. 349. On the allusions to Wordsworth's "Ode" in "The Lighthouse," see Emily Kopley, *Virginia Woolf and Poetry* (Oxford: Oxford UP, 2021), pp. 95–96.

3. Wordsworth's "Ode: Intimations of Immortality" is echoed again: "Not for these I raise / The song of thanks and praise; / But for those obstinate questionings / Of sense and outward things, / Fallings from us, vanishings; / Blank misgivings of a Creature / Moving about in worlds not realised" (stanza 9, lines 139–45). *Norton Anthology of English Literature,* 10th ed., vol. D, p. 351.

sayings, and memories and ideas, like a fountain spurting over that glaring, hideously difficult white space, while she modelled it with greens and blues.

Charles Tansley used to say that, she remembered, women can't paint, can't write. Coming up behind her, he had stood close beside her, a thing she hated, as she painted here on this very spot. "Shag tobacco," he said, "fivepence an ounce," parading his poverty, his principles. (But the war had drawn the sting of her femininity. Poor devils, one thought, poor devils, of both sexes.) He was always carrying a book about under his arm—a purple book. He "worked." He sat, she remembered, working in a blaze of sun. At dinner he would sit right in the middle of the view. But after all, she reflected, there was the scene on the beach. One must remember that. It was a windy morning. They had all gone down to the beach. Mrs. Ramsay sat down and wrote letters by a rock. She wrote and wrote. "Oh," she said, looking up at something floating in the sea, "is it a lobster pot? Is it an upturned boat?" She was so short-sighted that she could not see, and then Charles Tansley became as nice as he could possibly be. He began playing ducks and drakes. They chose little flat black stones and sent them skipping over the waves. Every now and then Mrs. Ramsay looked up over her spectacles and laughed at them. What they said she could not remember, but only she and Charles throwing stones and getting on very well all of a sudden and Mrs. Ramsay watching them. She was highly conscious of that. Mrs. Ramsay, she thought, stepping back and screwing up her eyes. (It must have altered the design a good deal when she was sitting on the step with James. There must have been a shadow.) When she thought of herself and Charles throwing ducks and drakes and of the whole scene on the beach, it seemed to depend somehow upon Mrs. Ramsay sitting under the rock, with a pad on her knee, writing letters. (She wrote innumerable letters, and sometimes the wind took them and she and Charles just saved a page from the sea.) But what a power was in the human soul! she thought. That woman sitting there writing under the rock resolved everything into simplicity; made these angers, irritations fall off like old rags; she brought together this and that and then this, and so made out of that miserable silliness and spite (she and Charles squabbling, sparring, had been silly and spiteful) something—this scene on the beach for example, this moment of friendship and liking—which survived, after all these years complete, so that she dipped into it to re-fashion her memory of him, and there it stayed in the mind affecting one almost like a work of art.

"Like a work of art," she repeated, looking from her canvas to the drawing-room steps and back again. She must rest for a moment. And, resting, looking from one to the other vaguely, the old question which traversed the sky of the soul perpetually, the vast, the general question which was apt to particularise itself at such moments as these, when she released faculties that had been on the strain, stood over her, paused over her, darkened over her. What is the meaning of life? That was all—a simple question; one that tended to close in on one with years. The great revelation had never come. The great revelation perhaps never did come. Instead there were little daily miracles, illuminations, matches struck unexpectedly in the dark; here was one. This, that, and the other; herself and Charles Tansley and the breaking wave; Mrs. Ramsay bringing them together; Mrs. Ramsay saying, "Life stand still here"; Mrs. Ramsay making of the moment something permanent (as in another sphere Lily herself tried to make of the moment something permanent)—this was of the nature of a revelation. In the midst of chaos there was shape; this eternal passing and flowing (she looked at the clouds going and the leaves shaking) was struck into stability. Life stand still here, Mrs. Ramsay said. "Mrs. Ramsay! Mrs. Ramsay!" she repeated. She owed it all to her.

All was silence. Nobody seemed yet to be stirring in the house. She looked at it there sleeping in the early sunlight with its windows green and blue with the reflected leaves. The faint thought she was thinking of Mrs. Ramsay seemed in consonance with this quiet house; this smoke; this fine early morning air. Faint and unreal, it was amazingly pure and exciting. She hoped nobody would open the window or come out of the house, but that she might be left alone to go on thinking, to go on painting. She turned to her canvas. But impelled by some curiosity, driven by the discomfort of the sympathy which she held undischarged, she walked a pace or so to the end of the lawn to see whether, down there on the beach, she could see that little company setting sail. Down there among the little boats which floated, some with their sails furled, some slowly, for it was very calm moving away, there was one rather apart from the others. The sail was even now being hoisted. She decided that there in that very distant and entirely silent little boat Mr. Ramsay was sitting with Cam and James. Now they had got the sail up; now after a little flagging and hesitation the sails filled and, shrouded in profound silence, she watched the boat take its way with deliberation past the other boats out to sea.

IV

The sails flapped over their heads. The water chuckled and slapped the sides of the boat, which drowsed motionless in the sun. Now and then the sails rippled with a little breeze in them, but the ripple ran over them and ceased. The boat made no motion at all. Mr. Ramsay sat in the middle of the boat. He would be impatient in a moment, James thought, and Cam thought, looking at her father, who sat in

the middle of the boat between them (James steered; Cam sat alone
in the bow) with his legs tightly curled. He hated hanging about. Sure
enough, after fidgeting a second or two, he said something sharp to
Macalister's boy, who got out his oars and began to row. But their
father, they knew, would never be content until they were flying along.
He would keep looking for a breeze, fidgeting, saying things under his
breath, which Macalister and Macalister's boy would overhear, and
they would both be made horribly uncomfortable. He had made them
come. He had forced them to come. In their anger they hoped that the
breeze would never rise, that he might be thwarted in every possible
way, since he had forced them to come against their wills.

All the way down to the beach they had lagged behind together,
though he bade them "Walk up, walk up," without speaking. Their
heads were bent down, their heads were pressed down by some
remorseless gale. Speak to him they could not. They must come; they
must follow. They must walk behind him carrying brown paper parcels. But they vowed, in silence, as they walked, to stand by each
other and carry out the great compact—to resist tyranny to the death.
So there they would sit, one at one end of the boat, one at the other,
in silence. They would say nothing, only look at him now and then
where he sat with his legs twisted, frowning and fidgeting, and pish-
ing and pshawing and muttering things to himself, and waiting impatiently for a breeze. And they hoped it would be calm. They hoped he
would be thwarted. They hoped the whole expedition would fail, and
they would have to put back, with their parcels, to the beach.

But now, when Macalister's boy had rowed a little way out, the
sails slowly swung round, the boat quickened itself, flattened itself,
and shot off. Instantly, as if some great strain had been relieved,
Mr. Ramsay uncurled his legs, took out his tobacco pouch, handed
it with a little grunt to Macalister, and felt, they knew, for all they
suffered, perfectly content. Now they would sail on for hours like
this, and Mr. Ramsay would ask old Macalister a question—about
the great storm last winter probably—and old Macalister would
answer it, and they would puff their pipes together, and Macalister
would take a tarry rope in his fingers, tying or untying some knot,
and the boy would fish, and never say a word to any one. James would
be forced to keep his eye all the time on the sail. For if he forgot,
then the sail puckered and shivered, and the boat slackened, and
Mr. Ramsay would say sharply, "Look out! Look out!" and old Macalister would turn slowly on his seat. So they heard Mr. Ramsay asking some question about the great storm at Christmas. "She comes
driving round the point," old Macalister said, describing the great
storm last Christmas, when ten ships had been driven into the bay
for shelter, and he had seen "one there, one there, one there" (he
pointed slowly round the bay. Mr. Ramsay followed him, turning his

head). He had seen four men clinging to the mast. Then she was gone. "And at last we shoved her off," he went on (but in their anger and their silence they only caught a word here and there, sitting at opposite ends of the boat, united by their compact to fight tyranny to the death). At last they had shoved her off, they had launched the lifeboat, and they had got her out past the point—Macalister told the story; and though they only caught a word here and there, they were conscious all the time of their father—how he leant forward, how he brought his voice into tune with Macalister's voice; how, puffing at his pipe, and looking there and there where Macalister pointed, he relished the thought of the storm and the dark night and the fishermen striving there. He liked that men should labour and sweat on the windy beach at night; pitting muscle and brain against the waves and the wind; he liked men to work like that, and women to keep house, and sit beside sleeping children indoors, while men were drowned, out there in a storm. So James could tell, so Cam could tell (they looked at him, they looked at each other), from his toss and his vigilance and the ring in his voice, and the little tinge of Scottish accent which came into his voice, making him seem like a peasant himself, as he questioned Macalister about the eleven ships that had been driven into the bay in a storm. Three had sunk.

He looked proudly where Macalister pointed; and Cam thought, feeling proud of him without knowing quite why, had he been there he would have launched the lifeboat, he would have reached the wreck, Cam thought. He was so brave, he was so adventurous, Cam thought. But she remembered. There was the compact; to resist tyranny to the death. Their grievance weighed them down. They had been forced; they had been bidden. He had borne them down once more with his gloom and his authority, making them do his bidding, on this fine morning, come, because he wished it, carrying these parcels, to the Lighthouse; take part in these rites he went through for his own pleasure in memory of dead people, which they hated, so that they lagged after him, and all the pleasure of the day was spoilt.

Yes, the breeze was freshening. The boat was leaning, the water was sliced sharply and fell away in green cascades, in bubbles, in cataracts. Cam looked down into the foam, into the sea with all its treasure in it, and its speed hypnotised her, and the tie between her and James sagged a little. It slackened a little. She began to think, How fast it goes. Where are we going? and the movement hypnotised her, while James, with his eye fixed on the sail and on the horizon, steered grimly. But he began to think as he steered that he might escape; he might be quit of it all. They might land somewhere; and be free then. Both of them, looking at each other for a moment, had a sense of escape and exaltation, what with the speed and the change. But the breeze bred in Mr. Ramsay too the same excitement, and, as old Macalister turned to fling his line overboard, he cried out aloud,

"We perished," and then again, "each alone."[1] And then with his usual spasm of repentance or shyness, pulled himself up, and waved his hand towards the shore.

"See the little house," he said pointing, wishing Cam to look. She raised herself reluctantly and looked. But which was it? She could no longer make out, there on the hillside, which was their house. All looked distant and peaceful and strange. The shore seemed refined, far away, unreal. Already the little distance they had sailed had put them far from it and given it the changed look, the composed look, of something receding in which one has no longer any part. Which was their house? She could not see it.

"But I beneath a rougher sea," Mr. Ramsay murmured. He had found the house and so seeing it, he had also seen himself there; he had seen himself walking on the terrace, alone. He was walking up and down between the urns; and he seemed to himself very old and bowed. Sitting in the boat, he bowed, he crouched himself, acting instantly his part—the part of a desolate man, widowed, bereft; and so called up before him in hosts people sympathising with him; staged for himself as he sat in the boat, a little drama; which required of him decrepitude and exhaustion and sorrow (he raised his hands and looked at the thinness of them, to confirm his dream) and then there was given him in abundance women's sympathy, and he imagined how they would soothe him and sympathise with him, and so getting in his dream some reflection of the exquisite pleasure women's sympathy was to him, he sighed and said gently and mournfully,

> But I beneath a rougher sea
> Was whelmed in deeper gulfs than he,

so that the mournful words were heard quite clearly by them all. Cam half started on her seat. It shocked her—it outraged her. The movement roused her father; and he shuddered, and broke off, exclaiming: "Look! Look!" so urgently that James also turned his head to look over his shoulder at the island. They all looked. They looked at the island.

But Cam could see nothing. She was thinking how all those paths and the lawn, thick and knotted with the lives they had lived there, were gone: were rubbed out; were past; were unreal, and now this was real; the boat and the sail with its patch; Macalister with his earrings; the noise of the waves—all this was real. Thinking this, she was murmuring to herself, "We perished, each alone," for her father's words broke and broke again in her mind, when her father, seeing her gazing

1. Mr. Ramsay continues to recite Cowper's "The Castaway" (see note 1 p. 108).

so vaguely, began to tease her. Didn't she know the points of the
compass? he asked. Didn't she know the North from the South? Did
she really think they lived right out there? And he pointed again,
and showed her where their house was, there, by those trees. He
wished she would try to be more accurate, he said: "Tell me—which is
East, which is West?" he said, half laughing at her, half scolding her,
for he could not understand the state of mind of any one, not absolutely imbecile, who did not know the points of the compass. Yet
she did not know. And seeing her gazing, with her vague, now rather
frightened, eyes fixed where no house was Mr. Ramsay forgot his
dream; how he walked up and down between the urns on the terrace;
how the arms were stretched out to him. He thought, women are
always like that; the vagueness of their minds is hopeless; it was a
thing he had never been able to understand; but so it was. It had been
so with her—his wife. They could not keep anything clearly fixed in
their minds. But he had been wrong to be angry with her; moreover,
did he not rather like this vagueness in women? It was part of their
extraordinary charm. I will make her smile at me, he thought. She
looks frightened. She was so silent. He clutched his fingers, and
determined that his voice and his face and all the quick expressive
gestures which had been at his command making people pity him and
praise him all these years should subdue themselves. He would make
her smile at him. He would find some simple easy thing to say to her.
But what? For, wrapped up in his work as he was, he forgot the sort of
thing one said. There was a puppy. They had a puppy. Who was looking after the puppy today? he asked. Yes, thought James pitilessly, seeing his sister's head against the sail, now she will give way. I shall be
left to fight the tyrant alone. The compact would be left to him to
carry out. Cam would never resist tyranny to the death, he thought
grimly, watching her face, sad, sulky, yielding. And as sometimes happens when a cloud falls on a green hillside and gravity descends and
there among all the surrounding hills is gloom and sorrow, and it
seems as if the hills themselves must ponder the fate of the clouded,
the darkened, either in pity, or maliciously rejoicing in her dismay: so
Cam now felt herself overcast, as she sat there among calm, resolute
people and wondered how to answer her father about the puppy; how
to resist his entreaty—forgive me, care for me; while James the law-
giver, with the tablets of eternal wisdom laid open on his knee (his
hand on the tiller had become symbolical to her), said, Resist him.
Fight him. He said so rightly; justly. For they must fight tyranny to the
death, she thought. Of all human qualities she reverenced justice
most. Her brother was most god-like, her father most suppliant. And
to which did she yield, she thought, sitting between them, gazing at
the shore whose points were all unknown to her, and thinking how

the lawn and the terrace and the house were smoothed away now and peace dwelt there.

"Jasper," she said sullenly. He'd look after the puppy.

And what was she going to call him? her father persisted. He had had a dog when he was a little boy, called Frisk. She'll give way, James thought, as he watched a look come upon her face, a look he remembered. They look down he thought, at their knitting or something. Then suddenly they look up. There was a flash of blue, he remembered, and then somebody sitting with him laughed, surrendered, and he was very angry. It must have been his mother, he thought, sitting on a low chair, with his father standing over her. He began to search among the infinite series of impressions which time had laid down, leaf upon leaf, fold upon fold softly, incessantly upon his brain; among scents, sounds; voices, harsh, hollow, sweet; and lights passing, and brooms tapping; and the wash and hush of the sea, how a man had marched up and down and stopped dead, upright, over them. Meanwhile, he noticed, Cam dabbled her fingers in the water, and stared at the shore and said nothing. No, she won't give way, he thought; she's different, he thought. Well, if Cam would not answer him, he would not bother her Mr. Ramsay decided, feeling in his pocket for a book. But she would answer him; she wished, passionately, to move some obstacle that lay upon her tongue and to say, Oh, yes, Frisk. I'll call him Frisk. She wanted even to say, Was that the dog that found its way over the moor alone? But try as she might, she could think of nothing to say like that, fierce and loyal to the compact, yet passing on to her father, unsuspected by James, a private token of the love she felt for him. For she thought, dabbling her hand (and now Macalister's boy had caught a mackerel, and it lay kicking on the floor, with blood on its gills) for she thought, looking at James who kept his eyes dispassionately on the sail, or glanced now and then for a second at the horizon, you're not exposed to it, to this pressure and division of feeling, this extraordinary temptation. Her father was feeling in his pockets; in another second, he would have found his book. For no one attracted her more; his hands were beautiful, and his feet, and his voice, and his words, and his haste, and his temper, and his oddity, and his passion, and his saying straight out before every one, we perish, each alone, and his remoteness. (He had opened his book.) But what remained intolerable, she thought, sitting upright, and watching Macalister's boy tug the hook out of the gills of another fish, was that crass blindness and tyranny of his which had poisoned her childhood and raised bitter storms, so that even now she woke in the night trembling with rage and remembered some command of his; some insolence: "Do this," "Do that," his dominance: his "Submit to me."

So she said nothing, but looked doggedly and sadly at the shore, wrapped in its mantle of peace; as if the people there had fallen asleep, she thought; were free like smoke, were free to come and go like ghosts. They have no suffering there, she thought.

V

Yes, that is their boat, Lily Briscoe decided, standing on the edge of the lawn. It was the boat with greyish-brown sails, which she saw now flatten itself upon the water and shoot off across the bay. There he sits, she thought, and the children are quite silent still. And she could not reach him either. The sympathy she had not given him weighed her down. It made it difficult for her to paint.

She had always found him difficult. She never had been able to praise him to his face, she remembered. And that reduced their relationship to something neutral, without that element of sex in it which made his manner to Minta so gallant, almost gay. He would pick a flower for her, lend her his books. But could he believe that Minta read them? She dragged them about the garden, sticking in leaves to mark the place.

"D'you remember, Mr. Carmichael?" she was inclined to ask, looking at the old man. But he had pulled his hat half over his forehead; he was asleep, or he was dreaming, or he was lying there catching words, she supposed.

"D'you remember?" she felt inclined to ask him as she passed him, thinking again of Mrs. Ramsay on the beach; the cask bobbing up and down; and the pages flying. Why, after all these years had that survived, ringed round, lit up, visible to the last detail, with all before it blank and all after it blank, for miles and miles?

"Is it a boat? Is it a cork?" she would say, Lily repeated, turning back, reluctantly again, to her canvas. Heaven be praised for it, the problem of space remained, she thought, taking up her brush again. It glared at her. The whole mass of the picture was poised upon that weight. Beautiful and bright it should be on the surface, feathery and evanescent, one colour melting into another like the colours on a butterfly's wing; but beneath the fabric must be clamped together with bolts of iron. It was to be a thing you could ruffle with your breath; and a thing you could not dislodge with a team of horses. And she began to lay on a red, a grey, and she began to model her way into the hollow there. At the same time, she seemed to be sitting beside Mrs. Ramsay on the beach.

"Is it a boat? Is it a cask?" Mrs. Ramsay said. And she began hunting round for her spectacles. And she sat, having found them, silent, looking out to sea. And Lily, painting steadily, felt as if a door had opened, and one went in and stood gazing silently about in a high cathedral-like place, very dark, very solemn. Shouts came from a world far away. Steamers vanished in stalks of smoke on the horizon. Charles threw stones and sent them skipping.

Mrs. Ramsay sat silent. She was glad, Lily thought, to rest in silence, uncommunicative; to rest in the extreme obscurity of human relationships. Who knows what we are, what we feel? Who knows even at the moment of intimacy, This is knowledge? Aren't things spoilt then, Mrs. Ramsay may have asked (it seemed to have happened so often, this silence by her side) by saying them? Aren't we more expressive thus? The moment at least seemed extraordinarily fertile. She rammed a little hole in the sand and covered it up, by way of burying in it the perfection of the moment. It was like a drop of silver in which one dipped and illumined the darkness of the past.

Lily stepped back to get her canvas—so—into perspective. It was an odd road to be walking, this of painting. Out and out one went, further and further, until at last one seemed to be on a narrow plank, perfectly alone, over the sea. And as she dipped into the blue paint, she dipped too into the past there. Now Mrs. Ramsay got up, she remembered. It was time to go back to the house—time for luncheon. And they all walked up from the beach together, she walking behind with William Bankes, and there was Minta in front of them with a hole in her stocking. How that little round hole of pink heel seemed to flaunt itself before them! How William Bankes deplored it, without, so far as she could remember, saying anything about it! It meant to him the annihilation of womanhood, and dirt and disorder, and servants leaving and beds not made at mid-day— all the things he most abhorred. He had a way of shuddering and spreading his fingers out as if to cover an unsightly object which he did now—holding his hand in front of him. And Minta walked on ahead, and presumably Paul met her and she went off with Paul in the garden.

The Rayleys, thought Lily Briscoe, squeezing her tube of green paint. She collected her impressions of the Rayleys. Their lives appeared to her in a series of scenes; one, on the staircase at dawn. Paul had come in and gone to bed early; Minta was late. There was Minta, wreathed, tinted, garish on the stairs about three o'clock in the morning. Paul came out in his pyjamas carrying a poker in case of burglars. Minta was eating a sandwich, standing half-way up by a window, in the cadaverous early morning light, and the carpet had a hole in it. But what did they say? Lily asked herself, as if by looking she could hear them. Minta went on eating her sandwich, annoyingly, while he spoke something violent, abusing her, in a mutter so as not to wake the children, the two little boys. He was withered, drawn; she flamboyant, careless. For things had worked loose after the first year or so; the marriage had turned out rather badly.

And this, Lily thought, taking the green paint on her brush, this making up scenes about them, is what we call "knowing" people, "thinking" of them, "being fond" of them! Not a word of it was true; she had made it up; but it was what she knew them by all the same. She went on tunnelling her way into her picture, into the past.

Another time, Paul said he "played chess in coffee-houses." She had built up a whole structure of imagination on that saying too. She remembered how, as he said it, she thought how he rang up the servant, and she said, "Mrs. Rayley's out, sir," and he decided that he would not come home either. She saw him sitting in the corner of some lugubrious place where the smoke attached itself to the red plush seats, and the waitresses got to know you, and he played chess with a little man who was in the tea trade and lived at Surbiton,[1] but that was all Paul knew about him. And then Minta was out when he came home and then there was that scene on the stairs, when he got the poker in case of burglars (no doubt to frighten her too) and spoke so bitterly, saying she had ruined his life. At any rate when she went down to see them at a cottage near Rickmansworth,[2] things were horribly strained. Paul took her down the garden to look at the Belgian hares which he bred, and Minta followed them, singing, and put her bare arm on his shoulder, lest he should tell her anything.

Minta was bored by hares, Lily thought. But Minta never gave herself away. She never said things like that about playing chess in coffee-houses. She was far too conscious, far too wary. But to go on with their story—they had got through the dangerous stage by now. She had been staying with them last summer some time and the car broke down and Minta had to hand him his tools. He sat on the road mending the car, and it was the way she gave him the tools—business-like, straightforward, friendly—that proved it was all right now. They were "in love" no longer; no, he had taken up with another woman, a serious woman, with her hair in a plait and a case in her hand (Minta had described her gratefully, almost admiringly), who went to meetings and shared Paul's views (they had got more and more pronounced) about the taxation of land values and a capital levy.[3] Far from breaking up the marriage, that alliance had righted it. They were excellent friends, obviously, as he sat on the road and she handed him his tools.

So that was the story of the Rayleys, Lily thought. She imagined herself telling it to Mrs. Ramsay, who would be full of curiosity to

1. A suburban neighborhood of southwest London next to the River Thames.
2. A town in southwest Hertfordshire, England, about seventeen miles northwest of central London.
3. Liberal governments in early twentieth-century Britain proposed taxing wealth in the form of land or other privately owned assets (as distinct from taxing income) to reduce poverty and strengthen the social safety net: such proposals were part of the People's Budget of 1909, and in 1924 the nationalization of land was proposed. See note 4 p. 9.

know what had become of the Rayleys. She would feel a little triumphant, telling Mrs. Ramsay that the marriage had not been a
success.

But the dead, thought Lily, encountering some obstacle in her
design which made her pause and ponder, stepping back a foot or so,
oh, the dead! she murmured, one pitied them, one brushed them
aside, one had even a little contempt for them. They are at our mercy.
Mrs. Ramsay has faded and gone, she thought. We can over-ride her
wishes, improve away her limited, old-fashioned ideas. She recedes
further and further from us. Mockingly she seemed to see her there
at the end of the corridor of years saying, of all incongruous things,
"Marry, marry!" (sitting very upright early in the morning with the
birds beginning to cheep in the garden outside). And one would
have to say to her, It has all gone against your wishes. They're happy
like that; I'm happy like this. Life has changed completely. At that all
her being, even her beauty, became for a moment, dusty and out of
date. For a moment Lily, standing there, with the sun hot on her back,
summing up the Rayleys, triumphed over Mrs. Ramsay, who would
never know how Paul went to coffee-houses and had a mistress; how
he sat on the ground and Minta handed him his tools; how she stood
here painting, had never married, not even William Bankes.

Mrs. Ramsay had planned it. Perhaps, had she lived, she would
have compelled it. Already that summer he was "the kindest of men."
He was "the first scientist of his age, my husband says." He was also
"poor William—it makes me so unhappy, when I go to see him, to
find nothing nice in his house—no one to arrange the flowers." So
they were sent for walks together, and she was told, with that faint
touch of irony that made Mrs. Ramsay slip through one's fingers,
that she had a scientific mind; she liked flowers; she was so exact.
What was this mania of hers for marriage? Lily wondered, stepping
to and fro from her easel.

(Suddenly, as suddenly as a star slides in the sky, a reddish light
seemed to burn in her mind, covering Paul Rayley, issuing from him.
It rose like a fire sent up in token of some celebration by savages on
a distant beach. She heard the roar and the crackle. The whole sea
for miles round ran red and gold. Some winey smell mixed with it
and intoxicated her, for she felt again her own headlong desire to
throw herself off the cliff and be drowned looking for a pearl brooch
on a beach. And the roar and the crackle repelled her with fear and
disgust, as if while she saw its splendour and power she saw too how
it fed on the treasure of the house, greedily, disgustingly, and she
loathed it. But for a sight, for a glory it surpassed everything in her
experience, and burnt year after year like a signal fire on a desert
island at the edge of the sea, and one had only to say "in love" and
instantly, as happened now, up rose Paul's fire again. And it sank

and she said to herself, laughing, "The Rayleys"; how Paul went to coffee-houses and played chess.)

She had only escaped by the skin of her teeth though, she thought. She had been looking at the table-cloth, and it had flashed upon her that she would move the tree to the middle, and need never marry anybody, and she had felt an enormous exultation. She had felt, now she could stand up to Mrs. Ramsay—a tribute to the astonishing power that Mrs. Ramsay had over one. Do this, she said, and one did it. Even her shadow at the window with James was full of authority. She remembered how William Bankes had been shocked by her neglect of the significance of mother and son. Did she not admire their beauty? he said. But William, she remembered, had listened to her with his wise child's eyes when she explained how it was not irreverence: how a light there needed a shadow there and so on. She did not intend to disparage a subject which, they agreed, Raphael had treated divinely.[4] She was not cynical. Quite the contrary. Thanks to his scientific mind he understood—a proof of disinterested intelligence which had pleased her and comforted her enormously. One could talk of painting then seriously to a man. Indeed, his friendship had been one of the pleasures of her life. She loved William Bankes.

They went to Hampton Court[5] and he always left her, like the perfect gentleman he was, plenty of time to wash her hands, while he strolled by the river. That was typical of their relationship. Many things were left unsaid. Then they strolled through the courtyards, and admired, summer after summer, the proportions and the flowers, and he would tell her things, about perspective, about architecture, as they walked, and he would stop to look at a tree, or the view over the lake, and admire a child—(it was his great grief—he had no daughter) in the vague aloof way that was natural to a man who spent so much time in laboratories that the world when he came out seemed to dazzle him, so that he walked slowly, lifted his hand to screen his eyes and paused, with his head thrown back, merely to breathe the air. Then he would tell her how his housekeeper was on her holiday; he must buy a new carpet for the staircase. Perhaps she would go with him to buy a new carpet for the staircase. And once something led him to talk about the Ramsays and he had said how when he first saw her she had been wearing a grey hat; she was not more than nineteen or twenty. She was astonishingly beautiful. There he stood looking down the avenue at Hampton Court as if he could see her there among the fountains.

4. See note 6 p. 42.
5. A palace built in the sixteenth century on the Thames River southwest of London, once a residence of Henry VIII (1491–1547, king of England 1509 until his death); known for its formal gardens, including a maze, and a popular excursion for Londoners.

She looked now at the drawing-room step. She saw, through William's eyes, the shape of a woman, peaceful and silent, with downcast eyes. She sat musing, pondering (she was in grey that day, Lily thought). Her eyes were bent. She would never lift them. Yes, thought Lily, looking intently, I must have seen her look like that, but not in grey; nor so still, nor so young, nor so peaceful. The figure came readily enough. She was astonishingly beautiful, as William said. But beauty was not everything. Beauty had this penalty—it came too readily, came too completely. It stilled life—froze it. One forgot the little agitations; the flush, the pallor, some queer distortion, some light or shadow, which made the face unrecognisable for a moment and yet added a quality one saw for ever after. It was simpler to smooth that all out under the cover of beauty. But what was the look she had, Lily wondered, when she clapped her deer-stalker's hat on her head, or ran across the grass, or scolded Kennedy, the gardener? Who could tell her? Who could help her?

Against her will she had come to the surface, and found herself half out of the picture, looking, a little dazedly, as if at unreal things, at Mr. Carmichael. He lay on his chair with his hands clasped above his paunch not reading, or sleeping, but basking like a creature gorged with existence. His book had fallen on to the grass.

She wanted to go straight up to him and say, "Mr. Carmichael!" Then he would look up benevolently as always, from his smoky vague green eyes. But one only woke people if one knew what one wanted to say to them. And she wanted to say not one thing, but everything. Little words that broke up the thought and dismembered it said nothing. "About life, about death; about Mrs. Ramsay"—no, she thought, one could say nothing to nobody. The urgency of the moment always missed its mark. Words fluttered sideways and struck the object inches too low. Then one gave it up; then the idea sunk back again; then one became like most middle-aged people, cautious, furtive, with wrinkles between the eyes and a look of perpetual apprehension. For how could one express in words these emotions of the body? express that emptiness there? (She was looking at the drawing-room steps; they looked extraordinarily empty.) It was one's body feeling, not one's mind. The physical sensations that went with the bare look of the steps had become suddenly extremely unpleasant. To want and not to have, sent all up her body a hardness, a hollowness, a strain. And then to want and not to have—to want and want—how that wrung the heart, and wrung it again and again! Oh, Mrs. Ramsay! she called out silently, to that essence which sat by the boat, that abstract one made of her, that woman in grey, as if to abuse her for having gone, and then having gone, come back again. It had seemed so safe, thinking of her. Ghost, air, nothingness, a thing you could play with easily and safely at any time of day or night, she had been that, and then suddenly she put her hand out and wrung the heart thus. Suddenly, the empty drawing-room steps, the frill of the chair inside, the puppy tumbling on the terrace, the whole wave and whisper of the garden became like curves and arabesques flourishing round a centre of complete emptiness.

"What does it mean? How do you explain it all?" she wanted to say, turning to Mr. Carmichael again. For the whole world seemed to have dissolved in this early morning hour into a pool of thought, a deep basin of reality, and one could almost fancy that had Mr. Carmichael spoken, for instance, a little tear would have rent the surface pool. And then? Something would emerge. A hand would be shoved up, a blade would be flashed.[6] It was nonsense of course.

A curious notion came to her that he did after all hear the things she could not say. He was an inscrutable old man, with the yellow stain on his beard, and his poetry, and his puzzles, sailing serenely through a world which satisfied all his wants, so that she thought he had only to put down his hand where he lay on the lawn to fish up anything he wanted. She looked at her picture. That would have been his answer, presumably—how "you" and "I" and "she" pass and vanish; nothing stays; all changes; but not words, not paint. Yet it would be hung in the attics, she thought; it would be rolled up and flung under a sofa; yet even so, even of a picture like that, it was true. One might say, even of this scrawl, not of that actual picture, perhaps, but of what it attempted, that it "remained for ever," she was going to say, or, for the words spoken sounded even to herself, too boastful, to hint, wordlessly; when, looking at the picture, she was surprised to find that she could not see it. Her eyes were full of a hot liquid (she did not think of tears at first) which, without disturbing the firmness of her lips, made the air thick, rolled down her cheeks. She had perfect control of herself—Oh, yes!—in every other way. Was she crying then for Mrs. Ramsay, without being aware of any unhappiness? She addressed old Mr. Carmichael again. What was it then? What did it mean? Could things thrust their hands up and grip one; could the blade cut; the fist grasp? Was there no safety? No learning by heart of the ways of the world? No guide, no shelter, but all was miracle, and leaping from the pinnacle of a tower into the air? Could it be, even for elderly people, that this was life?— startling, unexpected, unknown? For one moment she felt that if

6. Evokes an episode from the legend of King Arthur and the knights of the Round Table, as retold in Tennyson's *Idylls of the King* (published serially between 1857 and 1888). Near the end, as King Arthur is dying, the Lady of the Lake reclaims his magic sword: "So flashed and fell the brand Excalibur: / But ere he dipped the surface, rose an arm / Clothed in white samite, mystic, wonderful, / And caught him by the hilt" ("The Passing of Arthur," 1869, lines 310–313; *The Norton Anthology of English Literature*, 10th ed., vol. E, p. 241).

they both got up, here, now on the lawn, and demanded an explanation, why was it so short, why was it so inexplicable, said it with violence, as two fully equipped human beings from whom nothing should be hid might speak, then, beauty would roll itself up; the space would fill; those empty flourishes would form into shape; if they shouted loud enough Mrs. Ramsay would return. "Mrs. Ramsay!" she said aloud, "Mrs. Ramsay!" The tears ran down her face.

VI

[Macalister's boy took one of the fish and cut a square out of its side to bait his hook with. The mutilated body (it was alive still) was thrown back into the sea.]

VII

"Mrs. Ramsay!" Lily cried, "Mrs. Ramsay!" But nothing happened. The pain increased. That anguish could reduce one to such a pitch of imbecility, she thought! Anyhow the old man had not heard her. He remained benignant, calm—if one chose to think it, sublime. Heaven be praised, no one had heard her cry that ignominious cry, stop pain, stop! She had not obviously taken leave of her senses. No one had seen her step off her strip of board into the waters of annihilation. She remained a skimpy old maid, holding a paint-brush.

And now slowly the pain of the want, and the bitter anger (to be called back, just as she thought she would never feel sorrow for Mrs. Ramsay again. Had she missed her among the coffee cups at breakfast? not in the least) lessened; and of their anguish left, as antidote, a relief that was balm in itself, and also, but more mysteriously, a sense of some one there, of Mrs. Ramsay, relieved for a moment of the weight that the world had put on her, staying lightly by her side and then (for this was Mrs. Ramsay in all her beauty) raising to her forehead a wreath of white flowers with which she went. Lily squeezed her tubes again. She attacked that problem of the hedge. It was strange how clearly she saw her, stepping with her usual quickness across fields among whose folds, purplish and soft, among whose flowers, hyacinths or lilies, she vanished. It was some trick of the painter's eye. For days after she had heard of her death she had seen her thus, putting her wreath to her forehead and going unquestioningly with her companion, a shade across the fields.[1] The sight, the phrase, had its power to console. Wherever she happened to be, painting, here, in the country or in London, the vision would come to her, and her eyes, half closing, sought something to base

1. Lily's vision of Mrs. Ramsay as a shade with a wreath of white flowers evokes the Elysian fields in the classical underworld; see also note 4 p. 25.

her vision on. She looked down the railway carriage, the omnibus; took a line from shoulder or cheek; looked at the windows opposite; at Piccadilly,[2] lamp-strung in the evening. All had been part of the fields of death. But always something—it might be a face, a voice, a paper boy crying *Standard, News*[3]—thrust through, snubbed her, waked her, required and got in the end an effort of attention, so that the vision must be perpetually remade. Now again, moved as she was by some instinctive need of distance and blue, she looked at the bay beneath her, making hillocks of the blue bars of the waves, and stony fields of the purpler spaces, again she was roused as usual by something incongruous. There was a brown spot in the middle of the bay. It was a boat. Yes, she realised that after a second. But whose boat? Mr. Ramsay's boat, she replied. Mr. Ramsay; the man who had marched past her, with his hand raised, aloof, at the head of a procession, in his beautiful boots, asking her for sympathy, which she had refused. The boat was now half way across the bay.

So fine was the morning except for a streak of wind here and there that the sea and sky looked all one fabric, as if sails were stuck high up in the sky, or the clouds had dropped down into the sea. A steamer far out at sea had drawn in the air a great scroll of smoke which stayed there curving and circling decoratively, as if the air were a fine gauze which held things and kept them softly in its mesh, only gently swaying them this way and that. And as happens sometimes when the weather is very fine, the cliffs looked as if they were conscious of the ships, and the ships looked as if they were conscious of the cliffs, as if they signalled to each other some message of their own. For sometimes quite close to the shore, the Lighthouse looked this morning in the haze an enormous distance away.

"Where are they now?" Lily thought, looking out to sea. Where was he, that very old man who had gone past her silently, holding a brown paper parcel under his arm? The boat was in the middle of the bay.

VIII

They don't feel a thing there, Cam thought, looking at the shore, which, rising and falling, became steadily more distant and more peaceful. Her hand cut a trail in the sea, as her mind made the green swirls and streaks into patterns and, numbed and shrouded, wandered in imagination in that underworld of waters where the pearls stuck in clusters to white sprays, where in the green light a change

2. A major road in the West End of London, with hotels and theaters.
3. The *Evening Standard* and the *Daily News* were the two evening newspapers in London at the time.

came over one's entire mind and one's body shone half transparent enveloped in a green cloak.

Then the eddy slackened round her hand. The rush of the water ceased; the world became full of little creaking and squeaking sounds. One heard the waves breaking and flapping against the side of the boat as if they were anchored in harbour. Everything became very close to one. For the sail, upon which James had his eyes fixed until it had become to him like a person whom he knew, sagged entirely; there they came to a stop, flapping about waiting for a breeze, in the hot sun, miles from shore, miles from the Lighthouse. Everything in the whole world seemed to stand still. The Lighthouse became immovable, and the line of the distant shore became fixed. The sun grew hotter and everybody seemed to come very close together and to feel each other's presence, which they had almost forgotten. Macalister's fishing line went plumb down into the sea. But Mr. Ramsay went on reading with his legs curled under him.

He was reading a little shiny book with covers mottled like a plover's egg.[1] Now and again, as they hung about in that horrid calm, he turned a page. And James felt that each page was turned with a peculiar gesture aimed at him: now assertively, now commandingly; now with the intention of making people pity him; and all the time, as his father read and turned one after another of those little pages, James kept dreading the moment when he would look up and speak sharply to him about something or other. Why were they lagging about here? he would demand, or something quite unreasonable like that. And if he does, James thought, then I shall take a knife and strike him to the heart.

He had always kept this old symbol of taking a knife and striking his father to the heart. Only now, as he grew older, and sat staring at his father in an impotent rage, it was not him, that old man reading, whom he wanted to kill, but it was the thing that descended on him—without his knowing it perhaps: that fierce sudden black-winged harpy,[2] with its talons and its beak all cold and hard, that struck and struck at you (he could feel the beak on his bare legs, where it had struck when he was a child) and then made off, and there he was again, an old man, very sad, reading his book. That he would kill, that he would strike to the heart. Whatever he did—(and he might do anything, he felt, looking at the Lighthouse and the distant shore) whether he was in a business, in a bank, a barrister, a

---

1. Plovers are small shorebirds; their eggs are typically tan or greenish and speckled with darker brown spots. They were once considered a delicacy, eaten boiled.
2. In classical mythology, a monster with a woman's face and body and a bird's wings and claws, often a minister of divine vengeance.

man at the head of some enterprise, that he would fight, that he would track down and stamp out—tyranny, despotism, he called it—making people do what they did not want to do, cutting off their right to speak. How could any of them say, But I won't, when he said, Come to the Lighthouse. Do this. Fetch me that. The black wings spread, and the hard beak tore. And then next moment, there he sat reading his book; and he might look up—one never knew—quite reasonably. He might talk to the Macalisters. He might be pressing a sovereign into some frozen old woman's hand in the street, James thought, and he might be shouting out at some fisherman's sports; he might be waving his arms in the air with excitement. Or he might sit at the head of the table dead silent from one end of dinner to the other. Yes, thought James, while the boat slapped and dawdled there in the hot sun; there was a waste of snow and rock very lonely and austere; and there he had come to feel, quite often lately, when his father said something or did something which surprised the others, there were two pairs of footprints only; his own and his father's. They alone knew each other. What then was this terror, this hatred? Turning back among the many leaves which the past had folded in him, peering into the heart of that forest where light and shade so chequer each other that all shape is distorted, and one blunders, now with the sun in one's eyes, now with a dark shadow, he sought an image to cool and detach and round off his feeling in a concrete shape. Suppose then that as a child sitting helpless in a perambula-tor, or on some one's knee, he had seen a waggon crush ignorantly and innocently, some one's foot? Suppose he had seen the foot first, in the grass, smooth, and whole; then the wheel; and the same foot, purple, crushed. But the wheel was innocent. So now, when his father came striding down the passage knocking them up early in the morning to go to the Lighthouse down it came over his foot, over Cam's foot, over anybody's foot. One sat and watched it.

But whose foot was he thinking of, and in what garden did all this happen? For one had settings for these scenes; trees that grew there; flowers; a certain light; a few figures. Everything tended to set itself in a garden where there was none of this gloom. None of this throw-ing of hands about; people spoke in an ordinary tone of voice. They went in and out all day long. There was an old woman gossiping in the kitchen; and the blinds were sucked in and out by the breeze; all was blowing, all was growing; and over all those plates and bowls and tall brandishing red and yellow flowers a very thin yellow veil would be drawn, like a vine leaf, at night. Things became stiller and darker at night. But the leaf-like veil was so fine, that lights lifted it, voices crinkled it; he could see through it a figure stooping, hear, coming close, going away, some dress rustling, some chain tinkling.

It was in this world that the wheel went over the person's foot. Something, he remembered, stayed and darkened over him; would not move; something flourished up in the air, something arid and sharp descended even there, like a blade, a scimitar, smiting through the leaves and flowers even of that happy world and making it shrivel and fall.

"It will rain," he remembered his father saying. "You won't be able to go to the Lighthouse."

The Lighthouse was then a silvery, misty-looking tower with a yellow eye, that opened suddenly, and softly in the evening. Now—

James looked at the Lighthouse. He could see the white-washed rocks; the tower, stark and straight; he could see that it was barred with black and white; he could see windows in it; he could even see washing spread on the rocks to dry. So that was the Lighthouse, was it?

No, the other was also the Lighthouse. For nothing was simply one thing. The other Lighthouse was true too. It was sometimes hardly to be seen across the bay. In the evening one looked up and saw the eye opening and shutting and the light seemed to reach them in that airy sunny garden where they sat.

But he pulled himself up. Whenever he said "they" or "a person," and then began hearing the rustle of some one coming, the tinkle of some one going, he became extremely sensitive to the presence of whoever might be in the room. It was his father now. The strain was acute. For in one moment if there was no breeze, his father would slap the covers of his book together, and say: "What's happening now? What are we dawdling about here for, eh?" as, once before he had brought his blade down among them on the terrace and she had gone stiff all over, and if there had been an axe handy, a knife, or anything with a sharp point he would have seized it and struck his father through the heart. She had gone stiff all over, and then, her arm slackening, so that he felt she listened to him no longer, she had risen somehow and gone away and left him there, impotent, ridiculous, sitting on the floor grasping a pair of scissors.

Not a breath of wind blew. The water chuckled and gurgled in the bottom of the boat where three or four mackerel beat their tails up and down in a pool of water not deep enough to cover them. At any moment Mr. Ramsay (he scarcely dared look at him) might rouse himself, shut his book, and say something sharp; but for the moment he was reading, so that James stealthily, as if he were stealing downstairs on bare feet, afraid of waking a watchdog by a creaking board, went on thinking what was she like, where did she go that day? He began following her from room to room and at last they came to a room where in a blue light, as if the reflection came from many china

dishes, she talked to somebody; he listened to her talking. She talked
to a servant, saying simply whatever came into her head. She alone
spoke the truth; to her alone could he speak it. That was the source
of her everlasting attraction for him, perhaps; she was a person to
whom one could say what came into one's head. But all the time he
thought of her, he was conscious of his father following his thought,
surveying it, making it shiver and falter. At last he ceased to think.

There he sat with his hand on the tiller in the sun, staring at the
Lighthouse, powerless to move, powerless to flick off these grains
of misery which settled on his mind one after another. A rope seemed
to bind him there, and his father had knotted it and he could only
escape by taking a knife and plunging it. . . . But at that moment the
sail swung slowly round, filled slowly out, the boat seemed to shake
herself, and then to move off half conscious in her sleep, and then
she woke and shot through the waves. The relief was extraordinary.
They all seemed to fall away from each other again and to be at their
ease and the fishing-lines slanted taut across the side of the boat.
But his father did not rouse himself. He only raised his right hand
mysteriously high in the air, and let it fall upon his knee again as if
he were conducting some secret symphony.

IX

(The sea without a stain on it, thought Lily Briscoe, still standing
and looking out over the bay. The sea stretched like silk across the
bay. Distance had an extraordinary power; they had been swallowed
up in it, she felt, they were gone for ever, they had become part of
the nature of things. It was so calm; it was so quiet. The steamer
itself had vanished, but the great scroll of smoke still hung in the
air and drooped like a flag mournfully in valediction.)

X

It was like that then, the island, thought Cam, once more drawing her fingers through the waves. She had never seen it from out at
sea before. It lay like that on the sea, did it, with a dent in the middle
and two sharp crags, and the sea swept in there, and spread away
for miles and miles on either side of the island. It was very small;
shaped something like a leaf stood on end. So we took a little boat,
she thought, beginning to tell herself a story of adventure about
escaping from a sinking ship. But with the sea streaming through
her fingers, a spray of seaweed vanishing behind them, she did not
want to tell herself seriously a story; it was the sense of adventure
and escape that she wanted, for she was thinking, as the boat sailed
on, how her father's anger about the points of the compass, James's
obstinacy about the compact, and her own anguish, all had slipped,

all had passed, all had streamed away. What then came next? Where were they going? From her hand, ice cold, held deep in the sea, there spurted up a fountain of joy at the change, at the escape, at the adventure (that she should be alive, that she should be there). And the drops falling from this sudden and unthinking fountain of joy fell here and there on the dark, the slumbrous shapes in her mind; shapes of a world not realised[1] but turning in their darkness, catching here and there, a spark of light; Greece, Rome, Constantinople. Small as it was, and shaped something like a leaf stood on its end with the gold-sprinkled waters flowing in and about it, it had, she supposed, a place in the universe—even that little island? The old gentlemen in the study she thought could have told her. Sometimes she strayed in from the garden purposely to catch them at it. There they were (it might be Mr. Carmichael or Mr. Bankes who was sitting with her father) sitting opposite each other in their low armchairs. They were crackling in front of them the pages of *The Times*, when she came in from the garden, all in a muddle, about something some one had said about Christ, or hearing that a mammoth had been dug up in a London street, or wondering what Napoleon was like.[2] Then they took all this with their clean hands (they wore grey-coloured clothes; they smelt of heather) and they brushed the scraps together, turning the paper, crossing their knees, and said something now and then very brief. Just to please herself she would take a book from the shelf and stand there, watching her father write, so equally, so neatly from one side of the page to another, with a little cough now and then, or something said briefly to the other old gentleman opposite. And she thought, standing there with her book open, one could let whatever one thought expand here like a leaf in water; and if it did well here, among the old gentlemen smoking and *The Times* crackling then it was right. And watching her father as he wrote in his study, she thought (now sitting in the boat) he was not vain, nor a tyrant and did not wish to make you pity him. Indeed, if he saw she was there, reading a book, he would ask her, as gently as any one could, Was there nothing he could give her?

Lest this should be wrong, she looked at him reading the little book with the shiny cover mottled like a plover's egg. No; it was right. Look at him now, she wanted to say aloud to James. (But James had his eye on the sail.) He is a sarcastic brute, James would say. He brings the talk round to himself and his books, James would say. He is intolerably egotistical. Worst of all, he is a tyrant. But look! she said,

1. Alludes to "Ode: Intimations of Immortality" by William Wordsworth, lines 139–45; see note 3 p. 116.
2. The topics the men discuss include the theory of evolution, based in part on the discovery of extinct species ("a mammoth had been dug up in a London street") and still controversial at the time.

looking at him. Look at him now. She looked at him reading the little book with his legs curled; the little book whose yellowish pages she knew, without knowing what was written on them. It was small; it was closely printed; on the fly-leaf, she knew, he had written that he had spent fifteen francs on dinner;[3] the wine had been so much; he had given so much to the waiter; all was added up neatly at the bottom of the page. But what might be written in the book which had rounded its edges off in his pocket, she did not know. What he thought they none of them knew. But he was absorbed in it, so that when he looked up, as he did now for an instant, it was not to see anything; it was to pin down some thought more exactly. That done, his mind flew back again and he plunged into his reading. He read, she thought, as if he were guiding something, or wheedling a large flock of sheep, or pushing his way up and up a single narrow path; and sometimes he went fast and straight, and broke his way through the bramble, and sometimes it seemed a branch struck at him, a bramble blinded him, but he was not going to let himself be beaten by that; on he went, tossing over page after page. And she went on telling herself a story about escaping from a sinking ship, for she was safe, while he sat there; safe, as she felt herself when she crept in from the garden, and took a book down, and the old gentleman, lowering the paper suddenly, said something very brief over the top of it about the character of Napoleon.

She gazed back over the sea, at the island. But the leaf was losing its sharpness. It was very small; it was very distant. The sea was more important now than the shore. Waves were all round them, tossing and sinking, with a log wallowing down one wave; a gull riding on another. About here, she thought, dabbling her fingers in the water, a ship had sunk, and she murmured, dreamily half asleep, how we perished, each alone.

XI

So much depends then, thought Lily Briscoe, looking at the sea which had scarcely a stain on it, which was so soft that the sails and the clouds seemed set in its blue, so much depends, she thought, upon distance: whether people are near us or far from us; for her feeling for Mr. Ramsay changed as he sailed further and further across the bay. It seemed to be elongated, stretched out; he seemed to become more and more remote. He and his children seemed to be swallowed up in that blue, that distance; but here, on the lawn, close at hand, Mr. Carmichael suddenly grunted. She laughed. He

---

3. Leslie Stephen owned a pocket-sized copy of Plato in which he had jotted the cost of a restaurant meal in France; *francs*: French currency, a franc being worth about twenty US cents at that time.

clawed his book up from the grass. He settled into his chair again puffing and blowing like some sea monster. That was different altogether, because he was so near. And now again all was quiet. They must be out of bed by this time, she supposed, looking at the house, but nothing appeared there. But then, she remembered, they had always made off directly a meal was over, on business of their own. It was all in keeping with this silence, this emptiness, and the unreality of the early morning hour. It was a way things had sometimes, she thought, lingering for a moment and looking at the long glittering windows and the plume of blue smoke: they became unreal. So coming back from a journey, or after an illness, before habits had spun themselves across the surface, one felt that same unreality, which was so startling; felt something emerge. Life was most vivid then. One could be at one's ease. Mercifully one need not say, very briskly, crossing the lawn to greet old Mrs. Beckwith, who would be coming out to find a corner to sit in, "Oh, good-morning, Mrs. Beckwith! What a lovely day! Are you going to be so bold as to sit in the sun? Jasper's hidden the chairs. Do let me find you one!" and all the rest of the usual chatter. One need not speak at all. One glided, one shook one's sails (there was a good deal of movement in the bay, boats were starting off) between things, beyond things. Empty it was not, but full to the brim. She seemed to be standing up to the lips in some substance, to move and float and sink in it, yes, for these waters were unfathomably deep. Into them had spilled so many lives. The Ramsays'; the children's; and all sorts of waifs and strays of things besides. A washer-woman with her basket; a rook, a red-hot poker; the purples and grey-greens of flowers: some common feeling held the whole.

It was some such feeling of completeness perhaps which, ten years ago, standing almost where she stood now, had made her say that she must be in love with the place. Love had a thousand shapes. There might be lovers whose gift it was to choose out the elements of things and place them together and so, giving them a wholeness not theirs in life, make of some scene, or meeting of people (all now gone and separate), one of those globed compacted things over which thought lingers, and love plays.

Her eyes rested on the brown speck of Mr. Ramsay's sailing boat. They would be at the Lighthouse by lunch time she supposed. But the wind had freshened, and, as the sky changed slightly and the sea changed slightly and the boats altered their positions, the view, which a moment before had seemed miraculously fixed, was now unsatisfactory. The wind had blown the trail of smoke about; there was something displeasing about the placing of the ships.

The disproportion there seemed to upset some harmony in her own mind. She felt an obscure distress. It was confirmed when she

turned to her picture. She had been wasting her morning. For whatever reason she could not achieve that razor edge of balance between
two opposite forces; Mr. Ramsay and the picture; which was necessary. There was something perhaps wrong with the design? Was it,
she wondered, that the line of the wall wanted breaking, was it that
the mass of the trees was too heavy? She smiled ironically; for had
she not thought, when she began, that she had solved her problem?

What was the problem then? She must try to get hold of something
that evaded her. It evaded her when she thought of Mrs. Ramsay; it
evaded her now when she thought of her picture. Phrases came.
Visions came. Beautiful pictures. Beautiful phrases. But what she
wished to get hold of was that very jar on the nerves, the thing itself
before it has been made anything. Get that and start afresh; get that
and start afresh; she said desperately, pitching herself firmly again
before her easel. It was a miserable machine, an inefficient machine,
she thought, the human apparatus for painting or for feeling; it always
broke down at the critical moment; heroically, one must force it on.
She stared, frowning. There was the hedge, sure enough. But one got
nothing by soliciting urgently. One got only a glare in the eye from
looking at the line of the wall, or from thinking—she wore a grey hat.
She was astonishingly beautiful. Let it come, she thought, if it will
come. For there are moments when one can neither think nor feel.
And if one can neither think nor feel, she thought, where is one?

Here on the grass, on the ground, she thought, sitting down, and
examining with her brush a little colony of plantains.[1] For the lawn
was very rough. Here sitting on the world, she thought, for she could
not shake herself free from the sense that everything this morning
was happening for the first time, perhaps for the last time, as a traveller, even though he is half asleep, knows, looking out of the train window, that he must look now, for he will never see that town, or that
mule-cart, or that woman at work in the fields, again. The lawn was
the world; they were up here together, on this exalted station, she
thought, looking at old Mr. Carmichael, who seemed (though they
had not said a word all this time) to share her thoughts. And she
would never see him again perhaps. He was growing old. Also, she
remembered, smiling at the slipper that dangled from his foot, he was
growing famous. People said that his poetry was "so beautiful." They
went and published things he had written forty years ago. There was
a famous man now called Carmichael, she smiled, thinking how
many shapes one person might wear, how he was that in the newspapers, but here the same as he had always been. He looked the same—
greyer, rather. Yes, he looked the same, but somebody had said, she
recalled, that when he had heard of Andrew Ramsay's death (he was

---

1. *Plantago major*, a broadleaf plant that is considered a weed when it grows in a grass lawn.

killed in a second by a shell; he should have been a great mathematician) Mr. Carmichael had "lost all interest in life." What did it mean—that? she wondered. Had he marched through Trafalgar Square grasping a big stick?[2] Had he turned pages over and over, without reading them, sitting in his room in St. John's Wood alone? She did not know what he had done, when he heard that Andrew was killed, but she felt it in him all the same. They only mumbled at each other on staircases; they looked up at the sky and said it will be fine or it won't be fine. But this was one way of knowing people, she thought: to know the outline, not the detail, to sit in one's garden and look at the slopes of a hill running purple down into the distant heather. She knew him in that way. She knew that he had changed somehow. She had never read a line of his poetry. She thought that she knew how it went though, slowly and sonorously. It was seasoned and mellow. It was about the desert and the camel. It was about the palm tree and the sunset. It was extremely impersonal; it said something about death; it said very little about love. There was an impersonality about him. He wanted very little of other people. Had he not always lurched rather awkwardly past the drawing-room window with some newspaper under his arm, trying to avoid Mrs. Ramsay whom for some reason he did not much like? On that account, of course, she would always try to make him stop. He would bow to her. He would halt unwillingly and bow profoundly. Annoyed that he did not want anything of her, Mrs. Ramsay would ask him (Lily could hear her) wouldn't he like a coat, a rug, a newspaper? No, he wanted nothing. (Here he bowed.) There was some quality in her which he did not much like. It was perhaps her masterfulness, her positiveness, something matter-of-fact in her. She was so direct.

(A noise drew her attention to the drawing-room window—the squeak of a hinge. The light breeze was toying with the window.)

There must have been people who disliked her very much, Lily thought (Yes; she realised that the drawing-room step was empty, but it had no effect on her whatever. She did not want Mrs. Ramsay now.)—People who thought her too sure, too drastic. Also her beauty offended people probably. How monotonous, they would say, and the same always! They preferred another type—the dark, the vivacious. Then she was weak with her husband. She let him make those scenes. Then she was reserved. Nobody knew exactly what had happened to her. And (to go back to Mr. Carmichael and his dislike) one could not imagine Mrs. Ramsay standing painting, lying reading, a whole morning on the lawn. It was unthinkable. Without saying a word, the only

2. Trafalgar Square is located in central London at the north end of Whitehall, the site of many British government offices; it commemorates Admiral Horatio Nelson's victory over the French and Spanish navies at the Battle of Trafalgar in 1805, and it has long been used as a center of demonstrations and protests.

token of her errand a basket on her arm, she went off to the town, to the poor, to sit in some stuffy little bedroom. Often and often Lily had seen her go silently in the midst of some game, some discussion, with her basket on her arm, very upright. She had noted her return. She had thought, half laughing (she was so methodical with the tea cups), half moved (her beauty took one's breath away), eyes that are closing in pain have looked on you. You have been with them there.

And then Mrs. Ramsay would be annoyed because somebody was late, or the butter not fresh, or the teapot chipped. And all the time she was saying that the butter was not fresh one would be thinking of Greek temples, and how beauty had been with them there in that stuffy little room. She never talked of it—she went, punctually, directly. It was her instinct to go, an instinct like the swallows for the south, the artichokes for the sun, turning her infallibly to the human race, making her nest in its heart. And this, like all instincts, was a little distressing to people who did not share it; to Mr. Carmichael perhaps, to herself certainly. Some notion was in both of them about the ineffectiveness of action, the supremacy of thought. Her going was a reproach to them, gave a different twist to the world, so that they were led to protest, seeing their own prepossessions disappear, and clutch at them vanishing. Charles Tansley did that too: it was part of the reason why one disliked him. He upset the proportions of one's world. And what had happened to him, she wondered, idly stirring the plantains with her brush. He had got his fellowship. He had married; he lived at Golder's Green.[3]

She had gone one day into a Hall and heard him speaking during the war. He was denouncing something: he was condemning somebody. He was preaching brotherly love. And all she felt was how could he love his kind who did not know one picture from another, who had stood behind her smoking shag ("fivepence an ounce, Miss Briscoe") and making it his business to tell her women can't write, women can't paint, not so much that he believed it, as that for some odd reason he wished it? There he was lean and red and raucous, preaching love from a platform (there were ants crawling about among the plantains which she disturbed with her brush—red, energetic, shiny ants, rather like Charles Tansley). She had looked at him ironically from her seat in the half-empty hall, pumping love into that chilly space, and suddenly, there was the old cask or whatever it was bobbing up and down among the waves and Mrs. Ramsay looking for her spectacle case among the pebbles. "Oh, dear! What a nuisance! Lost again. Don't bother, Mr. Tansley. I lose thousands every summer," at which he pressed his chin back against his collar, as if

---

3. A residential area in the suburban London borough of Barnet, newly developed at the beginning of the twentieth century and known for its large Jewish population.

afraid to sanction such exaggeration, but could stand it in her whom he liked, and smiled very charmingly. He must have confided in her on one of those long expeditions when people got separated and walked back alone. He was educating his little sister, Mrs. Ramsay had told her. It was immensely to his credit. Her own idea of him was grotesque, Lily knew well, stirring the plantains with her brush. Half one's notions of other people were, after all, grotesque. They served private purposes of one's own. He did for her instead of a whipping-boy. She found herself flagellating his lean flanks when she was out of temper. If she wanted to be serious about him she had to help herself to Mrs. Ramsay's sayings, to look at him through her eyes.

She raised a little mountain for the ants to climb over. She reduced them to a frenzy of indecision by this interference in their cosmogony. Some ran this way, others that.

One wanted fifty pairs of eyes to see with, she reflected. Fifty pairs of eyes were not enough to get round that one woman with, she thought. Among them, must be one that was stone blind to her beauty. One wanted most some secret sense, fine as air, with which to steal through keyholes and surround her where she sat knitting, talking, sitting silent in the window alone; which took to itself and treasured up like the air which held the smoke of the steamer, her thoughts, her imaginations, her desires. What did the hedge mean to her, what did the garden mean to her, what did it mean to her when a wave broke? (Lily looked up, as she had seen Mrs. Ramsay look up; she too heard a wave falling on the beach.) And then what stirred and trembled in her mind when the children cried, "How's that? How's that?" cricketing? She would stop knitting for a second. She would look intent. Then she would lapse again, and suddenly Mr. Ramsay stopped dead in his pacing in front of her and some curious shock passed through her and seemed to rock her in profound agitation on its breast when stopping there he stood over her and looked down at her. Lily could see him.

He stretched out his hand and raised her from her chair. It seemed somehow as if he had done it before; as if he had once bent in the same way and raised her from a boat which, lying a few inches off some island, had required that the ladies should thus be helped on shore by the gentlemen. An old-fashioned scene that was, which required, very nearly, crinolines and peg-top trousers.[4] Letting herself be helped by him, Mrs. Ramsay had thought (Lily supposed) the time has come now. Yes, she would say it now. Yes, she would marry him. And she stepped slowly, quietly on shore. Probably she said one

---

4. Trousers cut very wide in the hips and narrow at the ankles, originally in fashion ca. 1858–65; *crinolines*: petticoats made of a stiff cloth woven from horsehair and cotton or linen; worn as undergarments, they held out the wide skirts fashionable in the mid-nineteenth century.

word only, letting her hand rest still in his. I will marry you, she might have said, with her hand in his; but no more. Time after time the same thrill had passed between them—obviously it had, Lily thought, smoothing a way for her ants. She was not inventing; she was only trying to smooth out something she had been given years ago folded up; something she had seen. For in the rough and tumble of daily life, with all those children about, all those visitors, one had constantly a sense of repetition—of one thing falling where another had fallen, and so setting up an echo which chimed in the air and made it full of vibrations.

But it would be a mistake, she thought, thinking how they walked off together, arm in arm, past the greenhouse, to simplify their relationship. It was no monotony of bliss—she with her impulses and quicknesses; he with his shudders and glooms. Oh, no. The bedroom door would slam violently early in the morning. He would start from the table in a temper. He would whizz his plate through the window. Then all through the house there would be a sense of doors slamming and blinds fluttering, as if a gusty wind were blowing and people scudded about trying in a hasty way to fasten hatches and make things shipshape. She had met Paul Rayley like that one day on the stairs. It had been an earwig, apparently. Other people might find centipedes. They had laughed and laughed.

But it tired Mrs. Ramsay, it cowed her a little—the plates whizzing and the doors slamming. And there would fall between them sometimes long rigid silences, when, in a state of mind which annoyed Lily in her, half plaintive, half resentful, she seemed unable to surmount the tempest calmly, or to laugh as they laughed, but in her weariness perhaps concealed something. She brooded and sat silent. After a time he would hang stealthily about the places where she was—roaming under the window where she sat writing letters or talking, for she would take care to be busy when he passed, and evade him, and pretend not to see him. Then he would turn smooth as silk, affable, urbane, and try to win her so. Still she would hold off, and now she would assert for a brief season some of those prides and airs the due of her beauty which she was generally utterly without; would turn her head; would look so, over her shoulder, always with some Minta, Paul, or William Bankes at her side. At length, standing outside the group the very figure of a famished wolfhound (Lily got up off the grass and stood looking at the steps, at the window, where she had seen him), he would say her name, once only, for all the world like a wolf barking in the snow, but still she held back; and he would say it once more, and this time something in the tone would rouse her, and she would go to him, leaving them all of a sudden, and they would walk off together among the pear trees, the cabbages, and the raspberry beds. They would have it out together. But with what attitudes and with what words? Such a dignity was theirs in this relationship that, turning away, she and Paul and Minta would hide their curiosity and their discomfort, and begin picking flowers, throwing balls, chattering, until it was time for dinner, and there they were, he at one end of the table, she at the other, as usual.

"Why don't some of you take up botany? . . . With all those legs and arms why doesn't one of you . . . ?" So they would talk as usual, laughing, among the children. All would be as usual, save only for some quiver, as of a blade in the air, which came and went between them as if the usual sight of the children sitting round their soup plates had freshened itself in their eyes after that hour among the pears and the cabbages. Especially, Lily thought, Mrs. Ramsay would glance at Prue. She sat in the middle between brothers and sisters, always occupied, it seemed, seeing that nothing went wrong so that she scarcely spoke herself. How Prue must have blamed herself for that earwig in the milk! How white she had gone when Mr. Ramsay threw his plate through the window! How she drooped under those long silences between them! Anyhow, her mother now would seem to be making it up to her; assuring her that everything was well; promising her that one of these days that same happiness would be hers. She had enjoyed it for less than a year, however.

She had let the flowers fall from her basket, Lily thought, screwing up her eyes and standing back as if to look at her picture, which she was not touching, however, with all her faculties in a trance, frozen over superficially but moving underneath with extreme speed.

She let her flowers fall from her basket, scattered and tumbled them on to the grass and, reluctantly and hesitatingly, but without question or complaint—had she not the faculty of obedience to perfection?—went too. Down fields, across valleys, white, flower-strewn—that was how she would have painted it. The hills were austere. It was rocky; it was steep. The waves sounded hoarse on the stones beneath. They went, the three of them together, Mrs. Ramsay walking rather fast in front, as if she expected to meet some one round the corner.

Suddenly the window at which she was looking was whitened by some light stuff behind it. At last then somebody had come into the drawing-room; somebody was sitting in the chair. For Heaven's sake, she prayed, let them sit still there and not come floundering out to talk to her. Mercifully, whoever it was stayed still inside; had settled by some stroke of luck so as to throw an odd-shaped triangular shadow over the step. It altered the composition of the picture a little. It was interesting. It might be useful. Her mood was coming back to her. One must keep on looking without for a second relaxing the intensity of emotion, the determination not to be put off, not to be bamboozled. One must hold the scene—so—in a vise and let nothing come in and spoil it. One wanted, she thought, dipping her brush deliberately, to be on a level with ordinary experience, to feel simply that's a chair, that's a table, and yet at the same time, It's a miracle, it's an ecstasy. The problem might be solved after all. Ah, but what had happened? Some wave of white went over the window pane. The air must have stirred some flounce in the room. Her heart leapt at her and seized her and tortured her.

"Mrs. Ramsay! Mrs. Ramsay!" she cried, feeling the old horror come back—to want and want and not to have. Could she inflict that still? And then, quietly, as if she refrained, that too became part of ordinary experience, was on a level with the chair, with the table. Mrs. Ramsay—it was part of her perfect goodness—sat there quite simply, in the chair, flicked her needles to and fro, knitted her reddish-brown stocking, cast her shadow on the step. There she sat.

And as if she had something she must share, yet could hardly leave her easel, so full her mind was of what she was thinking, of what she was seeing, Lily went past Mr. Carmichael holding her brush to the edge of the lawn. Where was that boat now? And Mr. Ramsay? She wanted him.

XII

Mr. Ramsay had almost done reading. One hand hovered over the page as if to be in readiness to turn it the very instant he had finished it. He sat there bareheaded with the wind blowing his hair about, extraordinarily exposed to everything. He looked very old. He looked, James thought, getting his head now against the Lighthouse, now against the waste of waters running away into the open, like some old stone lying on the sand; he looked as if he had become physically what was always at the back of both of their minds—that loneliness which was for both of them the truth about things.

He was reading very quickly, as if he were eager to get to the end. Indeed they were very close to the Lighthouse now. There it loomed up, stark and straight, glaring white and black, and one could see the waves breaking in white splinters like smashed glass upon the rocks. One could see lines and creases in the rocks. One could see the windows clearly; a dab of white on one of them, and a little tuft of green on the rock. A man had come out and looked at them through a glass and gone in again. So it was like that, James thought, the Lighthouse one had seen across the bay all these years; it was a stark tower on a bare rock. It satisfied him. It confirmed some obscure feeling of his about his own character. The old ladies, he thought, thinking of the

garden at home, went dragging their chairs about on the lawn. Old
Mrs. Beckwith, for example, was always saying how nice it was and
how sweet it was and how they ought to be so proud and they ought to
be so happy, but as a matter of fact, James thought, looking at the
Lighthouse stood there on its rock, it's like that. He looked at his
father reading fiercely with his legs curled tight. They shared that
knowledge. "We are driving before a gale—we must sink," he began
saying to himself, half aloud, exactly as his father said it.

Nobody seemed to have spoken for an age. Cam was tired of looking at the sea. Little bits of black cork had floated past; the fish were
dead in the bottom of the boat. Still her father read, and James looked
at him and she looked at him, and they vowed that they would fight
tyranny to the death, and he went on reading quite unconscious of
what they thought. It was thus that he escaped, she thought. Yes, with
his great forehead and his great nose, holding his little mottled book
firmly in front of him, he escaped. You might try to lay hands on him,
but then like a bird, he spread his wings, he floated off to settle out of
your reach somewhere far away on some desolate stump. She gazed at
the immense expanse of the sea. The island had grown so small that
it scarcely looked like a leaf any longer. It looked like the top of a rock
which some wave bigger than the rest would cover. Yet in its frailty
were all those paths, those terraces, those bedrooms—all those innumerable things. But as, just before sleep, things simplify themselves
so that only one of all the myriad details has power to assert itself, so,
she felt, looking drowsily at the island, all those paths and terraces
and bedrooms were fading and disappearing, and nothing was left but
a pale blue censer swinging rhythmically this way and that across her
mind. It was a hanging garden; it was a valley, full of birds, and flowers, and antelopes. . . . She was falling asleep.

"Come now," said Mr. Ramsay, suddenly shutting his book.

Come where? To what extraordinary adventure? She woke with
a start. To land somewhere, to climb somewhere? Where was he
leading them? For after his immense silence the words startled them.
But it was absurd. He was hungry, he said. It was time for lunch.
Besides, look, he said. "There's the Lighthouse. We're almost there."

"He's doing very well," said Macalister, praising James. "He's keeping her very steady."

But his father never praised him, James thought grimly.

Mr. Ramsay opened the parcel and shared out the sandwiches
among them. Now he was happy, eating bread and cheese with
these fishermen. He would have liked to live in a cottage and lounge
about in the harbour spitting with the other old men, James
thought, watching him slice his cheese into thin yellow sheets with
his penknife.

This is right, this is it, Cam kept feeling, as she peeled her hard-boiled egg. Now she felt as she did in the study when the old men were reading *The Times*. Now I can go on thinking whatever I like, and I shan't fall over a precipice or be drowned, for there he is, keeping his eye on me, she thought.

At the same time they were sailing so fast along by the rocks that it was very exciting—it seemed as if they were doing two things at once; they were eating their lunch here in the sun and they were also making for safety in a great storm after a shipwreck. Would the water last? Would the provisions last? she asked herself, telling herself a story but knowing at the same time what was the truth.

They would soon be out of it, Mr. Ramsay was saying to old Macalister; but their children would see some strange things. Macalister said he was seventy-five last March; Mr. Ramsay was seventy-one. Macalister said he had never seen a doctor; he had never lost a tooth. And that's the way I'd like my children to live—Cam was sure that her father was thinking that, for he stopped her throwing a sandwich into the sea and told her, as if he were thinking of the fishermen and how they lived, that if she did not want it she should put it back in the parcel. She should not waste it. He said it so wisely, as if he knew so well all the things that happened in the world that she put it back at once, and then he gave her, from his own parcel, a gingerbread nut, as if he were a great Spanish gentleman, she thought, handing a flower to a lady at a window (so courteous his manner was). He was shabby, and simple, eating bread and cheese; and yet he was leading them on a great expedition where, for all she knew, they would be drowned.

"That was where she sunk," said Macalister's boy suddenly.

Three men were drowned where we are now, the old man said. He had seen them clinging to the mast himself. And Mr. Ramsay taking a look at the spot was about, James and Cam were afraid, to burst out:

But I beneath a rougher sea,

and if he did, they could not bear it; they would shriek aloud; they could not endure another explosion of the passion that boiled in him; but to their surprise all he said was "Ah" as if he thought to himself, But why make a fuss about that? Naturally men are drowned in a storm, but it is a perfectly straightforward affair, and the depths of the sea (he sprinkled the crumbs from his sandwich paper over them) are only water after all. Then having lighted his pipe he took out his watch. He looked at it attentively; he made, perhaps, some mathematical calculation. At last he said, triumphantly:

"Well done!" James had steered them like a born sailor.

There! Cam thought, addressing herself silently to James. You've got it at last. For she knew that this was what James had been wanting, and she knew that now he had got it he was so pleased that he would not look at her or at his father or at any one. There he sat with his hand on the tiller sitting bolt upright, looking rather sulky and frowning slightly. He was so pleased that he was not going to let anybody share a grain of his pleasure. His father had praised him. They must think that he was perfectly indifferent. But you've got it now, Cam thought.

They had tacked, and they were sailing swiftly, buoyantly on long rocking waves which handed them on from one to another with an extraordinary lilt and exhilaration beside the reef. On the left a row of rocks showed brown through the water which thinned and became greener and on one, a higher rock, a wave incessantly broke and spurted a little column of drops which fell down in a shower. One could hear the slap of the water and the patter of falling drops and a kind of hushing and hissing sound from the waves rolling and gambolling and slapping the rocks as if they were wild creatures who were perfectly free and tossed and tumbled and sported like this for ever.

Now they could see two men on the Lighthouse, watching them and making ready to meet them.

Mr. Ramsay buttoned his coat, and turned up his trousers. He took the large, badly packed, brown paper parcel which Nancy had got ready and sat with it on his knee. Thus in complete readiness to land he sat looking back at the island. With his long-sighted eyes perhaps he could see the dwindled leaf-like shape standing on end on a plate of gold quite clearly. What could he see? Cam wondered. It was all a blur to her. What was he thinking now? she wondered. What was it he sought, so fixedly, so intently, so silently? They watched him, both of them, sitting bareheaded with his parcel on his knee staring and staring at the frail blue shape which seemed like the vapour of something that had burnt itself away. What do you want? they both wanted to ask. They both wanted to say, Ask us anything and we will give it you. But he did not ask them anything. He sat and looked at the island and he might be thinking, We perished, each alone, or he might be thinking, I have reached it. I have found it; but he said nothing.

Then he put on his hat.

"Bring those parcels," he said, nodding his head at the things Nancy had done up for them to take to the Lighthouse. "The parcels for the Lighthouse men," he said. He rose and stood in the bow of the boat, very straight and tall, for all the world, James thought, as if he were saying, "There is no God," and Cam thought, as if he were leaping into space, and they both rose to follow him as he sprang, lightly like a young man, holding his parcel, on to the rock.

XIII

"He must have reached it," said Lily Briscoe aloud, feeling suddenly completely tired out. For the Lighthouse had become almost invisible, had melted away into a blue haze, and the effort of looking at it and the effort of thinking of him landing there, which both seemed to be one and the same effort, had stretched her body and mind to the utmost. Ah, but she was relieved. Whatever she had wanted to give him, when he left her that morning, she had given him at last.

"He has landed," she said aloud. "It is finished."[1] Then, surging up, puffing slightly, old Mr. Carmichael stood beside her, looking like an old pagan god, shaggy, with weeds in his hair and the trident (it was only a French novel) in his hand. He stood by her on the edge of the lawn, swaying a little in his bulk and said, shading his eyes with his hand: "They will have landed," and she felt that she had been right. They had not needed to speak. They had been thinking the same things and he had answered her without her asking him anything. He stood there as if he were spreading his hands over all the weakness and suffering of mankind; she thought he was surveying, tolerantly and compassionately, their final destiny. Now he has crowned the occasion, she thought, when his hand slowly fell, as if she had seen him let fall from his great height a wreath of violets and asphodels which, fluttering slowly, lay at length upon the earth.

Quickly, as if she were recalled by something over there, she turned to her canvas. There it was—her picture. Yes, with all its greens and blues, its lines running up and across, its attempt at something. It would be hung in the attics, she thought; it would be destroyed. But what did that matter? she asked herself, taking up her brush again. She looked at the steps;[2] they were empty; she looked at her canvas; it was blurred. With a sudden intensity, as if she saw it clear for a second, she drew a line there, in the centre. It was done; it was finished. Yes, she thought, laying down her brush in extreme fatigue, I have had my vision.

---

1. Echoes the last words of Jesus Christ on the cross; John 19:30.
2. In the holograph, Woolf wrote in the margin: "The white shape stayed perfectly still," with a mark possibly indicating the words were to be inserted between "she looked at the step" and "She drew a line, there, in the centre" (*Original Holograph*, p. 366).

MARK HUSSEY

Note on Woolf Online[†]

* * *

The most ambitious published digital project in Woolf studies to date is Woolf Online. This site (for which I serve as coordinator of scholarly content) provides high-resolution digital images of each page of the three holograph notebooks that comprise the extant draft of *To the Lighthouse* (in the Berg Collection of New York Public Library). Behind each image is a transcription that can be revealed by moving the cursor over the holograph. Each edition of the novel published before Woolf's death in 1941 is represented by high-resolution scans of each page, as is every page of extant proof (the proofs are held in the Mortimer Rare Book Room of the Allan Neilson Library, Smith College). All reviews of the novel published prior to 1941 are included as image and as transcription, as well as several essays on which Woolf worked or which were published during the period she was writing *To the Lighthouse*. Additionally, there is a time line of composition with links to Woolf's diary and letters wherever she refers to the novel, or to dates in the holograph. Ancillary materials provide an extensive context, and include photographs of the Stephen family from Leslie Stephen's album (Smith College), postcard images of late nineteenth-century St. Ives, scans of newspapers produced during the 1926 General Strike, when Woolf was composing the "Time Passes" section of the novel, an Ordnance Survey map of Talland House—altogether, Woolf Online comprises nearly 4,200 digital objects that represent materials from archives in New York, London, and Sussex. Apart from the obvious benefit of not having to travel to various collections to peruse these materials, Woolf Online's gathering of so many relevant objects in a searchable database offers to scholars the potential for recontextualizing *To the Lighthouse* in hitherto unforeseen ways, as well as providing a comprehensive map of Woolf's creative process from early stirrings recorded in her diary through drafting and revision.

[†] From "Digital Woolf," in *A Companion to Virginia Woolf,* ed. Jessica Berman (Oxford: Wiley-Blackwell, 2016), p. 272. Reprinted by permission of Wiley. Pamela L. Caughie, Nick Hayward, Mark Hussey, Peter Shillingsburg, and George K. Thiruvathukal, eds. Woolf Online. Web. In addition to the many materials described in this note, Woolf Online also maintains and regularly updates a lengthy list of literary criticism on *To the Lighthouse.*

Selected Textual Variants

This table of variants presents just some of the many substantive differences among three versions of the novel: the uncorrected page proofs and the first US and British editions. There are many other small and large differences, which can be found in Woolf Online and in recent editions of the novel: Virginia Woolf, *To the Lighthouse*, ed. David Bradshaw, Oxford World's Classics (Oxford: Oxford UP, 2006); Virginia Woolf, *To the Lighthouse*, ed. Susan Dick, Shakespeare Head Edition (Oxford: Blackwell, 1992).

Two passages about Mrs. McNab from the typescript of "Time Passes" as Woolf prepared it for translation into French (an intermediate version, between the holograph and the proofs) appear here for comparison with the later versions.

The differences between the three printed versions, the "Time Passes" typescript, and the holograph manuscript are so many and so lengthy that they cannot be presented in this format, but they can be observed in Woolf Online, and some are mentioned in the footnotes to this edition.

These variants were collated and transcribed by the editor of this Norton Critical Edition.

Abbreviations:

US = this Norton Critical Edition, which replicates the first US edition
UK = British first edition
UP = Uncorrected proof
TP TYPESCRIPT = typescript prepared for translation

The Window

US (8–9): reflect himself and disparage them—he was not satisfied. And he would go to picture galleries, they said, and he would ask one
UK: reflect himself and disparage them, put them all on edge somehow with his acid way of peeling the flesh and blood off everything, he was not satisfied. And he would go to picture galleries, they said, and he would ask one
UP: reflect himself, and made them all feel in the wrong somehow—if it was fine well; then, the farmers, he would say, wanted rain—he was not satisfied. And he would go to picture galleries—could one imagine him looking at pictures?—and he would ask one

US (23): things must spoil. Every door was left open

UK and UP: things must spoil. What was the use of flinging a green Cashmere shawl over the edge of a picture frame? In two weeks it would be the colour of pea soup. But it was the doors that annoyed her; every door was left open.

US (24–25) (UK same with minor differences): ("Nature has but little clay," said Mr. Bankes once, much moved by her voice on the telephone, though she was only telling him a fact about a train, "like that of which she moulded you." He saw her at the end of the line very clearly Greek, straight, blue-eyed. How incongruous it seemed to be telephoning to a woman like that. The Graces assembling seemed to have joined hands in meadows of asphodel to compose that face. He would catch the 10:30 at Euston.

"Yet she's no more aware

UP: ("Nature has but little clay," said Mr. Bankes once, hearing her voice on the telephone, and much moved by it though she was only telling him a fact about a train, "like that of which she moulded you." For her beauty seemed to imply all that. Generous, noble, true—the obvious words came quicker to the lips because such qualities—he thought of her at the end of the telephone—seemed in her to have dipped their disembodied shapes in flesh and so assembling, like a ring of Graces joining hands in meadows of asphodel, to have combined together to compose her face.

"But she's no more aware

US (39), UK: something critical. She had been annoyed
UP: something critical. ("She isn't altogether what she looks like," she would have said.) Its humour would have disguised the fact that she had been annoyed

US (80), UK: amounted to. "I—I—I."
UP: amounted to. "It's time someone attended to me."

US (93) and UP: partly because she remembered how beautiful it often is—the sea at night. But she knew
UK: partly because she did not mind looking now, with him watching, at the Lighthouse. For she knew

US (93): It's going to be wet tomorrow. You won't be able to go." And she looked at him smiling. For she had triumphed again. She had not said it: yet he knew.
UK: It's going to be wet tomorrow." She had not said it, but he knew it. And she looked at him smiling. For she had triumphed again.
UP: It's going to be wet tomorrow. You won't be able to go." And she looked at him smiling. For she had triumphed again.

Time Passes

US (96): [Mr. Ramsay, stumbling along a passage one dark morning, stretched his arms out, but Mrs. Ramsay having died rather suddenly the night before, his arms, though stretched out, remained empty.]
UK: [Mr. Ramsay stumbling along a passage stretched his arms out one dark morning, but Mrs. Ramsay having died rather suddenly the night before he stretched his arms out. They remained empty.]
UP: (One dark morning, Mr. Ramsay stumbling along a passage stretched his arms out, but Mrs. Ramsay having died rather suddenly the night before he stumbled along the passage stretching his arms out.)

US (98) (UK and UP same with minor differences): putting down china, looking sideways in the glass, as if, after all, she had her consolations, as if indeed there twined about her dirge some incorrigible hope. Visions of joy there must have been at the wash-tub
TP TYPESCRIPT: (putting down china) granting, as she stood the chair straight by the dressing table, her forgiveness of it all. <leaning her bony breast on the hard thorn.>
   Was it then that she had her consolations, when, with the breeze in the west and the clouds white in the sun she stood at her cottage door? For what reason did there twine about her dirge this incorrigible hope? and why, with no gift to bestow and no gift to take did she yet prefer to live; singing, ~~and~~ dusting? Were there then for Mrs. McNab who had been trampled into the mud for generations, had been a mat for King and Kaiser, moments of illumination, visions of joy, at the wash tub

US (98) (UK same with minor differences): old music hall song. The mystic, the visionary, walking the beach on a fine night, stirring a puddle, looking at a stone, asking themselves "What am I," "What is this?" had suddenly an answer vouchsafed them: (they could not say what it was) so that they were warm in the frost and had comfort in the desert. But Mrs. McNab continued to drink and gossip as before.
UP: old music hall song, while the mystic, the visionary, walking the beach on a fine night, stirring a puddle, looking at a stone, asking themselves "What am I," "What is this?" had suddenly an answer vouchsafed them: ("We are in the hands of the Lord") so that that they were warm in the frost and had comfort in the desert. But Mrs. McNab continued to drink and gossip as before.
TP TYPESCRIPT: old Music hall song.
   Walking the beach the mystic, the visionary, were possessed of intervals of comprehension perhaps; suddenly, unexpectedly, looking at a stone, stirring a puddle with a stick, heard an absolute answer, so

that they were warm in the frost and had comfort in the desert. The truth had been made known to them. But Mrs. McNab was none of these. She was no skeleton lover, who voluntarily surrenders and makes abstract and reduces the multiplicity of the world to unity and its volume and anguish to one voice piping clear and sweet an unmistakable message. The inspired, the lofty minded, might walk the beach, hear in the lull of the storm a voice, behold in some serene clearing a vision, and so mount the pulpit and make public how it is simple, it is certain, our duty, our hope; we are one. Mrs. McNab continued to drink and gossip as before. She was toothless almost; she had pains in all her limbs. She never divulged her reasons for opening windows and dusting bedrooms, and singing, when her voice was gone, her old silly song. Her message to a world now beginning to break into the voluntary and irrepressible loveliness of spring was transmitted by the lurch of her body and the leer of her smile and in them no less than in the bleat of lamb and the bud of cowslip were the broken syllables of a revelation more confused but more profound (could one have read it) than any accorded to solitary watchers, pacing the beach at midnight, and receiving as they stirred the pool, revelations of an extraordinary kind.

US (99): [Prue Ramsay died that summer in some illness connected with childbirth, which was indeed a tragedy, people said, everything, they said, had promised so well.]
UK: [Prue Ramsay died that summer in some illness connected with childbirth, which was indeed a tragedy, people said. They said nobody deserved happiness more.]
UP: (Prue that summer in some illness connected with childbirth died, which was indeed a tragedy, people said. Everything, they said, had promised so well.)

The Lighthouse

US (107) and UK: What does it mean then, what can it all mean?
UP: "I'll go and see about it," said Nancy, going out of the room. What does it mean, then, what can it all mean?

US (117) and UP: There must have been a shadow.) When she thought
UK: There must have been a shadow.). Mrs. Ramsay. When she thought

US (118): She owed it all to her
UK: She owed this revelation to her.
UP: "I owe that to you."

US (130) and UK: "What does it mean? How do you
UP: "What is death? How do you

US (135), UP: The other Lighthouse was true too.
UK: The other was the Lighthouse too.

US (135): some one going, he became extremely sensitive to the presence of whoever might be in the room. It was his father now. The
strain was acute.
UK: some one going, he became extremely sensitive to the presence
of whoever might be in the room. It was his father now. The strain
became acute.
UP: some one going, or that laugh which ended with three separate
"ahs," each less than the last, like drops wrung from the heart of merriment, it meant that he was drawing near the thing he did not want
to think about (his mother), since it was terrible and horrible to think
of her with his father near; it meant that something had started the
sense of her, as still by opening a drawer in a cupboard or looking at a
face—Rose's for instance—through one's fingers one could recover
her absolutely for a moment. But it was horrible; the strain was acute.

US (136): one's head. But all the time he thought of her, he was conscious of his father following his thought, surveying it, making it
shiver and falter. At last he ceased to think
   There he sat
UK: one's head. But all the time he thought of her, he was conscious
of his father following his thought, shadowing it, making it shiver
and falter
   At last he ceased to think; there he sat
UP: one's head. Now in London, now wherever they lived, they were
surrounded by distortions; lamentations; and long speeches and violence; and old ladies like Mrs. Beckwith being kind, and bald men
sipping tea and being clever while bread and butter turned brown in
the saucer, and there one twiddled one's thumbs in the heart of unreality, sitting in the background on a stool, and if in the middle of all
this sighing and being clever some one sneezed or a dog was sick,
nobody dared laugh. And the house grew darker, he thought, and
turned the colour of dusty plush, and there were shrines in corners
and nothing could be moved, and nothing could be broken. In the
depths of the winter, or in those long twilight months which seemed
interminable, his father, standing up very stiff and straight on a platform in the city (to get there they must dine early and drive eternally), proved conclusively (but they could none of them listen) how
there is no God; one must be brave; for there is no God, he said,
while rows and rows of the ugliest people in the world gaped up at

him, in that greenish hall, hung with brown pictures of great men. If she had been there now, what would she have done? he wondered. Laughed? Even she might have found it difficult to tell the truth. He could only see her twitching her cloak round her, feeling the cold. But she was dead by that time. The war was beginning. Andrew was killed. Prue died. Still his father lectured. Even when his hall was full of fog, and only sprinkled with elderly women whose heads rose and fell, like hens sipping, as they listened and wrote down, about being brave, and there is no God, still he lectured.

Often they quarreled among themselves afterwards, what could one say to him? How could one appease him? For he wanted praise. He wanted sympathy. He wanted them to go with him and listen to him, and to say how good it was; how it was the greatest success. Rose said it, forced herself to say it, but she said it wrongly and he was angry; he was depressed. And James himself wanted to say it, for there he[1] stood very straight and very stiff, facing that dismal group of people; one could not help admiring him; and liking him; as he stood there doggedly sticking it out about God and being brave. So that sometimes James would have liked to say it himself; how he admired him; what a brain he had; and would have done so, only his father found him once with a book of his and sneered at him for "it wasn't the kind of thing to interest *him*," he said; whereupon James made a vow; he would never praise his father as long as he lived.

There he sat[2]

US (137): he was not vain, nor a tyrant and did not wish to make you pity him. Indeed,
UK: he was most lovable, he was most wise; he was not vain nor a tyrant. Indeed,
UP: he was not vain, nor a tyrant (these were the things they hated him most for) and did not wish to make you pity him. Indeed,

US (140) and UK: Beautiful pictures. Beautiful phrases. But what she
UP: Beautiful pictures. Wreaths of flowers. Beautiful phrases. The Bride of Death. But what she

---

1. Before cancelling this entire passage, Woolf had corrected "he" to read "his father," and, in the next line, had crossed out "and liking him."
2. At the proof stage, Woolf learned that she needed to cut two pages so as to avoid an awkward last signature with mostly blank pages. (The proofs came in at 322 pages when 320 pages would make a neater fit.) The cut needed to come from near the end, because she was revising in batches and had already returned most of the proofs. This was the passage she chose. With different printing technology, the published book might have included this passage, but Woolf cut the passage for the US edition too, even though it was set in smaller type and didn't need to be shortened. See Mark Hussey and Peter Shillingsburg. "The Composition, Revision, Printing and Publications of *To the Lighthouse*," Part II: Production, Woolf Online. Ed. Pamela L. Caughie, Nick Hayward, Mark Hussey, Peter Shillingsburg, and George K. Thiruvathukal.

US (141) and UP: There was an impersonality about him.
UK: There was an aloofness about him.

US (143) and UK: Lily knew well, stirring the plantains with her brush. Half one's notions
UP: Lily knew well. Educating sandy-haired children in some bleak suburb, vegetarian, austere. Half one's notions

US (144) and UK: a temper. He would whizz his plate through the window. Then all
UP: a temper. Some letter or some article criticizing his books had burst on his plate. Then all

US (144): on the stairs. It had been an earwig, apparently. Other people might find centipedes. They had laughed and laughed.
   But it tired Mrs. Ramsay,
UK: on the stairs. They had laughed and laughed, like a couple of children, all because Mr. Ramsay, finding an earwig in his milk at breakfast had sent the whole thing flying through the air on to the terrace outside. "An earwig," Prue murmured, awestruck, "in his milk." Other people might find centipedes. But he had built round him such a fence of sanctity, and occupied the space with such a demeanor of majesty that an earwig in his milk was a monster.
   But it tired Mrs. Ramsay
UP: on the stairs. They had laughed and laughed, like a couple of children, all because Mr. Ramsay, finding an earwig in his cup at breakfast had sent the whole thing flying through the air on to the terrace outside. "An earwig," Prue murmured, awestruck, looking with round eyes. Other people might find centipedes. But he had built round him such a fence of sanctity, and occupied the space with such a demeanor of majesty that an earwig in his milk was a monster. Later he met them outside his study door, took them in, and showed them his map of the Hebrides. It was a wonderful map. He was charming, showing them his map. They forgave him instantly, as indeed he expected to be forgiven.
   But it tired Mrs. Ramsay[3]

US (149) and UK: as if he were leaping into space, and
UP: as if he were jumping into eternity, and

US (150): He stood there as if he were spreading his hands
UP and UK: He stood there spreading his hands

US (150) and UK: brush in extreme fatigue, I have had my vision.
UP: brush, I have had my vision.

---

3. Woolf Online, "The Composition . . ." includes a detailed analysis of this set of revisions.

CONTEXTS

VIRGINIA WOOLF

Undated Notes and an Outline†

<u>To the Lighthouse</u>

All character—<u>not</u> a view of the world.
Two blocks joined by a corridor.

Topics that may come in:
 How her beauty is to be conveyed by the impression that she makes
on all these people. One after another feeling it without knowing
exactly what she does to them, to charge her words.
Episode of taking Tansley to call on the poor. How they see her.
The great cleavages in to which the human race is split, through
 the Ramsays not liking Mr. Tansley.
But they liked Mr. Carmichael.
Her reverence for learning & painting.
Inherited, not very personal.
The look of the room—fiddle & sand shoes.
Great photographs covering bare patches.
The beauty is to be revealed the 2ⁿᵈ time Mr. R. stops.
Discourse on sentimentality.
He was quoting The Charge of the Light Brigade, & then impressed
 upon it was this picture of mother & Child.

How much more important divisions between people are than
 between countries.
The source of all evil.
She was lapsing into mere sensation—seeing things in the garden.*
The waves breaking. Tapping of cricket balls.
The bark "How's that?"
They did not speak to each other.
Tansley shed.
Tansley the product of universities had to assert the power
 of his intellect.

† From Woolf's notebook labeled "Notes for Writing," Berg Collection, New York Public
 Library, pp. 11–13. Transcribed from Woolf Online. Reprinted by permission of the
 Berg Collection, New York Public Library, and The Society of Authors as the Literary
 Representative of the Estate of Virginia Woolf. These undated notes appear directly
 following notes dated March 6 and 14, 1925 ("Notes for Writing," pp. 7–10) that include
 ideas related to To the Lighthouse (see Composition Chronology, 164–65).
 * She feels the glow of sensation—& how they are made up of all different things—(what
 she has just done) & wishes for some bell to strike & say this is it. It does strike. She
 guards her moment [Woolf's note].

To the Lighthouse[2]

<u>Ten chapters</u>

Now the question of the ten years.
The Seasons.
The Skull
The gradual dissolution of everything
This is to be contrasted with the permanence of——what?
Sun, moon & stars.
Hopeless gulfs of misery.
Cruelty.
The War.
Change. Oblivion. Human vitality. Old woman cleaning up. She
   bobbed up, valorous, as if a principle of human life projected
We are handed on by our children?
Shawls & shooting caps. A green-handled brush.
The devouringness of nature.
But all the time, this passes, accumulates.
Darkness.
The welter of winds & waves.
What then is the medium through wh. we regard human beings?
Tears. &c.
Slept through life.

---

2. On a separate sheet of blank paper (not part of a notebook), Berg Collection. Transcribed from Woolf Online.

The Composition, Revision, Publication, and Reception of *To the Lighthouse*—A Virginia Woolf Chronology, 1924–28[†]

In diary entries, in letters to family and friends, and in her handwritten draft, Woolf kept track of her progress in composing *To the Lighthouse*. She described the initial thoughts and feelings that went into its conception and planning, and she captured her struggles to meet the compositional challenges she had set herself and to manage the emotions stirred up by her story. After she had finished the draft, she recorded the work of revision and the moment of publication, on May 5, 1927. Once it was published, friends and family wrote to her celebrating her accomplishment—and then, as its success unfolded over the following months, she registered her afterthoughts on what she had achieved.

Taken together, these records offer extraordinary insight into Woolf's artistic process and into the novel itself, and they indicate how her work on the novel was embedded in a life filled with social events and other writing obligations. To provide all the relevant diary entries, letters, and manuscript records would take an entire book, so this Chronology excerpts just the relevant passages to create a candid narrative collage of the author's writing life during a period of outstanding creativity.

1924

September 22, to Roger Fry, Monk's House Papers, Sussex University[‡]
I have just finished your pamphlet, so I must write off at once & say how it fills me with admiration & stirs up in me, as you alone do, all sorts of bats & tadpoles—ideas, I mean, which have clung to my roof & lodged in my mind, & now I'm all alive with pleasure. * * * I'm puzzling, in my weak witted way, over some of your problems: about 'form' in literature. I've been writing about Percy Lubbock's book, & trying to make out what I mean by form in fiction. I say it is emotion put in the right relations; & has nothing to do with form as used

---

[†] This Chronology incorporates passages from Virginia Woolf's diaries, letters, and notebooks and from her holograph manuscript of *To the Lighthouse*, held in the Berg Collection, New York Public Library; it also includes passages from letters to her from other sources, as noted. Reprinted by permission of the Berg Collection, New York Public Library, and The Society of Authors as the Literary Representative of the Estate of Virginia Woolf.

To read more of Woolf's personal writings and correspondence with friends, see *Diary*, vols. 2 and 3; *Letters*, vol. 3; *Original Holograph*; and *The Letters of Vita Sackville-West to Virginia Woolf*, ed. Louise DeSalvo and Mitchell A. Leaska (London: Hutchinson, 1984). Woolf Online also provides access to some of the same diary entries, letters, and notes, and it enables readers to track her progress in writing the manuscript: see Pamela L. Caughie, Nick Hayward, Mark Hussey, Peter Shillingsburg, and George K. Thiruvathukal, eds., Woolf Online.

[‡] The following two letters were transcribed by the editor of this Norton Critical Edition at Sussex University Library. SxMs-18/1/D/58/1. Monk's House Papers, University of Sussex Special Collections at the Keep. Reprinted by permission of The Society of Authors as the Literary Representative of the Estate of Virginia Woolf.

of painting. But this you must tidy up for me when we meet, which must be soon, and often.[1]

October 3, to Jacques Raverat, Monk's House Papers, Sussex University
[T]he falsity of the past (by which I mean Bennett, Galsworthy & so on) is precisely I think that they adhere to a formal railway line of sentence, for its convenience, never reflecting that people don't & never did feel or think or dream for a second in that way; but all over the place, in your way.[2]

October 17, diary, Berg Collection, NYPL[†]
I did run up stairs thinking I'd make time to enter that astounding fact—the last words of the last page of Mrs Dalloway * * * The only difficulty is to hold myself back from writing others. My cul-de-sac, as they called it, stretches so far, & shows such vistas. I see already The Old Man.[3]

1925

January 6, diary, Berg Collection, NYPL
I'm always conceiving stories now. Short ones—scenes—for instance The Old Man (a character of L.S.)

March 6 and 14[4]
Notes for stories * * *
My idea is that these sketches will be a corridor leading from Mrs. Dalloway to a new book. What I expect to happen is that some two figures will detach themselves from the party & go off independently into another volume. * * *
<u>The Past</u> founded on images ancestor worship, what it amounts to, & means. Some middle aged woman of distinguished parents; her feelings for her father & mother— * * *.

---

1. Woolf refers to the manuscript of Roger Fry's *The Artist and Psycho-Analysis*, which Hogarth Press would publish in November 1924 (this edition, pp. 240–43), and to Percy Lubbock's *The Craft of Fiction* (1921).
2. Woolf's essay "Modern Fiction" criticizes contemporary novelists Arnold Bennett (1867–1931) and John Galsworthy (1867–1933) in similar terms; she had been revising her essays for inclusion in *The Common Reader* (1925). Jacques Raverat (1885–1925), French painter and friend with whom Woolf corresponded, as she did with Fry, about aesthetic theory.
† Unless otherwise indicated, the following selections from Virginia Woolf's letters and diaries are from the Berg Collection, New York Public Library. Reprinted by permission of the Berg Collection, New York Public Library, and The Society of Authors as the Literary Representative of the Estate of Virginia Woolf. Unless otherwise indicated, the following selections were transcribed by the editor of this Norton Critical Edition.
3. Woolf's father, Leslie Stephen (1832–1904).
4. This selection is from the notebook "Notes for Writing," Berg Collection, NYPL, pp. 7–10. Eight stories are described and given various titles in these notes. The story here titled "The Past" became "Ancestors." Six stories plus one written before *Mrs. Dalloway* were published as *Mrs. Dalloway's Party: A Short Story Sequence* by Stella McNichol in 1973. On the next page following the words "But what?" appear the undated notes and diagram under the title *To the Lighthouse* ("Notes for Writing," pp. 11–13); see Woolf's "Undated Notes and an Outline" (161–62).

One about people looking out of a window & realising the planets, or some quite other world. being recalled to this one. * * * It strikes me that it might all end with a picture. These stories about people would fill half the book; & then the other thing would loom up; & we should step into quite a different place & people? But what?

May 14, diary, Berg Collection, NYPL
I'm now all on the strain with desire to * * * get on to <u>To the Light-house</u>. This is going to be fairly short: to have father's character done complete in it; & mother's; & and St Ives; & childhood; & and all the usual things I try to put in—life, death &c. But the centre is father's character, sitting in a boat, reciting We perished, each alone, while he crushes a dying mackerel.

June 14, diary, Berg Collection, NYPL
After finishing those two books * * * one can't concentrate directly on a new one; & then the letters, the talk, the reviews, all serve to enlarge the pupil of my mind more & more. I cant settle in, contract, & shut myself off. I've written 6 little stories,[5] scrambled them down untidily, & have thought out, perhaps too clearly, To the Lighthouse.

June 27, diary, Berg Collection, NYPL
I am making up "To the Lighthouse"—the sea is to be heard all through it. I have an idea that I will invent a new name for my books to supplant "novel". A new—by Virginia Woolf. But what? Elegy?

July 20, diary, Berg Collection, NYPL
[T]his theme may be sentimental; father & mother & child in the garden: the death; the sail to the lighthouse. I think, though, that when I begin it I shall enrich it in all sorts of ways; thicken it; give it branches & roots which I do not perceive now. It might contain all characters boiled down; & childhood; & then this impersonal thing, which I'm dared to do by my friends, the flight of time, & the conse-quent break of unity in my design. That passage (I conceive the book in 3 parts: 1. at the drawing room window; 2. seven years passed; 3. the voyage:) interests me very much.

Aug. 6th[6]
The plan of this book is roughly that it shall consist of three parts: One, Mrs. Ramsay (?) sitting at the window: while Mr. R walks up & down in the dusk: the idea being that there shall be curves of

---

5. These are the stories described in "notes for stories," March 6 and 14, 1925; *those two books: The Common Reader* published on April 23 and *Mrs. Dalloway* on May 14, 1925.
6. The writing book (the first of three, in the Berg Collection) in which she drafted *To the Lighthouse* starts with the title, <u>To the Lighthouse</u>, centered as for a title page, with these dates: "Begun (August 6th 1925)—Jan. 18th 1926/Finished March 16th 1927." On the next page appears this three-part "plan." Virginia and Leonard stayed at Monk's House, their country home in Rodmell, Sussex, from August 5 to October 2, 1925.

conversation or reflection or description or in fact anything, modulated by his appearance & disappearance at the window: gradually it shall grow later; the child shall go to bed; the engaged couple shall appear: But this is all to be filled up as richly and variously as possible. My aim being to find a unit for the sentence which shall be less emphatic & intense than that in Mrs. D: an everyday sentence for carrying on the narrative easily. The theme of the 1st part shall <u>really</u> contribute to Mrs. R's character; at least Mrs. R's character shall be displayed, but finally in conjunction with his, so that one gets an impression of their relationship

To precipitate feeling, there should be a sense of waiting, of expectation: the child waiting to go to the Lighthouse: the woman awaiting the return of the couple.

2.) The passing of time. I am not sure how this is to be given: an interesting experiment, giving the sense of 10 years passing.

3) This is the voyage to the Lighthouse.

Several characters can be brought in: the young atheist, the old gentleman, the lovers: Episodes can be written on woman's beauty; on truth: but these should be greater and less knobbly than those in Mrs. D: making a more harmonious whole.

There need be no specification of date.

Whether this will be long or short, I do not know. The dominating impression is to be of Mrs. R's character.

September 3: Holograph date for "Indeed he almost knocked her easel over" (16).

December 7, diary, Berg Collection, NYPL

[T]here is Tom's postcard about *On Being Ill*—an article which I, & Leonard too, thought one of my best[7] * * * [H]e is not enthusiastic; so, reading the proof just now, I saw wordiness, feebleness, & all the vices in it. This increases my distaste for my own writing, & dejection at the thought of beginning another novel. What theme have I? Shan't I be held up for personal reasons? It will be too like father, or mother: &, oddly, I know so little of my own powers.

1926

January 15[8]

The idea has grown in the interval since I wrote the beginning. The presence of the 8 children; undifferentiated, should be important to bring out the sense of life in opposition to fate—i.e. waves,

---

7. Woolf had sent "On Being Ill" to T. S. Eliot in November, and it appeared in *The New Criterion* in January 1926.

8. This note was added at the beginning of the writing book now in the Berg Collection where, on the next page, she had already started writing the novel.

lighthouse. Then there is to be some movement as the evening passes: a great dinner scene, all the family, & <u>after</u> this I think, Minta and Charles go out to become engaged

Also a scene in Mrs. Rs. bedroom, with children choosing jewels while the birds rise & fall outside; a scene of her descending the stairs, smelling burning fat; but all is to draw in towards the end, & leave the two alone: she expecting the return of the young couple. That poetry should be used in quotations to give the character.

January 18: Holograph date for "They both smiled, standing there. They both felt a common hilarity" (18).

January 19, diary, Berg Collection, NYPL
Vita having this moment (20 minutes ago—it is now 7) left me, what are my feelings? * * * She is not clever; but abundant & fruitful. * * * Oh & mixed up with this is the invigoration of again beginning my novel, in the Studio, for the first time this morning. All these fountains play on my being and intermingle.[9]

January 21: Holograph date for start of section V: "And even if it isn't fine tomorrow" (22).

January 26, to Vita, Berg Collection, NYPL
I * * * have written I think 20 pages. To tell you the truth, I have been very excited, writing. I have never written so fast. Give me no illness for a year, 2 years, & I would write 3 novels straight off. * * * I think I can write now, never before—an illusion which attends me always for 50 pages. But its true I write quick—all in a splash.

January 31: Holograph date for "But his son hated him" (30).

February 3, to Vita, Berg Collection, NYPL
I am back again in the thick of my novel, & things are crowding into my head: millions of things I might put in—all sorts of incongruities, which I make up walking the streets, gazing into the gas fire. Then I struggle with them, from 10 to 1: then lie on the sofa & watch the sun behind the chimneys: & think of more things: then set up a page of poetry in the basement, & so up to tea——Morgan Forster. I've shirked 2 parties, & another Frenchman, & buying a hat, & going to tea with Hilda Trevelyan: for I really can't combine all this with keeping my imaginary people going. Not that they are people: what one imagines, in a novel, is a world. Then, when one has imagined this world,

9. Vita Sackville-West (1892–1962), Woolf's friend and her lover starting in December 1925. A wealthy aristocrat, often traveling with her diplomat husband, she published poetry, prose fiction, and nonfiction. Vita had left for a long trip to Persia; *the Studio*: Woolf's writing room in the basement of 52 Tavistock Square, next to the Hogarth Press office.

suddenly people come in—but I don't know why one does it, or why it should alleviate the misery of life, & yet not make one exactly happy; for the strain is too great. Oh, to have done it, & be free.

February 8, diary, Berg Collection, NYPL
I am rather tired, a little tired, from having thought too much about To the Lighthouse. Never never have I written so easily, imagined so profusely.

February 18: Holograph date for "Certainly, Nancy had gone with them" (57). (The position of this section was later changed.)

February 22: Holograph date for "No, she thought . . . children never forget" (49).

February 23, diary, Berg Collection, NYPL
I am blown like an old flag by my novel. This one is To the Lighthouse. I think it is worth saying for my own interest that at last at last, after that battle Jacob's Room, that agony—all agony but the end, Mrs Dalloway, I am now writing as fast & freely as I have written in the whole of my life; more so—20 times more so—than any novel yet. I think this is the proof that I was on the right path; & that what fruit hangs in my soul is to be reached there. Amusingly, I now invent theories that fertility & fluency are the things: I used to plead for a kind of close, terse, effort. Anyhow this goes on all the morning; & I have the devils own work not to be flogging my brain all the afternoon. I live entirely in it and come to the surface rather obscurely & am often unable to think what to say when we walk around the Square, which is bad I know.

February 24, diary, Berg Collection, NYPL
[W]e talked a lot, when L. was in the basement with the electrician, of father, who, said Francis, dominates the 20th Century. "He made it possible for me to have a decent life" he said. "He pulled down the whole edifice, & never knew what he was doing. He never realized that if God went, morality must follow. A remarkable man; for though he would not believe in God, he was stricter than those who did."

"He loved lamentation" said L. coming up. R.M. said her parents called him always "poor Leslie Stephen" because he had lost his faith. Also they said he was very gentle & charming. Gwen said her father & uncles[1] had a great respect for him. They had a very romantic feeling for my mother.

Because she was so beautiful, I said, proud that R.M. should know this; & felt rather queer, to think how much of this there is in To

---

1. Gwen Raverat and Rose and Francis Macauley had come to dinner; Gwen's father and uncles were sons of Charles Darwin.

the Lighthouse, & how all these people will read it & recognize poor Leslie Stephen and beautiful Mrs Stephen in it.

March 2, to Vita, Berg Collection, NYPL
But to write a novel in the heart of London is next to an impossibility. I feel as if I were nailing a flag to the top of a mast in a raging gale. What is so perplexing is the change of perspective: here I'm sitting thinking how to manage the passage of ten years, up in the Hebrides; then the telephone rings; then a charming bony pink cheeked Don called Lucas comes to tea: well, am I here, asking him about the Life of Webster, which he's editing, or in a bedroom up in the Hebrides?

March 5: Holograph date for "Well, then, Nancy had gone with them" (61).

March 16, to Vita, Berg Collection, NYPL
As for the <u>mot juste</u>, you are quite wrong. Style is a very simple matter; it is all rhythm. Once you get that, you can't use the wrong words. But on the other hand here am I sitting after half the morning, crammed with ideas, & visions, & so on, & can't dislodge them, for lack of the right rhythm. Now this is very profound, what rhythm is, and goes far deeper than words. A sight, an emotion, creates this wave in the mind, long before it makes words to fit it; and in writing (such is my present belief) one has to recapture this, & set this working (which has nothing apparently to do with words) & then, as it breaks & tumbles in the mind, it makes words to fit it.

March 17: Holograph date for draft of an anecdote about Mr. Carmichael and a bear in the Himalayan mountains, during the dinner scene, later cut.

March 29: Holograph date for "it had become . . . already the past" (84).

April 18, diary, Berg Collection, NYPL
Yesterday I finished the first part of To the Lighthouse, & today began the second. I cannot make it out—here is the most difficult abstract piece of writing—I have to give an empty house, no people's characters, the passage of time, all eyeless & featureless with nothing to cling to: well, I rush at it, & at once scatter out two pages. Is it nonsense, is it brilliance? Why am I so flown with words, & apparently free to do exactly what I like? When I read a bit it seems spirited too; needs compressing, but not much else.

April 30: Holograph date for start of "Time Passes," section 2: "So with the lamps all put out" (94).

May 5, diary, Berg Collection, NYPL
An exact Diary of the Strike[2] would be interesting. For instance, it is now a ¼ to 2: there is a brown fog; nobody is building; it is drizzling. The first thing in the morning we stand at the window & watch the traffic in Southampton Row. This is incessant. * * * There are no buses. No placards. No newspapers. The men are at work in the road; water, gas & electricity are allowed; but at 11 the light was turned off. I sat in the press in the brown fog, while L. wrote an article for the Herald.

May 9: Holograph date for description of Mrs. McNab (97–98).[3]

May 14: Holograph date for "The spring without a leaf to toss" (98).

May 27: Holograph date for start of "The Lighthouse", section 1, "What does it mean then, what can it all mean? Lily Briscoe asked herself" (107).

May 31: Holograph date for "She set her clean canvas" (109).

June 2, to Vanessa Bell,[4] Berg Collection, NYPL
I went to your show. * * * I expect the problem of empty spaces, & how to model them, has rather baffled you. There are flat passages, so that the design is not completely comprehended. * * * I am amazed, a little alarmed (for as you have the children, the fame by rights belongs to me) by your combination of pure artistic vision & brilliance of imagination. A mistress of the brush—you are now undoubtedly that; but still I think the problems of design on a large scale slightly baffle you.

June 7, to Vita, Berg Collection, NYPL
Are you writing poetry? If so, then tell me what is the difference between that emotion & the prose emotion? What drives you to one & not the other? I am trying to work this out. * * * My novel is very very bad: all my worst faults displayed.

---

2. The nationwide General Strike was started on May 2 by the Trades Union Congress in support of striking mineworkers. Taking the side of the strikers, Leonard helped to organize a petition calling on the government to negotiate. The General Strike ended May 12, but its "gloomy" effects continued, the coal miners continuing on strike for several more months. See Kate Flint, "Virginia Woolf and the General Strike," *Essays in Criticism: A Quarterly Journal of Literary Criticism* 36.4 (1986): 319–34.
3. Further lines about Mrs. McNab that were not used in the finished novel appear in Selected Textual Variants (154–55).
4. Woolf's sister, the painter; the letter refers to a group painting exhibition at Leicester Galleries that included works by Vanessa and by Duncan Grant and that had been delayed by the General Strike.

June 17, from Vita, Berg Collection, NYPL

About prose and poetry, and the difference between them. I don't believe there is any, with all due respect to Coleridge. *** None of the definitions fit. Matthew Arnold says that poetry describes the flowing, not the fixed; why should not prose?[5]

June 21: Holograph date for "Down in the hollow of one wave" (115).

July 25, diary, Berg Collection, NYPL

What impressed me was [Thomas Hardy's] freedom, ease, & vitality. He seemed very "Great Victorian" doing the whole thing with a sweep of his hand *** & setting no great stock by literature. *** Mrs. Hardy said to me, do you know Aldous Huxley? I said I did. They had been reading his book. *** "They've changed everything now he said. We used to think there was a beginning & a middle & an end. We believed in the Aristotelian theory. Now one of those stories came to an end with a woman going out of the room." He chuckled. But he no longer read novels.[6]

July–August, diary, Berg Collection, NYPL

Rodmell. 1926

As I am not going to milk my brains for a week, I shall here write the first pages of the greatest book in the world. This is what the book would be that was made entirely solely & with integrity of one's thoughts. Suppose one could catch them before they became "works of art."? Catch them hot & sudden as they rise in the mind— walking up Asheham hill for instance. Of course one cannot; for the process of language is slow & deluding. One must stop to find a word; then, there is the form of the sentence soliciting one to fill it.

Art & Thought[7]

What I thought was this: if art is based on thought, what is the transmuting process? I was telling myself the story of our visit to the Hardys. & I began to compose it. ***

My Own Brain

Here is a whole nervous breakdown in miniature. We came on Tuesday. Sank into a chair, could scarcely rise; Everything insipid;

---

5. Samuel Taylor Coleridge (1772–1834), Romantic poet and literary critic who claimed in his *Biographia Literaria* (1817) that poetry is unique in exercising the "magical power . . . of imagination;" Matthew Arnold (1822–1888), poet and author of *Culture and Anarchy* (1869). In June and July Woolf was working on her essay on Thomas De Quincey, "Impassioned Prose," which discusses the relation between prose and poetry; this edition, pp. 253–55.

6. Virginia and Leonard paid a visit to Thomas Hardy (1840–1928) at his home, Max Gate, in Dorchester; *his book: Two or Three Graces* (1926), by Aldous Huxley (1894–1963). Hardy had stopped writing novels by this time, and wrote only poetry.

7. For the period at Rodmell from July 27 through the end of August, she replaced dated entries with a series of reflections.

tasteless, colourless. Enourmous desire for rest. Wednesday—only wish to be alone in the open air. Air delicious—avoided speech; could not read. Thought of my own power of writing with veneration, as of something incredible, belonging to someone else; never again to be enjoyed by me. Mind a blank. Slept in my chair. Thursday. No pleasure in life whatsoever; but felt perhaps more attuned to existence. Character & idiosyncracy as Virginia Woolf completely sunk out. Humble & modest. Difficulty in thinking what to say. Read automatically, like a cow chewing cud. Slept in chair. Friday. Sense of physical tiredness; but slight activity of the brain. Beginning to take notice. * * * A desire to read poetry set in on Friday. This brings back a sense of my own individuality. * * * No 'making up' power yet; no desire to cast scenes in my book. * * *

    Returning Health

This is shown by the power to make images: the suggestive power of every sight & word is enormously increased. Shakespeare must have had this to an extent which makes my normal state the state of a person blind, deaf, dumb, stone-stockish & fish-blooded. And I have it compared with poor Mrs Bartholomew almost to the extent that Shre has it compared with me.[8]

August 4: Holograph date for "She could no longer make out, there on the hillside, which was their house. All looked distant and peaceful and strange" (121).

August 17: Holograph date for "the ships looked as if they were conscious of the cliffs, as if they signalled to each other" (132).

August 26: Holograph date for "(The sea without a stain on it, thought Lily Briscoe" (136).

September 1: Holograph date for "how could he love his kind" (142).

September 3, diary, Berg Collection, NYPL

For the rest, Charleston, Tilton, To the Lighthouse, Vita, expeditions: the summer dominated by a feeling of washing in boundless warm fresh air—such an August not come my way for years: bicycling; no settled work done, but advantage taken of air for going to the river, or over the downs. The novel is now easily within sight of the end, but this, mysteriously, comes no nearer. I am doing Lily on the lawn: but whether its her last lap, I don't know. Nor am I sure of the quality; the only certainty seems to be that after tapping my antennae in the air

---

8. Mrs. Bartholomew sometimes worked as a cook at Monk's House.

vaguely for an hour every morning I generally write with heat & ease till 12.30: & thus do my two pages.

[September 5] diary, Berg Collection, NYPL
So it will be done, written over that is, in 3 weeks, I forecast, from today. What emerges? At this moment I'm casting about for an end. The problem is how to bring Lily & Mr R. together & make a combination of interest at the end. I am feathering about with various ideas. The last chapter which I begin tomorrow is In the Boat: I had meant to end with R. climbing on to the rock. If so, what becomes & Lily & her picture? Should there be a final page about her & Carmichael looking at the picture & summing up R.'s character? In that case I lose the intensity of the moment. If this intervenes, between R. & the lighthouse, there's too much chop & change, I think. Could I do it in a parenthesis? So that one had the sense of reading the two things at the same time?

September 6: Holograph date for "Indeed they were very close to the lighthouse now" (146).

September 12: Holograph date for "So it was like that, James thought" (146).

September 13, diary, Berg Collection, NYPL
The blessed thing is coming to an[9] I say to myself with a groan. Its like some prolonged rather painful & yet exciting process of nature, which one desires inexpressibly to have over. Oh the relief of waking & thinking its done—the relief & the disappointment, I suppose. * * * Morgan[1] said he felt 'This is a failure' as he finished The passage to India. I feel—what? A little stale this last week or two from steady writing. But also a little triumphant. If my feeling is correct, this is the greatest stretch I've put my method to, & I think it holds. By this I mean that I have been dredging up more feelings & character, I imagine. * * * And this last lap, in the boat, is hard, because the material is not so rich as it is with Lily on the lawn: I am forced to be more direct & more intense. I am making some use of symbolism, I observe; & I go in dread of 'sentimentality'.

September 15: Holograph date for "'He must have reached it,' said Lily Briscoe aloud" (150).

---

9. Woolf probably meant to write "end" here.
1. E. M. Forster (1879–1970), author of *A Passage to India* (1924).

September 28, diary, Berg Collection, NYPL
Intense depression: I have to confess this has overcome me several times since September 6th. * * * We had been walking, expeditioning, in the fine hot weather. I was writing the last pages of To the Lighthouse (finished, provisionally, Sept 16th). Somehow, my reading had lapsed. I was hunting no hares. * * * [N]o one came to stay, & I got very few letters; & the high pure hot days went on & on; & this blankness persisted, & I began to suspect my book of the same thing. * * *

But it is always a question whether I wish to avoid these glooms. * * * These 9 weeks give one a plunge into deep waters; which is a little alarming, but full of interest. All the rest of the year one's (I daresay rightly) curbing & controlling this odd immeasurable soul. When it expands, though one is frightened & bored & gloomy, it is as I say to myself, awfully queer. There is an edge to it which I feel of great importance, once in a way. One goes down into the well & nothing protects one from the assault of truth. Down there I cant write or read; I exist however. I am. Then I ask myself what I am? & get a closer though less flattering answer than I should on the surface— where, to tell the truth, I get more praise than is right. But the praise will go; one will be left alone with this queer being in old age.

September 30, diary, Berg Collection, NYPL
I wished to add some remarks to this, on the mystical side of this solitude; how it is not oneself but something in the universe that one's left with. It is this that is frightening & exciting in the midst of my profound gloom, depression, boredom, whatever it is: One sees a fin passing far out. What image can I reach to convey what I mean? Really there is none I think. The interesting thing is that in all my feeling & thinking I have never come up against this before. Life is, soberly & accurately, the oddest affair; has in it the essence of reality. I used to feel this as a child—couldn't step across a puddle once I remember, for thinking, how strange—what am I? &c.[2]

November 23, diary, Berg Collection, NYPL
I am re-doing six pages of Lighthouse daily. * * * My present opinion is that it is easily the best of my books. * * * Yet I have no idea yet of any other to follow it: which may mean that I have made my method perfect, & it will now stay like this, & serve whatever use I wish to put it to. Before, some development of the method brought fresh subjects in view, because I saw the chance of being able to say them. Yet I am now & then haunted by some semi mystic very profound life of

---

2. Woolf speculates that this state of mind may lead to a new book, and she later added a note in the margin: "Perhaps The Waves or moths (Oct. 1929)."

a woman, which shall all be told on one occasion; & time shall be utterly obliterated; future shall somehow blossom out of the past.

December 21, from Roger Fry to Marie Mauron[†]
I have sent off the proofs of Virginia Woolf. * * * Good Lord, how difficult she is to translate, but I think Charles has managed to keep the atmosphere marvellously. To tell the truth I do not think this piece is quite of her best vintage. I have noticed one peculiarity. She is so splendid as soon as a character is involved—for example the old *concièrge* is superb—but when she tries to give her impression of inanimate objects, she exaggerates, she underlines, she poeticizes just a little bit. Several times I felt it was better in the translation, because in translation everything is slightly reduced, less accentuated.

1927

January__, Sunday, to Edward Sackville West, Berg Collection, NYPL
I'm glad, but surprised, that you like Time Passes. I thought that between the Princesse Bassiano & the translator it had got into a hopeless mess, and was too ashamed to read it.[3]

January 14, diary, Berg Collection, NYPL
This moment I have finished the final drudgery. It is now complete for Leonard to read on Monday. Thus I have done it some days under the year, & feel thankful to be out of it again. Since October 25th I have been revising & retyping (some parts 3 times over) & no doubt I should work at it again; but I cannot. What I feel is that it is a hard muscular book, which at this age proves that I have something in me. It has not run out & gone flabby, at least such is my feeling before reading it over.

January 23, diary, Berg Collection, NYPL
Well Leonard has read To the Lighthouse, & says it is much my best book, & it is a 'masterpiece'. He said this without my asking. * * * He calls it entirely new 'a psychological poem', is his name for it. An improvement upon Dalloway: more interesting. Having won this great relief, my mind dismisses the whole thing, as usual; & I forget

---

[†] The letter appears in *Letters of Roger Fry*, vol. 2, ed. Denys Sutton (London: Chatto & Windus, 1972), p. 598. Reprinted with permission. On October 19 Woolf had written to Charles Mauron asking if he would be willing to translate a chapter of her book. Fry was handling the proofs because the Maurons were his friends.

3. "Le Temps Passe," a version of "Time Passes" translated by Charles Mauron, appeared in January 1927, in the Winter 1926 issue of the French journal *Commerce*, whose publisher was the Princesse Bassiano. In March Woolf wrote to Mauron to thank him, apparently without having read his translation.

it, & shall only wake up & be worried again over proofs & then when
it appears.

February 12, diary, Berg Collection, NYPL
I have to read To the L. tomorrow & Monday, straight through in
print: straight through, owing to my curious methods, for the first
time. * * * I may note that the first symptoms of Lighthouse are
unfavourable. Roger, it is clear did not like Time Passes. Harpers &
the Forum have refused serial rights. * * * But these opinions refer
to the rough copy, unrevised. And anyhow I feel callous: L.'s opinion keeps me steady.[4]

February 21, to Vita, Berg Collection, NYPL
[I have been] laboriously correcting two sets of proofs. My goodness
how you'll dislike that book! Honestly you will. * * * Whether its
good or bad, I know not: I'm dazed, I'm bored, I'm sick to death: I go
on crossing out commas & putting in semi-colons in a state of mar-
moreal despair.

March 5, to Vanessa, Berg Collection, NYPL
I think we are now at the same point: both mistresses of our
medium as never before: both therefore confronted with entirely new
problems of structure. Of course your colour intrigues me, seduces,
& satisfies me exquisitely. * * * I should like you to paint a large,
large picture; where everything would be brought perfectly firmly
together, yet all half flying off the canvas in rapture.

March 21, diary, Berg Collection, NYPL
Dear me, how lovely some parts of The Lighthouse are! Soft & pli-
able, & I think deep, & never a word wrong for a page at a time. This
I feel about the dinner party, & the children in the boat; but not of
Lily on the lawn. That I do not much like. But I like the end.

May 5, diary, Berg Collection, NYPL
Book out. We have sold (I think) 1690 before publication—twice
Dalloway. I write however in the shadow of the damp cloud of
the Times Lit Sup. Review, which is an exact copy of the Js R
Mrs Dalloway review, gentlemanly, kindly, timid & praising beauty,
doubting character, & leaving me moderately depressed. I am anxious
about Time Passes. Think the whole thing may be pronounced soft,
shallow, insipid, sentimental. Yet, honestly, don't much care. * * *

4. Proofs of *To the Lighthouse* had been printed by R. & R. Clark, Edinburgh, between
   January 31 and February 12. Because Roger Fry had sent the typescript of "Time Passes"
   to Mauron, he had formed his critical view of it before it was revised for incorporation
   into the novel.

I am excited about my article on Poetry & Fiction. Writing for an audience always stirs me.[5]

May 8, to Vanessa (in France), Berg Collection, NYPL
I sent you two copies of the Lighthouse * * * I hope you'll write & criticise it. I would like your good opinion, which is more than one can say of most people. Probably the subject was a little unwise: But then one falls into these things all in a second—I made it up one afternoon in the Square—without any premeditation, that I can see. How do you make up pictures? Suddenly all in a second? * * * Leonard says its my best book; but then I think he has to. * * *
God! How you'll laugh at the painting bits in the Lighthouse!

May 12, from Vita, Berg Collection, NYPL
[E]verything real is blurred to a haze by your book of which I have just read the last words, and that is the only thing which seems real. I can only say that I am dazzled and bewitched. How did you do it? how did you walk along that razor-edge without falling? why did you say anything so silly as that I "shouldn't like it"? You can never have meant that though.
    Darling, it makes me afraid of you. Afraid of your penetration and loveliness and genius.
    The dinner is the part I like best perhaps. Then the deserted house, and the passage of time, which must have been so difficult to manage and in which you've succeeded so completely. And odd bits, like the shawl over the skull, and a phrase about the unity of things on page 101—oh, and hundreds of phrases, scattered about, which are so like you (the flesh-and-blood Virginia, warming grey milk by the gas,) that it looks odd to see them in print. And of course the relationship of Mr and Mrs Ramsay. And her shadow in the window. But I could go on for ever like that. * * *
    Of course it is perfectly ridiculous to call it a novel.
    I wonder if you know how like Mrs Ramsay you are yourself? But perhaps that's because she is your mother.

May 13, to Vita, Berg Collection, NYPL
What a generous woman you are! Your letter has just come. * * * I was honest though in thinking you wouldn't care for The Lighthouse: too psychological; too many personal relationships, I think. * * * The dinner party the best thing I ever wrote: the one thing that I think justifies my faults as a writer: This damned 'method'.

5. For the *TLS* review see this edition, pp. 281–82. On May 18, Woolf gave (for the Oxford University English Club) the lecture that became the essay "Poetry, Fiction and the Future," published in the *New York Herald Tribune*, August 14 and 21, 1927, and later retitled "The Narrow Bridge of Art;" this edition, pp. 257–65.

Because I don't think one could have reached those particular emotions in any other way. I was doubtful about Time Passes. It was written in the gloom of the Strike: then I re-wrote it: then I thought it impossible as prose—I thought you could have written it as poetry. I don't know if I'm like Mrs Ramsay: as my mother died when I was 13 probably it is a child's view of her: but I have some sentimental delight in thinking that you like her. She has haunted me: but then so did that old wretch my father. Do you think it sentimental? Do you think it irreverent about him? I should like to know. I was more like him than her, I think; & therefore more critical: but he was an adorable man, & somehow, tremendous. * * *

May 15, to Vanessa, Berg Collection, NYPL
Dearest,
No letter from you—But I see how it is—
Scene: after dinner: Nessa sewing: Duncan doing absolutely nothing.
<u>Nessa:</u> (throwing down her work) Christ! There's the Lighthouse! I've only got to page 86 & I see there are 320. Now I can't write to Virginia because she'll expect me to tell her what I think of it.
<u>Duncan</u> Well, I should just tell her that you think it a masterpiece.
<u>Nessa</u> But she's sure to find out. They always do. She'll want to know why I think it's a masterpiece
<u>Duncan</u> Well Nessa, I'm afraid I can't help you, because I've only read 5 pages so far, & really I dont see much prospect of doing much reading this month, or next month, or indeed before Christmas.
<u>Nessa</u> Oh its all very well for you. But I shall have to say something: And I dont know who in the name of Jupiter all these people are (turns over some pages desperately) I think I shall make a timetable: its the only way: ten pages a day for 20 days is—
<u>Duncan</u> But you'll never be able to keep up ten pages a day.
<u>Nessa</u> (rather dashed) No—I suppose I shant. * * *6

May 16, received; dated May 11, from Vanessa, Berg Collection, NYPL†
* * * I dont flatter myself that my literary opinion is really of any interest to you & it would be difficult or impossible to give it to you in a nutshell. In fact I think I am more incapable than anyone else in the world of making an aesthetic judgment on it—only I know that I have somewhere a feeling about it as a work of art which will

---

6. Woolf's humorous imagined scene continues at length; Vanessa's response to the novel had already been written and sent from France but hadn't arrived.
†

perhaps gradually take shape & which must be enormously strong
to make any impression on me at all beside the other feelings which
you have roused in me—I suppose Im the only person in the world
who can have these feelings, at any rate to such an extent—so though
probably they dont matter to you at all you may be interested to know
how much you did make me feel. Besides I daresay they do show
something about aesthetic merits in your curious art of writing. Anyhow it seemed to me that in the first part of the book you have given
a portrait of mother which is more like her to me than anything I
could ever have conceived of as possible. It is almost painful to have
her so raised from the dead. You have made one feel the extraordinary beauty of her character, which must be the most difficult thing
in the world to do. It was like meeting her again with oneself grown
up & on equal terms & it seems to me the most astonishing feat of
creation to have been able to see her in such a way. You have given
father too I think as clearly but perhaps, I may be wrong, that isnt
quite so difficult. There is more to catch hold of. Still it seems to
me to be the only thing about him which ever gave a true idea. So
you see as far as portrait painting goes you seem to me to be a
supreme artist & it is so shattering to find oneself face to face with
those two again that I can hardly consider anything else. In fact for
the last two days I have hardly been able to attend to daily life. Duncan & I have talked about them, as each had a copy, whenever we
could get alone together, Roger too furious at being out of it for us
to be able to do so when he was there. I dont think it is only that I
knew them though that makes me feel all this, for Duncan who
didnt know them says too that for the first time he understands
mother. So your vision of her stands as a whole by itself & not only
as reminding one of facts.

But I am very bad at describing my feelings—I daresay youll
understand.   Then of course there is the relationship between
the two, which perhaps is more your subject—but it is so mixed
with the other that one cant feel only one alone. But that too is
complete & seemed to me to be understood & imagined as a
whole.   I agree with Leonard, I think it is your best work—
you see I cant quite avoid an opinion. I know that in spite of all my
personal interest I shouldnt have been moved as I was if it hadnt
moved me impersonally too, only at the moment I dont feel capable of much analysis. I am excited & thrilled & taken into another
world as one only is by a great work of art, only now also it has
this curious other interest which I cant help feeling too.   I
daresay you'll think all Ive said is nonsense. You can put it down
to the imbecile ravings of a painter on paper. By the way surely
Lily Briscoe must have been rather a good painter—before her

time perhaps, but with great gifts really? No, we didnt laugh at the bits about painting—though I'm a little doubtful about covering paints with damp cloths, but it <u>might</u> be done. But how do you make Boeuf en Daube? Does it have to be eaten on the moment after cooking 3 days?

May 16, diary, Berg Collection, NYPL
The book. Now on its feet so far as praise is concerned. * * * Nessa enthusiastic—a sublime, almost upsetting spectacle. She says it is an amazing portrait of mother; a supreme portrait painter; has lived in it; found the rising of the dead almost painful. * * * Sold 1802 of The L.: if it makes 3,000 I shall be as they say more than content.[7]

May 22, to Vanessa, Berg Collection, NYPL
I was so pleased & excited by your letter that I trotted about all day like a puppy with a bone. In fact you entirely destroyed my powers of work: I was always taking it out & reading it again, until I thought perhaps I exaggerated, & ran off to Leonard with it to ask him if he thought you really meant it. Taking into account your well known character, he decided, finally, that you probably did. So then I settled down to complete satisfaction, which no one else's letters have given me. * * *

But what do you think I did know about mother? It can't have been much. What would Quentin have known of you if you had died when he was 13? I suppose one broods over some germ; but I specially refrained either from reading her letters, or father's life. He was easier to do, but I was very much afraid you would think me sentimental. I seem to make people think that the Stephen family was one of insane gloom. I thought it was a cheerful enough book. * * * Lord Olivier writes that my horticulture & natural history is in every instance wrong: there are no rooks, elms, or dahlias in the Hebrides; my sparrows are wrong; so are my carnations: and it is impossible for women to die of childbirth in the 3rd month. He infers that Prue had had a slip (which is common in the Hebrides) & was 9 months gone. This is the sort of thing that painters know nothing of.[8]

May 25, to Vanessa, Berg Collection, NYPL
I'm in a terrible state of pleasure that you should think Mrs Ramsay so like mother. At the same time, it is a psychological mystery why she should be: how a child could know about her; except that she has always haunted me, partly, I suppose, her beauty; & then dying

---

7. Woolf later added in the margin: "This it did on July 13th."
8. About Prue's "slip:" Woolf implies this is a ridiculous idea, and the inference is especially egregious if Prue is a portrait of their older half-sister Stella Duckworth.

at that moment, I suppose she cut a great figure in one's mind when it was just awake, & had not any experience of life. Only then one would have suspected that one had made up a sham—an ideal. Probably there is a great deal of you in Mrs Ramsay; though, in fact, I think you & mother are very different in my mind. Why do I attach so much importance to what you & Duncan think? Illiterate, simpletons, as you are? I daresay you are qualified however, much more than many of my literary friends to judge of things as a whole, as works of art.

May 17, from Roger Fry, Monk's House Papers, Sussex University[†]

Well I've just finished 'To the Lighthouse'. You won't want or expect criticisms from me—I'm not du métier. How little, I realized when I tried to imagine how I should describe the problems of a writer à la Lily Briscoe (in which by the by Vanessa and I both think you come through unscathed and triumphant though a little breathless and anxious perhaps). I know I should make a great mess of that.

So you won't get a criticism only you can't help my thinking it the best thing you've done, actually better than Mrs. Dalloway. You're no longer bothered by the simultaneity of things and go backwards and forwards in time with an extraordinary enrichment of each moment of consciousness.

I'm sure that there's lots I haven't understood and that when I talk it over with Morgan he'll have discovered a lot of hidden meanings. I suspect for instance that arriving at the Lighthouse has a symbolic meaning which escapes me. But I wonder if it matters. I think vague overtones of the actual events (I do not know what else to call them though thank goodness nothing happens on the stage—How wise you are to kill people such a long way behind the scene) count in the effect without one's knowing all they may imply or did imply to you.

My own private suspicion (which is not you must note an appreciation) is that it is rather a great book. It's certainly the most intensely human thing you've done. Also you've created or perhaps realized and transmitted a great character. I'd give anything to know—though probably even you can't tell me—how much you may unconsciously have drawn on Vanessa or whether it's just what is like in both.

Well I wish intensely that you had dedicated it to me. I think I must exact a copy with a private dedication. But I should have been enormously proud if my name had got linked on to that book.

† The following two letters were transcribed by the editor of this Norton Critical Edition at Sussex University Library. SxMs-18/1/D/58/2. Monk's House Papers, University of Sussex Special Collections at the Keep. Reprinted with permission.

May 27, to Roger Fry, Monk's House Papers, Sussex University

Thank you very much for your letter. I am immensely glad that you like the Lighthouse. Now I wish I had dedicated it to you. But when I read it over it seemed to me so bad that I couldn't face asking you. And then, as it happened, that very day, I met you somewhere,—was so overcome (did you guess it?) by your magnificence, splendour & purity (of intellect, not body) that I went home & was positive it was out of the question—dedicating such a book to such a man. Really therefore the not-dedication is a greater compliment than the dedication would have been. But you shall have a private copy, if you'll accept it. What I meant was (but would not have said in print) that besides all your surpassing private virtues, you have I think kept me on the right path, so far as writing goes, more than anyone—if the right path it is.

I meant <u>nothing</u> by The Lighthouse. One has to have a central line down the middle of the book to hold the design together. I saw that all sorts of feelings would accrue to this, but I refused to think them out, & trusted that people would make it the deposit for their own emotions—which they have done, one thinking it means one thing another another. I can't manage Symbolism except in this vague, generalised way. Whether it's right or wrong I don't know; but directly I'm told what a thing means, it becomes hateful to me.

I did not consciously think of Nessa when I was doing Mrs. Ramsay. In fact she & my mother seemed to me very different people. But no doubt something of Nessa leaked in. After all, my mother died when I was 13, so that the idea must have been developed somehow.

June 6, diary, Berg Collection, NYPL

And now, with Morgan's morganatic, evasive, elusive letter[9] this morning, The Lighthouse is behind me. * * * I think * * * I am now almost an established figure—as a writer. They dont laugh at me any longer. Soon they will take me for granted. Possibly I shall be a celebrated writer. Anyhow, The Lighthouse is much more nearly a success, in the usual sense of the word, than any other book of mine.

July 11 [misdated July 10], diary, Berg Collection, NYPL

I have never mentioned the absorbing subject—the subject which has filled our thoughts to the exclusion of Clive & Mary & literature & death & life—motor cars.[1] * * * We have decided on a Singer.

9. E. M. Forster had written to her that it was difficult for him to formulate his thoughts about her book and that he would like to speak with her about it. He found it both sad and beautiful, raising questions in his mind while also striking him as perhaps her best work. For the text of his letter, see *Selected Letters of E. M. Forster,* ed. Mary Lago and P. N. Furbank, 2 vols. (Cambridge: Harvard UP, 1983), vol. 2, pp. 76–78.

1. On October 3, 1926, Woolf had written to a young friend, the writer Gerald Brenan, that she had just finished writing her novel and now wanted only "to buy a motor

And, the reason why I am distracted now is that Fred is going to ring me up & say if I am to have my first lesson this evening. * * * This is a great opening up in our lives. One may go to Bodiam, to Arundel, explore the Chichester downs, expand that curious thing, the map of the world in one's mind. It will I think demolish loneliness, & may of course imperil complete privacy.

July 23, diary, Berg Collection, NYPL
Since making the last entry I have learnt enough to drive a car in the country alone. On backs of paper I write down instructions for starting cars. We have a nice light little shut up car in which we can travel thousands of miles. It is very dark blue, with a paler line around it. The world gave me this for writing The Lighthouse, I reflect, a book which has now sold 3,160 (perhaps) copies: will sell 3,500 before it dies, & thus far exceeds any other of mine.

September 4, diary, Berg Collection, NYPL
Many scenes have come & gone unwritten, since it is today the 4th Sept, a cold grey blowy day, made memorable by the sight of a kingfisher, & by my sense, waking early, of being again visited by 'the spirit of delight'. "Rarely rarely comest thou, spirit of delight." That was I singing this time last year; & sang so poignantly that I have never forgotten it, or my vision of a fin rising on a wide blank sea.[2] No biographer could possibly guess this important fact about my life in the late summer of 1926; yet biographers pretend they know people.

November 20, diary, Berg Collection, NYPL
I think on the whole this is our happiest autumn. So much work; & success now; & life on easy terms. * * * Fame increases; I think. Young men write about me in their absurd random books.

1928

May 4, diary, Berg Collection, NYPL
The prize was an affair of dull stupid horror: a function; not alarming; stupefying. Hugh Walpole saying how much he disliked my books; rather, how much he feared for his own.[3] * * * Also the 'fame' is becoming vulgar & a nuisance. It means nothing; & yet takes one's time. Americans perpetually.

---

car . . . and wander over The Continent, poking into ruined cities, basking, drinking, writing, like you, in cafés" (*Letters* 3: 296).

2. The quotation is from Percy Shelley; for the vision of the fin, see above, diary, September 30, 1926 (174).

3. On May 2, Woolf was awarded the 1927–28 Femina Vie Heureuse prize (for a foreign book) for *To the Lighthouse*; Hugh Walpole (1884–1941), a British novelist and friend of Woolf's, gave the award.

November 28, diary, Berg Collection, NYPL
                              1928
Father's birthday. He would have been <u>1832</u> 96, yes, today; & could
                                        96
have been 96, like other people one has known; but mercifully was
not. His life would have entirely ended mine. What would have
happened? No writing; no books;—inconceivable. I used to think of
him & mother daily; but writing The Lighthouse, laid them in my
mind. And now he comes back sometimes, but differently. (I believe
this to be true—that I was obsessed by them both, unhealthily; &
writing of them was a necessary act.) He comes back now more as a
contemporary. I must read him some day. I wonder if I can feel again,
I hear his voice, I know this by heart?

Autobiographical Writings

VIRGINIA WOOLF

Although 22 Hyde Park Gate was the family home in London, the Stephen children continued to produce the *News* at Talland House, in St. Ives, Cornwall, where the family annually stayed from July or August to early October. The handwritten, double-column issues were composed and illustrated by Virginia and Vanessa, with occasional contributions by Thoby, surely delighting their parents with their dry wit and arch use of journalistic conventions (the authors refer to themselves as "the juveniles"). Issues survive from 1891 to April 1895, a month before Julia Stephen's death. In the summer of 1892, when Virginia was ten years old, among reports of family games and outings, guests arriving and leaving, Julia's matchmaking, troublesome rats and the dog acquired to dispatch them, and installments of a serial story titled "A Cockney's Farming Experiences," the *News* reports on matters that resonate in *To the Lighthouse*.

Hyde Park Gate News[†]

Vol. II, No. 35 *Monday, 12th September* 1892

On Saturday morning Master Hilary Hunt and Master Basil Smith came up to Talland House and asked Master Thoby and Miss Virginia Stephen to accompany them to the light-house as Freeman the boatman said that there was a perfect tide and wind for going there. Master Adrian Stephen was much disappointed at not being allowed to go.[1] On arriving at the light-house Miss Virginia Stephen saw a small and dilapidated bird standing on one leg on the light-house. Mrs Hunt called the man and asked him how it had got there. He said that it had been blown there and they then saw that it's eyes had been picked out. On the way home Master Basil Smith "spued like fury".

---

† From *Hyde Park Gate News*, vol. II, No. 35 (Monday, 12th September 1892) and vol. II, No. 38 (Monday, 3rd October 1892) as it appeared in *Hyde Park Gate News: The Stephen Family Newspaper*, ed. Gill Lowe (London: Hesperus Press, 2005), pp. 108–9, 118. Reprinted by permission of The Society of Authors as the Literary Representative of the Estate of Virginia Woolf.

1. Adrian was Julia and Leslie Stephen's youngest child, often taken to be a model for James. The Godrevy Island lighthouse visitors' log lists Virginia and other Stephen family members as visitors in 1892 and 1894.

Vol. II, No. 38 Monday, 3rd October 1892

On Monday Mr Stephen with his youngest son and daughter went down to the pier and there looked about for a boat. After a long time of waiting a man appeared. They were soon out and sailing merrily along. There was a good breeze and it not being too calm the party was in high spirits. "The music of the water" as Mr Mitchel says "beating against the boat the gulls puffins and other sea birds making so harmonious a sound that it would delight the ears of a musician. The sail ended hapily by seeing the sea pig or porpoise.

Mrs Stephen who is really like a "Good Angel" to the poor of St Ives is now trying to get enough "Filthy Lucre" to start a nurse in the town. In her pilgrimages among the poor she has discovered the real want of one and with Mrs Hain Mrs Staff and a few other ladies she has already made a start. This is not at all a new scheme of Mrs Stephen's but it seems that few other ladies have had the courage or wit to start a similar adventure. We heartily wish the plan all the success it deserves.

———————

In 1905 the four Stephen siblings traveled back to Cornwall for a summer holiday, staying in Trevose House overlooking Carbis Bay from August to early October. Their last visit had been in 1894, the summer before their mother's death. Although houses, hotels, and roads had urbanized the neighborhood of Talland House, Woolf records the pleasures of revisiting people and places and rediscovering familiar walking routes where nothing seemed to have changed. At the start of her writing career, she alternates between vivid, straightforward diary entries and the self-consciously literary style of a late-Victorian local color writer. She reread the diary volume in which these entries appear while writing *To the Lighthouse*. The journal entries begin with the train journey from London.

Diary: Cornwall 1905[†]

* * *

Ah, how strange it was, then, to watch the familiar shapes of land & sea unroll themselves once more, as though a magicians hand had

[†] From *A Passionate Apprentice: The Early Journals, 1897–1909*, ed. Mitchell A. Leaska (London: Hogarth Press and San Diego: Harcourt Brace Jovanovich, 1990), pp. 281–82, 286–90. Published by Chatto & Windus. Text copyright © 1990 by Quentin Bell and Angelica Garnett. Used by permission of HarperCollins Publishers and Random House Group Ltd.

raised the curtain that hung between us, & to see once more the silent but palpable forms, which for more than ten years we had seen only in dreams, or in the visions of waking hours.

It was dusk when we came, so that there still seemed to be a film between us & the reality. We could fancy that we were but coming home along the high road after some long day's outing, & that when we reached the gate at Talland House, we should thrust it open, & find ourselves among the familiar sights again. In the dark, indeed, we made bold to humour this fancy of ours further than we had a right to; we passed through the gate, groped stealthily but with sure feet up the carriage drive, mounted the little flight of rough steps, & peered through a chink in the escalonia hedge. There was the house, with its two lighted windows; there on the terrace were the stone urns, against the bank of tall flowers; all, so far as we could see was as though we had but left it in the morning. But yet, as we knew well, we could go no further; if we advanced the spell was broken. The lights were not our lights; the voices were the voices of strangers. [ ] We hung there like ghosts in the shade of the hedge, & at the sound of footsteps we turned away.

From the raised platform of the high road we beheld the curve wh. seemed to enclose a great sweep of bay full tonight of liquid mist, set with silver stars & we traced the promontory of the island, & saw the cluster of lights which nestle in its warm hollow.

The dawn however rose upon that dim twilight & showed us a country of bright hill sides, of cliffs tumbling in a cascade of brown rocks into the sea, &, alas, we saw also not a few solid white mansions where the heather used to spring. They have cut a broad public road too, where we stumbled along a foot path on the side of the moor, & there are signs, as [A.] said, that the whole place has been tidied up since our day. There are differences though, which only strike a very fresh eye, & in two days time we see only the permanent outlines of the moor & island, & the place is in substance & detail unchanged.

* * *

Today we set apart as a day of pilgrimage to certain old St Ives people, who in spite of the passage of eleven years, still cherish some faithful memory of us. So at least we were told, though I think we delayed the expedition a little from fear we might find that this statement had been exaggerated. The farmers daughter who used to bring us our chickens & help in the house, the woman who took in our washing, the old man who kept the bathing tents & his wife; these were the people we proposed to visit in their cottages in St Ives.

There was no doubt, at any rate that Jinny Berryman, as she was, did cordially remember & welcome us. It was a pleasure to see the blank respectful face of the woman behind the counter in the eating shop glow with sudden recognition when we spoke our name. We were made to sit down, & hear how we had changed, or had remained the same; whom we were like & whom we in no way resembled, how we climbed the tree in the garden, & how in short, we were much as other children are, but to this woman at least, remarkable in all we did & said.

* * *

At Mrs Daniels the same story was repeated. * * * All kinds of trivial half forgotten memories revived & we did our share of question, & anecdote; we asserted that there was no place like St Ives, & that we had never forgotten its washer woman. Indeed, we were not guilty of insincerity; her portrait had been lying unexposed in some dim recess of our brains, & at the first sight of her face the old picture became clear again, & with it a multitude of slighter impressions which seem to cluster round it. I could see her once more tramping up the drive with her basket of clean clothes, leaning away from her burden, & ready to put it down & talk good humouredly if we stopped her.

* * *

* * * At ebb tide in the evening the stretch of the sands here is vast & melancholy; the waves spread themselves one over lapping the other in thin fan shaped layers of water; so shallow that the break of the wave is hardly more than a ripple. The slope of the beach gleams as though laid with a film of mother o' pearl where the sea has been, & a row of sea gulls sits on the skirts of the repeating wave. The pallor of the sandhills makes the scene yet more ghostly, but the beautiful sights are often melancholy & very lonely.

* * *

———

After Woolf's father, Leslie Stephen, died in February 1904, Frederic W. Maitland undertook to write the authorized biography. He invited Virginia to select and copy passages from letters between Leslie and Julia that he could use, and to write something about her father's later years. Incorporated into *The Life and Letters of Leslie Stephen* (1906) as a contribution from "one of his daughters," this essay is among her earliest publications. In addition to this remembrance and passages about him in her memoirs, Woolf also wrote "Leslie Stephen, the Philosopher at Home: A Daughter's Memories" (1932), in which she recalled, as she does here, his habit of reciting poetry as if he were speaking his own words. In "The Philosopher at Home," she celebrates his approach to educating her—"allowing a girl of 15 the free run of a large and quite unexpurgated library," with instructions "to read what one liked because one liked it, never to pretend to admire what one did not"—and quotes tributes by his eminent friends George Meredith and James Russell Lowell, who called him "the most lovable of men" (Virginia Woolf, *The Essays of Virginia Woolf*, transpose *Woolf*, vol. 5: *1929–1932*, ed. Stuart N. Clarke [Orlando: Harcourt, 2009], pp. 585–93, quotations pp. 588–89).

Impressions of Sir Leslie Stephen[†]

* * *

'My impression as a child always was that my father was not very much older than we were. He used to take us to sail our boats in the Round Pond, and with his own hands fitted one out with masts and sails after the pattern of a Cornish lugger; and we knew that his interest was no 'grown-up' pretence; it was as genuine as our own; so there was a perfectly equal companionship between us. Every evening we spent an hour and a half in the drawing-room, and, as far back as I can remember, he found some way of amusing us himself. At first he drew pictures of animals as fast as we could demand them, or cut them out of paper with a pair of scissors. Then when we were old enough he spent the time in reading aloud to us. I cannot remember any book before "Tom Brown's School Days" and "Treasure Island";[1] but it must have been very soon that we attacked the first of that long line of red backs—the thirty-two volumes of the Waverley Novels, which provided reading for many years of evenings, because when we had finished the last he was ready to begin the first over again. At the end of a volume my father always gravely asked our opinion as to its merits, and we were required to say which of the characters we liked best and why. I can remember his indignation when one of us preferred the hero to the far more life-like villain. My father always loved reading aloud, and of all books, I think, he loved Scott's the best. In the last years of his life, when he was tired of reading anything else, he would send one of us to the bookshelf to take down the first of the Waverley Novels that happened to present itself, and this he would open at random and read with quiet satisfaction till bedtime. * * *

'His memory for poetry was wonderful; he could absorb a poem that he liked almost unconsciously from a single reading, and it amused him to discover what odd fragments and often quite second-rate pieces had "stuck" to him, as he said, in this way. He had long

---

[†] From Frederic W. Maitland, *The Life and Letters of Leslie Stephen* (London: Duckworth, 1906), pp. 474–76.

1. Thomas Hughes, *Tom Brown's School Days* (1857); Robert Louis Stevenson, *Treasure Island* (1883).

ago acquired all the most famous poems of Wordsworth, Tennyson, Keats, and Matthew Arnold, among moderns. Milton of old writers was the one he knew best; he specially loved the "Ode on the Nativity," which he said to us regularly on Christmas night. This was indeed the last poem he tried to say on the Christmas night before he died; he remembered the words, but was then too weak to speak them. * * * He very much disliked reading poems from a book, and if he could not speak from memory he generally refused to recite at all. His recitation, or whatever it may be called, gained immensely from this fact, for as he lay back in his chair and spoke the beautiful words with closed eyes, we felt that he was speaking not merely the words of Tennyson or Wordsworth but what he himself felt and knew. Thus many of the great English poems now seem to me inseparable from my father; I hear in them not only his voice, but in some sort his teaching and belief.

* * *

Written in 1907–8 and addressed to her sister Vanessa Bell's first son Julian around the time of his birth, "Reminiscences" began as a "life" of Vanessa but evolved into an account of Woolf's early memories, especially of the deaths of her mother and her older half-sister Stella, whose death in turn left Vanessa (at eighteen) to manage the household and bear the brunt of Leslie's grief and bad temper. Woolf's portrait of her mother here differs markedly from her father's portrait of Julia in his *Mausoleum Book*; "Reminiscences" was not intended for publication, and Woolf's private portrayal of her father as a "tyrant" differs even more markedly from the public tribute she contributed to Maitland's *Life and Letters* and from her later "Leslie Stephen: The Philosopher at Home" (1932).

The publication in 1975 of the first edition of *Moments of Being: Unpublished Autobiographical Writings of Virginia Woolf,* in which "Reminiscences" and "A Sketch of the Past" (see next selection) appeared in print for the first time, transformed readers' understanding of *To the Lighthouse,* as these two memoirs reveal what many readers believe to be "the autobiographical origins of *To the Lighthouse*" and, too, the reason "why Virginia Woolf was impelled to write that novel;" Jane Lilienfeld, " 'The Deceptiveness of Beauty': Mother Love and Mother Hate in *To the Lighthouse," Twentieth-Century Literature* 23 (1977): 345–76, quotations p. 345.

From Reminiscences[†]

* * *

In this sense your grandmother's death was disastrous; for you must conceive that she was not only the most beautiful of women as her portraits will tell you, but also one of the most distinct. Her life had been so swift, it was to be so short, that experiences which in most have space to expand themselves and bear leisurely fruit, were all compressed in her; she had married, borne children, and mourned her husband by the time she was twenty-four. For eight years she pondered that active season, and as I guess, formulated then in great part the judgement of life which underlay her future. She had been happy as few people are happy, for she had passed like a princess in a pageant from her supremely beautiful youth to marriage and mother-hood, without awakenment. * * * [S]he had lived with a man, stain-less of his kind, exalted in a world of pure love and beauty. The effect of his death then was doubly tremendous, because it was a disillu-sionment as well as a tragic human loss. * * * She flung aside her religion, and became, as I have heard, the most positive of disbelievers. She reversed those natural instincts which were so strong in her of happiness and joy in a generous and abundant life, and pressed the bitterest fruit only to her lips. She visited the poor, nursed the dying, and felt herself possessed of the true secret of life at last, which is still obscured from a few, though they too must come to know it, that sorrow is our lot, and at best we can but face it bravely. * * *

Fate, who is thought by some to arrange human lives to her lik-ing, chose that your grandfather, with his first wife, should live in the same street with your grandmother and further decreed that Minny was to die there, and that your grandmother thus should be thrown into contact with her learned and formidable friend under the conditions which she of all people felt most poignantly. Would any other arrangement of circumstances have so brought about the miracle? For she found one who had equal reasons with herself to believe in the sorrow of life and every incentive to adopt her own stoic philosophy; he also was of the giant breed, no light lover, no superficial optimist. She might go hand in hand with him through the shadows of the Valley—but, of a sudden, her companion became her guide, pointed on, urged her to follow, to hope, to strive once

† From *Moments of Being*, ed. Jeanne Schulkind, 2nd ed. (San Diego: Harcourt Brace Jova-novich, 1985), pp. 32–37, 40, 55–56. Published by Chatto & Windus. Text copyright © 1985, 1976 by Quentin Bell and Angelica Garnett. Introduction and editorial matter copy-right © 1985, 1976 by Jeanne Schulkind. Used by permission of HarperCollins Publishers, Random House Group Ltd., and The Society of Authors as the Literary Representative of the Estate of Virginia Woolf.

more. She could not so soon throw off what had come to be a habit of suffering almost, and yet his reason was the stronger, his need was the greater. At length with pain and remorse she, courageous as she was, more truly courageous perhaps than her husband, bade herself face the truth and realize in all its aspects the fact that joy was to be endured as well as sorrow. * * *

These circumstances had taken their part in forming your grandmother's character; and by the time we, her children, knew her, she was the most prompt, practical and vivid of human beings. It was as though she had made up her mind definitely upon certain great matters and was never after troubled to consider herself at all; but every deed and word had the bright, inexorable, swift stamp of something struck clearly by a mass of hoarded experience. Four children were born to her; there were four others already, older, demanding other care;[1] she taught us, was their companion, and soothed, cheered, inspired, nursed, deceived your grandfather; and any one coming for help found her invincibly upright in her place, with time to give, earnest consideration, and the most practical sympathy. * * * Her intellectual gifts had always been those that find their closest expression in action; she had great clearness of insight, sound judgement, humour, and a power of grasping very quickly the real nature of someone's circumstances, and so arranging that the matter, whatever it was, fell into its true proportions at once. Sometimes with her natural impetuosity, she took it on herself to despatch difficulties with a high hand, like some commanding Empress. But most often I think her service, when it was not purely practical, lay in simply helping people by the light of her judgement and experience, to see what they really meant or felt. But any sensible woman may have these qualities, and yet be none of the things that your grandmother was. All her gifts had something swift, decisive, witty even, in their nature; so that there could be no question of dulness or drudgery in her daily work, however lugubrious it seemed of itself. * * *

* * *

* * * You will not find in what I say, or again in those sincere but conventional phrases in the life of your grandfather, or in the noble lamentations with which he fills the pages of his autobiography,[2] any semblance of a woman whom you can love. It has often occurred to me to regret that no one ever wrote down her sayings and vivid ways of speech since she had the gift of turning words in a manner peculiar to her, rubbing her hands swiftly, or raising them in gesticulation as she spoke. I can see her, standing by the open door of a

---

1. The "four others" were Julia's three children by her first husband, Herbert Duckworth, and Laura, the daughter of Leslie Stephen and his first wife, Minny.
2. *The Mausoleum Book*, this edition, pp. 210–15.

railway carriage which was taking Stella and some others to Cambridge, and striking out in a phrase or two pictures of all the people who came past her along the platform, and so she kept them laughing till the train went.

What would one not give to recapture a single phrase even! or the tone of the clear round voice, or the sight of the beautiful figure, so upright and so distinct, in its long shabby cloak, with the head held at a certain angle, a little upwards, so that the eye looked straight out at you. "Come children," she would say directly she had waved her last fantastic farewell, and one would grasp her umbrella, and another her arm, and one no doubt would stand gaping, and she would call sharply, "Quick, quick". And so she would pass with her swift step, through the crowds, and into some dingy train or omnibus, where perhaps she would ask the conductor why the company did not give him straw to stand on—"Your feet must be cold"—and hear his story and make her comment, until we were home just in time for lunch. * * *

* * * The relationship between your grandfather and mother was, as the saying is, perfect, nor would I for a moment dispute that, believing as I do that each of these much tried and by no means easy-going people found in the other the highest and most perfect harmony which their natures could respond to. Beautiful often, even to our eyes, were their gestures, their glances of pure and unutterable delight in each other. But, if I can convey my meaning by the metaphor, the high consonance, the flute voices of two birds in tune, was only reached by rich, rapid scales of discord, and incongruity. After all she was fifteen years the younger, and his age was made emphatic by the keen intellect, always voyaging, as she must have thought, alone in ice-bound seas. * * *

* * * But she never belittled her own works, thinking them, if properly discharged, of equal, though other, importance with her husband's. Thus in those moments, breathing spaces in the incessant conflict, when each rested secure for a second in the other's embrace, she knew with just but always delighted pride, that he worshipped in her something as unchallengeably high as the lofty remote peak which she honoured in him. * * *

* * * She died when she was forty-eight, and your mother was a child of fifteen. If what I have said of her has any meaning you will believe that her death was the greatest disaster that could happen; it was as though on some brilliant day of spring the racing clouds of a sudden stood still, grew dark, and massed themselves; the wind flagged, and all creatures on the earth moaned or wandered seeking aimlessly. But what figures or variety of figures will do justice to the shapes which since then she has taken in countless lives? The dead, so people say, are forgotten, or they should rather say, that life has for the most part little significance to any of us. But now and again

on more occasions than I can number, in bed at night, or in the street, or as I come into the room, there she is; beautiful, emphatic, with her familiar phrase and her laugh; closer than any of the living are, lighting our random lives as with a burning torch, infinitely noble and delightful to her children.

* * *

[Two years after the death of Julia Stephen, her oldest daughter, Stella, died, leaving Virginia and Vanessa virtually alone with their father.]

* * * [F]or us the tragedy was but just beginning; as in the case of other wounds the pain was drugged at the moment, and made itself felt afterwards when we began to move. There was pain in all our circumstances, or a dull discomfort, a kind of restlessness and aimlessness which was even worse. Misery of this kind tends to concentrate itself upon an object, if it can find one, and there was a figure, unfortunately, who would serve our purpose very well. Your grandfather showed himself strangely brisk, and so soon as we came to think, we fastened our eyes upon him, and found just cause for anger. We remembered how he had tasked Stella's strength, embittered her few months of joy, and now when he should be penitent, he showed less grief than anyone. On the contrary none was more vigorous, and there were signs at once which woke us to a sort of frenzy, that he was quite prepared to take Vanessa for his next victim. When he was sad, he explained, she should be sad; when he was angry, as he was periodically when she asked him for a cheque, she should weep; instead she stood before him like a stone. A girl who had character would not tolerate such speeches, and when she connected them with other words of the same kind, addressed to the sister lately dead, to her mother even, it was not strange that an uncompromising anger took possession of her. We made him the type of all that we hated in our lives; he was the tyrant of inconceivable selfishness, who had replaced the beauty and merriment of the dead with ugliness and gloom. We were bitter, harsh, and to a great extent, unjust; but even now it seems to me that there was some truth in our complaint; and sufficient reason why both parties should be unable at the time and without fault, to come to a good understanding. If he had been ten years younger, or we older, or had there been a mother or sister to intervene, much pain and anger and loneliness might have been spared. But again, death spoilt what should have been so fair.

* * *

"A Sketch of the Past," written 1939–40 and neither finished nor prepared for publication, is an episodic memoir and a meditation on memory, on writing about the self, and on the transformation of memory into
art. (See headnote to "Reminiscences" for the impact of the 1975 first
publication of "A Sketch of the Past" on reading *To the Lighthouse*.) Woolf
wrote it under the growing threat of German bombing campaigns, which
endangered life in the countryside south of London and which eventually destroyed her London home. She was also under pressure to complete her biography of Roger Fry, which was published in July 1940; and
she was writing under the influence of reading Freud seriously for the
first time and absorbing his views on the family romance, on the lasting impact of childhood trauma, and on the subjectivity of memory.
These selections sample both the memories that relate to the composition of *To the Lighthouse* and her meditations on transforming those
memories into novel form.

From A Sketch of the Past[†]

* * *

* * * If life has a base that it stands upon, if it is a bowl that one fills
and fills and fills—then my bowl without a doubt stands upon this
memory. It is of lying half asleep, half awake, in bed in the nursery
at St Ives. It is of hearing the waves breaking, one, two, one, two,
and sending a splash of water over the beach; and then breaking,
one, two, one, two, behind a yellow blind. It is of hearing the blind
draw its little acorn across the floor as the wind blew the blind out.
It is of lying and hearing this splash and seeing this light, and feeling, it is almost impossible that I should be here; of feeling the pur-
est ecstasy I can conceive.

* * *

* * * [T]here was one external reason for the intensity of this first
impression: the impression of the waves and the acorn on the blind;
the feeling, as I describe it sometimes to myself, of lying in a grape
and seeing through a film of semi-transparent yellow—it was due
partly to the many months we spent in London. The change of
nursery was a great change. And there was the long train journey;

† From *Moments of Being*, ed. Jeanne Schulkind, 2nd ed. (San Diego: Harcourt Brace
  Jovanovich, 1985), pp. 64–66, 71–72, 80–84, 107–08, 127–31, 134–35. Published by
  Chatto & Windus. Text copyright © 1985, 1976 by Quentin Bell and Angelica Garnett.
  Introduction and editorial matter copyright © 1985, 1976 by Jeanne Schulkind. Used by
  permission of HarperCollins Publishers, Random House Group Ltd., and The Society
  of Authors as the Literary Representative of the Estate of Virginia Woolf.

and the excitement. I remember the dark; the lights; the stir of the going up to bed.

But to fix my mind upon the nursery—it had a balcony; there was a partition, but it joined the balcony of my father's and mother's bedroom. My mother would come out on to her balcony in a white dressing gown. There were passion flowers growing on the wall; they were great starry blossoms, with purple streaks, and large green buds, part empty, part full.

If I were a painter I should paint these first impressions in pale yellow, silver, and green. There was the pale yellow blind; the green sea; and the silver of the passion flowers. I should make a picture that was globular; semi-transparent. I should make a picture of curved petals; of shells; of things that were semi-transparent; I should make curved shapes, showing the light through, but not giving a clear outline. Everything would be large and dim; and what was seen would at the same time be heard; sounds would come through this petal or leaf—sounds indistinguishable from sights. Sound and sight seem to make equal parts of these first impressions. When I think of the early morning in bed I also hear the caw of rooks falling from a great height. The sound seems to fall through an elastic, gummy air; which holds it up; which prevents it from being sharp and distinct. The quality of the air above Talland House seemed to suspend sound, to let it sink down slowly, as if it were caught in a blue gummy veil. The rooks cawing is part of the waves breaking— one, two, one, two—and the splash as the wave drew back and then it gathered again, and I lay there half awake, half asleep, drawing in such ecstasy as I cannot describe.

The next memory—all these colour-and-sound memories hang together at St Ives—was much more robust; it was highly sensual. It was later. It still makes me feel warm; as if everything were ripe; humming; sunny; smelling so many smells at once; and all making a whole that even now makes me stop—as I stopped then going down to the beach; I stopped at the top to look down at the gardens. They were sunk beneath the road. The apples were on a level with one's head. The gardens gave off a murmur of bees; the apples were red and gold; there were also pink flowers; and grey and silver leaves. The buzz, the croon, the smell, all seemed to press voluptuously against some membrane; not to burst it; but to hum round one such a complete rapture of pleasure that I stopped, smelt; looked. * * *

* * *

* * * Week after week passed at St Ives and nothing made any dint upon me. Then, for no reason that I know about, there was a sudden violent shock; something happened so violently that I have remembered it all my life. I will give a few instances. The first: I was fighting

with Thoby on the lawn. We were pommelling each other with our fists. Just as I raised my fist to hit him, I felt: why hurt another person? I dropped my hand instantly, and stood there, and let him beat me. I remember the feeling. It was a feeling of hopeless sadness. It was as if I became aware of something terrible; and of my own powerlessness. I slunk off alone, feeling horribly depressed. The second instance was also in the garden at St Ives. I was looking at the flower bed by the front door; "That is the whole", I said. I was looking at a plant with a spread of leaves; and it seemed suddenly plain that the flower itself was a part of the earth; that a ring enclosed what was the flower; and that was the real flower; part earth; part flower. It was a thought I put away as being likely to be very useful to me later. The third case was also at St Ives. Some people called Valpy had been staying at St Ives, and had left. We were waiting at dinner one night, when somehow I overheard my father or my mother say that Mr Valpy had killed himself. The next thing I remember is being in the garden at night and walking on the path by the apple tree. It seemed to me that the apple tree was connected with the horror of Mr Valpy's suicide. I could not pass it. I stood there looking at the grey-green creases of the bark—it was a moonlit night—in a trance of horror. I seemed to be dragged down, hopelessly, into some pit of absolute despair from which I could not escape. My body seemed paralysed.

There are three instances of exceptional moments. I often tell them over, or rather they come to the surface unexpectedly. But now that for the first time I have written them down, I realise something that I have never realised before. Two of these moments ended in a state of despair. The other ended, on the contrary, in a state of satisfaction. *** I do not know if I was older when I saw the flower than I was when I had the other two experiences. I only know that many of these exceptional moments brought with them a peculiar horror and a physical collapse; they seemed dominant; myself passive. This suggests that as one gets older one has a greater power through reason to provide an explanation; and that this explanation blunts the sledge-hammer force of the blow. I think this is true, because though I still have the peculiarity that I receive these sudden shocks, they are now always welcome; after the first surprise, I always feel instantly that they are particularly valuable. And so I go on to suppose that the shock-receiving capacity is what makes me a writer. I hazard the explanation that a shock is at once in my case followed by the desire to explain it. I feel that I have had a blow; but it is not, as I thought as a child, simply a blow from an enemy hidden behind the cotton wool of daily life; it is or will become a revelation of some order; it is a token of some real thing behind appearances; and I make it real by putting it into words. It is only by putting it into words that I make it whole; this wholeness means that it has lost its power to hurt me; it gives me, perhaps because by doing so I take away the pain, a great delight to put the severed parts together. Perhaps this is the strongest pleasure known to me. It is the rapture I get when in writing I seem to be discovering what belongs to what; making a scene come right; making a character come together. From this I reach what I might call a philosophy; at any rate it is a constant idea of mine; that behind the cotton wool is hidden a pattern; that we—I mean all human beings—are connected with this; that the whole world is a work of art; that we are parts of the work of art. *Hamlet* or a Beethoven quartet is the truth about this vast mass that we call the world. But there is no Shakespeare, there is no Beethoven; certainly and emphatically there is no God; we are the words; we are the music; we are the thing itself. And I see this when I have a shock.

* * *

Until I was in the forties, * * * the presence of my mother obsessed me. I could hear her voice, see her, imagine what she would do or say as I went about my day's doings. She was one of the invisible presences who after all play so important a part in every life. * * *

* * *

* * * Then one day walking round Tavistock Square I made up, as I sometimes make up my books, *To the Lighthouse*; in a great, apparently involuntary, rush. One thing burst into another. Blowing bubbles out of a pipe gives the feeling of the rapid crowd of ideas and scenes which blew out of my mind, so that my lips seemed syllabling of their own accord as I walked. What blew the bubbles? Why then? I have no notion. But I wrote the book very quickly; and when it was written, I ceased to be obsessed by my mother. I no longer hear her voice; I do not see her.

I suppose that I did for myself what psycho-analysts do for their patients. I expressed some very long felt and deeply felt emotion. And in expressing it I explained it and then laid it to rest. But what is the meaning of "explained" it? Why, because I described her and my feeling for her in that book, should my vision of her and my feeling for her become so much dimmer and weaker? Perhaps one of these days I shall hit on the reason; and if so, I will give it, but at the moment I will go on, describing what I can remember, for it may be true that what I remember of her now will weaken still further. (This note is made provisionally, in order to explain in part why it is now so difficult to give any clear description of her.)

Certainly there she was, in the very centre of that great Cathedral space which was childhood; there she was from the very first. My first memory is of her lap; the scratch of some beads on her dress comes back to me as I pressed my cheek against it. Then I see her in her white dressing gown on the balcony; and the passion flower with the purple star on its petals. Her voice is still faintly in my ears—decided, quick; and in particular the little drops with which her laugh ended—three diminishing ahs . . . "Ah—ah—ah . . ." I sometimes end a laugh that way myself. * * * [L]ike all children, I lay awake sometimes and longed for her to come. Then she told me to think of all the lovely things I could imagine. Rainbows and bells . . . But besides these minute separate details, how did I first become conscious of what was always there—her astonishing beauty? Perhaps I never became conscious of it; I think I accepted her beauty as the natural quality that a mother—she seemed typical, universal, yet our own in particular—had by virtue of being our mother. It was part of her calling. I do not think that I separated her face from that general being; or from her whole body. Certainly I have a vision of her now, as she came up the path by the lawn at St Ives; slight, shapely—she held herself very straight. * * *

* * *

* * * She was the whole thing; Talland House was full of her; Hyde Park Gate was full of her. I see now, though the sentence is hasty, feeble and inexpressive, why it was that it was impossible for her to leave a very private and particular impression upon a child. She was keeping what I call in my shorthand the panoply of life— that which we all lived in common—in being. * * * I see now that a woman who had to keep all this in being and under control must have been a general presence rather than a particular person to a child of seven or eight. Can I remember ever being alone with her for more than a few minutes? Someone was always interrupting. * * * What a jumble of things I can remember, if I let my mind run, about my mother; but they are all of her in company; of her surrounded; of her generalised; dispersed, omnipresent, of her as the creator of that crowded merry world which spun so gaily in the centre of my childhood. It is true that I enclosed that world in another made by my own temperament; it is true that from the beginning I had many adventures outside that world; and often went far from it; and kept much back from it; but there it always was, the common life of the family, very merry, very stirring, crowded with people; and she was the centre; it was herself. This was proved on May 5th 1895. For after that day there was nothing left of it. * * *

* * *

My father now falls to be described, because it was during the seven years between Stella's death in 1897 and his death in 1904 that Nessa and I were fully exposed without protection to the full blast of

that strange character. * * * [J]ust as I rubbed out a good deal of the
force of my mother's memory by writing about her in *To the Lighthouse*, so I rubbed out much of his memory there too. Yet he too
obsessed me for years. Until I wrote it out, I would find my lips moving; I would be arguing with him; raging against him; saying to myself
all that I never said to him. How deep they drove themselves into me,
the things it was impossible to say aloud. They are still some of them
sayable; when Nessa for instance revives the memory of Wednesday
and its weekly books,[1] I still feel come over me that old frustrated fury.

But in me, though not in her, rage alternated with love. It was only
the other day when I read Freud for the first time, that I discovered
that this violently disturbing conflict of love and hate is a common
feeling; and is called ambivalence. * * *

* * *

Father on one of his walking tours, it must have been in 1881, I
think—discovered St Ives. He must have stayed there, and seen Talland House to let. He must have seen the town almost as it had
been in the sixteenth century, without hotels, or villas; and the Bay
as it had been since time began. It was the first year, I think, that
the line was made from St Erth to St Ives—before that, St Ives was
eight miles from a railway station. * * * [I]n retrospect nothing that
we had as children made as much difference, was quite so important to us, as our summer in Cornwall. The country was intensified,
after the months in London to go away to Cornwall; to have our own
house; our own garden; to have the Bay; the sea; the moors; Clodgy;
Halestown Bog; Carbis Bay; Lelant; Trevail; Zennor; the Gurnard's
Head; to hear the waves breaking that first night behind the yellow
blind; to dig in the sand; to go sailing in a fishing boat; to scrabble
over the rocks and see the red and yellow anemones flourishing their
antennae; or stuck like blobs of jelly to the rock; to find a small fish
flapping in a pool; to pick up cowries; to look over the grammar in
the dining room and see the lights changing on the bay; the leaves
of the escallonia grey or bright green; to go down to the town and
buy a penny box of tintacks or a pocket knife. * * * . . . I could fill
pages remember one thing after another. All together made the summer at St Ives the best beginning to life conceivable. * * *

The town was then much as it must have been in the sixteenth
century, unknown, unvisited, a scramble of granite houses crusting
the slope in the hollow under the Island. It must have been built for
shelter; for a few fishermen, when Cornwall was more remote from
England than Spain or Africa is now. * * *

---

1. The household accounts, for which Vanessa was made responsible at age eighteen, and
about which Leslie was invariably angry.

Our house, Talland House, was just beyond the town, on the hill.
* * * It stood in a garden that ran downhill; and had formed itself
into separate gardens, surrounded by thick escallonia hedges, whose
leaves, pressed, gave out a very sweet smell. It had so many angles
cut off, and lawns surrounded, that each had a name; there was the
coffee garden; the Fountain—a basin with a funnel that dripped,
hedged in with damp evergreens; the cricket lawn; the Love Corner, under the greenhouse, where the purple jackmanii grew. * * *

From the Lookout place one had then, a perfectly open view across
the Bay. * * * Every year, about the first week in September, we
would cry "The pilchard boats are out!" There they were being
hauled down the beach, where they lay one behind another all the
rest of the year. Horses were struggling to draw them over the
beach. * * * All the years we were at St Ives the pilchards never
came into the bay; and the pilchard boats lay there, anchored, waiting; and we used to swim out and hang on to the edge, and see the
old man lying in his brown tarpaulin tent, keeping watch. The waiting pilchard boats was [sic] a sight that made father pish and pshaw
at table. He had a curious sympathy for the poverty of the fisher
people: a respect for fishermen, like his respect for Alpine guides.
And mother, of course, got to know them in their houses; and went
about, "doing good" as Stella wished to have it said on her tomb-
stone; she visited, helped, and started her nursing society. * * *

* * *

[A] treat announced perhaps once a fortnight was an afternoon
sailing. We would hire a lugger; the fisherman went with us. But
once Thoby was allowed to steer us home. "Show them you can bring
her in, my boy," father said, with his usual trust and pride in Thoby.
And Thoby took the fisherman's place; and steered; flushed and with
his blue eyes very blue, and his mouth set, he sat there, bringing us
round the point, into harbour, without letting the sail flag. One day
the sea was full of pale jelly fish, like lamps, with streaming hair;
but they stung you if you touched them. Sometimes lines would be
handed us; baited by gobbets cut from fish; and the line thrilled in
one's fingers as the boat tossed and shot through the water; and
then—how can I convey the excitement?—there was a little leaping
tug; then another; up one hauled; up through the water at length
came the white twisting fish; and was slapped on the floor. There it
lay flapping this way and that in an inch or two of water.

Once, after we had hung about, tacking, and hauling in gurnard
after gurnard, dab after dab, father said to me: "Next time if you
are going to fish I shan't come; I don't like to see fish caught but you
can go if you like." It was a perfect lesson. It was not a rebuke; not
a forbidding; simply a statement of his own feeling, about which I

could think and decide for myself. Though my passion for the thrill and the tug had been perhaps the most acute I then knew, his words slowly extinguished it; leaving no grudge, I ceased to wish to catch fish. But from the memory of my own passion I am still able to construct an idea of the sporting passion. It is one of those invaluable seeds, from which, since it is impossible to have every experience fully, one can grow something that represents other people's experiences. Often one has to make do with seeds; the germs of what might have been, had one's life been different. I pigeonhole 'fishing' thus with other momentary glimpses; like those rapid glances, for example, that I cast into basements when I walk in London streets.

Oak apples, ferns with clusters of seeds on their backs, the regatta, Charlie Pearce, the click of the garden gate, the ants swarming on the hot front door step; buying tintacks; sailing; the smell of Halestown Bog; splits with Cornish cream for tea in the farm house at Trevail; the floor of the sea changing colour at lessons; old Mr Wolstenholme in his beehive chair; the spotted elm leaves on the lawn; the rooks cawing as they passed over the house in the early morning; the escallonia leaves showing their grey undersides: the arc in the air, like the pip of an orange, when the powder magazine at Hayle blew up; the boom of the buoy—these for some reason come uppermost at the moment in my mind thinking of St Ives—an incongruous miscellaneous catalogue, little corks that mark a sunken net.

* * *

Family and Domestic Values

COVENTRY PATMORE

This book-length poem by Coventry Patmore (1823–96), which the speaker calls his "Epic of the Hearth," was enormously popular with Victorian readers. It was first published in four installments—*The Betrothal* (1854), *The Espousals* (1856), *Faithful Forever* (1860), *The Victories of Love* (1862)—and later reprinted as one volume. The poem narrates the courtship and married life of Felix and Honoria, mostly from Felix's point of view, with the addition of letters between them and other family members. Woolf inherited the 1866 Macmillan fourth edition that Patmore had given, with an inscription ("kind regards"), to her mother before her first marriage. Patmore frequently describes Honoria as a queen, and these excerpts exhibit the poem's dynamic of chivalrous reverence.

From The Angel in the House[†]

From Book I, *The Betrothal,* Canto 3

The Lover

He meets, by heavenly chance express,
　　The destined maid; some hidden hand
Unveils to him that loveliness
　　Which others cannot understand.

*　*　*

His merits in her presence grow,　　　　　　　　　5
　　To match the promise in her eyes,
And round her happy footsteps blow
　　The authentic airs of Paradise.
For joy of her he cannot sleep;
　　Her beauty haunts him all the night;　　　　10
It melts his heart, it makes him weep
　　For wonder, worship, and delight.

*　*　*

---

† From *The Angel in the House* (London: Macmillan, 1863), pp. 37–39, 109–10.

Yet trusts he, with undaunted cheer,
    To vanquish heaven, and call her Wife.
He notes how queens of sweetness still   15
    Neglect their crowns, and stoop to mate.

From Book I, *The Betrothal,* Canto 9

The Wife's Tragedy

Man must be pleased; but him to please
    Is woman's pleasure; down the gulf
Of his condoled necessities
    She casts her best, she flings herself.
How often flings for nought! and yokes   5
    Her heart to an icicle or whim;
Whose each impatient word provokes
    Another, not from her, but him;
While she, too gentle even to force
    His penitence by kind replies,   10
Waits by, expecting his remorse,
    With pardon in her pitying eyes;
And if he once, by shame oppress'd,
    A comfortable word confers,
She leans and weeps against his breast,   15
    And seems to think the sin was hers;
And whilst his love has any life,
    Or any eye to see her charms,
At any time, she's still his wife,
    Dearly devoted to his arms;   20
She loves with love that cannot tire;
    And when, ah woe, she loves alone,
Through passionate duty love springs higher,
    As grass grows taller round a stone.

JOHN RUSKIN

John Ruskin (1819–1900) wrote this lecture in 1864, the second of a pair of lectures ("Of Kings' Treasuries" is the first) that circulated widely in print and helped to consolidate the Victorian ideology of "separate spheres" that constructed gender in rigidly binary and heteronormative terms. The lecture draws heavily on an ersatz medieval image of chivalry that places middle-class women (whom Ruskin calls "queens") on a pedestal yet grants all effective power to men. In the first part of the lecture Ruskin invokes famous authors to support his portrayal of the ideal woman, among them Shakespeare and Sir Walter Scott, the authors Mr. and Mrs. Ramsay turn to at the end of a long day. After this excerpt, Ruskin describes his educational program for producing domestic queens: "a girl's education should be nearly . . . the same as a boy's; but quite differently directed. A woman, in any rank of life, ought to know whatever her husband is likely to know, but to know it in a different way. . . . [A] man ought to know any language or science he learns, thoroughly, while a woman ought to know the same language, or science, only so far as may enable her to sympathise in her husband's pleasures, and in those of his best friends" (64–65).

From Of Queens' Gardens[†]

* * *

Now their separate characters are briefly these. The man's power is active, progressive, defensive. He is eminently the doer, the creator, the discoverer, the defender. His intellect is for speculation and invention; his energy for adventure, for war, and for conquest, wherever war is just, wherever conquest necessary. But the woman's power is for rule, not for battle,—and her intellect is not for invention or creation, but for sweet ordering, arrangement, and decision. She sees the qualities of things, their claims, and their places. Her great function is Praise: she enters into no contest, but infallibly adjudges the crown of contest. By her office, and place, she is protected from all danger and temptation. The man, in his rough work in open world, must encounter all peril and trial:—to him, therefore, the failure, the offence, the inevitable error: often he must be wounded, or subdued, often misled, and *always* hardened. But he guards the woman from all this; within his house, as ruled by her, unless she herself has sought it, need enter no danger, no temptation, no cause of error or offence. This is the true nature of home— it is the place of Peace; the shelter, not only from all injury, but from all terror, doubt, and division. In so far as it is not this, it is not home; so far as the anxieties of the outer life penetrate into it, and the inconsistently minded, unknown, unloved, or hostile society of the outer world is allowed by either husband or wife to cross the threshold, it ceases to be home; it is then only a part of that outer world which you have roofed over, and lighted fire in. But so far as it is a sacred place, a vestal temple, a temple of the hearth watched over by Household Gods, before whose faces none may come but those whom they can receive with love,—so far as it is this, and roof and fire are types only of a nobler shade and light,—shade as of the rock in a weary land, and light as of the Pharos in the stormy sea;—so far it vindicates the name, and fulfils the praise, of Home.

† From *Sesame and Lilies* (London: Everyman, 1907), p. 59.

JULIA STEPHEN

Julia Stephen (1846–1895) was the mother of Virginia and her three siblings—Thoby, Vanessa, and Adrian—and of Stella, George, and Gerald from her first marriage to Herbert Duckworth (who died in 1870), and stepmother to Leslie's daughter Laura. She was a famous beauty, painted and photographed by some of the prominent artists of her day, and a model Victorian wife and mother who embodied the selfless ideal of the "Angel in the House." She also homeschooled her children and worked as a skilled volunteer nurse and public health activist, publishing a book on nursing, *Notes from Sick Rooms* (London, 1883), excerpted here, as well as writing stories for children and essays on household management. Although she signed an anti-women's suffrage petition in 1889, she wanted middle-class women's work—including the management of large Victorian households such as her own—taken seriously and professionalized, and she started a nursing organization in St. Ives that was after her death renamed The Julia Prinsep Stephen Nursing Association. See Diane Gillespie's "The Elusive Julia Stephen" in *Stories for Children, Essays for Adults*, pp. 1–27. If Mrs. Ramsay—with her eight children, her demanding husband, her matchmaking, and her hostessing—is taken to be a portrait of Julia Stephen, readers may be surprised to learn that she was also a published author, but Mrs. Ramsay's visits to the poor and ill and her passion for good hospitals and clean dairies resonate with Julia Stephen's published writing.

From Notes from Sick Rooms[†]

I have often wondered why it is considered a proof of virtue in anyone to become a nurse. The ordinary relations between the sick and the well are far easier and pleasanter than between the well and the well.

There are no doubt people to whom the sight of physical suffering is so distasteful as to turn a sick room into a real Chamber of Horrors for them. That such unlucky persons should ever have authority in a sick room ought to be an impossibility; but if by some unlucky chance they ever have, we should surely reserve our pity for the unfortunate invalids in their charge.

Illness has, or ought to have, much of the levelling power of death. We forget, or at all events cease to dwell on, the unfavourable sides to a character when death has claimed its owner, and in illness we can afford to ignore the details which in health make familiar intercourse difficult.

[†] From *Stories for Children, Essays for Adults*, ed. Diane F. Gillespie and Elizabeth Steele (Syracuse, NY: Syracuse UP, 1987), pp. 217–19, 227–28, 234.

The ways in which our friends dress, bring up their children, or spend their money, are apt to cause disagreement more or less marked between us when there is no thought of suffering or loss; but the moment we are threatened by either, how slight such matters seem! We can contemplate without irritation the vivid fringe of hair when the head which it disfigures is aching and fevered. * * *

A nurse's life is certainly not a dull one, and the more skilful the nurse the less dull she will be. The more she cultivates the *art* of nursing, the more enjoyment she will get, and the same may be said of the patient. The art of being ill is no easy one to learn, but it is practised to perfection by many of the greatest sufferers.

The greatest sufferer is by no means the worst patient, and to give relief, even if it be only temporary, to such patients is perhaps a greater pleasure than can be found in the performance of any other duty.

Nursing Instinct

It ought to be quite immaterial to a nurse whom she is nursing. I have often heard it urged against trained nurses that they look upon their patients as *cases*. If to look on patients as a case is to feel indifference towards them, then the charge is indeed a reproof; but assuming that the nurse is not indifferent, how should she look on her patient but as a case; and further, why should she?

The genuine love of her "case" and not of the individual patient seems to me the sign of the true nursing instinct.

It would be hard if those who were specially charming, or whose antecedents interested, were alone to be tenderly nursed. Every nurse, whether trained or amateur, should look on her patient as a "case," nursing with the same undeviating tenderness and watchful care the entire stranger, the unsympathetic friend, or the one who is nearest and dearest.

* * *

* * * One imperative duty of all those in attendance on the sick is that they should be cheerful; not an elaborate, forced cheerfulness, but a quiet brightness which makes their presence a cheer and not an oppression. It may seem difficult to follow this advice, but it is not. Cheerfulness is a habit, and no one should venture to attend the sick who wears a gloomy face. The atmosphere of the sick room should be cheerful and peaceful. Domestic disturbances, money matters, worries, and discussions of all kinds should be kept away.

Lying

There can be no half dealing in such matters; hints and whispers are worse than the whole truth. There is no limit to a sick person's imagination, and this is a fact which is too often ignored, even by the tenderest friends. The answers, "Oh, it is nothing," "Don't worry you[r]self," when suspicion is once aroused, are enough to fret the unfortunate patient into a fever. She will torture herself with suspicion of every possible calamity, and at last, when she has nerved herself to insist on being told, her unconscious tormentor discloses the fact that one of the pipes has burst!

If trouble should come, and it is important that the invalid should be kept in ignorance, her watchers must make peace with their consciences as best they can; and if questions are asked, they must "lie freely."

Crumbs

Among the number of small evils which haunt illness, the greatest, in the misery which it can cause, though the smallest in size, is crumbs. The origin of most things has been decided on, but the origin of crumbs in bed has never excited sufficient attention among the scientific world, though it is a problem which has tormented many a weary sufferer. I will forbear to give my own explanation, which would be neither scientific nor orthodox, and will merely beg that their evil existence may be recognised and, as far as human nature allows, guarded against. The torment of crumbs should be stamped out of the sick bed as if it were the Colorado beetle in a potato field. Anyone who has been ill will at once take her precautions, feeble though they will prove. She will have a napkin under her chin, stretch her neck out of bed, eat in the most uncomfortable way, and watch that no crumbs get into the folds of her nightdress or jacket. When she lies back in bed, in the vain hope that she may have baffled the enemy, he is before her: a sharp crumb is buried in her back, and grains of sand seem sticking to her toes. If the patient is able to get up and have her bed made, when she returns to it she will find the crumbs are waiting for her. The housemaid will protest that the sheets were shaken, and the nurse that she swept out the crumbs, but there they are, and there they will remain unless the nurse determines to conquer them. To do this she must first believe in them, and there are few assertions that are met with such incredulity as the one—I have crumbs in my bed. After every meal the nurse should put her hand into the bed and feel for the crumbs. When the bed is made, the nurse and housemaid must not content themselves with shaking or sweeping. The tiny crumbs stick in the sheets, and the nurse must patiently take each crumb out; if there are many very small ones, she must even wet her fingers, and get the crumbs to stick to them. The patient's night-clothes must be searched; crumbs lurk in each tiny fold or frill. They go up the sleeve of the nightgown, and if the patient is in bed when the search is going on, her arms should hang out of bed, so that the crumbs which are certain to be there may be induced to fall down. When crumbs are banished—that is to say, temporarily, for with each meal they return, and for this the nurse must make up her mind—she must see that there are no rucks in the bed-sheets. A very good way of avoiding these is to pin the lower sheet firmly down on the mattress with nursery pins, first stretching the sheet smoothly and straightly over the mattress. Many people are not aware of the importance of putting on a sheet *straight*, but if it is not, it will certainly drag, and if pinned it will probably tear. * * *

* * *

Fancies

One of the many mistakes into which nurses fall is that of persuading patients, or at least trying to persuade them (for we know how seldom people well or ill *are* persuaded). A sick person will often give in from sheer fatigue; but she remains unconvinced, and her mind is not at rest; she goes over and over her reasons and the nurse's; and worries herself over a thing of small importance, because she does not like to reopen the discussion. I would impress on all nurses strongly that, as far as lies in their power, they should keep their patient's mind at rest. They cannot control the disturbing influences which find their way into the sick room, nor can they overcome all the varied miseries which beset the sick brain; but some of these miseries they can soothe, and they can and should always be careful not to cause any themselves.

Invalids' fancies seem, and often are, absurd; but arguing will not dissipate them; it will only increase them, as the patient will hide what she feels, and so increase her mental discomfort—a sure way of augmenting her physical suffering. One of the many rewards that come to a careful and considerate nurse is that the patient's fancies are not absurd. If the invalid knows that her nurse has undertaken to see that a thing is right, she will have an easy mind about it, and will not worry the nurse with useless questions and suggestions.

There are, of course, patients who, without meaning to be exacting, are so delicately organised, or whose senses have become so acute through suffering, that they can detect a draught or a smell where even careful and discerning nurses can find neither. The nurse must, therefore, not deny that the evil exists; a door or a window may have been opened without her knowledge, and the current of air may be felt by the sick though not by the well. Something may have been dropped on the kitchen fire, or there may be some minute escape of gas which is imperceptible to all but the invalid. The nurse must remove these evils should they exist, and thoroughly investigate the evil real or fancied. Cold cannot be taken through the imagination; but a nervous dread of chill can make a sick person thoroughly wretched, and one of the chief duties of a nurse is to make her patient thoroughly comfortable in mind and body.

If the patient be well enough to be left for any time she should always have a bell, and any small thing that she is likely to want in a hurry, close by her. The nurse should never leave her patient hastily, but wait to be certain that all the things are there, and that the invalid has said all she wants. The mind moves slowly to expression in illness, and the feeling that the words are impatiently waited for takes away the power to utter them.

*　　*　　*

Remedies

*　　*　　*

For any affection of the bladder the patient will frequently be ordered a milk diet.

The nurse must see the milkman herself and impress on him the importance of sweet fresh milk from one cow being always brought. When brought she must empty the milk into a flat pan, such as is used for rising cream in a dairy; this pan must be placed in a cool place, and must be well scalded each time it is emptied.

The nurse must skim the milk carefully herself, for in such cases the patient must have no cream. The tumbler of milk must be stood in some warm water before it is given to the patient, so that the milk may be of the warmth of new milk. This milk cure is much used and is most valuable, but the nurse must remember that a milk diet is not heating, and that the patient must be kept warm, and great care taken that she should never have a chill while she is undergoing it.

*　　*　　*

LESLIE STEPHEN

Woolf's father, Leslie Stephen (1836–1904) was a celebrated, prolific Victorian man of letters whose top-floor, book-lined study in the family home in London became, in the absence of "paid-for" education, her school and her university. He was the father of Laura, from his first marriage, and of Vanessa, Thoby, Virginia, and Adrian, and the stepfather of Julia's three children from her earlier marriage. A Victorian patriarch, he left household and parental cares to Julia and took off on

"Sunday tramps" with male friends when he wasn't reading, writing, or lecturing. His death in 1904 enabled the four younger Stephens to escape Victorian social conventions and invent new lives for themselves in Bloomsbury.

After Julia's death, Leslie Stephen wrote his *Mausoleum Book,* a memorial of her life in the form of a long letter addressed to their children. (He also assembled a memorial photo album, now in the Smith College library.) Elaborating the chronological narrative with reflections on "my beloved angel," he emphasizes her beauty, her embodiment of Victorian ideals, her love of her children, her self-sacrifices as a nurse, and her deference and generosity toward himself. Woolf said she refrained from reading "father's life" while writing *To the Lighthouse,* yet these selections include passages she could have drawn on for the ways male characters idolize Mrs. Ramsay as mother, wife, and hostess; for the relationship between Mr. and Mrs. Ramsay; and for glimpses of life at their summer home.

From The Mausoleum Book†

* * *

And now I come nearer to my darling's story. I do not know certainly when I saw her first: but the first time at which I remember to have seen her was at that picnic of 1866 of which I have already spoken. I remember standing on the little green before the inn at Abinger Hatch. I was talking to Jeanie Senior, * * * one of the sweetest and best of women, who, for reasons, had a kindness for me. Julia was standing near us among a little group of girls. 'What do you think of Julia Jackson?' asked Mrs. Senior. I forget the words of my reply, but the substance was, she is the most beautiful girl I ever saw. My sister tells me that she was impressed at the same time and place and remembers that Julia was in white with blue flowers in her hat. I do not remember that I spoke to her. I saw and remembered her, as I might have seen and remembered the Sistine Madonna[1] or any other presentation of superlative beauty.

I must dwell a little more upon her beauty: for beauty, as it seems to me, was of the very essence of her nature. I have never seen—I have no expectation that I ever shall see—anyone whose outward appearance might be described as so absolutely faultless. Her portrait was very often drawn and painted by various people. She was a model to Burne-Jones for his picture of the Annunciation.[2] * * * [He describes several portraits.] * * * The portraits fail, I think, because

---

† From *The Mausoleum Book* (Oxford: Oxford University Press, 1977), pp. 30–33, 83, 90, 92–93.
1. Oil painting by Raphael (Rafello Sanzio, 1483–1520), Italian Renaissance artist.
2. Oil painting, 1879, by Edward Burne-Jones (1833–98).

Raphael, *Sistine Madonna* (detail), ca. 1513–14.
Image: Giorgio Morara / Alamy Stock Photo.

her beauty depended upon an exquisite delicacy of line and form
such as I never saw approached and which would have required
singular felicity and skill in drawing to represent adequately. Most
fortunately, the beautiful series of portraits taken by Mrs. Cameron,[3]
chiefly, I think, from 1866 to 1875, remain to give an impression to
her children of what she really was. * * * Her beauty was of the kind
which seems to imply—as it most certainly did accompany—equal
beauty of soul, refinement, nobility and tenderness of character; and
which yet did not imply, as some beauty called 'spiritual' may seem to
do, any lack of 'material' beauty. It was just the perfect balance, the
harmony of mind and body which made me feel when I looked at her

3. Julia Margaret Cameron (1815–1879) was Woolf's great-aunt and a pioneering Victorian
   photographer. Cameron's sisters, including Julia's mother, Maria Jackson (1818–1892),
   were famous for their embodiment of Victorian beauty ideals, a legacy later amplified
   by Cameron's portraits that helped to cultivate the family myth of Julia's beauty. At the
   end of his book, Leslie writes that he gave Vanessa the Cameron photograph that "shows
   her mother's beauty better than any other" (*The Mausoleum Book*, p. 97). Vanessa hung
   several Cameron images of her mother in her home starting in 1905. The image
   included here could have been among them.

Edward Burne-Jones, *Annunciation*, 1879. Julia Stephen posed as Mary for this painting when she was thirty-three and pregnant with Vanessa. Image: The Picture Art Collection / Alamy Stock Photo.

the kind of pleasure which I suppose a keen artistic sense to derive from a masterpiece of Greek sculpture. It was the complete reconciliation and fulfilment of all conditions of feminine beauty. * * *

* * *

* * * You, my elder children, know fully, and you, my younger, will remember though with less fulness of knowledge, what she was to you as a mother. The love of a mother for her children is the most beautiful thing in the world; it is sometimes the redeeming quality in characters not otherwise attractive. She was a perfect mother, a very ideal type of mother; and in her the maternal instincts were, as it seemed, but the refined essence of the love which showed its strength in every other relation of life. Yet, because you know this so well, I feel it hard to dwell upon it at length. This much I will try to say: her love of you all was an enduring and constant source of happiness to her. * * *

* * * My humours and vagaries were part of my character and, though many men are far better than I, I could not become another

Julia Margaret Cameron, photograph of Julia Duckworth, 1872. One print is titled *A Beautiful Vision*; another bears this caption: "A Study and a Portrait/My own cherished Niece and God Child/Julia Duckworth/a widow at 24." Image: Artokoloro / Alamy Stock Photo.

man. This at least I can say. My irritability implied nothing worse. I loved her with my whole heart, and loved her without qualification. She knew it—as well as I know it. Never for an instant, I am quite certain, did she take my tempers and irritabilities for symptoms of any want of love or diminution of love. 'My mother says', she told me long ago, 'that you worship the ground I tread upon'; she said it with tender pleasure for she knew it to be true. After our marriage I used sometimes to complain to her that she would not say to me in so many words, 'I love you'. * * * My complaint was only in play for I loved even her reticence. In truth, husband and wife, living together as we did in the most unreserved intimacy, confiding to each other every thought and feeling as it arises, do not require the language of words. In every action, in her whole conduct, she showed her love; it shone through her life; and the use of the set of words was a trifle. * * *

    There is another part of our relations of which I must say something. * * * I used often to grumble about my literary performances.

In my early letters, I used, I see, to point out my inferiority * * * and in later years I used to describe myself summarily as a 'failure'. Now, partly for my own sake, I will tell you what my view about myself really is. I know, of course, that I am a man of not inconsiderable literary ability. I think again that I am a man of greater ability than a good many much more popular authors. I have been approved by many men whose approval is worth having. * * * My darling used to tell me that I was the most ungrateful of men for not being more pleased. Certainly I will admit that I am not a 'failure' pure and simple; and if my books have not sold largely, I admit that reasons may be given, not all uncomplimentary, and that in any case failure to win such popularity would not justify whining. The sense in which I do take myself to be a failure is this: I have scattered myself too much. I think that I had it in me to make something like a real contribution to philosophical or ethical thought. Unluckily, what with journalism and dictionary making, I have been a jack of all trades; and instead of striking home have only done enough to persuade friendly judges that I could have struck. I am far indeed from thinking that this matters very much; but I do feel that if, for example, the history of English thought in the nineteenth century should ever be written, my name will only be mentioned in small type and footnotes whereas, had my energies been wisely directed, I might have had the honour of a paragraph in full sized type or even a section in a chapter all to myself. One cause has undoubtedly been my want of proper self-confidence or, in early days, of ambition.

Well, I state this that I may the better explain my Julia's feeling. She used to accuse me of excessive modesty, though I hope that she did not dislike the quality on the whole—whatever its right name. I used sometimes I must confess (as indeed I confessed to her) to profess a rather exaggerated self-depreciation in order to extort some of her delicious compliments. They were delicious, for even if I could not accept her critical judgement as correct, I could feel that it was distorted mainly by her tender love. Although she could perceive that I was 'fishing for a compliment' she could not find it in her heart to refuse me. * * *

BOEUF EN DAUBE FOR FOURTEEN

The beautiful savory dish that graces the dinner in "The Window," laboriously prepared over the course of three days by Mildred the cook but credited to Mrs. Ramsay's art, was a specialty of Roger Fry's, who loved the South of France, where this dish originates. He owned a small farmhouse in Provence, and in her biography of Fry Woolf describes him writing happily to a visitor, "'I've made a *boeuf en daube* which is a dream and will last us about five days so all I need do is boil peas or something,' and he could read or write while he watched the pot" (*Roger Fry*, p. 283). While the appearance and scent of the dish in its "huge brown pot" are described in the novel along with some of its ingredients and mode of preparation (75–76), Woolf initially included even more information in her manuscript, detailing ingredients such as bay leaf and sherry and emphasizing the importance of never allowing the dish to boil. A *daube* is a marinade; the dish is sometimes called *daube de boeuf*. A *daubière*—the pot in which a properly Provençal *boeuf en daube* is cooked—is a large round earthenware pot that is taller than it is wide, but Mildred's "masterpiece" can be cooked in any heavy cast iron or earthenware pot or casserole dish that has a tight-fitting lid.

The recipe below serves fourteen, the number of guests at Mrs. Ramsay's table, but the ingredients (except for the herb bouquets and the clove-stuck onion) and the cooking time can be halved to feed a smaller group.

Day One:

Make the marinade by combining these ingredients in a large, non-metallic bowl:

1 herb bouquet: 6 sprigs parsley, 4 sprigs thyme, 1 bay leaf, 1 stalk of celery cut in half: bundle together and tie with string so it can be removed
6 strips orange zest, without pith
2 medium red onions, thinly sliced (not chopped)
6 freshly crushed cloves garlic
6 cloves garlic, chopped
8 carrots, sliced into thin rounds
2 T chopped fresh parsley
1 T fresh thyme leaves (less if using dried)
1 tsp ground black pepper
1/2 tsp freshly ground nutmeg
2/3 C olive oil
4 cups full-bodied red wine (Burgundy is recommended)
6 T cognac

To the marinade, add the meat and mix well:

7–8 pounds of beef sirloin, chuck roast, or any combination of
cuts that are well-marbled with fat, with any large chunks of fat
discarded, cut into 2-inch cubes (they will shrink)
8 slices (or 4 ounces) of Canadian bacon or back bacon, trimmed
of fat, cut into 1-inch strips

Cover tightly and refrigerate for 24 hours, stirring occasionally.

Day Two:

Ingredients for the second day:

4 T olive oil
4 C beef stock (preferably homemade, see below*)
2 T tomato paste
1 whole, peeled onion stuck with 6 cloves
6 medium tomatoes cut in 1-inch chunks
1 herb bouquet, as above for the marinade
1½ C salt-cured, pitted niçoise olives (any kind of black olive may
be substituted)
Salt and pepper to taste
* For 4 cups of beef stock: boil together in about 5 cups of water:
1–2 pounds of beef bones, with or without meat; 1 onion, 1 carrot,
1 stalk celery, all roughly chopped; 1 bay leaf; 6 sprigs parsley. Simmer for about 2 hours, occasionally skimming off any foam that
forms, until the meat falls off the bones and the bones fall apart.
Cool to room temperature, skim off the fat, and strain through a
sieve, reserving the liquid for use.

Directions:

Preheat the oven to 265 degrees.
Remove the chunks of meat from the marinade, brushing off any
bits of vegetables that stick to them, and dry them on paper towels.
Cut the bacon into bite-sized pieces. Heat the olive oil in a large cast-
iron or earthenware casserole dish on top of the stove. Brown the
beef pieces and the bacon, a single layer at a time. Remove the
browned meat to a plate.
Pour the beef stock into the pot, adding the tomato paste and
scraping into the stock any browned bits of meat that stick to the
pan. Remove the orange peel from the marinade and replace the
old herb bouquet with the new one. Add the marinade, the fresh

tomatoes, the clove-stuck onion, and the olives to the pot and bring it gently to a boil.

Simmer on top of the stove for 20 minutes. Return the meat to the pot and season with salt and pepper. Seal the pot: if the lid doesn't fit tightly, cover the dish with foil before putting on the lid. Cook in the middle of the oven for 5–6 hours. The dish should bubble gently but not boil.

Remove from the oven and allow to cool slowly. Discard the herb bouquet and the whole onion. When cool, refrigerate overnight.

Day Three:

Directions for serving:

Skim off any excess fat. Preheat the oven to 265 degrees. Reheat the *boeuf en daube* gently, about 1 hour, until it begins to bubble. Adjust the seasonings with salt and pepper. Serve with peas and with egg noodles, rice, farro, or any other absorbent starch or grain.

Reality, Philosophy, and Science

LESLIE STEPHEN

Despite his deeply Victorian attitude toward his family, Leslie Stephen was in his day a radical thinker, renouncing religious belief, embracing Darwin's then controversial scientific discoveries and invigorating a variety of nonfiction literary genres including literary criticism, social and intellectual history, the history of philosophy, and—as the first editor of the *Dictionary of National Biography*—biography. He also critiqued the Victorian sage Thomas Carlyle's widely accepted "hero" theory that the progress of civilization depends on outstanding individuals, arguing instead that even great art reflects the common life of the people, in his *English Literature and Society in the Eighteenth Century*.

Modeling the intellectual qualities of rigor and honesty that Leslie Stephen most admired, the Scottish Enlightenment philosopher David Hume is the central figure in his 1876 *The History of English Thought*, which Woolf later described as her father's "masterpiece." Hume, in Leslie's view, "unflinchingly enquired into the profoundest of all questions, and . . . dared to give the result of his enquiries without fear or favour" (vol. 1, p. 314). While Woolf and her circle understood Mr. Ramsay to be a portrait of Leslie Stephen, Leslie's vision of Hume in particular offers a model for Mr. Ramsay as a philosopher: he ponders Hume's key question, "subject and object and the nature of reality," as Andrew Ramsay lightly summarizes it. Leslie wrote on this question as a philosopher in his own right, too, in essays such as "What Is Materialism?"

On Leslie Stephen's philosophical writings, his indebtedness to Hume, and the resemblance of his thought to Mr. Ramsay's, see Gillian Beer, "Hume, Stephen, and Elegy in *To the Lighthouse*," in *Virginia Woolf: The Common Ground* (Ann Arbor: U of Michigan P, 1996), pp. 29–47, and Ann Banfield, *The Phantom Table: Woolf, Fry, Russell and the Epistemology of Modernism* (Cambridge: Cambridge UP, 2000).

[On David Hume]†

* * *

47. How then do we come by the distinction between external and internal? If every object of thought is either a sensation or the representative of a sensation, an actual or a decaying impression, how can we even think of things as existing outside of us? 'It is impossible for us,' says Hume, 'so much as to conceive or form an idea of anything specifically different from ideas and impressions. Let us fix our attention out of ourselves as much as possible. Let us chase our imaginations to the heavens, or to the utmost limits of the universe; we never can really advance a step beyond ourselves, nor can conceive any kind of existence but those perceptions which have appeared in that narrow compass. This is the universe of the Imagination, nor have we any idea but what is there produced. * * * The mind is supposed to have no faculty except that of reviewing past impressions, modified only by their gradual decay.

48. Yet it is a plain fact of consciousness that we think of a table or a house as somehow existing independently of our perception of it. The mind is conscious of a series of sensations of colour, form, and so forth. Some of these recur frequently in the same relative positions, though interrupted by other terms of the series. Why does the mind, which can only, as Hume says, reproduce its impressions and ideas, and reproduce them as they occurred, identify the recurrent terms, and then suppose them to exist behind the interrupting terms? Why are not the group of sensations which we call table supposed to vanish when they are not felt like the group of sensations which we call toothache? 'As far as the senses are judges,' he says, 'all perceptions are the same in the manner of their existence.' The so-called qualities of bodies are sensations; the pain caused by a blow, the colours of the striking body, its extension and solidity, are equally feelings in the mind. We have, it would seem, in each case, the same ground, or absence of ground, for inferring a corresponding external existence in one case as in the other. Both inferences are alike reasonable or unreasonable. As reason does not infer the external existence in the case of a pain, it should not do so in the case of colour; and we must therefore refer to the imagination as the source of our belief in external existence. * * * The subjective element implies unreality. All perceptions have a subjective element. Therefore, the supposed reality must be a 'fiction.'

49. * * * A simple inspection of a sensation will not reveal an external object to which it corresponds. * * * The whole history of

† From *The History of English Thought in the Eighteenth Century*, 2 vols. (London: Smith, Elder, 1876), vol. 1, pp. 46–49.

philosophical thought is but a history of attempts to separate the object and the subject, and each new attempt implies that the previous line of separation was erroneously drawn or partly 'fictitious.' Such a familiar fact again as the belief that an object felt in the dark is coloured as we see it in the light, illustrates the popular tendency described by Hume to attribute an objective existence to our own sensations—in other words, to believe in a 'fiction.'

50. In what direction, then, are we to escape? Granting that Hume has exposed certain contradictions involved in contemporary philosophy and in all popular conceptions, are we to regard those contradictions as insoluble? The first remark will probably be that Hume's 'fiction' implies the existence of a condition which he tends to ignore. If we are unable accurately to draw the line between the objective and subjective, and even forced to admit that the attempt to separate the two elements in perceptions common to the race implies a contradictory attempt to get outside of our own minds, we must still admit that the primitive elements of consciousness imply the necessity of recognising the distinction. They have, that is, an objective and subjective aspect, and the power of thus organising impressions implies the existence of an organised mind. Hume's analysis seems to recognise no difference between the mind of a man and a polyp, between the intellectual and the merely sensitive animal. The mind is a bare faculty for repeating impressions; the power of grouping and arranging them is regarded as somehow illegitimate. Agreeing that all materials of thought are derived from experience, we yet have to account for the form impressed upon them. The destruction of innate ideas seemed to him, as to the philosophers whom he assailed, almost to imply the annihilation even of mental faculties. He could not allow that the function depended upon the organ without seeming to admit that the organ either created materials for itself, or was supplied with them from some source independent of experience. And, in the next place, the doctrine that belief in the external world is a 'fiction' is apparently self-destructive. If all reason is fiction, fiction is reason. * * *

What Is Materialism?[†]

* * * I shut my eyes for an instant, and believe that my pen and paper are still there. I believe that I should see them if my eyes were open, and that other persons may see them still. If I look back to the past, or forward to the future, or away to the furthest abysses of space, I am carrying on the same construction. I am 'producing' the curve of

† From *An Agnostic's Apology and Other Essays* (London: Smith, Elder, 1893), pp. 136–39, 142–44.

which a minute element is before my eyes. I form, then, a kind of hypothetical consciousness, of which my own is an essential part, but which extends indefinitely beyond it. By this artifice (if it may be called so) I state a general truth without explicit reference to my own perceptions. I do so when upon seeing a man first at one window and then at another I supply the intermediate positions and infer his relations to other objects by correcting my own perspective. Kepler constructed the solar system in the same way. He observed a planet in certain positions; he supplied the intermediate positions by discovering the curve which passed through all the observed positions; and to do so he had to place himself in imagination at a different point of view from which the relations asserted to exist might be matters of direct observation. All scientific progress is a development and a more distinct articulation of the same procedure.

* * *

'This is a table' is a phrase which in the first place asserts that I have a certain set of organised sense-impressions. But it also means that you have an analogous set of impressions, and that if we changed places we should also change sensations. It is a compact formula, which not only indicates the sensations of an observer at a particular time and place, but also gives the sensations of every other observer as those which would be perceived by the same observer at other times and places. It is a general formula with an indefinite term, such that when that term is filled in or defined it indicates the sensations corresponding to any particular case. We are, as it were, postulating an omnipresent consciousness, which may be for the moment focussed at any particular point, and the one phrase defines what will be its perceptions at that point. This habitual reference to the common instead of the particular generates the impression that I am somehow laying down truths, 'objective' in the sense of having no reference at all to my individual experience. Such formulae have been constructed from the experience of the race at large, and therefore are independent in one sense of my personal experience. Yet, in fact, each man is necessarily his own base, from which all things are measured for him; and he only discovers wider formulæ in which his own experience is included, not formulæ from which it is excluded. We do not get a step nearer towards the abolition of the subject. When we speak of what happened when the solar system was still an incandescent mist, we are only extending our experience, as we do when we say that the fire is still burning in the room we have left. * * *
* * * So far we are at the materialist point of view. We are enabled to see what we should see with increased faculties, and to trace the changes of the vision backwards and forwards. But nothing is so far

revealed to us which is not an object of sight, or of one of the senses. * * *

* * * We fancy that we thus get an 'objective' universe in the sense in which 'objective' means outside all consciousness, instead of meaning a formula common to all consciousness. The formula which is true for you and me, and for all other conscious beings, is taken to be true without any reference to consciousness at all. We forget that not only the sensations of light and heat, for example, have no meaning apart from a sentient being, but even that light and heat as used for the supposed physical causes of the sensations, vibrating atoms and so forth, have no meaning apart from the percipient being. * * * Thus, we first forget that all knowledge of the facts implies an inference from our sensations; then we attribute a reality to sensations apart from the sensitive being; and we suppose the other modifications of consciousness revealed to us through the sensations to be less real, or to be dependent upon the sensations for what reality they possess.

The argument which I have thus tried to express has, I should say, two applications. In the first place, it condemns Materialism so far as Materialism professes to state that 'matter' is an ultimate reality, and that thoughts and emotions are mere nothings or phantasms. * * * I cannot get into a world outside of all experience. We try to do so, verbally at least, when we invent the imaginary substratum in which sensible qualities somehow stick, instead of using the word as a mere name for the coherence of certain groups of sensation. We cannot peep behind the curtain.

> Immerst in darkness, round the drama rolled,
> Which for the pastime of eternity
> Thou didst thyself enact, conceive, behold.

The curtain is the reality. The effort to look behind it is an effort to get out of ourselves. It only plunges us into the transcendental region of antinomies and cobwebs of the brain. The unknowable, which lies beyond, is not made into a reality by its capital letter. It is a mere blank, with which we have nothing to do. * * *

BERTRAND RUSSELL

The eminent philosopher Bertrand Russell (1872–1970)—one of the founders of analytic philosophy, pioneering mathematical logician, influential antiwar activist, and winner of the 1950 Nobel Prize for literature—was part of the circle of Cambridge University intellectuals to which Woolf was connected through Bloomsbury family and friends.

Like Leslie Stephen, and in the tradition of Berkeley and Hume, Russell worked on the problem of "subject and object and the nature of reality" (or "think of a kitchen table . . . when you're not there"); he read Leslie's work and resolved some of its paradoxes through the notions of "unperceived perspectives" and "sensibilia," which allow for the existence of unobserved objects even though all knowledge of them is perceptual. Russell's advances reflected new developments in physics that revealed that an object is changed by being perceived, that it changes depending on the position of the observer, and that multiple points of view produce a multiplicity of objects. In the selection below, he formulates the problem in terms that resonate with *To the Lighthouse*. See Banfield and Beer, cited in the headnote to Leslie Stephen (219), and Holly Henry, *Virginia Woolf and the Discourse of Science* (Cambridge: Cambridge UP, 2003).

From The Problems of Philosophy†

Is there any knowledge in the world which is so certain that no reasonable man could doubt it? This question, which at first sight might not seem difficult, is really one of the most difficult that can be asked. * * *

To make our difficulties plain, let us concentrate attention on the table. To the eye it is oblong, brown and shiny, to the touch it is smooth and cool and hard; when I tap it, it gives out a wooden sound. Any one else who sees and feels and hears the table will agree with this description, so that it might seem as if no difficulty would arise; but as soon as we try to be more precise our troubles begin. Although I believe that the table is "really" of the same colour all over, the parts that reflect the light look much brighter than the other parts, and some parts look white because of reflected light. I know that, if I move, the parts that reflect the light will be different, so that the apparent distribution of colours on the table will change. It follows that if several people are looking at the table at the same moment, no two of them will see exactly the same distribution of colours, because no two can see it from exactly the same point of view, and any change in the point of view makes some change in the way the light is reflected.

For most practical purposes these differences are unimportant, but to the painter they are all-important: the painter has to unlearn the habit of thinking that things seem to have the colour which common sense says they "really" have, and to learn the habit of seeing things as they appear. Here we have already the beginning of one of

† From *The Problems of Philosophy* (New York: Henry Holt, 1912), pp. 9, 11–12, 17–18, 23, 26, 31–33.

the distinctions that cause most trouble in philosophy—the distinction between "appearance" and "reality." * * *

* * * Let us give the name of "sense-data" to the things that are immediately known in sensation: such things as colours, sounds, smells, hardnesses, roughnesses, and so on. We shall give the name "sensation" to the experience of being immediately aware of these things. Thus, whenever we see a colour, we have a sensation *of* the colour, but the colour itself is a sense-datum, not a sensation. The colour is that *of* which we are immediately aware, and the awareness itself is the sensation. It is plain that if we are to know anything about the table, it must be by means of the sense-data—brown colour, oblong shape, smoothness, etc.—which we associate with the table; but for the reasons which have been given, we cannot say that the table *is* the sense-data, or even that the sense-data are directly properties of the table. Thus a problem arises as to the relation of the sense-data to the real table, supposing there is such a thing.

The real table, if it exists, we will call a "physical object." * * *

* * * [I]f we take any common object of the sort that is supposed to be known by the senses, what the senses *immediately* tell us is not the truth about the object as it is apart from us, but only the truth about certain sense-data which, so far as we can see, depend upon the relations between us and the object. * * *

* * * [W]e have to ask ourselves whether, in any sense at all, there is such a thing as matter. Is there a table which has a certain intrinsic nature, and continues to exist when I am not looking, or is the table merely a product of my imagination, a dream-table in a very prolonged dream? * * *

* * * When ten people are sitting round a dinner-table, it seems preposterous to maintain that they are not seeing the same table-cloth, the same knives and forks and spoons and glasses. But the sense-data are private to each separate person; what is immediately present to the sight of one is not immediately present to the sight of another: they all see things from slightly different points of view, and therefore see them slightly differently. Thus, if there are to be public neutral objects, which can be in some sense known to many different people, there must be something over and above the private and particular sense-data which appear to various people. What reason, then, have we for believing that there are such public neutral objects?

The first answer that naturally occurs to one is that, although different people may see the table slightly differently, still they all see more or less similar things when they look at the table, and the variations in what they see follow the laws of perspective and reflection of light, so that it is easy to arrive at a permanent object underlying all the different people's sense-data. I bought my table from the former occupant of my room; I could not buy *his* sense-data, which died when he went away, but I could and did buy the confident expectation of more or less similar sense-data. Thus it is the fact that different people have similar sense-data, and that one person in a given place at different times has similar sense-data, which makes us suppose that over and above the sense-data there is a permanent public object which underlies or causes the sense-data of various people and various times.

* * *

PAUL TOLLIVER BROWN

Relativity, Quantum Physics, and Consciousness in Virginia Woolf's *To the Lighthouse*†

* * *

* * * Woolf was certainly exposed to Einstein's ideas through her relationship with Bertrand Russell and the prevalence of scientific discoveries in the popular media, and she makes direct references to Einstein in both her fiction and nonfiction. It is perhaps not surprising that she would have found his theory of a non-absolute space-time continuum of particular interest to the development of her own writing style. The role of a central narrator increasingly diminished in her novels and was replaced by the internal monologues of— and sometimes internal *dialogues* between—different characters in relative motion to one another.

In addition to noting the commonalities between Woolf's work and Einstein's, several critics have also proposed that Woolf was aware of and influenced by a number of other findings in contemporary science. Ann Banfield asserts that "Planck's discovery of the quantum in 1900, [. . .] Bohr's theory of the atom between 1913 and 1925 [. . . and] the discoveries of de Broglie, Heisenberg, P. Jordan, Dirac and Schrödinger on wave and particle theories in 1925–6 [. . .]" had an impact on Woolf's work and thought (*Phantom* 6). Sue Sun Yom asserts that her "ideas about writing [. . .] had some tangible relationship to the wave-particle duality and other associated characteristics of light posited in the mid-1920s and 1930s" (145), whereas Michael H. Whitworth contends that "Woolf had developed many aspects of her own wave/particle model [. . .] in anticipation of the physicists" (162). * * *

† From *Journal of Modern Literature* 32.3 (Spring 2009): 39–45, 47–48, 51–52, 54. Copyright © 2009 by Indiana University Press. Reprinted by permission of Indiana University Press. Page numbers for *To the Lighthouse* refer to this Norton Critical Edition. Ellipses in brackets are Brown's.

It may be impossible to determine the degree of influence discoveries in contemporary science may have had on Woolf's fiction or in what measure her own ideas preceded them. However, it is certain that, because of her father, she had considerable exposure to the philosophical questions underlying the debates among physicists in the early twentieth century regarding objective reality. Leslie Stephen invested a large portion of his scholarly energies into nineteenth-century realist-idealist debates in which the topics of objectivity and the role of perception are paramount. Einstein himself struggled with a belief in objective realism. Problems analogous to those with which Stephen contended resurfaced in a slightly altered form during the scientist's career at around the same time Woolf was writing *Mrs. Dalloway* and *To the Lighthouse*. Woolf's characters' fluid and oftentimes paranormal connection to one another, and to the objects around them, indicate she does not share all of Einstein's or her father's beliefs regarding objectivity. In *To the Lighthouse*, however, her concept of space and time remains relative, and she melds Einstein's theories with an additional sense of the permeable boundaries of consciousness between entities that reflects the holistic nature of subatomic phenomena.[1]

One of the thought problems that Stephen addressed, which informs Einstein's ideological crisis and Woolf's own ideas, involves the existence of unperceived objects. Paradigmatic examples of this thought problem include the following questions: does a table exist when you're not looking at it? If a tree falls in the woods and nobody hears it, does it make a sound? George Berkeley, an idealist, claimed that nothing could be said to exist independently of the senses that perceived it, to which Samuel Johnson, a realist, responded, "I refute [Berkeley] thus," and then proceeded to kick a stone (qtd. in Fogelin 79). Of course, Johnson's retort could not disprove Berkeley's claim but was, nevertheless, an argument Einstein would have supported because of its assertion of an objective reality. * * *

* * * For Stephen, objective existence could neither be proved nor disproved. At the same time, he also believed that human thought and perception were as real as external objects, but bound to an individual consciousness that could not reach beyond itself ("What Is Materialism?" 135).

Einstein dealt with a similar but slightly different formulation of the realist-idealist dilemma. He struggled to substantiate his heartfelt belief in an objective reality and further maintained, like Stephen, that the boundaries of consciousness were fixed. Unlike Stephen,

1. Although Woolf's exposure to quantum theories may not have been direct, Yom observes that "Frequent ruminations on the nature of light, including detailed consideration of the wave-particle duality, appeared in such widely read newspapers as *The Times* and the *Saturday Evening Post*" (145).

however, Einstein had to contend with the additional implications of his and others' findings in the field of quantum mechanics. In sub-atomic science, an observation on a system cannot be made without irrevocably altering the system in an unpredictable way. For example, bombarding an electron with a beam of light of short enough wave-length to determine its position will unavoidably transfer energy to the electron, knocking it out of position and rendering it impossible to discern its momentum at the moment of observation. By the same token, measuring an electron with a correspondingly weak and long wavelength of light would enable a physicist to ascertain its momen-tum, but the increased distance between the crests and troughs of the longer wavelength make it difficult to accurately establish the elec-tron's position. Being unable to determine the simultaneous position and momentum of a particle makes a full description of it in space-time impossible. Therefore, the minimal conditions for its empirically objective existence are not met. *** Consequently, an element of ambiguity regarding the notion of objectivity can never be overcome and cannot be attributed to a simple lack of technical innovation.

In the world of quantum physics, the thought problem of the realist-idealist debate has to be reformulated. In terms of the Berkeley-Johnson example cited above, Johnson would not have been able to locate the stone either before or after he kicked it, so the action of kicking would be inseparable from it, and the independent existence of the stone would be even more difficult to surmise. For the idealists as well, perception must now be understood as a more quasi-creative phenomenon. In the study of subatomic particles, the same experi-mental set-up will yield unpredictably varied results with repeated trials. Therefore, Stephen's definition of objectivity as "that which is true for both you and me" ("What Is Materialism?" 149) is also severely complicated by a multiplicity of "facts." Einstein faced a virtual world mediating between an "object" and its perception, which allowed for an array of possible outcomes, none of which could be either validated or invalidated by additional observations. Bohr explains:

> relativity [. . .] by a profound analysis of the problem of obser-vation, was destined to reveal the subjective character of all the concepts of classical physics. In spite of the great demands that it makes upon our power of abstraction, the theory of relativity approaches, in a particularly high degree, the classical ideal of unity and causality in the description of nature [. . .] However, [. . .] the classical ideal cannot be attained in the description of atomic phenomena. (*Atomic* 1: 97)

*** Either the location *or* the momentum of an "object" can be dis-covered at one time, but never at the same time. Therefore, an unam-biguously stable identification of a subatomic particle as a classically bounded object or point in space is not possible, nor is it possible to predict its future course through time.

In *To the Lighthouse*, Woolf depicts a relative world but also directly interrogates the issues of objectivity and realism that interested her father and that Einstein spent the remainder of his career trying to prove. Woolf's exploration of the fuzzy boundaries between subjects and objects coincides with the quantum physical understanding of a holistic universe. * * *

* * * Mrs. Ramsay appears to affect space by recreating it on her terms and from her own particularized point of view. * * * [Her] greatest achievement of unification in the novel is relativistic and occurs at the dinner table where she orders her environment like a large body of mass influencing the curvature of spacetime. * * * Her husband sits at the far end of the table "all in a heap, frowning" (64). Mr. Tansley "had been reading in his room, and now he came down and it all seemed to him silly, superficial, flimsy" (65–66). Mr. Bankes thinks just how "trifling it all is, how boring [. . .] compared with [. . .] work" (68), while Lily copes with the situation by obsessing over her painting. All the dinner guests are initially separated by concerns with their own affairs, and the efforts of socializing seem like a weight that Mrs. Ramsay compels them to bear. Mr. Bankes in particular "must make himself talk. Unless he were very careful, [Mrs. Ramsay] would find out this treachery of his; that he did not care a straw for her, and that would not be at all pleasant" (68). Aware of her guests' unfavorable dispositions, Mrs. Ramsay realizes from the beginning that "the whole effort of merging and flowing and creating rested on her" (64) and achieves the unity she desires by a series of silent communiqués. * * * Through a combination of efforts, "Some change [. . .] went through them all [. . .] and they were [. . .] conscious of making a party together in a hollow, on an island" (74).

Mrs. Ramsay's orchestrations and influence also extend beyond the ordered table. Not only does she arrange the spaces that surround her according to a form she both intuits and creates, but she is capable of attracting and influencing elements that at first appear outside of her control. She thinks, "They must come now [. . .] looking at the door, and at that instant, Minta Doyle, Paul Rayley, and a maid carrying a great dish in her hands came in together" (74). Mrs. Ramsay's influence is such that even distant bodies come under her sway. As a force that is "irresistible [. . .] She put a spell on them all" (77), and only when she eventually decides to leave the room does "a sort of disintegration set in" (85). * * *

The difference between Woolf's viewpoint and that of her father and Einstein makes itself apparent through the contrast between the table as an object of permeability and connectivity versus the table

as an object of independence and separation. The dinner table that
acts as Mrs. Ramsay's primary domain of influence and unification
is juxtaposed in the novel with Mr. Ramsay's kitchen table that represents the isolated and unperceived object. According to Banfield,
"The table is interposed between Woolf's woman-artist and the philosopher, placing the problem of knowledge at the center of Woolf's
art. To Lily's consternation, she finds her gaze riveted to the same
object [of] the philosopher" (Banfield, *Phantom* 49). Throughout the
novel, Lily is both repelled by and attracted to Mr. and Mrs. Ramsay, pondering the character of each and incorporating their world-
views into her artistic vision. * * *

Woolf's choice of the kitchen table as an object of contemplation
for Lily not only serves to conveniently contrast with Mrs. Ramsay's
dinner table, but the table itself acts as "the paradigmatic object of
knowledge in 'the history of English thought'" (Banfield, *Phantom*
66) and the prototypical object referred to by Stephen. * * * Despite
the interests and beliefs that Woolf shares with Stephen and Einstein, * * * she overtly questions their shared presumption of subjects and objects that occupy distinct and impermeable locations.
The contrast set up between the two tables in the novel serves to
introduce the debate over objectivity. Mr. Ramsay's table exists independently of its observation, whereas Mrs. Ramsay's table is a par-
ticipatory "object," interacting and changing with the forces of her
consciousness.

Mrs. Ramsay has a holistic relationship to the world around her,
which confounds the notion that subjects and objects are specifically located and bounded. * * * The discord between Mr. and
Mrs. Ramsay is not simply personal, involving such issues as, for
example, telling James whether or not he'll be able to go to the lighthouse tomorrow. It centers on different conceptions of reality and
knowledge. Mrs. Ramsay's holistic vision is opposed to Mr. Ramsay's
compartmental one. He divides knowledge into letters of the alphabet, and wonders if "he had, or might have had, the power to repeat
every letter of the alphabet from A to Z accurately in order" (29).
* * * Like Woolf's father, Mr. Ramsay feels he must focus on facts
and laws and discernable cause and effect relationships. His quest
for R (reality), however, indicates that he is not quite willing to forego
the possibility of uncovering the world beyond the senses, despite
the fact that the real-life person upon whom he is based understood
such a quest as one that was likely to remain unfulfilled.

* * * Mrs. Ramsay, on the other hand, sometimes thinks that "To
pursue truth with such astonishing lack of consideration for other
people's feelings [. . .] was [. . . a] horrible [. . .] outrage of human
decency" (27), reflecting a sense that human beings cannot be

removed from the world in which they live; they cannot wholly objectify their environment. * * *

*   *   *

* * * For Woolf, reality is not contained within a single perceptual consciousness, nor does it exist as a collection of multiple but rigidly divided perceptual consciousnesses. It is not an entirely boundless collective, nor does it exist as some form of transcendent actuality. The reality depicted in *To the Lighthouse* seems to be composed of multiple interpenetrating consciousnesses interconnected with one another and loosely housed within fluid subjectivities and objectivities that interactively create, as well as observe, their environment.

*   *   *

WORKS CITED

Banfield, Ann. *The Phantom Table: Woolf, Fry, Russell and the Epistemology of Modernism*. Cambridge: Cambridge UP, 2000.

Bohr, Niels. *Atomic Theory and the Description of Nature: The Philosophical Writings of Niels Bohr*. 3 vols. Woodbridge, CT: Ox Bow Press, 1987.

Fogelin, Robert J. *Berkeley and the Principles of Human Knowledge*. New York: Routledge, 2001.

Stephen, Leslie. "What Is Materialism?" *An Agnostic's Apology and Other Essays*. London: Smith, Elder, 1893.

Yom, Sue Sun. "Bio-graphy and the Quantum Leap: Waves, Particles, and Light as a Theory of Writing the Human Life." *Virginia Woolf: Texts and Contexts*. Eds. Beth Rigel Daugherty and Eileen Barrett. New York: Pace UP, 1996.

Art and Reality

VANESSA BELL

Woolf's older sister Vanessa Stephen Bell (1879–1961) trained as a painter starting in her teens and pursued her art throughout her life while also centering the social lives of family and friends in households in Bloomsbury, London; at her farmhouse Charleston, in Firle, Sussex; and in Cassis, France. She married Clive Bell in 1907; raised three children—Julian (1908–1937), Quentin (1910–1996), and Angelica (1918–2012); and, from World War I until the end of her life, lived and collaborated with the painter Duncan Grant (1885–1978). Bloomsbury's artistic and intellectual life revolved around painters and art theorists as much as around writers and literary critics. The influence of her art on Woolf's writing was profound; the sisters were collaborators (Vanessa designed the covers of her sister's books, made illustrations for some of her stories, and decorated her homes) and rivals. Vanessa's painting *Studland Beach* (1912), reproduced here, shows that Vanessa had dealt with compositional problems similar to those Lily confronts in *To the Lighthouse* and, too, that Vanessa was engaged as her sister was with the tug and pull between formal design and representation in art. For Woolf's comments on these issues in Vanessa's art, see Composition Chronology (170 and 176) and Woolf's essay "Pictures" (250–53). See also Lisa Tickner, "Vanessa Bell: *Studland Beach*, Domesticity, and 'Significant Form'," *Representations* 65 (Winter 1999): 63–92.

Also reproduced here is Vanessa's original design for the dust jacket of *To the Lighthouse*. In December 1926, in a letter suggesting how routine such a request had become, Virginia wrote to Vanessa that she was "in a hideous rush putting the last touches to my novel—what about the cover?" (*Letters* 3: 311–12). It is clear from Vanessa's response to the novel once it was published (see Composition Chronology, 178–80) that she hadn't read it before designing the cover. In June 1927, Woolf praised the cover as "lovely" and called Vanessa's style "unique; because so truthful" (*Letters* 3: 391). On the cover design, see "Cover to Cover: Newhaven Lighthouse as Vanessa Bell's Muse," this edition, pp. 243–46.

Vanessa Bell, *Studland Beach* (verso: Group of Male Nudes by Duncan Grant), c. 1912. Purchased from Anthony d'Offay Gallery 1976. © 2023 Artists Rights Society (ARS), New York/DACS, London. © Estate of Vanessa Bell. Image: Tate.

Vanessa Bell, original dust jacket for *To the Lighthouse*, 1927. © 2023 Artists Rights Society (ARS), New York/DACS, London. Image: NYPL.

CLIVE BELL

Vanessa Stephen married Clive Bell (1881–1964), her brother Thoby's Cambridge friend, shortly after Thoby's untimely death in 1906. Father of her sons Julian and Quentin, he remained part of her household at Charleston and in Cassis, France, even after the marriage ended and Vanessa formed her life partnership with Duncan Grant. Bell was an art critic and advocate for modern art who collaborated with Roger Fry on the Post-Impressionist Exhibitions of 1910 and 1912 and, as he recounts in the preface to *Art* (1914), engaged in long-running debates with Fry about art history and aesthetics. Woolf was part of the conversation; his ideas about art influenced hers, and his book *Civilization* (1928), which he was finishing while she was writing *To the Lighthouse*, is dedicated to her. In *Art*, excerpted here, he celebrates "primitive" art (such as early medieval European art and the arts of ancient Japan and China), declares that the art of the Renaissance, the paintings of Rembrandt, and most art made in eighteenth- and nineteenth-century Europe doesn't qualify as art, and insists on the timelessness and universality of the aesthetic value he names "significant form." Like Fry, he saw the paintings of Paul Cézanne (1839–1906) as the epitome of great art that made possible the modernist innovations of the Post-Impressionists.

[Significant Form]†

* * *

* * * All works of visual art have some common quality, or when we speak of "works of art" we gibber. Everyone speaks of "art," making a mental classification by which he distinguishes the class "works of art" from all other classes. What is the justification of this classification? What is the quality common and peculiar to all members of this class? Whatever it be, no doubt it is often found in company with other qualities; but they are adventitious—it is essential. There must be some one quality without which a work of art cannot exist; possessing which, in the least degree, no work is altogether worthless. What is this quality? What quality is shared by all objects that provoke our aesthetic emotions? What quality is common to Sta. Sophia and the windows at Chartres, Mexican sculpture, a Persian bowl, Chinese carpets, Giotto's frescoes at Padua, and the masterpieces of Poussin, Piero della Francesca, and Cézanne? Only one answer seems possible—significant form. In each, lines and colours combined in a particular way, certain forms and relations of forms, stir our aesthetic emotions. These relations and combinations of lines and colours,

† From *Art* (New York: Frederic Stokes, 1914), pp. 7–8, 49–54, 220–31.

these aesthetically moving forms, I call "Significant Form"; and "Significant Form" is the one quality common to all works of visual art.

*   *   *

* * * I want now to consider that metaphysical question—"Why do certain arrangements and combinations of form move us so strangely?" * * * It seems to me possible, though by no means certain, that created form moves us so profoundly because it expresses the emotion of its creator. Perhaps the lines and colours of a work of art convey to us something that the artist felt. If this be so, it will explain that curious but undeniable fact, to which I have already referred, that what I call material beauty (*e.g.* the wing of a butterfly) does not move most of us in at all the same way as a work of art moves us. It is beautiful form, but it is not significant form. It moves us, but it does not move us aesthetically. It is tempting to explain the difference between "significant form" and "beauty"—that is to say, the difference between form that provokes our aesthetic emotions and form that does not—by saying that significant form conveys to us an emotion felt by its creator and that beauty conveys nothing.

For what, then, does the artist feel the emotion that he is supposed to express? * * *

* * * One account of the matter, given me by a very good artist, is that what he tries to express in a picture is "a passionate apprehension of form." I have set myself to discover what is meant by "a passionate apprehension of form," and, after much talking and more listening, I have arrived at the following result. Occasionally when an artist—a real artist—looks at objects (the contents of a room, for instance) he perceives them as pure forms in certain relations to each other, and feels emotion for them as such. These are his moments of inspiration: follows the desire to express what has been felt. The emotion that the artist felt in his moment of inspiration he did not feel for objects seen as means, but for objects seen as pure forms—that is, as ends in themselves. He did not feel emotion for a chair as a means to physical well-being, nor as an object associated with the intimate life of a family, nor as the place where someone sat saying things unforgettable, nor yet as a thing bound to the lives of hundreds of men and women, dead or alive, by a hundred subtle ties; doubtless an artist does often feel emotions such as these for the things that he sees, but in the moment of aesthetic vision he sees objects, not as means shrouded in associations, but as pure forms. It is for, or at any rate through, pure form that he feels his inspired emotion.

Now to see objects as pure forms is to see them as ends in themselves. * * * What is the significance of anything as an end in itself? What is that which is left when we have stripped a thing of all its associations, of all its significance as a means? What is left to provoke our emotion? What but that which philosophers used to call "the thing in itself" and now call "ultimate reality"? Shall I be altogether fantastic in suggesting, what some of the profoundest thinkers have believed, that the significance of the thing in itself is the significance of Reality? Is it possible that the answer to my question, "Why are we so profoundly moved by certain combinations of lines and colours?" should be, "Because artists can express in combinations of lines and colours an emotion felt for reality which reveals itself through line and colour"? If this suggestion were accepted it would follow that "significant form" was form behind which we catch a sense of ultimate reality. * * *

* * *

* * * To instance simplification as a peculiarity of the art of any particular age seems queer, since simplification is essential to all art. Without it art cannot exist; for art is the creation of significant form, and simplification is the liberating of what is significant from what is not. Yet to such depths had art sunk in the nineteenth century, that in the eyes of the rabble the greatest crime of Whistler and the Impressionists was their by no means drastic simplification. * * *

The contemporary movement has pushed simplification a great deal further than Manet and his friends pushed it, thereby distinguishing itself from anything we have seen since the twelfth century. Since the twelfth century, in sculpture and glass, the thirteenth, in painting and drawing, the drift has been towards realism and away from art. Now the essence of realism is detail. Since Zola, every novelist has known that nothing gives so imposing an air of reality as a mass of irrelevant facts, and very few have cared to give much else. Detail is the heart of realism, and the fatty degeneration of art. The tendency of the movement is to simplify away all this mess of detail which painters have introduced into pictures in order to state facts. * * *

* * * In a work of art nothing is relevant but what contributes to formal significance. Therefore all informatory matter is irrelevant and should be eliminated. But what most painters have to express can only be expressed in designs so complex and subtle that without some clue they would be almost unintelligible. * * * [I]t is tempting and, indeed, reasonable, for him to wish to provide a clue; and to do so he has only to work into his design some familiar object, a tree or a figure, and the business is done. * * * Enter by the backdoor representation in the quality of a clue to the nature of design. I have no objection to its presence. Only, if the representative element is not to ruin the picture as a work of art, it must be fused into the design. It must do double duty; as well as giving information, it must create aesthetic emotion. It must be simplified into significant form.

Let us make no mistake about this. To help the spectator to appreciate our design we have introduced into our picture a representative
or cognitive element. This element has nothing whatever to do with
art. The recognition of a correspondence between the forms of a work
of art and the familiar forms of life cannot possibly provoke aesthetic
emotion. Only significant form can do that. Of course realistic forms
may be aesthetically significant, and out of them an artist may create
a superb work of art, but it is with their aesthetic and not with their
cognitive value that we shall then be concerned. We shall treat them
as though they were not representative of anything. The cognitive or
representative element in a work of art can be useful as a means to
the perception of formal relations and in no other way. * * *

* * *

To assure his design, the artist makes it his first care to simplify.
But mere simplification, the elimination of detail, is not enough. The
informatory forms that remain have got to be made significant. The
representative element, if it is not to injure the design, must become a
part of it; besides giving information it has got to provoke aesthetic
emotion. That is where symbolism fails. The symbolist eliminates,
but does not assimilate. His symbols, as a rule, are not significant
forms, but formal intelligencers. They are not integral parts of a plastic conception, but intellectual abbreviations. They are not
informed by the artist's emotion, they are invented by his intellect.
They are dead matter in a living organism. They are rigid and tight
because they are not traversed by the rhythm of the design. * * *

* * *

It seems that an artist creates a good design when, having been
possessed by a real emotional conception, he is able to hold and
translate it. We all agree, I think, that till the artist has had his
moment of emotional vision there can be no very considerable work
of art; but, the vision seen and felt, it still remains uncertain whether
he has the force to hold and the skill to translate it. Of course the
vast majority of pictures fail in design because they correspond to
no emotional vision; but the interesting failures are those in which
the vision came but was incompletely grasped. * * *
There is an absolute necessity about a good design arising, I imagine, from the fact that the nature of each form and its relation to all
the other forms is determined by the artist's need of expressing
exactly what he felt. Of course, a perfect correspondence between
expression and conception may not be established at the first or the
second attempt. But if the work is to be a success there will come a
moment in which the artist will be able to hold and express completely his hour or minute of inspiration. If that moment does not

come the design will lack necessity. For though an artist's aesthetic sense enables him, as we shall see, to say whether a design is right or wrong, only this masterful power of seizing and holding his vision enables him to make it right. * * *

ROGER FRY

Art historian and painter Roger Fry (1866–1934) was one of Woolf's most important influences as well as a deeply valued friend, and she drew on their conversations for her portrayal of visual arts in *To the Lighthouse*. In 1910 and 1912 Fry organized London exhibitions of paintings by the French Post-Impressionists that celebrated compositional form over representational illusion or likeness. Like Clive Bell, Fry valued the so-called "primitive" arts of Africa and Asia as resources for revolutionizing British art (see "Orienting Virginia Woolf: Race, Aesthetics, and Politics in *To the Lighthouse*," this edition, pp. 312–26). In her 1940 biography, Woolf articulated Fry's lifelong effort to balance the claims of form and representation: addressing Fry's notion of "aesthetic emotion," or the emotion aroused by an artwork's compositional form, she admiringly cites his view that "those who experience it feel it to have a peculiar quality of 'reality,'" which it had long been the aim of her art, too, to convey (*Roger Fry*, p. 229). Woolf valued Fry's delight in extending art theory to writing: he thought that writers should follow the Post-Impressionists and "fling representation to the winds" (*Roger Fry*, p. 172). He admired Woolf's use of "language as a medium of art," and he arranged for "Time Passes" to be translated into French and published a few months before the novel.

Fry eventually recognized the contribution of representational elements to art's capacity to evoke emotional response. While his catalogue introduction for the 1912 Post-Impressionist Exhibition (the first selection here) boldly states the argument for form, "The Artist and Psycho-Analysis"—a lecture for the British Psychological Society in 1924, when Hogarth Press began publishing Freud's writings in English translation—concedes, in closing, that emotions aroused by art may derive in part from deeply buried responses to lived experience. See Composition Chronology (163) for Woolf's letter to him about Hogarth Press publishing this lecture as a pamphlet and (181–82) for their discussion of the novel after its publication.

The French Post-Impressionists†

When the first Post-Impressionist Exhibition was held in these Galleries two years ago the English public became for the first time fully aware of the existence of a new movement in art, a movement which

---

† From "The French Group," in *Catalogue of the Second Post-Impressionist Exhibition*, Grafton Galleries, 1912, rpt. *Vision and Design*, pp. 156–57.

was the more disconcerting in that it was no mere variation upon
accepted themes but implied a reconsideration of the very purpose
and aim as well as the methods of pictorial and plastic art. It was not
surprising, therefore, that a public which had come to admire above
everything in a picture the skill with which the artist produced illusion
should have resented an art in which such skill was completely subordinated to the direct expression of feeling. Accusations of clumsiness and
incapacity were freely made, even against so singularly accomplished
an artist as Cézanne. Such darts, however, fall wide of the mark, since
it is not the object of these artists to exhibit their skill or proclaim their
knowledge, but only to attempt to express by pictorial and plastic form
certain spiritual experiences; and in conveying these, ostentation of
skill is likely to be even more fatal than downright incapacity.

* * *

* * * But the feeling on the part of the public may, and I think in
this case does, arise from a simple misunderstanding of what these
artists set out to do. The difficulty springs from a deep-rooted conviction, due to long-established custom, that the aim of painting is
the descriptive imitation of natural forms. Now, these artists do not
seek to give what can, after all, be but a pale reflex of actual appearance, but to arouse the conviction of a new and definite reality. They
do not seek to imitate form, but to create form; not to imitate life,
but to find an equivalent for life. By that I mean that they wish to
make images which by the clearness of their logical structure, and
by their closely-knit unity of texture, shall appeal to our disinterested
and contemplative imagination with something of the same vividness as the things of actual life appeal to our practical activities. In
fact, they aim not at illusion but at reality.

* * *

From The Artist and Psycho-Analysis[†]

* * *

* * * The form of a work of art has a meaning of its own and the contemplation of the form in and for itself gives rise in some people to a
special emotion which does not depend upon the association of the
form with anything else whatever. But that form may by various
means either by casual opposition or by some resemblance to things
or people or ideas in the outside world, become intimately associated
in our minds with those other things, and if these things are objects

---

[†] From *The Artist and Psycho-Analysis* (London: Hogarth Press, 1924), pp. 8–9, 15–16,
19–20.

of emotional feeling, we shall get from the contemplation of the form the echo of all the feelings belonging to the associated objects.

Now since very few people are so constituted by nature or training as to have developed the special feeling about formal design, and since everyone has in the course of his life accumulated a vast mass of feeling about all sorts of objects, persons, and ideas, for the greater part of mankind the associated emotions of a work of art are far stronger than the purely esthetic ones.

So far does this go that they hardly notice the form, but pass at once into the world of associated emotions which that form calls up in them. Thus, to go back to our example, the vast majority of people have no notion whether the form of "God Save the King" is finely constructed and capable of arousing esthetic emotion or not. They have never, properly speaking, heard the form because they have always passed at once into that richly varied world of racial and social emotion which has gathered round it.

And what is true of certain pieces of music is even more true of the graphic arts. Here we have forms which quite visibly resemble certain objects in nature, and not unfrequently these objects, such for instance as a beautiful woman, are charged for us with a great deal of emotion. When to this we add that people are far less sensitive to the meaning of visible formal design than they are to audible design, we need not be surprised that pictures are almost always estimated for qualities which have nothing, or almost nothing, to do with their formal design or their esthetic quality in the strict sense.

To satisfy this emotional pleasure in the associated ideas of images which the mass of mankind feel so strongly there has arisen a vast production of pictures, writings, music, etc., in which formal design is entirely subordinated to the excitation of the emotions associated with objects. And this is what we may call popular, commercial, or impure art, and to this category belongs nowadays the vast majority of so called artistic productions. On the other hand in each generation there are likely to be a certain number of people who have a sensitiveness to purely formal relations. To such people these relations have meaning and arouse keen emotions of pleasure. And these people create such systems of formal relations and do not sacrifice willingly or consciously anything of those formal relations to the arousing of emotions connected with objects in the outside world. Their whole attention is directed towards establishing the completest relationship of all parts within the system of the work of art.

It so happens that these systems of formal relations the meaning of which is apprehended by a comparatively few people in each generation, have a curious vitality and longevity, whereas those works in which appeal is made chiefly to the associated ideas of images rarely survive the generation for whose pleasure they were made.

This may be because the emotions about objects change more rapidly than the emotions about form. But whatever the reason, the result is that the accumulated and inherited artistic treasure of mankind is made up almost entirely of those works in which formal design is the predominant consideration.

*   *   *

* * * I have elsewhere expressed the belief that in a world of symbolists only two kinds of people are entirely opposed to symbolism, and they are the man of science and the artist, since they alone are seeking to make constructions which are completely self-consistent, self-supporting and self-contained—constructions which do not stand for something else, but appear to have ultimate value and in that sense to be real.

It is, of course, perfectly natural that people should always be looking for symbolism in works of art. Since most people are unable to perceive the meaning of purely formal relations, are unable to derive from them the profound satisfaction that the creator and those that understand him feel, they always look for some meaning that can be attached to the values of actual life, they always hope to translate a work of art into terms of *ideas* with which they are familiar. None the less in proportion as an artist is pure he is opposed to all symbolism.

You will have noticed that in all these psycho-analytical enquiries into pictorial art the attention of the investigator is fixed on the nature of the images, on what choice the painter has made of the object he represents. Now I venture to say that no one who has a real understanding of the art of painting attaches any importance to what we call the subject of a picture—what is represented. To one who feels the language of pictorial form all depends on *how* it is presented, *nothing* on what. Rembrandt expressed his profoundest feelings just as well when he painted a carcass hanging up in a butcher's shop as when he painted the Crucifixion or his mistress. Cézanne whom most of us believe to be the greatest artist of modern times expressed some of his grandest conceptions in pictures of fruit and crockery on a common kitchen table.

*   *   *

One thing I think we may clearly say, namely, that there is a pleasure in the recognition of order, of inevitability in relations, and that the more complex the relations of which we are able to recognize the inevitable interdependence and correspondence, the greater is the pleasure; this of course will come very near to the pleasure derived from the contemplation of intellectual constructions united by logical inevitability. What the source of that satisfaction is would clearly be a problem for psychology.

But in art there is, I think, an affective quality which lies outside that. It is not a mere recognition of order and inter-relation; every part, as well as the whole, becomes suffused with an emotional tone. Now, from our definition of this pure beauty, the emotional tone is not due to any recognizable reminiscence or suggestion of the emotional experiences of life; but I sometimes wonder if it nevertheless does not get its force from arousing some very deep, very vague, and immensely generalized reminiscences. It looks as though art had got access to the substratum of all the emotional colours of life, to something which underlies all the particular and specialized emotions of actual life. It seems to derive an emotional energy from the very conditions of our existence by its relation of an emotional significance in time and space. Or it may be that art really calls up, as it were, the residual traces left on the spirit by the different emotions of life, without however recalling the actual experiences, so that we get an echo of the emotion without the limitation and particular direction which it had in experience.

*　*　*

KABE WILSON

Cover to Cover: Newhaven Lighthouse as Vanessa Bell's Muse†

The lighthouse of Godrevy Island near St. Ives in Cornwall has often been credited as the inspiration for *To the Lighthouse*, owing to the way the novel was drawn from Woolf's impressions of family holidays there in childhood. In recent years, the novel's Isle of Skye setting has meant that the nearby Eilean Bàn lighthouse has also been discussed as having played a role in the work's creation. By comparison, Newhaven Lighthouse in Sussex, despite being the closest lighthouse to both Monk's House and Charleston, has received relatively little attention in the study of the coastal landmarks that would have been significant to the creative lives of Woolf and her sister Vanessa Bell. [1] The fact that the novel was mostly written and its famous cover designed within five miles of this structure has been generally overlooked.

This oversight could well be because Woolf never showed much positive creative interest in Newhaven as a place. It is often referred to in her diaries but generally in relation to its role as a transport hub—it hosts the ferry to Dieppe and was therefore an important

---

† Written for this Norton Critical Edition.
1. There were two lighthouses at Newhaven Harbour in the sisters' era, one at the end of the breakwater, which still stands, and one at the shore side of the harbour on the West Pier, which was damaged in the 1970s and replaced with a simple pole lamp.

Newhaven Lighthouse. © 2023 Artists Rights Society (ARS), New York/DACS, London. Image: Charleston.

point of access to Europe in that era. In *Mrs. Dalloway* Septimus Smith's return to England is recounted as having been via this port:

> It might be possible, Septimus thought, looking at England from the train window, as they left Newhaven; it might be possible that the world itself is without meaning.[2]

Referencing the town as a geographical prompt for Septimus' existential anxiety does not suggest a place she held in high regard.

The same was not necessarily true of Vanessa Bell. In a letter to her son Julian in August 1936 she reveals:

> Meanwhile Duncan and I have taken to going constantly to Newhaven to paint and I am getting more and more fascinated by boats on water—to look at—not to be in or on.[3]

A number of oil paintings of the harbour came out of this period for Bell, culminating in her work *Newhaven Lighthouse.* The painting shows the further of the harbour's two lighthouses as it appeared then, a white cast-iron Victorian structure flagged with smaller buildings at its base.

My painting on the cover of this Norton Critical Edition was inspired by Bell's scene. Painted in 2020, it depicts a much wider vista of the Sussex coastline viewed from further west than Newhaven, and though it shows two lighthouses, only one of them belongs

2. Virginia Woolf, *Mrs. Dalloway*, ed. Anne Fernald, Norton Critical Edition (1925; New York: Norton, 2021), p. 63.
3. From Vanessa Bell's letter to Julian Bell, August 29, 1936. *Selected Letters of Vanessa Bell*, ed. Regina Marler (New York: Pantheon, 1993), p. 420.

to Newhaven Harbour. The other, on the right of the painting, is the Belle Tout Lighthouse, which is four miles east along the coast. Belle Tout, both in Bell's time and now, undoubtedly has the more scenic setting. It sits atop Beachy Head, a popular tourist spot next to the Seven Sisters hills, which are themselves famed for their beauty and regarded as an iconic part of the Sussex landscape. It is now decommissioned, privately owned and maintained, and the site has been used as a location in both the James Bond and Harry Potter film series. Even though both of these lighthouses are visible in my acrylic scene, as an homage to Bell's painting the title is also *Newhaven Lighthouse*, and this is the one that is compositionally centred. By repeating her title despite depicting both structures, I wanted to underscore what is notable about Bell's painting—that of the two, she painted the lighthouse far out on the concrete breakwater of an industrial port, rather than the one surrounded by internationally renowned landscape. Belle Tout is admittedly a few miles further from Charleston but would still have been very reachable by various routes.

What makes this contrast even more stark is that her painting shows Newhaven Lighthouse when it had been modified for the imminence of war. As a Europe-facing port, Newhaven was likely to be a target for the Nazis and the base of the building was therefore given reinforcements and an armoury. The tranquil foreboding of the painting speaks to the changes to come—the rising threat to these provincial shores and the great shifts in human history wrought by war, which of course had been so powerfully detailed by Virginia Woolf in *To the Lighthouse* a decade earlier.

Unearthed in the cataloguing of the Angelica Garnett Gift to Charleston in 2014, a pencil sketch of an unidentified lighthouse

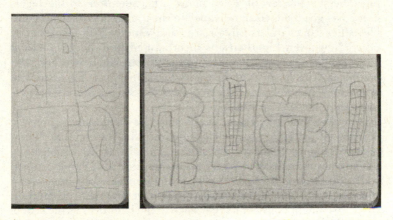

further signals Newhaven's significance. Though it is a simplistic line study, the rounded shape of the tower top, the prominence of the lower structure and the placement of a single window all suggest this depicts Newhaven's harbourside West Pier Lighthouse.

Judging by the portable scale of the sketchbook, we might guess that it was sketched from life. Intriguingly, on the following page there is a geometric design of solid rectangles surrounded by cloud-like swirls that could easily be read as an early plan for what would become Vanessa's *To the Lighthouse* Hogarth Press dust jacket. The chronology of the letters exchanged between the sisters in 1927 shows that Vanessa was tasked with designing a cover before she had read the novel. Without a full textual prompt, might she have taken the title as instruction? Is it possible she sought inspiration from real life and walked from Charleston to the nearest lighthouse looking for a visual guide for this project?

Whether or not this is the order of events, it is not hard to imagine that lighthouses took on a greater meaning for Bell in the years after Virginia's novel had been published. So the fact that she repeatedly travelled to and ended up painting Newhaven Lighthouse gives that particular beacon (and potentially its harbourside twin) a notable role in the longer history of the novel, and the personal history of Bell's connection to the text. That Lily Briscoe was likely modelled on Bell adds to this connection—between the novel's publication and the painting's completion, a cyclical historical link is created. The novel depicts an artist returning to the view of a lighthouse a decade after the lighthouse has been imbued with significance to the characters around her, and then she completes her work. In real life, the character inspired *by* Bell then in turn inspires Bell to place herself in view of a lighthouse a decade after *To the Lighthouse* has given added significance to the scene. She likewise completes her work, and as Lily Briscoe and Vanessa Bell inspire each other, Newhaven Lighthouse is incorporated into the metatextual loop. While we don't know the full extent of when it began, the presence of this harbour in the creative imagination of the artist who gave us the first visual representation of her sister's literary masterpiece should not go unnoticed.

On even a moderately clear day Newhaven's breakwater lighthouse is visible, if not from Monk's House or the Charleston estate themselves (due to their low lying positions), then from various points in the surrounding South Downs where Virginia and Vanessa often walked or cycled. As such, its role as a landmark in the area where both women lived, worked, and died deserves further recognition, so that we might consider its relevance to the later lives of the sisters in much the same manner that Godrevy is accorded great significance to their childhood.

Essays by Virginia Woolf

Thunder at Wembley[†]

It is nature that is the ruin of Wembley, yet it is difficult to see what steps Lord Stevenson, Lieut.-General Sir Travers Clarke, and the Duke of Devonshire could have taken to keep her out. They might have eradicated the grass and felled the chestnut trees; even so the thrushes would have got in, and there would always have been the sky. At Earl's Court and the White City, so far as memory serves, there was little trouble from this source. The area was too small; the light too brilliant. If a single real moth strayed in to dally with the arc lamps he was at once transformed into a dizzy reveller; if a laburnum tree shook her tassels, spangles of limelight floated in the violet and crimson air. Everything was intoxicated and transformed. But at Wembley nothing is changed and nobody is drunk. They say, indeed, that there is a restaurant where each diner is forced to spend a guinea upon his dinner. What vistas of cold ham that statement calls forth! What pyramids of rolls! What gallons of tea and coffee! For it is unthinkable that there should be champagne, plovers' eggs, or peaches at Wembley. And for six and eightpence two people can buy as much ham and bread as they need. Six and eightpence is not a large sum; but neither is it a small sum. It is a moderate sum, a mediocre sum. It is the prevailing sum at Wembley. You look through an open door at a regiment of motor-cars aligned in avenues. They are not opulent and powerful; they are not flimsy and cheap. Six and eightpence seems to be the price of each of them. It is the same with the machines for crushing gravel. One can imagine better; one can imagine worse. The machine before us is a serviceable type, and costs, inevitably, six and eightpence. Dress fabrics, rope, table linen,

† From *Nation & Athenaeum,* 35.13 (June 28, 1924): 409–10. The 1924–25 British Empire Exhibition was built on 220 acres in Wembley Park in suburban London. With pavilions for the British colonies and territories, "palaces" of Industry, Engineering, and Science, and kiosks for commercial brands such as Lipton and Wedgwood, the Exhibition allowed 27 million visitors to "see all of Empire at once" and showed off the empire's vast extent and profitability. Leonard and Virginia visited on May 29, 1924. See Scott Cohen, "The Empire from the Street: Virginia Woolf, Wembley, and Imperial Monuments," *MFS Modern Fiction Studies* 50:1 (2004): 85–109.

old masters, sugar, wheat, filigree silver, pepper, birds' nests (edible, and exported to Hong-Kong), camphor, bees-wax, rattans, and the rest—why trouble to ask the price? One knows beforehand—six and eightpence. As for the buildings themselves, those vast, smooth, grey palaces, no vulgar riot of ideas tumbled expensively in their architect's head; equally, cheapness was abhorrent to him, and vulgarity anathema. Per perch, rod, or square foot, however ferro-concrete palaces are sold, they too work out at six and eightpence.

But then, just as one is beginning a little wearily to fumble with those two fine words—democracy, mediocrity—nature asserts herself where one would least look to find her—in clergymen, school children, girls, young men, invalids in bath-chairs. They pass, quietly, silently, in coveys, in groups, sometimes alone. They mount the enormous staircases; they stand in queues to have their spectacles rectified gratis; to have their fountain pens filled gratis; they gaze respectfully into sacks of grain; glance reverently at mowing machines from Canada; now and again stoop to remove some paper bag or banana skin and place it in the receptacles provided for that purpose at frequent intervals along the avenues. But what has happened to our contemporaries? Each is beautiful; each is stately. Can it be that one is seeing human beings for the first time? In streets they hurry; in houses they talk; they are bankers in banks; sell shoes in shops. Here against the enormous background of ferro-concrete Britain, of rosy Burma, at large, unoccupied, they reveal themselves simply as human beings, creatures of leisure, civilization, and dignity; a little languid perhaps, a little attenuated, but a product to be proud of. Indeed, they are the ruin of the Exhibition. The Duke of Devonshire and his colleagues should have kept them out. As you watch them trailing and flowing, dreaming and speculating, admiring this coffee-grinder, that milk and cream separator, the rest of the show becomes insignificant. And what, one asks, is the spell it lays upon them? How, with all this dignity of their own, can they bring themselves to believe in that?

But this cynical reflection, at once so chill and so superior, was made, of course, by the thrush. Down in the Amusement Compound by some grave oversight on the part of the Committee several trees and rhododendron bushes have been allowed to remain; and these, as anybody could have foretold, attract the birds. As you wait your turn to be hoisted into mid-air, it is impossible not to hear the thrush singing. You look up, and discover a whole chestnut tree with its blossoms standing; you look down, and see ordinary grass, scattered with petals, harbouring insects, sprinkled with stray wild flowers. The gramophone does its best; they light a horse-shoe of fairy lamps above the Jack and Jill; a man bangs a bladder and implores you to come and tickle monkeys; boatloads of serious men are poised on the heights of the scenic railway; but all is vain. The cry of ecstasy that should have split the sky as the boat dropped to its doom patters from leaf to leaf, dies, falls flat, while the thrush proceeds with his statement. And then some woman, in the row of red-brick villas outside the grounds, comes out and wrings a dish-cloth in her backyard. All this the Duke of Devonshire should have prevented.

The problem of the sky, however, remains. Is it, one wonders, lying back limp but acquiescent in a green deck-chair, part of the Exhibition? Is it lending itself with exquisite tact to show off to the best advantage snowy Palestine, ruddy Burma, sand-coloured Canada, and the minarets and pagodas of our possessions in the East? So quietly it suffers all these domes and palaces to melt into its breast; receives them with such sombre and tender discretion; so exquisitely allows the rare lamps of Jack and Jill and the Monkey-Teasers to bear themselves like stars. But even as we watch and admire what we would fain credit to the forethought of Lieut.-General Sir Travers Clarke, a rushing sound is heard. Is it the wind or is it the British Empire Exhibition? It is both. The wind is rising and shuffling along the avenues; the Massed Bands of Empire are assembling and marching to the Stadium. Men like pincushions, men like pouter pigeons, men like pillar-boxes pass in procession. Dust swirls after them. Admirably impassive, the bands of Empire march on. Soon they will have entered the fortress; soon the gates will have clanged. But let them hasten! For either the sky has misread her directions or some appalling catastrophe is impending. The sky is livid, lurid, sulphurine. It is in violent commotion. It is whirling water-spouts of cloud into the air; of dust in the Exhibition. Dust swirls down the avenues, hisses and hurries like erected cobras round the corners. Pagodas are dissolving in dust. Ferro-concrete is fallible. Colonies are perishing and dispersing in spray of inconceivable beauty and terror which some malignant power illuminates. Ash and violet are the colours of its decay. From every quarter human beings come flying— clergymen, school children, invalids in bath-chairs. They fly with outstretched arms, and a vast sound of wailing rolls before them, but there is neither confusion nor dismay. Humanity is rushing to destruction, but humanity is accepting its doom. Canada opens a frail tent of shelter. Clergymen and school children gain its portals. Out in the open, under a cloud of electric silver, the bands of Empire strike up. The bagpipes neigh. Clergy, school children, and invalids group themselves round the Prince of Wales in butter. Cracks like the white roots of trees spread themselves across the firmament. The Empire is perishing; the bands are playing; the Exhibition is in ruins. For that is what comes of letting in the sky.

Pictures[†]

Probably some Professor has written a book on the subject, but it has not come our way. "The Loves of the Arts,"—that is more or less the title it would bear, and it would be concerned with the flirtations between music, letters, sculpture, and architecture, and the effects that the arts have had upon each other throughout the ages. Pending his inquiry, it would seem on the face of it that literature has always been the most sociable and the most impressionable of them all; that sculpture influenced Greek literature, music Elizabethan, architecture the English of the eighteenth century, and now, undoubtedly, we are under the dominion of painting. Were all modern paintings to be destroyed, a critic of the twenty-fifth century would be able to deduce from the works of Proust alone the existence of Matisse, Cézanne, Derain, and Picasso;[1] he would be able to say with those books before him that painters of the highest originality and power must be covering canvas after canvas, squeezing tube after tube, in the room next door.

Yet it is extremely difficult to put one's finger on the precise spot where paint makes itself felt in the work of so complete a writer. In the partial and incomplete writers it is much easier to detect. The world is full of cripples at the moment, victims of the art of painting, who paint apples, roses, china, pomegranates, tamarinds, and glass jars as well as words can paint them, which is, of course, not very well. We can say for certain that a writer whose writing appeals mainly to the eye is a bad writer; that if, in describing, say, a meeting in a garden, he describes roses, lilies, carnations, and shadows on the grass, so that we can see them, but allows to be inferred from them ideas, motives, impulses, and emotions, it is that he is incapable of using his medium for the purposes for which it was created, and is, as a writer, a man without legs.

But it is impossible to bring that charge against Proust, Hardy, Flaubert, or Conrad.[2] They are using their eyes without in the least impeding their pens, and they are using them as novelists have never used them before. Moors and woods, tropical seas, ships, harbours, streets, drawing-rooms, flowers, clothes, attitudes, effects of light and shade—all this they have given us with an accuracy and a subtlety that make us exclaim that now at last writers have begun to use their

† From *Nation & Athenaeum* 37.4 (April 25, 1925): 101–02. Woolf's praise for "silent painters" reflects both Roger Fry's views and her life-long admiration for her sister Vanessa Bell's art.
1. Pablo Picasso (1881–1973), Spanish painter; Marcel Proust (1871–1922), French novelist; painters Henri Matisse (1869–1954), Paul Cézanne (1839–1906), and André Derain (1880–1954).
2. Joseph Conrad (1857–1924), Thomas Hardy (1840–1928), and Gustave Flaubert (1821–1880) are Polish, British, and French writers respectively.

eyes. Not, indeed, that any of these great writers stops for a moment to describe a crystal jar as if that were an end in itself; the jars on their mantelpieces are always seen through the eyes of women in the room. The whole scene, however solidly and pictorially built up, is always dominated by an emotion which has nothing to do with the eye. But it is the eye that has fertilized their thought; it is the eye, in Proust above all, that has come to the help of the other senses, combined with them, and produced effects of extreme beauty and of a subtlety hitherto unknown. Here is a scene in a theatre, for example. We have to understand the emotions of a young man for a lady in a box below. With an abundance of images and comparisons we are made to appreciate the forms, the colours, the very fibre and texture of the plush seats and the ladies' dresses and the dullness or glow, sparkle or colour, of the light. At the same time that our senses drink in all this our minds are tunnelling, logically and intellectually, into the obscurity of the young man's emotions which, as they ramify and modulate and stretch further and further, at last penetrate so far, peter out into such a shred of meaning, that we can scarcely follow any more, were it not that suddenly, in flash after flash, metaphor after metaphor, the eye lights up that cave of darkness, and we are shown the hard, tangible, material shapes of bodiless thoughts hanging like bats in the primeval darkness where light has never visited them before.

A writer thus has need of a third eye whose function it is to help out the other senses when they flag. But it is extremely doubtful whether he learns anything directly from painting. Indeed, it would seem to be true that writers are of all critics of painting the worst— the most prejudiced, the most distorted in their judgments; if we accost them in picture galleries, disarm their suspicions, and get them to tell us honestly what it is that pleases them in pictures, they will confess that it is not the art of painting in the least. They are not there to understand the problems of the painter's art. They are after something that may be helpful to themselves. It is only thus that they can turn these long galleries from torture chambers of boredom and despair into smiling avenues, pleasant places filled with birds, sanctuaries where silence reigns supreme. Free to go their own way, to pick and choose at their will, they find modern pictures, they say, very helpful, very stimulating. Cézanne, for example—no painter is more provocative to the literary sense, because his pictures are so audaciously and provocatively content to be paint and not words that the very pigment, they say, seems to challenge us, to press on some nerve, to stimulate, to excite. That picture, for example, they explain (standing before a rocky landscape, all cleft in ridges of opal colour as if by a giant's hammer, silent, solid, serene), stirs words in us where we had not thought words to exist; suggests forms where we had never seen anything but thin air. As we gaze, words begin to raise their feeble limbs in the pale border land of no man's language, to sink down again in despair. We fling them like nets upon a rocky and inhospitable shore; they fade and disappear. It is vain, it is futile; but we can never resist the temptation. The silent painters, Cézanne and Mr. Sickert,[3] make fools of us as often as they choose.

But painters lose their power directly they attempt to speak. They must say what they have to say by shading greens into blues, posing block upon block. They must weave their spells like mackerel behind the glass at the aquarium, mutely, mysteriously. Once let them raise the glass and begin to speak and the spell is broken. * * * With half a sheet of notepaper we can tell all the stories of all the pictures in the world.

Nevertheless, they admit, moving round the gallery, even when they do not tempt us to the heroic efforts which have produced so many abortive monsters, pictures are very pleasant things. There is a great deal to be learnt from them. That picture of a wet marsh on a blowing day shows us much more clearly than we could see for ourselves the greens and silvers, the sliding streams, the gusty willows shivering in the wind, and sets us trying to find phrases for them, suggests even a figure lying there among the bulrushes, or coming out at the farmyard gate in top boots and mackintosh. That still life, they proceed, pointing to a jar of red-hot pokers, is to us what a beefsteak is to an invalid—an orgy of blood and nourishment, so starved we are on our diet of thin black print. We nestle into its colour, feed and fill ourselves with yellow and red and gold, till we drop off, nourished and content. Our sense of colour seems miraculously sharpened. We carry those roses and red-hot pokers about with us for days, working them over again in words. From a portrait, too, we get almost always something worth having—somebody's room, nose, or hands, some little effect of character or circumstance, some knick-knack to put in our pockets and take away. But again, the portrait painter must not attempt to speak; he must not say, "This is maternity: that intellect"; the utmost he must do is to tap on the wall of the room, or the glass of the aquarium; he must come very close, but something must always separate us from him.

There are artists, indeed, who are born tappers; no sooner do we see a picture of a dancer tying up her shoe by Degas than we exclaim, "How witty!" exactly as if we had read a speech by Congreve.[4] Degas detaches a scene and comments upon it exactly as a great comic writer detaches and comments, but silently, without for a moment infringing the reticence of paint. We laugh, but not with the muscles that laugh in reading. * * * Matisse taps; Derain taps; Mr. Grant taps; Picasso, Sickert, Mrs. Bell, on the other hand, are all mute as mackerel.

---

3. Walter Sickert (1860–1942), British painter.
4. William Congreve (1670–1729), British playwright; Edgar Degas (1834–1917), French artist.

But the writers have said enough. Their consciences are uneasy. No one knows better than they do, they murmur, that this is not the way to look at pictures; that they are irresponsible dragon-flies, mere insects, children wantonly destroying works of art by pulling petal from petal. In short, they had better be off, for here, oaring his way through the waters, mooning, abstract, contemplative, comes a painter, and, stuffing their pilferings into their pockets, out they bolt, lest they should be caught at their mischief and made to suffer the most extreme of penalties, the most exquisite of tortures—to be made to look at pictures with a painter.

Impassioned Prose[†]

When he was still a boy, his own discrimination led De Quincey to doubt whether "his natural vocation lay towards poetry."[1] He wrote poetry, eloquently and profusely, and his poetry was praised; but even so he decided that he was no poet, and the sixteen volumes of his collected works are written entirely in prose. After the fashion of his time, he wrote on many subjects—on political economy, on philosophy, on history; he wrote essays and biographies and confessions and memoirs. But as we stand before the long row of his books and make, as we are bound to make after all these years, our own selection, * * * we have to confess that, prose writer though he is, it is for his poetry that we read him and not for his prose.

What could be more damaging, to him as writer, to us as readers, than this confession? For if the critics agree on any point it is on this, that nothing is more reprehensible than for a prose writer to write like a poet. Poetry is poetry and prose is prose—how often have we not heard that! Poetry has one mission and prose another. Prose, Mr. Binyon wrote the other day, "is a medium primarily addressed to the intelligence, poetry to feeling and imagination."[2] * * * It is impossible not to admit, in part at least, the truth of these remarks. Memory supplies but too many instances of discomfort, of anguish, when in the midst of sober prose suddenly the temperature rises,

---

[†] From *Times Literary Supplement* 1285 (Sept. 16, 1926): 601–02. Woolf began this essay on the multivolume *The Works of Thomas De Quincey* in spring 1926 while writing "Time Passes," and she finished it during the summer before writing the novel's last section. She drafted some lines of the essay in the manuscript of the novel. While working on the essay in July, she queried Vita—who wrote both—about the "difference between prose and poetry," a question of relevance both for this essay, which advocates for a style that merges poetry and prose, and for *To the Lighthouse*. See Composition Chronology (170–71). Leslie Stephen had also written admiringly on De Quincey in *Hours in a Library* (1874) and the *Dictionary of National Biography*.

1. *The Works of Thomas De Quincey*, 15 vols. (Adam and Charles Black, 1862–63), vol. 14, p. 197.
2. Laurence Binyon, *Tradition and Reaction in Modern Poetry* (The English Association Pamphlet no. 63, April 1926), p. 12.

the rhythm changes, we go up with a lurch, come down with a bang, and wake, roused and angry. But memory supplies also a number of passages—in Browne, in Landor, in Carlyle, in Ruskin, in Emily Brontë[3]—where there is no such jerk, no such sense (for this perhaps is at the root of our discomfort) of something unfused, unwrought, incongruous and casting ridicule upon the rest. The prose writer has subdued his army of facts; he has brought them all under the same law of perspective. They work upon our minds as poetry works upon them. We are not woken; we reach the next point—and it may well be highly commonplace—without any sense of strain.

But, unfortunately for those who would wish to see a great many more things said in prose than are now thought proper, we live under the rule of the novelists. If we talk of prose we mean in fact prose fiction. And of all writers the novelist has his hands fullest of facts. Smith gets up, shaves, has his breakfast, taps his egg, reads *The Times*. How can we ask the panting, the perspiring, the industrious scribe with all this on his hands to modulate beautifully off into rhapsodies about Time and Death and what the hunters are doing at the Antipodes? It would upset the whole proportions of his day. It would cast grave doubt upon his veracity. Moreover, the greatest of his order seem deliberately to prefer a method which is the antithesis of prose poetry. A shrug of the shoulders, a turn of the head, a few words spoken in a hurry at a moment of crisis—that is all. But the train has been laid so deep beneath page after page and chapter after chapter that the single word when it is spoken is enough to start an explosion. We have so lived and thought with these men and women that they need only raise a finger and it seems to reach the skies. To elaborate that gesture would be to spoil it. The whole tendency therefore of fiction is against prose poetry. The lesser novelists are not going to take risks which the greater deliberately avoid. They trust that, if only the egg is real and the kettle boils, stars and nightingales will somehow be thrown in by the imagination of the reader. And therefore all that side of the mind which is exposed in solitude they ignore. They ignore its thoughts, its rhapsodies, its dreams, with the result that the people of fiction bursting with energy on one side are atrophied on the other; while prose itself, so long in service to this drastic master, has suffered the same deformity, and will be fit, after another hundred years of such discipline, to write nothing but the immortal works of Bradshaw and Baedeker.[4]

But happily there are in every age some writers who puzzle the critics, who refuse to go in with the herd. They stand obstinately

3. Emily Brontë (1818–1848), Sir Thomas Browne (1605–1682), Walter Savage Landor (1775–1864), Thomas Carlyle (1795–1881), and John Ruskin (1819–1900)—British writers.
4. Karl Baedeker (1801–1859) originated a famous series of travel guides; George Bradshaw (1801–1853) published *Bradshaw's Railway Guide*.

across the boundary lines, and do a greater service by enlarging and fertilizing and influencing than by their actual achievement, which, indeed, is often too eccentric to be satisfactory. * * * [O]ne of De Quincey's claims to our gratitude, one of his main holds upon our interest, is that he was an exception and a solitary. He made a class for himself. He widened the choice for others. * * *

* * *

* * * He was a born autobiographer. If the "Opium Eater" remains his masterpiece, a longer and less perfect book, the "Autobiographic Sketches," runs it very close.[5] For here it is fitting that he should stand a little apart, should look back, under cover of his raised hand, at scenes which had almost melted into the past. His enemy, the hard fact, became cloudlike and supple under his hands. * * * It was his object to record impressions, to render states of mind without particularizing the features of the precise person who had experienced them. A serene and lovely light lies over the whole of that distant prospect of his childhood. * * * [T]hese scenes have something of the soundlessness and the lustre of dreams. They swim up to the surface, they sink down again into the depths. They have, into the bargain, the strange power of growing in our minds, so that it is always a surprise to come upon them again and see what, in the interval, our minds have done to alter and expand.

Meanwhile, all these scenes compose an autobiography of a kind, but of a kind which is so unusual that one is forced to ask what one has learnt from it about De Quincey in the end. Of facts, scarcely anything. One has been told only what De Quincey wished us to know; and even that has been chosen for the sake of some adventitious quality—as that it fitted in here, or was the right colour to go there—never for its truth. * * *

Life and the Novelist[†]

The novelist—it is his distinction and his danger—is terribly exposed to life. Other artists, partially, at least, withdraw; they shut themselves up for weeks alone with a dish of apples and a paint box, or a roll of music paper and a piano. When they emerge it is to forget and distract themselves. But the novelist never forgets and is seldom distracted. He fills his glass and lights his cigarette, he enjoys presumably all the pleasures of talk and table, but always with a sense that he is

---

5. Woolf drafted this sentence in the holograph of *To the Lighthouse*.
† From *New York Herald Tribune* (Nov. 7, 1926): F1. The essay was a review of *A Deputy Was King* by G. B. Stern (1890–1973), excerpted here to focus on Woolf's general remarks on writing fiction.

being stimulated and played on by the subject matter of his art. Taste, sound, movement, a few words here, a gesture there, a man coming in, a woman going out, even the motor that passes in the street or the beggar who shuffles along the pavement, and all the reds and blues and lights and shades of the scene claim his attention and rouse his curiosity. He can no more cease to receive impressions than a fish in mid-ocean can cease to let the water rush through his gills.

But if this sensibility is one of the conditions of the novelist's life, it is obvious that all writers whose books survive have known how to master it and make it serve their purposes. They have finished the wine and paid the bill and gone off, alone, into some solitary room where, with toil and pause, in agony (like Flaubert) with struggle and rush, tumultuously (like Dostoievsky) they have mastered their perceptions, hardened them, and changed them into the fabrics of their art.[1]

So drastic is the process of selection that in its final state we can often find no trace of the actual scene upon which the chapter was based. For in that solitary room, whose door the critics are forever trying to unlock, processes of the strangest kind are gone through. Life is subjected to a thousand disciplines and exercises. It is curbed; it is killed. It is mixed with this, stiffened with that, brought into contrast with something else; so that when we get our scene at a cafe a year later the surface signs by which we remembered it have disappeared. There emerges from the mist something stark, formidable and enduring, the bone and substance upon which our rush of indiscriminating emotion was founded.

Of these two processes, the first—to receive impressions—is undoubtedly the easier, the simpler and the pleasanter. And it is quite possible, provided one is gifted with a sufficiently receptive temperament and a vocabulary rich enough to meet its demands, to make a book out of this preliminary emotion alone. Three quarters of the novels that appear to-day are concocted of experience to which no discipline, except the mild curb of grammar and the occasional rigors of chapter divisions, has been applied. * * *

* * *

* * * The writer's task is to take one thing and let it stand for twenty: a task of danger and difficulty; but only so is the reader relieved of the swarm and confusion of life and branded effectively with the particular aspect which the writer wishes him to see. * * *

* * * [The novelist] is faced by a problem which does not afflict the workers in other arts to the same extent. Stridently, clamorously,

1. Fyodor Dostoevsky (1821–1881), Russian writer.

life is forever pleading that she is the proper end of fiction and that the more he sees of her and catches of her the better his book will be. She does not add, however, that she is grossly impure; and that the side she flaunts uppermost is often, for the novelist, of no value whatever. Appearance and movement are the lures she trails to entice him after her, as if these were her essence, and by catching them he gained his goal. So believing, he rushes feverishly in her wake, ascertains what fox-trot is being played at the Embassy, what skirt is being worn in Bond Street, worms and winds his way into the last flings of topical slang, and imitates to perfection the last toss of colloquial jargon. He becomes terrified more than anything of falling behind the times: his chief concern is that the thing described shall be fresh from the shell with the down on its head.

* * *

On the other hand, to retire to one's study in fear of life is equally fatal. * * * To survive, each sentence must have, at its heart, a little spark of fire and this, whatever the risk, the novelist must pluck with his own hands from the blaze. His state then is a precarious one. He must expose himself to life; he must risk the danger of being led away and tricked by her deceitfulness: he must seize her treasure from her and let her trash run to waste. But at a certain moment he must leave the company and withdraw, alone, to that mysterious room where his booty is hardened and fashioned into permanence by processes which, if they elude the critic, hold for him so profound a fascination.

Poetry, Fiction and the Future†

Far the greater number of critics turn their backs upon the present and gaze steadily into the past. Wisely, no doubt, they make no comment upon what is being actually written at the moment; they leave that duty to the race of reviewers whose very title seems to imply transiency in themselves and in the objects they survey. But one has sometimes asked one's self, must the duty of a critic always be to the past, must his gaze always be fixed backward? Could he not sometimes turn round and, shading his eyes in the manner of Robinson Crusoe on the desert island, look into the future and trace on its mist

† First published in *New York Herald Tribune* (August 14 and 21, 1927): E1; based on a lecture Woolf gave at Oxford University, May 18, 1927. It was given the title "The Narrow Bridge of Art," by which it is better known, for reprinting in the essay collection *Granite & Rainbow* (New York: Harcourt Brace, 1958), which Leonard published after Woolf's death. Written just after she completed work on *To the Lighthouse*, this essay advances her thinking about the issues raised in "Impassioned Prose" a year earlier and anticipates her transition to writing *The Waves*, which she described as a "playpoem."

the faint lines of the land which some day perhaps we may reach? The truth of such speculations can never be proved, of course, but in an age like ours there is a great temptation to indulge in them. For it is an age clearly when we are not fast anchored where we are; things are moving round us; we are moving ourselves. Is it not the critic's duty to tell us, or to guess at least, where we are going?

Obviously the inquiry must narrow itself very strictly, but it might perhaps be possible in a short space to take one instance of dissatisfaction and difficulty, and, having examined into that, we might be the better able to guess the direction in which, when we have surmounted it, we shall go.

Nobody indeed can read much modern literature without being aware that some dissatisfaction, some difficulty, is lying in our way. On all sides writers are attempting what they cannot achieve, are forcing the form they use to contain a meaning which is strange to it. Many reasons might be given, but here let us select only one, and that is the failure of poetry to serve us as it has served so many generations of our fathers. Poetry is not lending her services to us nearly as freely as she did to them. The great channel of expression which has carried away so much energy, so much genius, seems to have narrowed itself or to have turned aside.

That is true only within certain limits of course; our age is rich in lyric poetry; no age perhaps has been richer. But for our generation and the generation that is coming the lyric cry of ecstasy or despair which is so intense, so personal and so limited, is not enough. The mind is full of monstrous, hybrid, unmanageable emotions. That the age of the earth is 3,000,000,000 years; that human life lasts but a second; that the capacity of the human mind is nevertheless boundless; that life is infinitely beautiful yet repulsive; that one's fellow creatures are adorable but disgusting; that science and religion have between them destroyed belief; that all bonds of union seem broken, yet some control must exist—it is in this atmosphere of doubt and conflict that writers have now to create, and the fine fabric of a lyric is no more fitted to contain this point of view than a rose leaf to envelop the rugged immensity of a rock.

But when we ask ourselves what has in the past served to express such an attitude as this—an attitude which is full of contrast and collision; an attitude which seems to demand the conflict of one character upon another, and at the same time to stand in need of some general shaping power, some conception which lends the whole harmony and force, we must reply that there was a form once, and it was not the form of lyrical poetry; it was the form of the drama, of the poetic drama of the Elizabethan age. And that is the one form which seems dead beyond all possibility of resurrection to-day.

For if we look at the state of the poetic play we must have grave
doubts that any force on earth can now revive it. It has been practiced and is still practiced by writers of the highest genius and ambition. Since the death of Dryden every great poet it seems has had
his fling. * * *

* * *

There is a vague, mysterious thing called an attitude to life. We all
know people—if we turn from literature to life for a moment—who
are at loggerheads with existence; unhappy people who never get
what they want; are baffled, complaining, who stand at an uncomfortable angle whence they see everything slightly askew. There are
others again who, though they appear perfectly content, seem to
have lost all touch with reality. They lavish all their affections upon
little dogs and old china. They take interest in nothing but the vicissitudes of their own health and the ups and downs of social snob-
bery. There are, however, others who strike us, why precisely it would
be difficult to say, as being by nature or by circumstances in a position where they can use their faculties to the full upon things that
are of importance. They are not necessarily happy or successful, but
there is a zest in their presence, an interest in their doings. They
seem alive all over. This may be partly the result of circumstances—
they have been born into surroundings that suit them—but much
more is the result of some happy balance of qualities in themselves
so that they see things not at an awkward angle, all askew; nor distorted through a mist; but four square, in proportion; they grasp
something hard; when they come into action they cut real ice.

A writer too has in the same way an attitude to life, though it is a
different life from the other. They, too, can stand at an uncomfortable angle; can be baffled, frustrated, unable to get at what they want
as writers. * * * Then, again, they can retire to the suburbs and lavish
their interest upon pet dogs and duchesses—prettinesses, sentimen-
talities, snobberies, and this is true of some of our most highly successful novelists. But there are others who seem by nature or
circumstances so placed that they can use their faculties freely upon
important things. It is not that they write quickly or easily, or become
at once successful or celebrated. One is rather trying to analyze a
quality which is present in most of the great ages of literature and is
most marked in the work of the Elizabethan dramatists. They seem
to have an attitude to life, a position which allows them to move their
limbs freely; a view which, though made up of all sorts of different
things, falls into the right perspective for their purposes.

In part, of course, this was the result of circumstances. The public appetite, not for books, but for the drama, the smallness of the

towns, the distance which separated people, the ignorance in which even the educated then lived, all made it natural for the Elizabethan imagination to fill itself with lions and unicorns, dukes and duchesses, violence and mystery. This was reinforced by something which we cannot explain so simply, but which we can certainly feel. They had an attitude to life which made them able to express themselves freely and fully. Shakespeare's plays are not the work of a baffled and frustrated mind; they are the perfectly elastic envelope of his thought. Without a hitch he turns from philosophy to a drunken brawl; from love songs to an argument; from simple merriment to profound speculation. And it is true of all the Elizabethan dramatists that though they may bore us—and they do—they never make us feel that they are afraid or self-conscious, or that there is anything hindering, hampering, inhibiting the full current of their minds.

Yet our first thought when we open a modern poetic play—and this applies to much modern poetry—is that the writer is not at his ease. * * * [T]hey lay their scene in the past because they are afraid of the present. They are aware that if they tried to express the thoughts, the visions, the sympathies and antipathies which are actually turning and tumbling in their brains in this year of grace 1927 the poetic decencies would be violated; they could only stammer and stumble and perhaps have to sit down or to leave the room. * * *

But can we explain ourselves a little more fully? What has changed, what has happened, what has put the writer now at such an angle that he cannot pour his mind straight into the old channels of English poetry? Some sort of answer may be suggested by a walk through the streets of any large town. The long avenue of brick is cut up into boxes, each of which is inhabited by a different human being who has put locks on his doors and bolts on his windows to insure some privacy, yet is linked to his fellows by wires which pass overhead, by waves of sound which pour through the roof and speak aloud to him of battles and murders and strikes and revolutions all over the world. And if we go in and talk to him we shall find that he is a wary, secretive, suspicious animal, extremely self-conscious, extremely careful not to give himself away. Indeed, there is nothing in modern life which forces him to do it. There is no violence in private life; we are polite, tolerant, agreeable, when we meet. War even is conducted by companies and communities rather than by individuals. Duelling is extinct. The marriage bond can stretch indefinitely without snapping. The ordinary person is calmer, smoother, more self-contained than he used to be.

But again we should find if we took a walk with our friend that he is extremely alive to everything—to ugliness, sordidity, beauty, amusement. He is immensely inquisitive. He follows every thought careless where it may lead him. He discusses openly what used never to be mentioned even privately. And this very freedom and curiosity are perhaps the cause of what appears to be his most marked characteristic—the strange way in which things that have no apparent connection are associated in his mind. Feelings which used to come simple and separate do so no longer. Beauty is part ugliness; amusement part disgust; pleasure part pain. Emotions which used to enter the mind whole are now broken up on the threshhold.

For example: It is a spring night, the moon is up, the nightingale singing, the willows bending over the river. Yes, but at the same time a diseased old woman is picking over her greasy rags on a hideous iron bench. She and the spring enter his mind together; they blend but do not mix. The two emotions, so incongruously coupled, bite and kick at each other in unison. But the emotion which Keats felt when he heard the song of a nightingale is one and entire, though it passes from joy in beauty to sorrow at the unhappiness of human fate. He makes no contrast. In his poem sorrow is the shadow which accompanies beauty. In the modern mind beauty is accompanied not by its shadow but by its opposite. The modern poet talks of the nightingale who sings "jug jug to dirty ears."[1] There trips along by the side of our modern beauty some mocking spirit which sneers at beauty for being beautiful; which turns the looking glass and shows us that the other side of her cheek is pitted and deformed. It is as if the modern mind, wishing always to verify its emotions, had lost the power of accepting anything simply for what it is. Undoubtedly this skeptical and testing spirit has led to a great freshening and quickening of soul. There is a candor, an honesty in modern writing which is salutary if not supremely delightful. * * * Naturally the poets were frightened away.

For of course poetry has always been overwhelmingly on the side of beauty. She has always insisted on certain rights, such as rhyme, meter, poetic diction. She has never been used for the common purpose of life. Prose has taken all the dirty work on to her own shoulders; has answered letters, paid bills, written articles, made speeches, served the needs of business men, shopkeepers, lawyers, soldiers, peasants.

Poetry has remained aloof in the possession of her priests. She has perhaps paid the penalty for this seclusion by becoming a little stiff. Her presence with all her apparatus—her veils, her garlands, her memories, her associations—affects us the moment she speaks. Thus when we ask poetry to express this discord, this incongruity, this sneer,

---

1. Woolf contrasts the melodious, haunting bird song in "To a Nightingale" (1819) by John Keats (1795–1821) with *The Waste Land* by T. S. Eliot (1888–1965): "the nightingale / Filled all the desert with inviolable voice / And still she cried, and still the world pursues, / 'Jug Jug' to dirty ears." *The Norton Anthology of English Literature,* 10th ed., 6 vols. (New York: Norton, 2018), vol. F, p. 663.

this contrast, this curiosity, the quick, queer emotions which are bred in small separate rooms, the wide, general ideas which civilization teaches, she cannot move quickly enough, simply enough, or broadly enough to do it. Her accent is too marked; her manner too emphatic. She gives us instead lovely lyric cries of passion; with a majestic sweep of her arm she bids us take refuge in the past; but she does not keep pace with the mind and fling herself subtly, quickly, passionately into its various sufferings and joys. * * *

Thus we are brought to reflect whether poetry is capable of the task which we are now setting her. It may be that the emotions here sketched in such rude outline and imputed to the modern mind submit more readily to prose than to poetry. It may be possible that prose is going to take over—has, indeed, already taken over—some of the duties which were once discharged by poetry.[2]

If, then, we are daring and risk ridicule and try to see in what direction we who seem to be moving so fast are going, we may guess that we are going in the direction of prose and that in ten or fifteen years' time prose will be used for purposes for which prose has never been used before. That cannibal, the novel, which has devoured so many forms of art will by then have devoured even more. We shall be forced to invent new names for the different books which masquerade under this one heading. And it is possible that there will be among the so-called novels one which we shall scarcely know how to christen. It will be written in prose, but in prose which has many of the characteristics of poetry. It will have something of the exaltation of poetry, but much of the ordinariness of prose. It will be dramatic, and yet not a play. It will be read, not acted. By what name we are to call it is not a matter of very great importance. What is important is that this book which we see on the horizon may serve to express some of those feelings which seem at the moment to be balked by poetry pure and simple and to find the drama equally inhospitable to them. Let us try, then, to come to closer terms with it and to imagine what may be its scope and its nature.

In the first place, one may guess that it will differ from the novel as we know it now chiefly in that it will stand further back from life. It will give, as poetry does, the outline rather than the detail. It will make little use of the marvelous fact-recording power, which is one of the attributes of fiction. It will tell us very little about the houses, incomes, occupations of its characters; it will have little kinship with the sociological novel or the novel of environment. With these limitations it will express the feelings and ideas of the characters closely and vividly, but from a different angle. It will resemble poetry in this

2. The first installment of the essay ended here.

that it will give not only or mainly people's relations to each other and their activities together, as the novel has hitherto done, but it will give the relation of the mind to general ideas and its soliloquy in solitude. For under the dominion of the novel we have scrutinized one part of the mind closely and left another unexplored. We have come to forget that a large and important part of life consists in our emotions toward such things as roses and nightingales, the dawn, the sunset, life, death and fate; we forget that we spend much time sleeping, dreaming, thinking, reading, alone; we are not entirely occupied in personal relations: all our energies are not absorbed in making our livings. The psychological novelist has been too prone to limit psychology to the psychology of personal intercourse; we long sometimes to escape from the incessant, the remorseless analysis of falling into love and falling out of love, of what Tom feels for Judith and Judith does or does not altogether feel for Tom. We long for some more impersonal relationship. We long for ideas, for dreams, for imaginations, for poetry.

* * *

In these respects then the novel or the variety of novel which will be written in time to come will take on some of the attributes of poetry. It will give the relations of man to nature, to fate; his imagination; his dreams. But it will also give the sneer, the contrast, the question, the closeness and complexity of life. It will take the mold of that queer conglomeration of incongruous things—the modern mind. Therefore it will clasp to its breast the precious prerogatives of the democratic art of prose; its freedom, its fearlessness, its flexibility. For prose is so humble that it can go anywhere; no place is too low, too sordid, or too mean for it to enter. It is infinitely patient, too, humbly acquisitive. It can lick up with its long glutinous tongue the most minute fragments of fact and mass them into the most subtle labyrinths, and listen silently at doors behind which only a murmur, only a whisper, is to be heard. With all the suppleness of a tool which is in constant use it can follow the windings and record the changes which are typical of the modern mind. To this, with Proust and Dostoievsky behind us, we must agree.

But can prose, we may ask, adequate though it is to deal with the common and the complex—can prose say the simple things which are so tremendous? Give the sudden emotions which are so surprising? Can it chant the elegy, or hymn the love, or shriek in terror, or praise the rose, the nightingale, or the beauty of night? Can it leap at one spring at the heart of its subject as the poet does? I think not. That is the penalty it pays for having dispensed with the incantation and the mystery, with rhyme and metre. It is true that prose writers are daring; they are constantly forcing their instrument to make the attempt. But one has always a feeling of discomfort in the presence of the purple patch or the prose poem. The objection to the purple patch, however, is not that it is purple but that it is a patch. * * * We feel the jerk and the effort; we are half woken from that trance of consent and illusion in which our submission to the power of the writer's imagination is most complete.

* * *

* * * [U]nfortunately, it seems true that some renunciation is inevitable. You cannot cross the narrow bridge of art carrying all its tools in your hands. Some you must leave behind, or you will drop them in midstream or, what is worse, over balance and be drowned yourself.

So, then, this unnamed variety of the novel will be written standing back from life, because in that way a larger view is to be obtained of some important features of it; it will be written in prose because prose, if you free it from the beast of burden work which so many novelists necessarily lay upon it of carrying loads of details, bushels of fact—prose thus treated will show itself capable of rising high from the ground, not in one dart, but in sweeps and circles, and of keeping at the same time in touch with the amusements and idiosyncrasies of human character in daily life.

There remains, however, a further question. Can prose be dramatic? It is obvious, of course, that Shaw and Ibsen[3] have used prose dramatically with the highest success, but they have been faithful to the dramatic form. This form one may prophesy is not the one which the poetic dramatist of the future will find fit for his needs. A prose play is too rigid, too limited, too emphatic for his purposes. It lets slip between its meshes half the things that he wants to say. He cannot compress into dialogue all the comment, all the analysis, all the richness that he wants to give. Yet he covets the explosive emotional effect of the drama; he wants to draw blood from his readers, and not merely to stroke and tickle their intellectual susceptibilities. * * * [I]t will be necessary for the writer of this exacting book to bring to bear upon his tumultuous and contradictory emotions the generalizing and simplifying power of a strict and logical imagination. Tumult is vile; confusion is hateful; everything in a work of art should be mastered and ordered. His effort will be to generalize rather than to split up. Instead of enumerating details he will mold blocks. His characters thus will have a dramatic power which the minutely realized characters of contemporary fiction often sacrifice in the interests of psychology. And then, though this is scarcely

---

3. Henrik Ibsen (1828–1906), Norwegian playwright; George Bernard Shaw (1856–1950), Irish playwright.

visible, so far distant it lies on the rim of the horizon—one can imagine that he will have extended the scope of his interest so as to dramatize some of those influences which play so large a part in life, yet have so far escaped the novelist—the power of music, the stimulus of sight, the effect on us of the shape of trees or the play of color, the emotions bred in us by crowds, the obscure terrors and hatreds which come so irrationally in certain places or from certain people, the delight of movement, the intoxication of wine. Every moment is the center and meeting place of an extraordinary number of perceptions which have not yet been expressed. Life is always and inevitably much richer than we who try to express it.

But it needs no great gift of prophecy to be certain that whoever attempts to do what is outlined above will have need of all his courage. Prose is not going to learn a new step at the bidding of the first comer. Yet if the signs of the times are worth anything the need of fresh developments is being felt. It is certain that there are scattered about in England, France and America writers who are trying to work themselves free from a bondage which has become irksome to them; writers who are trying to readjust their attitude so that they may once more stand easily and naturally in a position where their powers have full play upon important things. And it is when a book strikes us as the result of that attitude rather than by its beauty or its brilliancy that we know that it has in it the seeds of an enduring existence.

Literary Sources

ALFRED, LORD TENNYSON

The Charge of the Light Brigade[†]

> Half a league, half a league,
> Half a league onward,
> All in the valley of Death
> Rode the six hundred.
>
> 5 Into the valley of Death
> Rode the six hundred,
> For up came an order which
> Some one had blunder'd.
> 'Forward, the Light Brigade!
> 10 'Take the guns,' Nolan said:
> Into the valley of Death
> Rode the six hundred.
>
> 'Forward the Light Brigade!'
> No man was there dismay'd,
> 15 Not tho' the soldier knew
> Some one had blunder'd:
> Theirs not to make reply,
> Theirs not to reason why,
> Theirs but to do and die,
> 20 Into the valley of Death
> Rode the six hundred.

---

† From *The Examiner* (Dec. 9, 1854): 780. The poem is about the Crimean War battle of Balaklava on October 25, 1854. The British fought in support of the Ottoman Empire (modern-day Turkey) against Russia, which sought to expand its territory. The London newspaper *The Times* reported on the disastrous battle, in which the British cavalry ("the six hundred" of the Light Brigade) was ordered to make a suicidal attack on the cannons of the Russian artillery. Few soldiers or horses survived. Tennyson recorded that he wrote the poem immediately on reading this news report, which included the phrase, "some hideous blunder." On Woolf's use of the poem in *To the Lighthouse*, see Susan Stanford Friedman, *Mappings*, pp. 121–25.

Cannon to right of them,
Cannon to left of them,
Cannon in front of them
25   Volley'd and thunder'd;
Storm'd at with shot and shell,
Boldly they rode and well,
Into the jaws of Death,
Into the mouth of Hell
30   Rode the six hundred.

Flash'd all their sabres bare
Flash'd all at once in air
Sabring the gunners there,
Charging an army, while
35   All the world wonder'd:
Plunged in the battery smoke,
With many a desperate stroke
The Russian line they broke;
Then they rode back, but not
40   Not the six hundred.

Cannon to right of them,
Cannon to left of them,
Cannon behind them
    Volley'd and thunder'd;
45   Storm'd at with shot and shell,
While horse and hero fell,
Those that had fought so well
Came from the jaws of Death,
Back from the mouth of Hell,
50   All that was left of them,
    Left of six hundred.

When can their glory fade?
O the wild charge they made!
    All the world wonder'd.
55   Honour the charge they made!
Honour the Light Brigade,
    Noble six hundred!

THE BROTHERS GRIMM

The Fisherman and His Wife[†]

There was once on a time a Fisherman who lived with his wife in a miserable hovel close by the sea, and every day he went out fishing. And once as he was sitting with his rod, looking at the clear water, his line suddenly went down, far down below, and when he drew it up again, he brought out a large Flounder. Then the Flounder said to him, "Hark, you Fisherman, I pray you, let me live, I am no Flounder really, but an enchanted prince. What good will it do you to kill me? I should not be good to eat, put me in the water again, and let me go." "Come," said the Fisherman, "there is no need for so many words about it—a fish that can talk I should certainly let go, anyhow," with that he put him back again into the clear water, and the Flounder went to the bottom, leaving a long streak of blood behind him. Then the Fisherman got up and went home to his wife in the hovel.

"Husband," said the woman, "have you caught nothing to-day?" "No," said the man, "I did catch a Flounder, who said he was an enchanted prince, so I let him go again." "Did you not wish for anything first?" said the woman. "No," said the man; "what should I wish for?" "Ah," said the woman, "it is surely hard to have to live always in this dirty hovel; you might have wished for a small cottage for us. Go back and call him. Tell him we want to have a small cottage, he will certainly give us that." "Ah," said the man, "why should I go there again?" "Why," said the woman, "you did catch him, and you let him go again; he is sure to do it. Go at once." The man still did not quite like to go, but did not like to oppose his wife, and went to the sea.

When he got there the sea was all green and yellow, and no longer so smooth; so he stood and said,

> "Flounder, flounder in the sea,
> Come, I pray thee, here to me;
> For my wife, good Ilsabil,
> Wills not as I'd have her will."

Then the Flounder came swimming to him and said, "Well, what does she want, then?" "Ah," said the man, "I did catch you, and my wife says I really ought to have wished for something. She does not

† From *Grimm's Household Tales*, trans. Margaret Hunt, vol. 1 (London: George Bell and Sons, 1884), pp. 78–85. For readings of the novel through the lens of the fairy tale, see "Sexual Lines in *To the Lighthouse*," this edition, pp. 293–305, and David Ellison's chapter "Fishing the Waters" in his *Ethics and Aesthetics in European Modernist Literature: From the Sublime to the Uncanny* (Cambridge: Cambridge University Press, 2001).

like to live in a wretched hovel any longer; she would like to have a cottage." "Go, then," said the Flounder, "she has it already."

When the man went home, his wife was no longer in the hovel, but instead of it there stood a small cottage, and she was sitting on a bench before the door. Then she took him by the hand and said to him, "Just come inside, look, now isn't this a great deal better?" So they went in, and there was a small porch, and a pretty little parlour and bedroom, and a kitchen and pantry, with the best of furniture, and fitted up with the most beautiful things made of tin and brass, whatsoever was wanted. And behind the cottage there was a small yard, with hens and ducks, and a little garden with flowers and fruit. "Look," said the wife, "is not that nice!" "Yes," said the husband, "and so we must always think it,—now we will live quite contented." "We will think about that," said the wife. With that they ate something and went to bed.

Everything went well for a week or a fortnight, and then the woman said, "Hark you, husband, this cottage is far too small for us, and the garden and yard are little; the Flounder might just as well have given us a larger house. I should like to live in a great stone castle; go to the Flounder, and tell him to give us a castle." "Ah, wife," said the man, "the cottage is quite good enough; why should we live in a castle?" "What!" said the woman; "just go there, the Flounder can always do that." "No, wife," said the man, "the Flounder has just given us the cottage, I do not like to go back so soon, it might make him angry." "Go," said the woman, "he can do it quite easily, and will be glad to do it; just you go to him."

The man's heart grew heavy, and he would not go. He said to himself, "It is not right," and yet he went. And when he came to the sea the water was quite purple and dark-blue, and grey and thick, and no longer so green and yellow, but it was still quiet. And he stood there and said—

> "Flounder, flounder in the sea,
> Come, I pray thee, here to me;
> For my wife, good Ilsabil,
> Wills not as I'd have her will."

"Well, what does she want, then?" said the Flounder. "Alas," said the man, half scared, "she wants to live in a great stone castle." "Go to it, then, she is standing before the door," said the Flounder.

Then the man went away, intending to go home, but when he got there, he found a great stone palace, and his wife was just standing on the steps going in, and she took him by the hand and said, "Come in." So he went in with her, and in the castle was a great hall paved with marble, and many servants, who flung wide the doors; and the walls were all bright with beautiful hangings. * * * [S]aid the woman, "isn't that beautiful?" "Yes, indeed," said the man, "now let it be; and we will live in this beautiful castle and be content." "We will consider about that," said the woman, "and sleep upon it;" thereupon they went to bed.

Next morning the wife awoke first, and it was just daybreak, and from her bed she saw the beautiful country lying before her. Her husband was still stretching himself, so she poked him in the side with her elbow, and said, "Get up, husband, and just peep out of the window. Look you, couldn't we be the King over all that land? Go to the Flounder, we will be the King."

[The wife's desires increase from King to Emperor to Pope, each time the husband reluctantly summoning the Flounder with the same verse, each time the sea growing more stormy, each time her wish being instantly granted. At last the husband returns home to find his wife is the Pope.]

* * *

* * * [H]is wife was clad in gold, and she was sitting on a much higher throne, and had three great golden crowns on, and round about her there was much ecclesiastical splendour; and on both sides of her was a row of candles the largest of which was as tall as the very tallest tower, down to the very smallest kitchen candle, and all the emperors and kings were on their knees before her, kissing her shoe. "Wife," said the man, and looked attentively at her, "are you now Pope?" "Yes," said she, "I am Pope." So he stood and looked at her, and it was just as if he was looking at the bright sun. When he had stood looking at her thus for a short time, he said, "Ah, wife, if you are Pope, do let well alone!" But she looked as stiff as a post, and did not move or show any signs of life. Then said he, "Wife, now that you are Pope, be satisfied, you cannot become anything greater now." "I will consider about that," said the woman. Thereupon they both went to bed, but she was not satisfied, and greediness let her have no sleep, for she was continually thinking what there was left for her to be.

The man slept well and soundly, for he had run about a great deal during the day; but the woman could not fall asleep at all, and flung herself from one side to the other the whole night through, thinking always what more was left for her to be, but unable to call to mind anything else. At length the sun began to rise, and when the woman saw the red of dawn, she sat up in bed and looked at it. And when, through the window, she saw the sun thus rising, she said, "Cannot I, too, order the sun and moon to rise?" "Husband," said she, poking him in the ribs with her elbows, "wake up! go to the Flounder, for I wish to be even as God is." The man was still half asleep, but he was so horrified that he fell out of bed. He thought he must have heard amiss, and rubbed his eyes, and said, "Alas, wife, what are you saying?" "Husband," said she, "if I can't order the sun and moon to rise, and have to look on and see the sun and moon rising, I can't bear it. I shall not know what it is to have another happy hour, unless I can make them rise myself." Then she looked at him so terribly that a shudder ran over him, and said, "Go at once; I wish to be like unto God." "Alas, wife," said the man, falling on his knees before her, "the Flounder cannot do that; he can make an emperor and a pope; I beseech you, go on as you are, and be Pope." Then she fell into a rage, and her hair flew wildly about her head, and she cried, "I will not endure this, I'll not bear it any longer; wilt thou go?" Then he put on his trousers and ran away like a madman. But outside a great storm was raging, and blowing so hard that he could scarcely keep his feet; houses and trees toppled over, the mountains trembled, rocks rolled into the sea, the sky was pitch black, and it thundered and lightened, and the sea came in with black waves as high as church-towers and mountains, and all with crests of white foam at the top. Then he cried, but could not hear his own words,

> "Flounder, flounder in the sea,
> Come, I pray thee, here to me;
> For my wife, good Ilsabil,
> Wills not as I'd have her will."

"Well, what does she want, then?" said the Flounder. "Alas," said he, "she wants to be like unto God." "Go to her, and you will find her back again in the dirty hovel." And there they are living still at this very time.

ANONYMOUS

Sam Hall[†]

Oh, me name it is Sam Hall, chimney sweep, chimney sweep
Oh, me name it is Sam Hall, chimney sweep
Oh, me name it is Sam Hall, and I've robbed both great and small
And me neck will pay for all, when I die, when I die
5 And me neck will pay for all, when I die

I have 20 pounds in store, that's not all, that's not all . . .
I have 20 pounds in store, and I'll rob for twenty more
For the rich must help the poor, so must I, so must I . . .

---

† A popular traditional ballad about an unrepentant Robin Hood–like criminal who has been condemned to death, "Sam Hall" is still sung with regional variations in the UK, Ireland, and the United States. You can access a version of the ballad at Roud Folk Music Index #369.

Oh, they brought me to Coote Hill in a cart, in a cart . . .
10 Oh, they brought me to Coote Hill, there I stopped to make my will
For the best of friends must part, so must I, so must I . . .

Up the ladder I did grope, that's no joke, that's no joke . . .
Up the ladder I did grope, and the hangman pulled the rope
Oh, and ne'er a word I spoke, tumblin' down, tumblin' down . . .

15 Oh, me name it is Sam Hall, chimney sweep, chimney sweep . . .
Oh, me name it is Sam Hall, and I hate yas one and all
You're a bunch of muggers all, damn your eyes, damn your eyes . . .

CHARLES ELTON

Luriana, Lurilee†

Come out and climb the garden path
    Luriana, Lurilee.
The China rose is all abloom
And buzzing with the yellow bee.
5 We'll swing you on the cedar bough,
    Luriana, Lurilee.

I wonder if it seems to you,
    Luriana, Lurilee,
That all the lives we ever lived
10 And all the lives to be,
Are full of trees and changing leaves,
    Luriana, Lurilee.

How long it seems since you and I,
    Luriana, Lurilee,
15 Roamed in the forest where our kind
Had just begun to be,
And laughed and chattered in the flowers,
    Luriana, Lurilee.

How long since you and I went out,
20   Luriana, Lurilee,
To see the Kings go riding by
Over lawn and daisy lea,

† From *Another World Than This: An Anthology,* ed. Vita Sackville-West and Harold
Nicolson (London: Michael Joseph, 1945), p. 108. Although this poem wasn't published
until 1945, Charles Elton (1839–1900) was related by marriage to Lytton Strachey,
who recited it in Woolf's hearing and who had given a copy of it to Leonard when they
were students at Cambridge in the early 1900s.

With their palm leaves and cedar sheaves,
    Luriana, Lurilee.

25 Swing, swing, swing on a bough,
        Luriana, Lurilee,
    Till you sleep in a humble heap
    Or under a gloomy churchyard tree,
    And then fly back to swing on a bough,
30   Luriana, Lurilee.

SIR WALTER SCOTT

From The Antiquary[†]

Chapter XXXI

* * *

The body was laid in its coffin within the wooden bedstead which the young fisher had occupied while alive. At a little distance stood the father, whose rugged weather-beaten countenance, shaded by his grizzled hair, had faced many a stormy night and night-like day. He was apparently revolving his loss in his mind, with that strong feeling of painful grief peculiar to harsh and rough characters, which almost breaks forth into hatred against the world, and all that remain in it, after the beloved object is withdrawn. The old man had made the most desperate efforts to save his son, and had only been withheld by main force from renewing them at a moment when, without the possibility of assisting the sufferer, he must himself have perished. All this apparently was boiling in his recollection. His glance was directed sidelong towards the coffin, as to an object on which he could not steadfastly look, and yet from which he could not withdraw his eyes. His answers to the necessary questions which were occasionally put to him, were brief, harsh, and almost fierce. His family had not yet

---

† From *The Antiquary* (New York: Hurst, 1816), pp. 182–84. One of the Waverley novels and a best-seller when published in 1816, *The Antiquary* is set in 1794, in Scotland's Border country. Jonathan Oldbuck is "the Antiquary" of the title, the Laird of Monkbarns and the landlord of the family he visits here. When Mr. Ramsay reads this scene after dinner in "The Window," the deep pleasure Scott still provides reassures him about his own posterity. Leslie Stephen included an admiring essay on Scott in his *Hours in a Library* (1874), and his daughter had noted his love of Scott in her "Impressions of Sir Leslie Stephen," this edition, pp. 188–90. In Woolf's 1924 essay on *The Antiquary* she laughs at the stilted language of Scott's young lovers, yet she singles out Steenie's funeral for its vividness, its "complete presentation of life" (*The Essays of Virginia Woolf*, vol. 3: *1919–1924*, ed. Andrew McNeillie [Orlando: Harcourt Brace Jovanovich, 1988], p. 457). This scene is one of many about shipwrecks alluded to in *To the Lighthouse*.

dared to address to him a word, either of sympathy or consolation. His masculine wife, virago as she was, and absolute mistress of the family, as she justly boasted herself, on all ordinary occasions, was, by this great loss terrified into silence and submission, and compelled to hide from her husband's observation the bursts of her female sorrow. As he had rejected food ever since the disaster had happened, not daring herself to approach him, she had that morning, with affectionate artifice, employed the youngest and favourite child to present her husband with some nourishment. His first action was to put it from him with an angry violence that frightened the child; his next, to snatch up the boy and devour him with kisses. "Ye'll be a bra' fallow, an ye be spared, Patie,—but ye'll never—never can be—what he was to me!—He has sailed the coble wi' me since he was ten years auld, and there wasna the like o' him drew a net betwixt this and Buchan-ness.— They say folks maun submit—I will try."

And he had been silent from that moment until compelled to answer the necessary questions we have already noticed. Such was the disconsolate state of the father.

In another corner of the cottage, her face covered by her apron, which was flung over it, sat the mother—the nature of her grief sufficiently indicated by the wringing of her hands, and the convulsive agitation of the bosom, which the covering could not conceal. Two of her gossips, officiously whispering into her ear the common-place topic of resignation under irremediable misfortune, seemed as if they were endeavouring to stun the grief which they could not console.

The sorrow of the children was mingled with wonder at the preparations they beheld around them, and at the unusual display of wheaten bread and wine, which the poorest peasant, or fisher, offers to the guests on these mournful occasions; and thus their grief for their brother's death was almost already lost in admiration of the splendour of his funeral.

* * *

When Oldbuck entered this house of mourning, he was received by a general and silent inclination of the head, and, according to the fashion of Scotland on such occasions, wine and spirits and bread were offered round to the guests. * * *

At this moment the clergyman, entered the cottage. * * *

* * * [H]e edged himself towards the unfortunate father, and seemed to endeavour to slide in a few words of condolence or of consolation. But the old man was incapable as yet of receiving either; he nodded, however, gruffly, and shook the clergyman's hand in acknowledgment of his good intentions, but was either unable or unwilling to make any verbal reply.

The minister next passed to the mother, moving along the floor as slowly, silently, and gradually, as if he had been afraid that the ground would, like unsafe ice, break beneath his feet, or that the first echo of a footstep, was to dissolve some magic spell, and plunge the hut, with all its inmates, into a subterranean abyss. The tenor of what he had said to the poor woman could only be judged by her answers, as, half-stifled by sobs ill-repressed, and by the covering which she still kept over her countenance, she faintly answered at each pause in his speech—"Yes, sir, yes!—Ye're very gude—ye're very gude!—Nae doubt, nae doubt!—It's our duty to submit!—But, O dear, my poor Steenie! the pride o' my very heart, that was sae hand-some and comely, and a help to his family, and a comfort to us a', and a pleasure to a' that lookit on him!—O my bairn! my bairn! my bairn! what for is thou lying there!—and eh! what for am I left to greet for ye!"

There was no contending with this burst of sorrow and natural affection. Oldbuck had repeated recourse to his snuff-box to con-ceal the tears which, despite his shrewd and caustic temper, were apt to start on such occasions. * * *

WILLIAM SHAKESPEARE

Sonnet XCVIII[†]

> From you have I been absent in the spring,
> When proud-pied April dress'd in all his trim
> Hath put a spirit of youth in every thing,
> That heavy Saturn laugh'd and leap'd with him.
> 5 Yet nor the lays of birds nor the sweet smell
> Of different flowers in odour and in hue
> Could make me any summer's story tell,
> Or from their proud lap pluck them where they grew;
> Nor did I wonder at the lily's white,
> 10 Nor praise the deep vermilion in the rose:
> They were but sweet, but figures of delight,
> Drawn after you, you pattern of all those.
>   Yet seem'd it winter still, and, you away,
>   As with your shadow I with these did play.

---

† From *Shakespeare's Sonnets*, ed. William J. Rolfe (New York: Harper & Brothers, 1891), p. 96.

WILLIAM COWPER

The Castaway†

Obscurest night involved the sky;
  Th' Atlantic billows roared,
When such a destined wretch as I,
  Washed headlong from on board,
5 Of friends, of hopes, of all bereft,
His floating home for ever left.

No braver chief could Albion boast,
  Than he, with whom we went,
Nor ever ship left Albion's coast,
10 With warmer wishes sent.
He loved them both, but both in vain,
Nor him beheld, nor her again.

Not long beneath the whelming brine,
  Expert to swim he lay;
15 Nor soon he felt his strength decline,
  Or courage die away;
But waged with death a lasting strife,
Supported by despair of life.

He shouted; nor his friends had failed
20 To check the vessel's course,
But so the furious blast prevailed,
  That, pitiless, perforce,
They left their outcast mate behind,
And scudded still before the wind.

25 Some succour yet they could afford;
  And, such as storms allow,
The cask, the coop, the floated-cord,
  Delayed not to bestow;
But he (they knew) nor ship nor shore,
30 Whate'er they gave should visit more.

Nor, cruel as it seemed, could he,
  Their haste himself condemn,

---

† From *The Poems of William Cowper* (Boston: Crosby, Nichols, Lee, & Company, 1860), pp. 459–61. Written in 1799, this was the last poem Cowper (1731–1800) published before he died.

Aware that flight, in such a sea,
   Alone could rescue them;
35 Yet bitter felt it still to die
   Deserted, and his friends so nigh.

He long survives, who lives an hour
   In ocean self-upheld:
And so long he, with unspent power
40   His destiny repelled:
And ever as the minutes flew,
   Entreated help, or cried—"Adieu!"

At length, his transient respite past,
   His comrades, who before
45 Had heard his voice in every blast,
   Could catch the sound no more.
For then, by toil subdued, he drank
The stifling wave, and then he sank.

No poet wept him: but the page
50   Of narrative sincere,
That tells his name, his worth, his age,
   Is wet with Anson's[1] tear.
And tears by bards or heroes shed
Alike immortalize the dead.

55 I therefore purpose not, or dream,
   Descanting on his fate,
To give the melancholy theme
   A more enduring date.
But misery still delights to trace
60 It's semblance in another's case.

No voice divine the storm allayed
   No light propitious shone;
When, snatched from all effectual aid,
   We perished each alone:
65 But I beneath a rougher sea,
And whelmed in deeper gulfs than he.

---

1. George Anson (1697–1762), whose story of a sailor swept overboard in his *Voyage around the World* (1748) Cowper had read.

CRITICISM

Early Reviews

[ARTHUR SYDNEY McDOWELL]
Mrs. Woolf's New Novel†

* * *

In form "To the Lighthouse" is as elastic as a novel can be. It has no plot, though it has a scheme and a motive; it shows characters in outline rather than in the round; and while it depends almost entirely on the passing of time, it expands or contracts the time-sense very freely. The first and longest part of the book is almost stationary. * * *

* * * The book has its own motion: a soft stir and light of perceptions, meeting or crossing, of the gestures and attitudes, the feelings and thoughts of people: of instants in which these are radiant or absurd, have the burden of sadness or of the inexplicable. It is a reflective book, with an ironical or wistful questioning of life and reality. Somehow this steals into the pages, whether there is a sunny peace in the garden, or Mrs. Ramsay is interrupted in a fairy-tale, or a couple is late for dinner, so that one is inclined to say that this question of the meaning of things, however masked, is not only the essence but the real protagonist in the story. * * *

* * *

* * * The people in Mrs. Woolf's book seem to be looking through each other at some farther question; and, although they interact vividly, they are not completely real. * * * While you know quite well the kind of people represented in the story, they lack something as individuals. Mr. Ramsay, certainly—masterful and helpless, egotist and hero—does leave a deep mark by the end. His wife, with her calm beauty, her sympathy and swift decided actions, is more of a type, though her personality is subtly pervasive even when she has ceased to live. But there is a significant curtness in the parenthesis which (surely with a slip in punctuation) announces her death:—

† From an unsigned review, *Times Literary Supplement* 1318 (May 5, 1927): 315. More early reviews of *To the Lighthouse* can be found in Woolf Online and in Robin Majumdar and Allen McLaurin, eds., *Virginia Woolf: The Critical Heritage* (London and Boston: Routledge and Kegan Paul, 1975).

Mr. Ramsay stumbling along a passage stretched his arms out
one dark morning, but Mrs. Ramsay having died rather suddenly the night before he stretched his arms out. They remained
empty.

Here Mrs. Woolf's detachment seems a little strained, and, in fact,
this transitional part of the book is not its strongest part.

One comes back, however, to the charm and pleasure of her
design. It is carried through with a rare subtlety. Every little thread
in it—Mr. Ramsay writing a book, Lily Brisooe struggling with her
picture, the lights in the bay, the pathos and the absurdity—is
woven in one texture, which has piquancy and poetry by turns. * * *

LOUIS KRONENBERGER

Virginia Woolf Explores an English Country Home[†]

It was with "Mrs. Dalloway" that Virginia Woolf achieved a novel of
first-rate importance rather than of great promise and talent. * * *
The method of "Mrs. Dalloway" is substantially retained by Mrs. Woolf
in this new novel, "To the Lighthouse," but though one encounters
again her strikingly individual mingling of inward thought with outward action in which the "stream of consciousness" style is liberated
from its usual chaos and by means of selection and a sense of order,
made formally compact—one finds the method applied to somewhat
different aims.

"Mrs. Dalloway," of course, is Clarissa Dalloway from cover to
cover, and for that reason it has a magnificently concentrated clar-
ity. It is Clarissa in relation to herself, her family, her friends, her
servants, her milieu; it is her servants, her family, her friends, in
relation to her. "To the Lighthouse," on the other hand, is a book of
interrelationships among people, and though there are major and
minor characters, the major ones are not, as Clarissa Dalloway was,
the alpha and omega of the story, but more truly the means for giving to the story its harmony and unity, its focal points. Those who
reject "To the Lighthouse" as inferior to "Mrs. Dalloway" because it
offers no one with half the memorable lucidity of Clarissa Dalloway
must fail to perceive its larger and, artistically, more difficult aims.
They must fail to notice the richer qualities of mind and imagination and emotion which Mrs. Woolf, perhaps not wanting them,
omitted from "Mrs. Dalloway." They must fail to appreciate that as
an author develops he will always break down the perfection he has

† From *New York Times* (May 8, 1927): BR, p. 2.

achieved in an earlier stage of his writing in order to reach new objectives.

*   *   *

It is the final portion of the book which is most perplexing. It seems to sound in the minor what the long first portion sounded in the major, to persist as an ironical mood, to re-establish a scene with the sorry changes time has wrought, to reduce a symbolical achievement when it is finally made to the level of negation. The long opening portion seems to be carrying you ahead toward something which will be magnificently expressive, and then this final portion becomes obscure, a matter of arcs, of fractions, of uncoordinated notes. By comparison with the rest this final portion seems pale and weak. Perhaps there is a reason for this, perhaps Mrs. Woolf meant to show that with Mrs. Ramsay's death things fall apart, get beyond correlation. Mr. Ramsay is no longer interesting—can it be because he is no longer counterpoised against his wife? Life seems drifting, as the Ramsays drift over the bay in their boat, and all their physical vigor and all their reaching of the lighthouse at last conveys no significance.

*   *   *

It is, I think, in the superb interlude called "Time Passes" that Mrs. Woolf reaches the most impressive height of the book, and there one can find a new note in her work, something beyond the ironic sophistication and civilized human values of "Mrs. Dalloway." In this description of the unused house in the Hebrides, entered for ten years only by old and forlorn women caretakers and the wind and the sea air and the light of the lighthouse lamp, she has told the story of all life passing on, of change and destruction and solitude and waste—the story which more than a little embodies the plot action of the rest of the book, but above all the story which has for man the profoundest human values of all, though for ten years the house itself never received a human guest. The great beauty of these eighteen pages of prose carries in it an emotional and ironical undertone that is superior to anything else that the first-class technician, the expert stylist, the deft student of human life in Mrs. Woolf ever has done. Here is prose of extraordinary distinction in our time: here is poetry.

*   *   *

MARY M. COLUM

Woman as Artist[†]

Despite her modernity, Virginia Woolf is the best living example of that sort of mind which had its innings in letters in the eighteenth century—a mind partly critical, partly philosophical, highly imaginative, incapable of the vaster emotions but so subtle in its emotionalized intellectuality, so polished, that it makes most other contemporary writers appear to be parvenus of the intellect, stumbling self-consciously under their knowledge and their clevernesses. "Women can't write, women can't paint," says a character in her newest book, and the crabbed and cranky expression arrests one as one proceeds slowly through this leisurely, melancholy, whimsical book—this book by a woman who in a few years has become one of the foremost living English novelists—who, indeed, of all contemporary English novelists, has the most high-bred, the most accomplished mind. Her intellect is as natural to her as the color of her hair or the shape of her hands—it gives a sinewy nervousness to her style, a glamour to her learning, and a queer reality to her ideas. We feel that, although her heart may be deceived sometimes, her intellect never is. * * *

She has written half a dozen novels and a couple of books of criticism, all of unique distinction. * * * [W]ho in our time * * * has stood out more broad-mindedly, more proudly for the civilization that has been handed down to us as against the shocking crudenesses and the more shocking genteelnesses that are invading us, and invading us particularly in America? As she herself says of Addison—she is on "the side of sense, taste and civilization." No book of contemporary critical essays really surpasses her "Common Reader" in just these qualities—sense, taste and civilization. * * *

To write of any novel of hers without taking her critical powers into account is impossible. For hers is the critical mind turned on to fiction. * * * So frequently are the characters of her books intellectuals, or people whose main interests are intellectual, that we get the same impression as we get when we read her criticism, of the flashlight of the intellect being turned on life and on a few human beings, which are then revealed to us with a bright reality. Her people, in spite of their domesticity and their large families, seem hardly at all concerned in that major occupation of humanity, passing on life to other people, or even with the minor occupations that are incident to this. They seem to be concerned chiefly with

† From *New York Herald Tribune* (May 8, 1927): Section 7, pp. 1, 6.

something that is happening in their minds. Her women characters are all intellectuals, even when they aren't in the least erudite, passing their lives in reverie, as intellectual women so frequently do in old countries, dreaming their lives away, not bustling on to some sort of achievement as they do in America. For this reason her women are all fascinating, with a fascination that the intellectual woman has always had in real life when her intellect and her learning are an integral, unassumed part of her and do not stand out with the obviousness and the prickliness of quills on a porcupine. She can portray as no other living writer can these charming modern intellectual women, mysteriously sunk into themselves, revolving within their minds the mysteriousness of life, like Mrs. Ramsay in "To the Lighthouse," feeling "alone with her old protagonist—life." All of them are disappointed in some way, all unhappy in some way, as perhaps everybody is in this world who is not a clod of earth. They can be affectionate mothers, absorbed mothers, but they seem to be mothers, incidentally, in spite of the children who are forever hanging to their skirts, being read to, being soothed, being petted. Virginia Woolf can create like no other writer an atmosphere of cultivated English domesticity, that family life which is so different from American family life and which is in so many respects common to all old countries—that English family life where everybody is a distinct and separate individuality, with his own reserves, his own private happinesses and unhappinesses, his own interior life, his own loneliness—a household where there are doors to every room that close tightly and where people do not casually call each other by their Christian names. * * *

FRANCIS BROWN

An Allegorical Novel[†]

    The Editor sat in his chair
    With his usual cheerful smile.
    His voice was low, but his speech was fair
    And apparently void of guile.
5   "Write—write—write
    A review of this book!" said he;
    And plunged me deep in a woeful plight
    With my limited brain—ah, me!

---

† From *Daily Herald*, London (May 23, 1927): Among the Books, p. 7.

Words! words! words!
10 That jostle, and gallop, and rush!
Words—words—words—
An intangible, mystical mush!
Words—till I sit and stare
Like one in a darksome dream,
15 Groping about in a region where
Verbosity reigns supreme!

A tale of an egotist;
Of his wife, with a mind to give;
Of their children, eight; and of guests, a list;
20 But none of them seemed to live.
For nothing they seemed to yearn
(Save the husband, and praise he sought),
And little they did, but we read and learn
The myriad things they thought.

25 Thoughts—thoughts—thoughts—
That off at a tangent fly,
With Life dragged in by the scruff of its neck
With its how? and what? and why?
Thoughts that wander about
30 In a weird parenthetical style,
With meanings enmeshed in a web of doubt
Till their finding is scarce worthwhile.

The story is told with vim—
With a fevered, violent stress;
35 Its moral, however, is more than dim
To me, as I must confess.
But if I, with a mild amaze,
Found the task of reading it hard,
Mrs. Woolf, no doubt, will account it praise,
40 For I'm but a doggerel bard.

Foundational Critical Views

ERICH AUERBACH

From The Brown Stocking[†]

* * *

Our analysis of the passage[1] yields a number of distinguishing stylistic characteristics, which we shall now attempt to formulate.

The writer as narrator of objective facts has almost completely vanished; almost everything stated appears by way of reflection in the consciousness of the dramatis personae. When it is a question of the house, for example, or of the Swiss maid, we are not given the objective information which Virginia Woolf possesses regarding these objects of her creative imagination but what Mrs. Ramsay thinks or feels about them at a particular moment. Similarly we are not taken into Virginia Woolf's confidence and allowed to share her knowledge of Mrs. Ramsay's character; we are given her character as it is reflected in and as it affects various figures in the novel: the nameless spirits which assume certain things about a tear, the people who wonder about her, and Mr. Bankes. In our passage this goes so far that there actually seems to be no viewpoint at all outside the novel from which the people and events within it are observed, any more than there seems to be an objective reality apart from what is in the consciousness of the characters. Remnants of such a reality survive at best in brief references to the exterior frame of the action, such as "said Mrs. Ramsay, raising her eyes . . ." or "said Mr. Bankes once, hearing her voice." The last paragraph ("Knitting her reddish-brown hairy stocking . . .") might perhaps also be mentioned in this

† From *Mimesis: The Representation of Reality in Western Literature,* trans. Willard R. Trask (Princeton: Princeton University Press, 1953), pp. 534–36, 538, 540–41, 549–52. Reprinted by permission of Princeton University Press. This excerpt is from the last chapter, which pairs Woolf with Proust and compares *To the Lighthouse* with Homer's *Odyssey* (both comparisons are omitted here). The prominent placement of *To the Lighthouse* as the culmination of Auerbach's study helped to establish Woolf's centrality not only to modernist literature but to a distinguished, millennia-long lineage of European literature.
1. The chapter begins by quoting and analyzing section 5 of "The Window," from "'And even if it isn't fine tomorrow,' said Mrs. Ramsay" to "'Let us find another picture to cut out,' she said," pp. 22–25.

connection. But this is already somewhat doubtful. The occurrence is described objectively, but as for its interpretation, the tone indicates that the author looks at Mrs. Ramsay not with knowing but with doubting and questioning eyes—even as some character in the novel would see her in the situation in which she is described, would hear her speak the words given.

* * * [T]his attitude differs entirely from that of authors who interpret the actions, situations, and characters of their personages with objective assurance, as was the general practice in earlier times. Goethe or Keller, Dickens or Meredith, Balzac or Zola told us out of their certain knowledge what their characters did, what they felt and thought while doing it, and how their actions and thoughts were to be interpreted. They knew everything about their characters. * * * [T]he author, with his knowledge of an objective truth, never abdicated his position as the final and governing authority. * * *

* * *

Another stylistic peculiarity to be observed in our text—though one that is closely and necessarily connected with the "multipersonal representation of consciousness" just discussed—has to do with the treatment of time. * * * [A] sharp contrast results between the brief span of time occupied by the exterior event and the dreamlike wealth of a process of consciousness which traverses a whole subjective universe. These are the characteristic and distinctively new features of the technique: a chance occasion releasing processes of consciousness; a natural and even, if you will, a naturalistic rendering of those processes in their peculiar freedom, which is neither restrained by a purpose nor directed by a specific subject of thought; elaboration of the contrast between "exterior" and "interior" time. The three have in common what they reveal of the author's attitude: he submits, much more than was done in earlier realistic works, to the random contingency of real phenomena; and even though he winnows and stylizes the material of the real world—as of course he cannot help doing—he does not proceed rationalistically, nor with a view to bringing a continuity of exterior events to a planned conclusion. In Virginia Woolf's case the exterior events have actually lost their hegemony, they serve to release and interpret inner events, whereas before her time (and still today in many instances) inner movements preponderantly function to prepare and motivate significant exterior happenings. This too is apparent in the randomness and contingency of the exterior occasion (looking up because James does not keep his foot still), which releases the much more significant inner process.

* * *

*** The important point is that an insignificant exterior occurrence releases ideas and chains of ideas which cut loose from the present of the exterior occurrence and range freely through the depths of time. *** This enables us also to understand the close relation between the treatment of time and the "multipersonal representation of consciousness" discussed earlier. The ideas arising in consciousness are not tied to the present of the exterior occurrence which releases them. ***

*　*　*

Here we have returned once again to the reflection of multiple consciousnesses. It is easy to understand that such a technique had to develop gradually and that it did so precisely during the decades of the first World War period and after. The widening of man's horizon, and the increase of his experiences, knowledge, ideas, and possible forms of existence, which began in the sixteenth century, continued through the nineteenth at an ever faster tempo—with such a tremendous acceleration since the beginning of the twentieth that synthetic and objective attempts at interpretation are produced and demolished every instant. The tremendous tempo of the changes proved the more confusing because they could not be surveyed as a whole. *** In all parts of the world crises of adjustment arose; they increased in number and coalesced. They led to the upheavals which we have not weathered yet. In Europe this violent clash of the most heterogeneous ways of life and kinds of endeavor undermined not only those religious, philosophical, ethical, and economic principles which were part of the traditional heritage and which, despite many earlier shocks, had maintained their position of authority through slow adaptation and transformation; nor yet only the ideas of the Enlightenment, the ideas of democracy and liberalism which had been revolutionary in the eighteenth century and were still so during the first half of the nineteenth; it undermined even the new revolutionary forces of socialism, whose origins did not go back beyond the heyday of the capitalist system. These forces threatened to split up and disintegrate. ***

*** At the time of the first World War and after—in a Europe unsure of itself, overflowing with unsettled ideologies and ways of life, and pregnant with disaster—certain writers distinguished by instinct and insight find a method which dissolves reality into multiple and multivalent reflections of consciousness. That this method should have been developed at this time is not hard to understand.

But the method is not only a symptom of the confusion and helplessness, not only a mirror of the decline of our world. ***

*** [S]omething entirely different takes place here too. Let us turn again to the text which was our starting-point. It breathes an

air of vague and hopeless sadness. We never come to learn what
Mrs. Ramsay's situation really is. Only the sadness, the vanity of her
beauty and vital force emerge from the depths of secrecy. Even when
we have read the whole novel, the meaning of the relationship
between the planned trip to the lighthouse and the actual trip many
years later remains unexpressed, enigmatic, only dimly to be con-
jectured, as does the content of Lily Briscoe's concluding vision
which enables her to finish her painting with one stroke of the brush.
It is one of the few books of this type which are filled with good and
genuine love but also, in its feminine way, with irony, amorphous
sadness, and doubt of life. Yet what realistic depth is achieved in
every individual occurrence, for example the measuring of the stocking! Aspects of the occurrence come to the fore, and links to other
occurrences, which, before this time, had hardly been sensed, which
had never been clearly seen and attended to, and yet they are deter-
mining factors in our real lives. What takes place here in Virginia
Woolf's novel is precisely what was attempted everywhere in works
of this kind (although not everywhere with the same insight and
mastery)—that is, to put the emphasis on the random occurrence,
to exploit it not in the service of a planned continuity of action but
in itself. And in the process something new and elemental appeared:
nothing less than the wealth of reality and depth of life in every
moment to which we surrender ourselves without prejudice. * * *

ADRIENNE RICH

[Mother–Daughter Loss in *To the Lighthouse*]†

* * *

In *To the Lighthouse* Virginia Woolf created what is still the most
complex and passionate vision of mother–daughter schism in modern
literature. It is significantly, one of the very few literary documents
in which a woman has portrayed her mother as a central figure.
Mrs. Ramsay is a kaleidoscopic character, and in successive readings of the novel, she changes, almost as our own mothers alter in

† From *Of Woman Born: Motherhood as Experience and Institution* (New York: Norton,
1976), pp. 228–30, 240. Copyright © 1986, 1976 by W. W. Norton & Company, Inc.
Used by permission of W. W. Norton & Company, Inc. Adrienne Rich (1929–2012) was
a widely read American poet and essayist and a powerful force in feminist movements
of her era, especially cultural feminism and lesbian feminism. Her volumes of poetry
from the 1970s include *Diving into the Wreck* (1973) and *The Dream of a Common Language* (1978). Her essays on women writers in *On Lies, Secrets, and Silence* (1979) and
other collections affirmed the existence of women's literary traditions in English. Rich's
brief reading of *To the Lighthouse* in her popular book helped to make the novel central
to feminist thought in the 1970s and '80s. Page numbers for *To the Lighthouse* refer to
this Norton Critical Edition.

perspective as we ourselves are changing. The feminist scholar Jane Lilienfeld[1] has pointed out that during Virginia's early years her mother, Julia Stephen, expended almost all her maternal energies in caring for her husband and his lifework, the *Dictionary of National Biography*. Both Virginia and her sister Vanessa were later to seek each other for mothering, and Lilienfeld suggests that Leonard Woolf was to provide Virginia with the kind of care and vigilance that her mother had given her father. In any case, Mrs. Ramsay, with her "strange severity, her extreme courtesy," her attentiveness to others' needs (chiefly those of men), her charismatic attractiveness, even as a woman of fifty who had borne eight children—Mrs. Ramsay is no simple idealization. She is the "delicious fecundity . . . [the] fountain and spray of life [into which] the fatal sterility of the male plunged itself"; at the same time that "she felt this thing that she called life terrible, hostile, and quick to pounce on you if you gave it a chance."

She perceives "without hostility, the sterility of men," yet as Lilienfeld notes, she doesn't like women very much, and her life is spent in attunement to male needs. The young painter Lily Briscoe, sitting with her arms clasped around Mrs. Ramsay's knees, her head on her lap, longs to become one with her, in "the chambers of the mind and heart of the woman who was, physically, touching her. . . . Could loving, as people called it, make her and Mrs. Ramsay one? for it was not knowledge but unity that she desired, not inscriptions on tablets, nothing that could be written in any language known to men, but intimacy itself . . ." (41).

Yet nothing happens. Mrs. Ramsay is not available to her. And since Woolf has clearly transcribed herself into Lily Briscoe, the scene has a double charge: the daughter seeking intimacy with her own mother, the woman seeking intimacy with another woman, not her mother but toward whom she turns those passionate longings. Much later she understands that it is only in her work that she can "stand up to Mrs. Ramsay" and her "extraordinary power." In her work, she can reject the grouping of Mrs. Ramsay and James, "mother and son," as a pictorial subject. Through her work, Lily is independent of men, as Mrs. Ramsay is not. In the most acute, unembittered ways, Woolf pierces the shimmer of Mrs. Ramsay's personality; she needs men as much as they need her, her power and strength are founded on the dependency, the "sterility" of others.

It is clear that Virginia the daughter had pondered Julia her mother for years before depicting her in *To the Lighthouse*. Again, that fascinated attention is ascribed to Lily Briscoe:

1. Rich's biographical reading reflects her knowledge of a 1975 paper by Jane Lilienfeld that became Lilienfeld's influential "'The Deceptiveness of Beauty': Mother Love and Mother Hate in *To the Lighthouse*," *Twentieth-Century Literature* 23 (1977): 345–76.

Fifty pairs of eyes were not enough to get around that one woman with, she thought. Among them, must be one that was stone blind to her beauty. One wanted most some secret sense, fine as air, with which to steal through keyholes and surround her where she sat knitting, talking, sitting silent in the window alone; which took to itself and treasured up like the air which held the smoke of the steamer, her thoughts, her imaginations, her desires. What did the hedge mean to her, what did the garden mean to her, what did it mean to her when a wave broke? (143)

And this, precisely, is what Virginia the artist achieved; but the achievement is testimony not merely to the power of her art but to the passion of the daughter for the mother, her need above all to understand this woman, so adored and so unavailable to her; to understand, in all complexity, the differences that separated her mother from herself.

*   *   *

The loss of the daughter to the mother, the mother to the daughter, is the essential female tragedy. We acknowledge Lear (father–daughter split), Hamlet (son and mother), and Oedipus (son and mother) as great embodiments of the human tragedy; but there is no presently enduring recognition of mother–daughter passion and rapture.

There was such a recognition, but we have lost it. It was expressed in the religious mystery of Eleusis, which constituted the spiritual foundation of Greek life for two thousand years. Based on the mother–daughter myth of Demeter and Korê, this rite was the most forbidden and secret of classical civilization, never acted on the stage, open only to initiates who underwent long purification beforehand. According to the Homeric hymn to Demeter of the seventh century B.C.E., the mysteries were established by the goddess herself, on her reunion with her daughter Korê, or Persephone, who had been raped and abducted, in one version of the myth by Poseidon as lord of the underworld, or, in a later version, by Hades or Pluto, king of death. Demeter revenges herself for the loss of her daughter by forbidding the grain—of which she is queen—to grow.

When her daughter is restored to her—for nine months of the year only—she restores fruitfulness and life to the land for those months. * * *

Critical Approaches

RACHEL BOWLBY

Sexual Lines in *To the Lighthouse*†

* * *

> He was safe, he was restored to his privacy. He stopped to light
> his pipe, looked once at his wife and son in the window, and as
> one raises one's eyes from a page in an express train and sees a
> farm, a tree, a cluster of cottages as an illustration, a confirma-
> tion of something on the printed page to which one returns, for-
> tified, and satisfied, so without his distinguishing either his son
> or his wife, the sight of them fortified him and satisfied him and
> consecrated his effort to arrive at a perfectly clear understanding
> of the problem which now engaged the energies of his splendid
> mind. (27–28)

This is Mr Ramsay securing sustenance from the image of his wife
and son. The picture of familial harmony is analogous to the distant sight of the emblems of a pastoral idyll (farm, tree, 'cluster' of
cottages), and the whole paragraph—a single sentence—is like an
enactment in miniature of the structure of masculine subjectivity
as Woolf analyses its impasses for both sexes in *To the Lighthouse*.

Mr Ramsay is (as if) on a train: he is moving at a fast rate along a
line with a precise destination, and his 'effort' is 'to arrive' at a solution to his current 'problem'. In this endeavour, Mr Ramsay or the
traveller is 'restored', 'fortified' and 'satisfied'—given strength, and
given enough, like adequate nourishment—by seeing the image of
rural completeness, and this is explicitly likened to the sight of the
wife and child. * * *

This passage is immediately followed by another, much more
famous one, which by picking up on the 'splendid mind' might seem
to act in turn as its 'confirmation':

† From "Getting to Q: Sexual Lines in *To the Lighthouse*" in *Virginia Woolf: Feminist
Destinations* (Oxford: Basil Blackwell, 1988), pp. 62–79, 176–77. Used by permission of
Wiley. Page numbers for *To the Lighthouse* refer to this Norton Critical Edition, but the
quotations are from the British edition.

293

It was a splendid mind. For if thought is like the keyboard of a piano, divided into so many notes, or like the alphabet is ranged in twenty-six letters all in order, then his splendid mind had no sort of difficulty in running over those letters one by one, firmly and accurately, until it had reached, say, the letter Q. He reached Q. Very few people in the whole of England ever reach Q. . . . But after Q? What comes next? After Q there are a number of letters the last of which is scarcely visible to mortal eyes, but glimmers red in the distance. Z is only reached by one man in a generation. Still, if he could reach R it would be something. . . . Q he could demonstrate. If Q then is Q—R— (28)

* * * If Mr Ramsay is still in some way (like) a train passenger, the rails along which he travels have now become the letters of the alphabet, which also lead to a preordained destination that 'glimmers red in the distance' like the lights of a station. * * * 'If Q then is Q—R—' takes up the notation of propositional logic, and suggests that each letter attained is an advance upon the previous one, not just a neutral point on a line made up of points of equal value. Woolf is able to get maximum comic mileage out of the fact that P and Q really are the letters conventionally used as signs in propositional logic, while Mr Ramsay's name begins with the 'next' letter, R. (There is extra mileage too, perhaps, for a certain V.W. from the fact that her own consecutive initials are further along; and in that R is indeed often wheeled on in formal logic examples where a third letter is required in addition to P and Q . . .)

* * *

In his *Three Essays on the Theory of Sexuality* (1905), Freud suggests a close connection between fantasies and trains: 'The shaking produced by driving in carriages and later by railway-travel exercises such a fascinating effect upon older children that every boy, at any rate, has at one time or other in his life wanted to be an engine driver or coachman.'[1] The fact that having first said that the fascination of trains affects 'older children' in general, Freud then signals this kind of dream as every boy's, is suggestive. Going back for a moment to Woolf's simile of the alphabet and piano ('If thought is like the keyboard . . .'), we might say: 'If masculine development is like a train journey . . .', and then see how far this takes us.

Woolf's explorations of what makes the difference of the sexes are uncannily close to Freud's in another key, and this may be related to the fact that his writings were much discussed in Woolf's social

---

1. Sigmund Freud, "Three Essays on the Theory of Sexuality," trans. and ed. James Strachey, *The Standard Edition of the Complete Psychological Works of Sigmund Freud*, 24 vols. (London: Hogarth Press, 1953–74), vol. 7, pp. 123–246.

circle. The Hogarth Press, which she founded with her husband Leonard Woolf, published the first translations of Freud in Britain (and later, in the fifties and sixties, the Standard Edition). Woolf drew directly on psychoanalytic insights in her prose writings (especially *Three Guineas*), but she also made use of them in her fiction. *To the Lighthouse* is particularly interesting in this regard because Woolf said of its writing: 'I suppose I did for myself what psychoanalysts do for their patients. I expressed some very long felt and deeply felt emotion. And in expressing it I explained it and then laid it to rest' ("A Sketch of the Past," 198). This declaration gives critics justification for the identification of Woolf with Lily Briscoe, the daughter figure and artist as outsider who then looks back at the relation between her 'parents' and hers to them.

In the psychoanalytic account of human development, there is no subjectivity without sexual difference, and there is no natural, programmed progression for those of either biological sex towards the achievement of the 'masculine' or 'feminine' identity socially ascribed. Because the dominant line is that of masculinity, the girl's understanding of the meaning of sexual difference implies coming to terms with her *defacto* eccentricity, forced to take up a position in relation to the norm from which she is by definition excluded: as the image of maternal fulfilment seen from the train window, as the 'woman' despised for her lack of the masculine attribute, or as an interloper into the compartment reserved for men.

One way of looking at masculine development would be to say, in the teleology of social purpose, that its object is to get the boy onto the train, headed for a respectable destination, but still fired at some level by the fantasy of being Casey Jones at the throttle. But this is to go too fast, or to look only from one direction: put the other way around, the same process appears also as an inevitable lack of fit between the situation of the social subject as passenger and his residual fantasy of being, in the end, a hero. The mother figures in both perspectives as the imagined plenitude of a childhood left behind, but still there as the source of meaning and authentification for the work or journey in progress. Freud says that a man seeks in adult life to find again, in the form of a wife, the figure of support to whom he 'returns' for reassurance of his powers and centrality. Yet this reassurance refers to what he none the less lacks, to the extent that the social train admits him only at the price of a ticket which makes him like every other conforming passenger who has accepted the conditions of travel.

Mr Ramsay's blundering towards a possible R which will never be the Z of 'one man in a generation' perfectly illustrates such a pattern. He is likened to the resigned leader of an unsuccessful expedition:

How many men in a thousand million, he asked himself, reach
Z after all? Surely the leader of a forlorn hope may ask himself
that . . . Mr Ramsay squared his shoulders and stood very
upright by the urn.

Who shall blame him, if, so standing for a moment, he dwells
upon fame, upon search parties, upon cairns raised by grateful
followers over his bones? Finally, who shall blame the leader of
the doomed expedition, if, having adventured to the uttermost,
and used his strength wholly to the last ounce and fallen asleep
not much caring if he wakes or not, he now perceives by some
pricking in his toes that he lives, and does not on the whole
object to live, but requires sympathy, and whisky, and some one
to tell the story of his suffering to at once? Who shall blame
him? Who will not secretly rejoice when the hero puts his
armour off, and halts by the window and gazes at his wife
and son . . . and bending his magnificent head before her—
who will blame him if he does homage to the beauty of the
world? (29–30)

The 'expedition'—a journey with a goal, the attainment of which
would ensure immortal fame to the leader—remains as the structuring fantasy for the philosopher resigned to getting no further than
half-way, to being one of the 'plodding and persevering' rather than
a man of 'genius': 'the gifted, the inspired who, miraculously, lump
all the letters together in one flash' (29). And in the age of the train,
the journey is figured in the more heroic imagery of the pioneering
explorer.

Even Mr Ramsay's 'abstract' philosophical speculations seem to
be related to the need to come to terms with a social hierarchy of
men in which he does not necessarily occupy the place of 'genius':

Does the progress of civilization depend upon great men? Is the
lot of the average human being better now than in the time of the
Pharoahs? Is the lot of the average human being, however,
he asked himself, the criterion by which we judge the measure of
civilization? Possibly not. Possibly the greatest good requires the
existence of a slave class. The liftman in the Tube is an eternal
necessity. (35)

Here the path of the individual is transposed to the field of 'civilization', which is also endowed with a hypothetical line of progression
whose 'measure' can be decided. In this context of the great man *man-
qué,* it is the picture of maternal plenitude—his own wife and child,
the reverenced 'beauty' of the woman—which provides, restores, a
form of compensation. This is not incompatible with the fact that
the acquisition of dependants in the form of wife and children—the

settling down to the normality of the 'average' man—is also, in
Mr Bankes's view, the reason for Mr Ramsay's failure to fulfil his early
promise as a philosopher. The woman is placed in the contradictory
position of being both source of meaning for the masculine project
(that which 'fortifies' the traveller) and a constraint, the scapegoat for
its necessary failure in the original heroic mode of its conception.

Mr Ramsay's relation to his wife suggests the man's wish to return
to the position of the child in relation to a woman like his mother.
According to Freud, it is in so far as she identifies with her mother
that the woman:

> acquires her attractiveness to a man, whose Oedipus attach-
> ment to his mother it kindles into passion. How often it hap-
> pens, however, that it is only his son who obtains what he
> himself aspired to! One gets an impression that a man's love and
> a woman's are a phase apart psychologically.[2]

The resentment of James—'hating his father' (26)—for Mr Ramsey's
prior claims to his mother parallels Freud's Oedipal scenario, where
the boy wants nothing less than to put out of the way the father who
asserts his rights to the mother. Looking at it from the husband's
point of view, Mr Ramsay attempts to recover, with another woman,
the relation of dependence and centrality in which he once stood,
or imagines he once stood, to his own mother: after receiving the
sympathy he claims from his wife, he is 'like a child who drops off
satisfied' (31). Yet this harmony of oneness with the mother figure,
which his wife is called upon to secure, can necessarily never be
restored completely once it is posed in terms of a constitutive loss.
Mr Ramsay's demands for reassurance of his uniqueness are doomed
to be endlessly repeated: 'This was one of those moments when an
enormous need urged him, without being conscious what it was, to
approach any woman, to force them, he did not care how, his need
was so great, to give him what he wanted: sympathy' (110–11). Only
in fantasy can the exorbitant request be satisfactorily answered:

> Sitting in the boat, he bowed, he crouched himself, acting
> instantly his part—the part of a desolate man, widowed, bereft;
> and so called up before him in hosts people sympathising with
> him; staged for himself as he sat in the boat, a little drama;
> which required of him decrepitude and exhaustion and sor-
> row . . . and then there was given him in abundance women's
> sympathy, and he imagined how they would soothe him and
> sympathise with him. (121)

2. Sigmund Freud, "Femininity" (1933), in *New Introductory Lectures on Psychoanalysis*, trans. James Strachey (New York: Norton, 1965), p. 134.

Other men in the novel are represented as threatened in similar ways in that identity, and seeking to have it given or restored to them through the intercession of an all-providing Mrs Ramsay. Charles Tansley, the young protégé of her husband, unburdens himself of his hard-luck story: 'He had wanted to tell her everything about himself' (13). She had first confided in him the story of Mr Carmichael's 'unfortunate marriage', with the comment that 'he should have been a great philosopher'. In reading this as a parable of proper relations between the sexes (and not, for example, noticing its ironic reference to Mrs Ramsay's own case, where the very dependence of Mr Ramsay, rather than the marriage's ending, is allegedly what has restrained his philosophizing), Tansley is 'flattered':

> Charles Tansley revived. Insinuating, too, as she did the greatness of man's intellect, even in its decay, the subjection of all wives . . . to their husband's labours, she made him feel better pleased with himself than he had done yet, and he would have liked, had they taken a cab, for example, to have paid for it. As for her little bag, might he not carry that? . . . He would like her to see him, gowned and hooded, walking in a procession. (11)

But the final result of 'that extraordinary emotion which had been growing all the walk' (13) is a revelation:

> In she came, stood for a moment silent . . . stood quite motionless for a moment against a picture of Queen Victoria wearing the blue ribbon of the Garter; when all at once he realised that it was this: it was this:—she was the most beautiful person he had ever seen.
> With stars in her eyes and veils in her hair, with cyclamen and wild violets—what nonsense was he thinking? She was fifty at least; she had eight children. (13)

Momentarily the virgin, the queen and the mother coalesce into a mute image which makes the man something more than what he took himself previously to be: 'for the first time in his life Charles Tansley felt an extraordinary pride' (13). The woman's perfection and summation of every part establishes the man's identity.

It is the asymmetry of Freud's 'phase apart' that now points the way towards a consideration of the difference in the developments of boys and girls. For if the metaphors of journey, destination, progression—indeed, of 'development' itself in so far as the word implies determinate stages towards an end already known—are useful in thinking of the case of the man, they are less obviously applied to that of the woman imagined as the sustaining object of the gaze from the window. It was the realization of this asymmetry, prompted by the criticisms of other analysts including women, which led Freud, in what can appear retroactively as his own logical 'line' of intellectual development, to consider what was different in the girl's development to what is called femininity rather than to assume it as a progression along parallel lines to the boy's development to what is called masculinity.

It would seem that girls are placed in a structurally untenable position in so far as the main line of human development is concerned. For if subjectivity is figured by the place on the train, with the mother in the distance, left behind and idealized, but women in general devalued and despised for their lack of the attribute of masculinity, then women are effectively put in two places at once, both of which are undesirable. The third possibility is the place on the train, as part of the 'procession', but that is by definition deemed unwomanly as being reserved for men. The difficulty of reaching 'femininity' is emphasized by Freud when he speaks of no less than three possible 'lines of development' for girls after they have understood the meaning of sexual difference. Only one of these lines goes to 'normal' femininity (heterosexuality and motherhood); the other two, frigidity and homosexuality, each represent different versions of the refusal of the 'normal' feminine position.

'Anatomy is destiny', so often taken as the Freudian condemnation of women to a conventionally feminine fate, is rather the marking of the way that determinate social meanings are arbitrarily imposed upon subjects of either anatomical sex, and in far less tenable ways for the woman. Freud's account of the trials of the girl on her way to what is prescribed as normal femininity makes her development sound like a switchback railway journey thwarted with upheavals and potential reversals at every turn.[3] As has often been pointed out, these very difficulties can be taken as a kind of

---

3. In two ways in particular the girl has to accomplish a more difficult journey, according to Freud: by changing the sex of the object of love (from female to male: the boy has only to substitute another woman for the mother) and by changing the chief site of erotic arousal (from clitoris to vagina). Initially, there is no difference in the sexuality of boys and girls; it is only after the girl has understood the meaning of sexual difference—an understanding which Freud mythically attaches to sightings of the genitals of the other sex—that (in the "normal" course of development) she regards herself as lacking and gives up the forms of sexuality that are now, retroactively, identified as masculine. In addition to the texts cited above, see also "Some Psychical Consequence of the Anatomical Distinction Between the Sexes" (1925) and "Female Sexuality" (1931), both in Sigmund Freud, *Sexuality and the Psychology of Love*, ed. Philip Rieff (New York: Macmillan, 1963).

Studies of *To the Lighthouse* that look at Woolf's undermining of the Freudian scenario of feminine development include: Margaret Homans, "Mothers and Daughters in Virginia Woolf's Victorian Novel," in *Bearing the Word: Language and Female Experience in Nineteenth-Century Women's Writing* (Chicago: U of Chicago P, 1986), pp. 277–88; Gayatri Spivak, "Unmaking and Making in *To the Lighthouse*," in Sally McConnell-Ginet, Ruth Borker, and Nelly Furman, eds., *Women and Language in Literature and Society* (New York: Praeger, 1980), pp. 310–27; and Elizabeth Abel, "'Cam the Wicked': Woolf's Portrait of the Artist as Her Father's Daughter," in *Virginia Woolf and Bloomsbury: A Centenary Celebration*, ed. Jane Marcus (Basingstoke: Macmillan, 1987), pp. 170–89 [adapted by the *Editor*].

allegory of the impossibility for 'woman' of finding an approximate
identity to match—to challenge and to fit in with—that of the masculine scenario which has already put her in certain contradictory
positions. Masculine identity is permanently under threat, but
'femininity' never has the pretence to any positive content to begin
with.

Mrs Ramsay seems to others the image of fulfilled womanhood,
but does not sustain the equanimity she constantly proffers to
assuage their doubts and floundering: 'For the most part, oddly
enough, she must admit that she felt this thing that she called life
terrible, hostile, and quick to pounce on you if you gave it a chance'
(47). Her perpetual mothering represents for her the only way of
holding at bay 'this thing' that is always ready to spring. 'She would
have liked always to have had a baby' (46), and her demand upon
others 'to say that people must marry, people must have children'
(47) is said to emanate not from assurance but from a negotiation
of what would otherwise be despair. Mrs Ramsay's own capacity to
ease the sufferings of those around her is exposed as resting on her
acknowledgement that the alleviation is only a patching over of a
fundamental discord:

> She had often the feeling, Why must they grow up and lose it
> all? And then she said to herself, brandishing her sword at life,
> Nonsense. They will be perfectly happy. And here she was, she
> reflected, feeling life rather sinister again, making Minta marry
> Paul Rayley. (47)

The incompatibility of the marital relations upon which Mrs Ramsay nonetheless so vehemently insists is brought to the surface in
the story she reads to James of the Fisherman's wife:

> Flounder, flounder, in the sea
> Come, I pray thee, here to me;
> For my wife, good Ilsabil,
> Wills not as I'd have her will. (45)

'"Well, what does she want then?" said the Flounder' (45), echoing—
or anticipating—Freud's famous formulation.[4] What he, Mr Ramsay, would have her will, she tries to will, and yet there remains a
discrepancy after she has 'satisfied' him, after 'there throbbed
through her . . . the rapture of successful creation' (32) which seems
then to create or to comfort her too:

---

4. Freud, after decades trying to solve what he called "the riddle of femininity" ("Femi-
ninity," p. 112), famously asked, "What does woman want?" in a letter to Marie
Bonaparte, quoted in Ernest Jones, *The Life and Work of Sigmund Freud*, 3 vols. (New
York: Basic Books, 1953–57), vol. 2, p. 421 [*Editor*].

Every throb of this pulse seemed, as he walked away, to enclose her and her husband, and to give to each that solace which two different notes, one high, one low, struck together, seem to give each other as they combine. Yet, as the resonance died, and she turned to the Fairy Tale again, Mrs Ramsay felt not only exhausted in body . . . but also there tinged her physical fatigue some faintly disagreeable sensation with another origin. (32)

Mrs Ramsay is 'discomposed' (32) by the 'disagreeable sensation' which itself has more than one part: not liking the public aspect of 'his coming to her like that, openly' for reassurance (32); not liking 'to feel finer than her husband' (32); 'not being entirely sure' (32) that he is as fine as she tells him he is to soothe him. Rather than 'the entire joy, the pure joy, of the two notes sounding together', the outcome of the exchange reminds her of a discordance, of what she calls (in the latest psychological language) 'the inadequacy of human relationships' (33). The image of perfect complementarity and reciprocity betwen the sexes shows itself to mask a basic disunity of parts that in fact do not fit, either within her or between the two of them.

If Mrs Ramsay endeavours to preserve the spectacle of the composure of feminine and masculine relationships, Lily Briscoe is placed outside this structure, fascinated by it but resisting incorporation into it as a woman who, in Mrs Ramsay's scheme, should marry Mr Bankes. Against Mrs Ramsay's urging that 'an unmarried woman has missed the best of life' (40), and Charles Tansley's running insistence that 'women can't paint, women can't write' (39), Lily 'would urge her own exemption from the universal law' (40); and this makes her, as when she is about to fail to give Mr Ramsay the solace he demands of her, 'not a woman' (111): 'That man, she thought, her anger rising in her, never gave; that man took. She, on the other hand, would be forced to give. Mrs Ramsay had given. Giving, giving, giving, she had died' (110).

In making of Lily a cultural and sexual rebel against 'the universal law', the novel seems to place her as the antithesis to Mrs Ramsay, whose energies are dedicated to the maintenance of all that Lily repudiates in her prescribed sexual destiny. Yet from another point of view, as has often been pointed out, their projects are analogous. The unification or bringing together of disparate things, of the 'discomposed', which Mrs Ramsay seeks to achieve by marryings and motherings, is also what Lily attempts in the field of art:

Mrs Ramsay making of the moment something permanent (as in another sphere Lily herself tried to make of the moment something permanent)—this was of the nature of a revelation.

> In the midst of chaos there was shape; this eternal passing and
> flowing was struck into stability. (118)

This 'revelation' itself stands out in the narrative as a 'moment' to
give coherence, a nodal point perhaps upon which to base a general
interpretation of *To the Lighthouse*. Such a view lends itself readily
to being brought into connection with Woolf's own interest in and
endorsement of a particular modernist conception of the function
of art: that the work of art makes in its own autonomous medium
the unity which in the world itself is lacking. In the biographical
reading of the Lily/Mrs Ramsay connection/opposition, Lily, like
Virginia Stephen, represents the virginal artist daughter of the Victorian 'Angel in the House', moving tentatively away from the restric-
tions on female expectations to become what Mrs Ramsay thinks of
as 'an independent little creature' (15–16). This parallel is borne out
by the statements in Woolf's memoirs and her diary indicating that
the writing of *To the Lighthouse* finally routed or put to rest the
ghost of a too angelic mother who had haunted her since her death,
when Virginia was only thirteen.

But it could be argued that the moment of unity, the apparently
resolved triple sequence of times collected together in the completion
of Lily Briscoe's picture, only emphasizes all the more strongly the
underlying lack of harmony in 'human relationships', as in the art or
institutions which attempt to cover over their 'inadequacy'. This is the
alternative I have stressed in examining what undermines the unity of
the most apparently unifying or unified of characters and episodes in
the novel. But this is not then to argue that it is more 'adequate' to
posit a general flux and fragmentation than a final unification. Rather,
To the Lighthouse explores both the insistence and the untenability of
the prevailing constructions of masculine and feminine identities,
showing how the two are neither complementary, making a whole,
nor ever reached in their imaginary completion by individuals of
either sex. In particular, the conquering hero and the angel in the
house are (masculine) fantasies, and it is in relation to them that men
and women have to take up their parts, more or less adequately.

The three sections of *To the Lighthouse* are distinguished by different forms of temporality. The first and third focus, as often in Woolf's
novels, on a single day and the associative links which connect it, in
the consciousnesses of the characters and along the narrative line, to
other times and places. The 'present moment' is divided and encom-
passes more than one time, and this effect is multiplied by the number of characters in such a way that their coming together as a
group—for instance, in the dinner party scene—constitutes only a
tenuous and ephemeral connection of many heterogeneous parts. * * *

The middle section, 'Time Passes', makes Mrs Ramsay's death parenthetical, literally, to a general lack of differentiation from which identifiable human agency is absent, except for the ambivalent questioning of 'sea airs' (97), or the half-acknowledged place of the narrator:

> Night after night, summer and winter, the torment of storms, the arrow-like stillness of fine weather, held their court without interference. Listening (had there been anyone to listen) from the upper rooms of the empty house, only gigantic chaos streaked with lightning could have been heard tumbling and tossing. (100–101)

In this part, 'time passing' is represented rather as cyclical repetition than as the multiple story lines or criss-cross networks—to the past, and to other places—of a day. Natural rhythms take precedence over the appeal to any kind of progression or linear development: there is no specificity of a differentiated past or elsewhere structuring the present. But the half-acknowledged narrator also identifies the abandoned house as a kind of aesthetic image of natural, self-contained peace:

> So loveliness reigned and stillness, and together made the shape of loveliness itself, a form from which life had parted; solitary like a pool at evening, far distant, seen from a train window, vanishing so quickly that the pool, pale in the evening, is scarcely robbed of its solitude, though once seen. (97)

Neither of these two forms of temporality, or atemporality—the changelessness of the 'form', 'the shape of loveliness', or the repeated movements of a chaotic nature—apparently bears any relation to the linearity identified as masculine: they are like obverse sides against which it appears as an arbitrary imposition.

The other kinds of time—that of night and day, of waves, of seasons and years, or that of still form, signify no progression but the bareness of natural cycles, permanent recurrence and alternation, or else static completeness. It is these times which are often associated with femininity as cyclical and 'reproductive', or as iconic and eternal, and which are differentiated in *To the Lighthouse* from the arbitrary sequences of masterful 'masculine' temporality.

Yet in terms of the sexual structuring of subjectivity, this difference is far from absolute: it is not a dualism of two unrelated types. As with the interconnection of repetition and linearity in the keyboard simile, the 'shape of loveliness itself', likened to a pool glimpsed from a train window, acquires its meaning in relation to the distance and direction of the place from which it is seen. What appears as

the pure origin of life in Mrs Ramsay ('this delicious fecundity' [31])
is so only by virtue of its capacity to symbolize the antithesis of the
end-directed cultural purposes of 'the fatal sterility of the male'
(31). It is at once the basis of meaning to authenticate the otherwise
indefinite and wavering series of A to Z, and a means of comfort,
representing an attempted restoration of infantile dependence and
centrality. It also represents freedom from the 'failure' (31) which
threatens to engulf from the point at which he joins the line of
ambitious males headed and herded towards the letter R and
beyond. The image of the succouring, nurturing woman serves to
supply—and necessarily to fail to supply—the gap betwen R and Z,
making up for the man's inevitable incapacity to get to the end of
his line.

The absoluteness of the distinction between different times is also
undermined in other ways. The repetitive work of the old women on
the decaying house prevents rather than inducing a return to a
natural state—'the whole house would have plunged to the depths
to lie upon the sands of oblivion' (104)—and is thus eminently a
cultural enterprise. As if to underline this almost ironically, the restoration work is precipitated by the women's receipt of an imperious
letter from the remnants of the Ramsay family: 'All of a sudden,
would Mrs McNab see that the house was ready, one of the young
ladies wrote' (104). This brings Mrs McNab close to what Mr Ramsay abstracts into the possible 'eternal necessity' of 'the liftman in
the Tube' (35) than to a figure for the eternal feminine. But Mrs
McNab's work against the dereliction of the house is also similar in
form to the time pattern of Mrs Ramsay's life of dailiness. For the
latter, 'the monotonous fall of the wave on the beach' (14) is either
consoling or admonitory, warning 'her whose day had slipped past
in one quick doing after another that it was all ephemeral as a rainbow' (15). So again, the clear division of different modes of temporality is made more complicated. The beat of the waves is not only a
soothing return to cradle songs: it can also signify a forward march
towards an end whose approach measures the dissipation of wasted
days. The forms of feminine subjectivity cannot be separated
from their position in relation to the governing order of masculine
temporality.

If the 'Time Passes' section of *To the Lighthouse* figures as the
antithesis against which the man's letters appear in sharpest outline
and opposition, the first and third parts also—but differently—depart
from that line, showing its multiple layers and complex crossings and
intersections, like Mrs Ramsay's knitting. So different a view of the
narrative line—without a place of mastery, and resembling a network
or imbrication of many times, places, memories and fantasies—could

be said to be feminine in that it looks beyond—just glimpses further than—the certainties of the recognizable, single line. If this is what constitutes the difference of modernist from realist narrative, it might also be what makes modernism in a certain sense 'feminine'. For the time being, that 'feminine' is so by virtue of its pursuing different, less direct lines from those identified as masculine: by its moving away from what it regards, from another position, as the false neutrality and universality of the principal, masculine line.

To the Lighthouse makes evident the mapping of human subjectivity in terms of figurations inseparable from sexual difference, and it also shows the lack of fit, the 'phase apart', entailed by the discrepancy between the train of masculinity and the various outsider positions into which the woman is cast:

> ('Nature has but little clay,' said Mr Bankes once, much moved by her voice on the telephone, though she was only telling him a fact about a train, 'like that of which she moulded you.' He saw her at the end of the line very clearly Greek, straight, blue-eyed. How incongruous it seemed to be telephoning to a woman like that . . .) (24)

The woman moves the man to a poetic language quite different from the factual language of timetables. He imagines her as a Greek statue or goddess, returning backwards along a cultural line where artistic and feminine purity can be clearly seen, and which is marked by pathos through its necessary difference from the here and now associated with the mechanical lines of the railway and the phone. 'How incongruous to be telephoning to a woman like that' could be taken to condense all the features of the unparallel lines of masculine and feminine journeys. Just as the simile of the train passenger contrasted the straight progression along an arbitrary line with the image of the woman as restorer or giver of meaning, so Mr Bankes casts the lady in a mould of aesthetic perfection and endows her with the function of making up for the mechanical and routinized lines in the modern world.

The eventual arrival at the lighthouse, and the eventual completion or composition of Lily Briscoe's picture of James and Mrs Ramsay, are so belated in the novel as to put in question the very progression of which their achievement appears, at length, as a kind of formal culmination. This is no Z at the end of the alphabet, but rather the discovery of a different kind of line, contrary to the 'doomed expedition' (30) ordained for the forward march of masculine history. * * *

PAMELA L. CAUGHIE

[The Artist Figure in *To the Lighthouse*][†]

* * *

With Lily Briscoe in *To the Lighthouse,* Woolf created her first artist figure to tell the story of her own artwork as well as the story in which her artwork figures, and it is this narrative function of the artist that led Woolf to question some of the modernist assumptions with which she began. The structure of Woolf's novel is the progression of Lily's painting: its inception in Lily's desire to paint Mrs. Ramsay (part 1); its dissolution following the death of Mrs. Ramsay (part 2); its renewal ten years later when Lily returns to the Ramsays' summer home (part 3); and its completion as the exhausted artist lays down her brush, declaring in the last line of the novel: "I have had my vision." * * * [T]he involuted structure of this and the other novels on the artist figure suggests not just a reflexive relation of the framed artwork to the artwork of the frame but also a spiral relation. That is, it suggests both the way the subject matter of the novel turns in on and reflects its method and the way it winds out from and back to its method. In other words, it is not that the meaning of the novel is its method, or that the form and content are one and the same; rather, the subject matter of the novel is a function of the novel's discourse. If *To the Lighthouse* is in quest of its own status as art, then in generalizing on this work we must remember that a particular kind of painting, and thus a particular kind of discourse, is at issue in this novel. As Lily explains to William Bankes in part 1, her painting makes "no attempt at likeness . . . the picture was not of them" (42). The painting, she continues, is a matter of *relations,* and it is these relations we must consider.

Throughout the novel, Woolf presents Lily's art as a matter of relating two things: the mass on the right of her canvas and the mass on the left; Mrs. Ramsay in the window and Mr. Ramsay in the boat; the shore on which she stands and the sea to which she looks. Early in the novel this relation is one of connection: "It was a question, [Lily] remembered, how to connect this mass on the right hand with that on the left. She might do it by bringing the line of the branch across so" (43). Most critics accept this connection between two things as the essence not only of this novel but of Woolf's art in general. "Throughout Mrs. Woolf's work," writes [James] Naremore,

---

† From *Virginia Woolf and Postmodernism: Literature in Quest and Question of Itself* (Urbana: University of Illinois Press, 1991), pp. 33–39. Reprinted by permission of the author. Page numbers for *To the Lighthouse* refer to this Norton Critical Edition. Some footnotes have been omitted.

"the chief problem for her and for her characters is to overcome the space between things, to attain an absolute unity with the world."[1] Certainly this line across the canvas that presages Lily's final brush stroke endorses such a reading. However, this is only one moment of Woolf's novel. By the time Lily completes her painting, the relation she seeks has changed from connecting two things to maintaining a balance between forces (140). As Lily nears the completion of her painting, she thinks: "One wanted . . . to be on a level with ordinary experience, to feel simply that's a chair, that's a table, and yet at the same time, It's a miracle, it's an ecstasy. The problem [of relations] might be solved after all" (146). The problem is solved, but neither by synthesizing two things nor by choosing between them. The problem is solved—or rather, removed—by a change in Lily's concerns: *the distinction to be made is no longer between two things but between different ways of relating things*. And what effects this change is Lily's function as narrator in part 3.

While Lily paints her picture in sections III–XIII of this third part, she moves back and forth between a loss of consciousness of outer things as she "tunnels" into the past, and a return to consciousness of external things as she looks out to sea. Both the memories Lily recreates from the first part of the novel and the events she observes in the third part somehow function in the production of her art, and thus we must consider the role of memory and the function of the trip to the lighthouse. In her presentation of those memories, those boat scenes, and the relation between them, Woolf checks two modernist tendencies in Lily's art. One is the withdrawal from the public world of facts into the private world of vision to achieve some form of order. The other is the effort to synthesize the two to achieve some kind of harmony. I want to consider each of these tendencies in turn by looking at the way the memories and the boat trip are presented to us.

Critics often focus on the role memory plays in the production of Lily's painting as well as Woolf's novel. Clearly Woolf believed that memory is necessary to the creative act. She felt a special sympathy with Proust and shared his sense of the involuntary memory, the moment when habit relaxes and memories well up, merging past and present in one stream of time. Yet Woolf's emphasis here is slightly different from Proust's. First, the memories do not enable Lily to express some hitherto unrealized experience, nor does the consciousness of the world around her disturb that vision, but the two together enable her to paint. Second, Lily's memories are not private but shared in that they activate the reader's memories. For example, when Lily hears a voice saying "women can't paint, women

---

1. James Naremore, *The World without a Self: Virginia Woolf and the Novel* (New Haven: Yale UP, 1973), p. 242 [*Editor*].

can't write," we have identified that voice long before Lily dips into her memory far enough to pull out the name Charles Tansley. * * * This reworking of earlier scenes implicates the reader in the narrative process, merging our memories with the artist's. We become aware of the person and the stories made up about the person, for the person does not exist outside those stories, yet failing to look at the person turns the imaginings in on the creator, allows one to accept one's own illusions as truth. This turning inward is the tendency toward subjectivism and aestheticism that Woolf evokes and disrupts in this novel.

Such disruption is dramatized in section IV when, at the moment of greatest intensity, Lily steps into the waters of annihilation in her frantic desire to bring back the dead Mrs. Ramsay. At that moment, Woolf breaks the spell with this scene:

> [Macalister's boy took one of the fish and cut a square out of its side to bait his hook with. The mutilated body (it was alive still) was thrown back into the sea]. (131)

This is life, "startling, unexpected, unknown" (130). The brackets, conventionally used to indicate an interruption, remind us of the reports of external events placed in brackets in "Time Passes." * * * Who tells us this scene? If, as I will argue, Lily narrates the scenes in the boat, it seems unlikely that she narrates this action. This scene seems to be outside Lily's consciousness, disconnected from her, yet it brings her back to herself and to her surroundings. The very ambiguity of the perceiver and reporter of this scene, the startling break from Lily's consciousness, and the indifferent cruelty of the action make us feel the shock of life intruding on our illusion. This section functions not only thematically but also structurally. It keeps us from wading into the waters of annihilation by manifesting the structure of the text and by checking the consoling power of art. It reminds us that there *is* something beyond the text, but that something cannot be assimilated until it is made part of a sequence. In the placement of this section, Woolf makes us conscious of the process she has been investigating through Lily's painting, the moving back and forth from outer world to inner and of the virtual boundary between the two.

This losing consciousness of outer things and returning to it suggests the balance between fact and vision that Lily desires. But the language of these boat scenes indicates that what she looks at is also narrated, not merely observed. At the end of section III, Lily walks across the lawn and looks at the boats going out to sea: "there was one rather apart from the others. The sail was even now being hoisted. She *decided* that there in that very distant and entirely silent little boat Mr. Ramsay was sitting with Cam and James. Now they had got the sail up; now after a little flagging and hesitation the sails filled and, shrouded in profound silence, she watched the boat take its way with deliberation past the other boats out to sea" (118; emphasis added). Lily *selects* one boat and *decides* that this is the Ramsays'. The boat, the whole scene, is "shrouded in profound silence" until someone, here the artist, gives it shape by giving it some sequence ("Now they had got the sail up; now . . . the sails filled"). It is as if Lily narrates the boat scene given to us in the next section. Earlier that morning Lily had wondered how to make sense of the chaos of emotions, actions, and voices that filled the house after ten years' passage of time: "If only she could put them together, she felt, write them out in some sentence, then she would have got at the truth of things" (108). Mr. Ramsay's trip to the lighthouse seems to be that sequence.

Throughout section IV, the boat scene, Woolf employs the conditional "would be," at times suggesting the children's thoughts—"He would be impatient in a moment, James thought"—at others suggesting someone imagining the scene: "Now they would sail on for hours like this, and Mr. Ramsay would ask old Macalister a question—about the great storm last winter probably—and old Macalister would answer it, and they would puff their pipes together, and Macalister would take a tarry rope in his fingers, tying or untying some knot, and the boy would fish, and never say a word to any one" (119). If we are in the minds of the children in such passages, the choice of verbs would suggest their knowledge of their father's behavior on such boat trips; yet this is supposedly their first trip to the lighthouse.[2] *Would* calls attention to the *telling* of the boat scene; we are not watching *what* happens but *how* what happens could be narrated. Someone is creating all this, while we watch, and that someone seems to be Lily, who stands on the shore watching the little boat: "Yes, the breeze was freshening" (120). *Yes* evokes the presence of a perceiver, someone creating and confirming this vision, and links the various sections: "Yes, that is their boat, Lily Briscoe decided" (124). The words *now, would,* and *yes* evoke the perceiving and connecting mind. The return to Lily on the shore in the next section (V) reminds us of the unreality of the scene in that boat, shrouded in silence, compared with Lily's actions on shore.

By means of Lily's function as narrator, Woolf stresses the reciprocal relation between life and art, how the creative process actualizes daily life. By calling attention to Lily's stories—of Mrs. Ramsay, of

2. *Would* suggests not only that this boat trip has occurred before but that it has occurred several times before. *Would* marks the *iterative* in narrative, a repeated event presented only once. Here, however, the narrative time (iterative) conflicts with the story time (this is their first trip), making the sequence clearly a function of the narration.

Paul and Minta, of Mr. Ramsay and the children—Woolf reveals that the nature of the relation between fact and vision, art and life, has changed. We are no longer concerned with *the* connection or *the* correspondence between two realms but with the connections we posit among a variety of elements selected from a range of possibilities. That is, we are no longer concerned with formal relations (as Lily is in part 1) but with narrative relations. Once we acknowledge this change in relations, we can better explain Lily's remark about the status of her artwork. Asking again the recurring question of this last part, "What does it mean?" Lily thinks of how Mr. Carmichael would presumably have answered: "nothing stays; all changes; but not words, not paint" (130). We can see why this attitude has brought Mr. Carmichael fame as a poet following World War I, for it validates the artist's activity in terms of its product, the thing that endures. When Lily thinks of her painting, however, she qualifies this view: "Yet it would be hung in the attics, she thought; it would be rolled up and flung under a sofa; yet even so, even of a picture like that, it was true. One might say, even of this scrawl, not of that actual picture, perhaps, but of what it attempted, that it 'remained for ever' . . ." (130). Lily judges her art not in terms of how it differs from life but in terms of what it attempts; that is, in terms of its commitment to a form of behavior, not its devotion to a type of painting.

* * * [A] particular conception of art is at issue here. What makes these assertions more modest than the wholesale endorsement of any artistic activity by women is *the change in motive,* from the desire to connect two things and make a lasting product, to the desire to maintain a multiple perspective and participate in an ongoing activity. * * *

Woolf expresses this relation in the wavelike rhythm of Lily's painting. Lily feels urged forward and held back simultaneously. Her pauses and strokes form one process, so that the moments when the artist is not painting are just as essential as the strokes themselves. *Waves,* a noun, would seem to suggest a thing, a mountain of water with white foam curling at the top. Yet it actually signifies an action: the momentary lull after the break and before the next towering mound of water is part of the continual movement that is the wave. There is no definitive opposition between the fixed state and the duration. *Painting* reveals a similar lack of clear-cut distinctions: it refers to the marks on a canvas and to the process of marking that canvas. In this last section, Woolf explores the oscillating relations between the thing and the process that produces the thing. The aesthetic object consists not just of the marks on a canvas, or the words on a page, but of the pauses or spaces between them, the ongoing rhythmic process in which they take on meaning. Without such pauses, we could not see the strokes; without spaces, the words would run together. * * *

*** This movement is what keeps our fictions from hardening into some permanent form. Even those moments when all seems to come together into a unified whole, as when Mrs. Ramsay says, "Life stand still here," even those moments disintegrate as we grasp them: the dinner scene breaks up and becomes the past as we look at it; Lily's vision becomes the past as she has it. ***

And so the final brush stroke signifies the artist's commitment to a certain behavior, not the answer to a general question—What is the value of art? What is the nature of women's art? What does it all mean? The dramatic gesture with which Lily completes her painting recalls the initial brush stroke. Early in the novel Woolf stresses the inception of the work, the courage of the artist to commit herself to the project before her, for the first strokes of the artist, like the first words of the novelist, eliminate other possibilities and both inscribe and fill in the space to be enclosed. After that gap of ten years, Lily, in part 3, stands empty before her canvas: "Where to begin?—that was the question[,] at what point to make the first mark? One line placed on the canvas committed her to innumerable risks, to frequent and irrevocable decisions. . . . Still the risk must be run; the mark made" (115). Similarly, the last stroke of the painting claims attention: "With a sudden intensity, as if she saw it clear for a second, she drew a line there, in the centre. It was done; it was finished. Yes, she thought, laying down her brush in extreme fatigue, I have had my vision" (150).

Already, with the last stroke of the brush, with the last words of the novel, the vision is past, receding as the harmony of the dinner scene recedes, as the wave recedes, for the vision must be perpetually remade, the relations must be forever reestablished. This line is not the union of two kinds of experience but the affirmation of one possible form of activity, a gesture that implies not so much the completion of the act as its exhaustion, the crossing out of the current enterprise and the crossing over to a new one.[3]

*   *   *

3. My reading of *To the Lighthouse* might usefully be compared with that of Marianne Hirsch in *The Mother/Daughter Plot: Narrative, Psychoanalysis, Feminism* (Bloomington: Indiana UP, 1989), pp. 108–116. Hirsch argues that "Lily's solution to what art should be and her completion of the painting" depend on her rejection of the aesthetic criteria of harmony, balance, order, and permanence (112–13). Thus, the end of the novel does not resolve the tensions between two forces but maintains them, and Lily's line can be said to connect the masses on the right and left of her canvas as well as to acknowledge their disconnection (114). Yet where Hirsch, like Rachel Blau DuPlessis (in "For the Etruscans: Sexual Difference and Artistic Production," in *The Future of Difference,* ed. Hester Eisenstein and Alice Jardine [Boston: G. K. Hall, 1980], pp. 128–56) discussed such writing by women in terms of "the aesthetic of 'both / and'" (Hirsch, 115), I argue for a pragmatic approach that emphasizes multiple and changing relations. Compare also Christine Froula's explanation of Woolf's continual experimentation and Lily's disposable art ("Rewriting Genesis: Gender and Culture in Twentieth-Century Texts," *Tulsa Studies in Women's Literature* 7 [Fall 1988]: 197–220) [adapted by the *Editor*].

URMILA SESHAGIRI

Orienting Virginia Woolf: Race, Aesthetics, and Politics in *To the Lighthouse*†

* * *

In this essay, I argue that some of Woolf's most radical literary innovations arise from a material and a formalist politics of race. * * * My
argument concentrates on *To the Lighthouse* (1927), Woolf's elegiac
novel about an English family and the brutal end of Victorianism, in
which racial alterity offers a provocative source of feminist artistic
inspiration. While *To the Lighthouse* critiques the imperialist master-
narratives of early twentieth-century England, it also transforms
Oriental perspectives—encoded in Lily Briscoe's Chinese eyes—into
arbiters of meaning in a barren postwar world. Subtle tropes of racial
difference in *To the Lighthouse* show us that modern subjects cannot
maintain faith in an ideal of seamless, unified, globally dominant
white Englishness. The well-known feminist politics and formalist
aesthetics that answer this novel's questions depend on the often-
overlooked narrative position of racial identity: Woolf's remaking
of modern English femininity emerges out of complex assumptions
about the history, peoples, and art objects of non-Western nations.
Recovering the crucial but repressed role of racial politics in *To the
Lighthouse* reveals that this novel makes its most radical moves away
from literary conventions because of the various aesthetic and political racialisms that inform Woolf's narrative technique.

Reading Woolf, Reading Race

* * *

* * * While Woolf's objections to British imperialism are widely
known, I find that her critique of the Empire is self-reflexive, focused
on imperialism's damage to *England* rather than to subject-nations.
Woolf always challenges the master narratives of patriarchy and
British imperialism, but she does not additionally trouble England's
representations of the world outside itself. And because her anti-
imperialism does not manifest itself through claims about racial or
cultural equality, Woolf's novels often reproduce a wide range of
assumptions about nonwhite otherness as well as inscribe tropes of

† From *MFS: Modern Fiction Studies* 50.1 (2004): 58–84. Copyright © 2004 The Pur-
due Research Foundation. Reprinted with permission of Johns Hopkins University
Press. This essay reappears in revised form in Seshagiri's book *Race and the Modernist
Imagination* (Ithaca, NY: Cornell University Press, 2010). Page numbers for *To the
Lighthouse* refer to this Norton Critical Edition. Footnotes have been edited.

racial difference onto white English identity. In *To the Lighthouse,* Woolf's uses of exoticism, primitivism, and Orientalism are frequently disconnected from material colonialist practice; I propose a critical model for reading this novel that accommodates the full range of Woolf's representations of ethnicity and alterity. My goal here is not to claim that Woolf is racist or that her anti-imperialism is false, but rather that the various racially defined threads of her fiction bridge her political interests and aesthetic goals.

* * *

It is helpful to examine how Woolf's engagement with specific political and artistic discourses contributed to her literary racial poetics, and although her personal relationships have been exhaustively documented and commented on, I mention a few of them here to establish that they encouraged Woolf to interrogate cultural, national, and racial differences. The core of the anti-imperialism that emerges so strongly in Woolf's 1938 polemic, *Three Guineas,* was a reaction against a family legacy of patriarchal nationalism and imperial administration. While Woolf's great-grandfather James Stephen (1758–1832) was an abolitionist in the West Indies, her grandfather Sir James Stephen (1789–1859) was a founding figure of Queen Victoria's empire. Sir James, who served as Counsel to the Colonial Board of Trade, was dubbed "Mister Mother-Country" for his zealous devotion to the ideals and bureaucracy of the burgeoning British Empire at midcentury. His son and Woolf's father, Leslie Stephen (1832–1904), immortalized England's nation-builders in his *Dictionary of National Biography* (first published in 1882). Allegiance to England's colonizing and civilizing mission carried over into Woolf's own generation, most notably in Dorothea Stephen (1871–1965), Woolf's first cousin. Dorothea worked as a Christian missionary in India and published a volume called *Studies in Indian Thought* (1919), and her commitment to conversion drove Woolf to comment that "tampering with beliefs seems to me impertinent, insolent, corrupt beyond measure".[1] The Stephen family's long-standing complicity with colonialism compelled Woolf to resist what she saw as the inevitably oppressive results of overseas conquest.

Leslie Stephen's death in 1904 prompted Woolf and her siblings Vanessa, Thoby, and Adrian to move to 46 Gordon Square in London's then-unfashionable Bloomsbury district, a physical relocation that corresponded to a realignment of Woolf's ideological compass. In Thoby Stephen's famous Thursday night "at-homes" with his Cambridge friends, matters of racial and cultural difference began to shift away from the context of imperialism; Woolf stood at the

1. Woolf, *Letters* 4: 333.

center of the crossovers and conflicts that characterized the frequently race-focused discussions of Bloomsbury's politics and art.
While she kept company with E. M. Forster and Maynard Keynes,
who maintained serious interests in colonialism and national politics, she also brushed up against London's Orientalist fashion craze
through her friendship with Lady Ottoline Morrell. In Lady
Ottoline's company, Woolf not only attended salons where guests
regularly wore East Asian garb, but she herself appeared at a fancy-
dress party costumed as Cleopatra. Nonwhite racial identities, freed
from their dominant association with colonized subjects, became in
Woolf's world—as they were becoming for the English avant-garde—
gateways into disruptive or subversive cultural possibilities. * * *

Woolf's involvement with racial and imperialist concerns was not
confined to abstract discussion and comfortable travel. Her roles in
two Bloomsbury incidents, the Dreadnought Hoax of 1910 and the
Post-Impressionist Ball of 1911, signal an active investment in racial
difference and its possibilities for undermining English cultural
authority.[2] * * * The Bloomsburyites' antimilitarism reveals an ironic
complicity with the very imperial violence the hoax intended to
deride, and Woolf's participation in the incident anticipates the
complex, racialized challenges to white British hegemony that crowd
her mature fiction.

In the year following the Dreadnought Hoax, Roger Fry's exhibit
"Manet and the Post-Impressionists" enabled Woolf to participate
in a second, smaller act of racially charged social subversion. * * *
[S]he used the racial politics of postimpressionism to achieve a minor
sexual and social liberation for herself. The exhibit itself, with its
works by Gauguin, Cézanne, Matisse, Picasso, Manet, and van Gogh,[3]
shocked London's museum-going public; art critics lambasted Fry
for his choice of artists and subject matter. The poster advertising
the exhibit, which Marianna Torgovnick hails as the "English debut
of the primitive in high culture" (85), featured a Gauguin painting of
a nude "native" woman standing next to a Tahitian statue. Both the
form and the content of the exhibit's works scandalized the public:
the nakedness of nonwhite subjects presented through postimpressionism's nonmimetic contours shattered the English art world's
assumptions about aesthetic civility. Gleefully aware that the exhibit's
focus on non-Western subjects appalled London audiences, Woolf
and her sister Vanessa Bell attended the Post-Impressionist Ball in
March 1911 dressed as savages "à la Gauguin" (Bishop 22). Vanessa

---

2. For the Dreadnought Hoax, for which Woolf, her brother Adrian, and some friends put on
   blackface and costumes and masqueraded as the Abyssinian emperor and his entou-
   rage in order to mock the authority of the British navy, see Hermione Lee, *Virginia
   Woolf*, pp. 278–79 [*Editor*].
3. See "The French Post-Impressionists," this edition, pp. 239–40 [*Editor*].

recalls that "we wore brilliant flowers and beads, we browned our legs and arms and had very little on beneath the draperies,"[4] and Virginia writes, "Vanessa and I were practically naked."[5] The spectacle of the "bare-shouldered bare-legged" sisters at the ball outraged "indignant ladies who swept out in protest" (Q. Bell, vol. 1, 170). * * * Virginia and Vanessa's cross-cultural masquerade rejected Victorian modesty in the same way the postimpressionist paintings rejected artistic conventions; like the Dreadnought Hoax, Woolf's challenge to English social norms at the Post-Impressionist Ball reveals an early interest in reordering the boundaries of Englishness through tropes of racial difference.

The 1910 postimpressionist exhibit marked the beginning of Woolf's engagement with the intersection of racial difference and the fine arts in London. The famously expansive circle of artists and writers in Bloomsbury connected Woolf to creative milieux where she encountered modernist aesthetic experimentation based on the forms and tropes of Asian and African arts. Between 1911 and 1918, several members of the Bloomsbury group attended performances by Sergei Diaghilev's fantastically eclectic Ballets Russes, which captivated Covent Garden audiences with performances that merged Western classicism with polyglot global traditions. * * *

In the same years that Diaghilev's ballets were the rage in London, Woolf began her loyal patronage of Roger Fry's many artistic ventures that advocated cross-cultural aesthetic dialogues. As I will discuss in detail later, Fry's formalist doctrines about mixing non-Western art with Western traditions would acquire a feminist dimension in Woolf's racially inflected narrative experimentation in *To the Lighthouse*. Woolf visited the exhibits Fry sponsored, attended his lectures on art history, and, of course, bought art objects from the short-lived Omega Workshops, whose pottery, textiles, furnishings, paintings, and sculptures bore traces of Asian, African, and Native American influences. * * * At a cultural moment when various factions of the London avant-garde were absorbed with expressing a new kind of English artistry through racial difference, Woolf similarly located stylistic potential in the art objects of non-Western cultures.

* * *

Lily Briscoe's Chinese Eyes

To the Lighthouse is Virginia Woolf's most private and domestic novel, set in a seaside house on the Isle of Skye. Of Woolf's major novels, *To the Lighthouse* is the least explicitly about race or Empire. * * *

4. Vanessa Bell, "Memories of Roger Fry," quoted in Lee, *Virginia Woolf*, p. 287.
5. Woolf, "Old Bloomsbury," in *Moments of Being*, p. 201.

Government, Empire, and war flicker on the novel's peripheries, subordinated to the details and politics of family life. But the marginal imperial, and racial paradigms in *To the Lighthouse* emerge as the sites where Woolf remakes the English self: Woolf's deployment of racial alterity in this novel enables her to envision the "life of Monday or Tuesday" in terms other than those dictated by masculine privilege,[6] and her feminist recuperation of narrative development overturns English patriarchy's worldview with discourses and tropes from non-English cultures. The historical, aesthetic, and imperial discourses running through *To the Lighthouse* meet at the site of racial difference, producing an extraordinary balance among three apparently contradictory ideological positions: this novel opposes imperialism, insists on racial hierarchies, *and* valorizes non-white otherness.

Each of the novel's three sections questions the stability of English identities rooted in the ideals of a racially exploitative Empire. The first section, "The Window," problematizes the Ramsay family's relationship to the British Empire through equal measures of nostalgia and critique; while the Ramsay house itself metonymically suggests the material and ideological goals of imperial enterprise, the members of the Ramsay family variously comply with and repudiate the Empire's values. In "Time Passes," the apocalyptic devastation that describes the Great War also suggests that imperially dictated identity is fundamentally hollow, prey to the same forces that supposedly protect it. And finally, in "The Lighthouse," Lily Briscoe supplies a new ending to an imperial English life-narrative, committing to an artistry that safeguards her from marriage and the violence of a postwar public sphere. Paradoxically, Woolf secures a new English feminism by attributing non-Western characteristics and perspectives to Lily, whose "little Chinese eyes" exclude her socially *and* elevate her artistically. To articulate a break with nineteenth-century literary mimesis, *To the Lighthouse* incorporates imperializing discourses about race as well as the racialized discourse of English formalism: Woolf's construction of Lily Briscoe as a modern feminist rests on a connection between essentializing, Orientalist attitudes and the visual arts.

Unremarkable events in a single day—taking a walk, going shopping, hosting a dinner party—present competing critical angles on colonialist and racist exploitation in the novel's opening section. Despite continually shifting centers of narrative consciousness, imperialism, like the lighthouse beam, remains a fixed, steady presence throughout the novel's first section, "The Window." On one hand, the Ramsay household, filled with artifacts of imperialist

6. Woolf, "Modern Fiction," *Essays* 4: 160.

exploitation, emblematizes the transformation of peoples and cultures into commodities for English consumption. These commodities—a book about "the Savage Customs of Polynesia" (23), Mrs. Ramsay's "opal necklace, which Uncle James had brought her from India" (62) and the "horrid skull" sent to the family as a hunting trophy (86)—serve as mute reminders of colonized nations whose resources have been plundered. Mr. Ramsay, the patriarch who presides over these commodities, possesses a colonizing, linear intelligence that assimilates the world in terms of power and struggle, hierarchy and history: "Does the progress of civilisation depend upon great men? Is the lot of the average human being better now than in the time of the Pharaohs? . . . Possibly the greatest good requires the existence of a slave class" (35). The Ramsay house and the patriarch at its helm buttress Victorian imperialism, providing the economic and ideological motivation for expanding England's global control. But Empire's solid material presence in the Ramsays' quotidian routine is only applauded by male characters. Woolf's female characters hint at England's progressively fading allegiance to imperialist principles, mocking narratives of colonial life and the Victorian reverence for national institutions. Mrs. Ramsay famously reconstitutes her husband's patriarchal authority as "the fatal sterility of the male" (31); her richly conceived interior life ironizes and subverts the masculine rhetoric of familial hierarchy. The life story and opium-stained beard of the poet Augustus Carmichael invite Mrs. Ramsay's skepticism; his past appears to her an exercise in futility: "an early marriage; poverty; going to India; translating a little poetry 'very beautifully, I believe,' being willing to teach the boys Persian or Hindustanee, but what really was the use of that?" (10–11). And the daughters of the Ramsay family suggest a resistance to the late Victorian Empire that will increase in future generations ("for there was in all their minds a mute questioning of deference and chivalry, of the Bank of England and the Indian Empire, of ringed fingers and lace" [7–8]). Thus, "The Window" represents imperialism through sexual polarities: the male characters embrace the imperialist saturation of English private life, while female characters struggle against a totalizing imperial worldview.

The cracks in imperialist and nationalist ideals broaden into chasms in "Time Passes." Using physical and metaphysical violence to represent the horrors of the Great War, Woolf annihilates the family network she has developed so carefully in the novel's opening. By truncating the stories of these characters and describing their deaths between indifferent parentheses, Woolf indicates that the larger life-narratives they represented—Mrs. Ramsay's all-encompassing maternalism, Prue Ramsay's marriage and implicit entry into her mother's role, Andrew Ramsay's dutifully enacted patriotic violence—can have no closure in the postwar modern world. The savage wrecking of these three lives exposes the impermanence of national identities rooted in conquest. By literally killing at-home support for imperialism abroad, Woolf uncovers a deep-rooted cultural need for new narratives of Englishness. Indeed, if the deaths of Mrs. Ramsay, Prue, and Andrew represent the end of Victorianism, the natural chaos assaulting the Ramsay house reaches back to the larger cultural instability of post-Elizabethan imperial Englishness. Although "Time Passes" never mentions a specific historical moment, Woolf's metaphors in this section evoke a historical chronology that begins long before World War I, intimating that English identity has been grounded in asymmetrical, racially exploitative power relations for centuries. Woolf does not illuminate racial inequalities by accommodating the perspectives of nonwhite characters or exploited colonial subjects; rather, she uses the recurring symbols of tea and china to render impossible any belief in the unified, undifferentiated white English subject.

Amid the storms and dust and dampness that beset the Ramsay house, Woolf's images of the family's teacups and china remind us that even the most banal signifiers of English civility stem from centuries of racial exploitation. At the war's inception, the china is "already furred, tarnished, cracked"; then, the "repeated shocks" of the war "cracked the tea-cups"; finally, the dishes silently embody postwar resignation to destruction: "Let the broken glass and the china lie out on the lawn and be tangled over with grass and wild berries" (97, 99, 103). Tea and china, although associated with Englishness for centuries, are nonetheless imported and appropriated from the East with the same violence as Mrs. Ramsay's jewels or the skull that hangs in the children's bedroom. To borrow from Sara Suleri, imperialist history-making is always "an act of cultural transcription so overdetermined as to dissipate the logic of origins, or the rational framework of chronologies" (9). Transforming tea and china into signifiers for Englishness stems from a similarly overdetermined historical process, and Woolf's multiple references to the Ramsays' tea sets and china form a palimpsest of absent colonial spaces and practices.

Porcelain-making and widespread tea-drinking both originally hail from the Tang dynasty in China during the sixth century AD; their migration to England was enabled by a vast network of British cultural appropriation. When Queen Elizabeth founded the British East India Company in 1600, Britain began its broad-based trade with China, importing silk, tea, and "China ware," as the British called Chinese porcelain dishes. In 1744, when "China ware" had become a commonplace feature of English homes, two porcelain factories opened in England to compete with and eventually undersell the Chinese imports. Although the fast-growing European porcelain industry influenced later designs in English porcelain, the first English manufacturers owed their methods as well as their aesthetics to East Asian traditions; English porcelain was for a long time derived directly from Chinese and Japanese techniques.[7] By the turn of the twentieth century, British porcelain factories ranged from small operations in Ireland and Wales to the great houses of Spode and Wedgwood in England, and the flood of Chinese imports had slowed to an economically insignificant trickle. "China ware," initially valued for its foreign cachet, became assimilated into the English domestic sphere until only the name bespoke its Eastern origins.

Like porcelain, tea's Eastern origins were overwritten by English practices that burgeoned as the Empire grew stronger. The East India Company first introduced tea into England in 1684, when the Company acquired a trading post in the Chinese province of Canton. Even more than porcelain, the history of tea drinking in England supplies a map of colonial brutality: the Opium Wars in 1839 and 1857, arising from Britain's enforced opium-for-tea exchange with China, are but the most extreme consequence.[8] As tea's popularity soared in England over the eighteenth and nineteenth centuries, the colonists worked to cultivate tea in their own territories and become less reliant on Chinese imports. Between 1850 and 1930, the English planted hybrid strains of Chinese tea in Assam, Malawi, and Uganda; Thomas Lipton founded his tea empire in Ceylon; the Brooke Bond Company began cultivating tea in Nairobi; and English colonists introduced the practice of tea drinking to Iran, Morocco, and Turkey.[9] In *To the Lighthouse,* the Ramsays' tea set, found decaying in "all oblivion" by Mrs. McNab, portends the larger destiny of a nation built on what is borrowed or taken by force (104). Tea—imported, transplanted, and imposed as social ritual—signifies the hybrid, culturally divided quality of Englishness.

The minutiae of "Time Passes," like the colonial artifacts that appear in "The Lighthouse," describe an imperial Englishness that has depended historically on the not-English and the not-white. And if the novel's second section begins by exposing the mutually constitutive relationship between racial and cultural violence and English selfhood, its conclusion foreshadows Woolf's final rewriting of white English identity:

> The sigh of all the seas breaking in measure round the isles soothed them; the night wrapped them; nothing broke their

7. For a detailed history of English porcelain, see Young and Battle.
8. For a historical overview of Britain's tea trade from the late seventeenth century through the twentieth century, see Forrest, Chow and Kramer, and Campbell.
9. See Beauthéae.

> sleep, until, the birds beginning and the dawn weaving their thin voices in to its whiteness, a cart grinding, a dog somewhere barking, the sun lifted the curtains, broke the veil on their eyes, and Lily Briscoe stirring in her sleep. She clutched at her blankets as a faller clutches at the turf on the edge of a cliff. Her eyes opened wide. Here she was again, she thought, sitting bolt upright in bed. Awake. (106)

The final emphasis on Lily Briscoe's eyes—which are repeatedly described as "little" and "Chinese" in the novel's opening section—hints that the novel's conflicts will end with a new visual order and that the fundamental act of perception holds the potential to transform English selfhood. Through Lily's "little Chinese eyes," the longstanding imperialist binaries (colonizer/colonized, white/nonwhite, civilized/primitive) symbolized by tea, china, and the other material evidence of British rule will lose their meaning in the postwar world. However, Woolf replaces these binaries with new racial divisions that make alternative modes of knowledge and perception available to the English subject. Although *To the Lighthouse* renders invisible the colonized subjects whose resources prop up the Ramsays' material existence, it offers a new racial alterity that severs the tie between the English individual and an imperial ideal of collective nationalism.

Reading Lily Briscoe's artistic development in dialogue with the racially derived doctrines of early twentieth-century English formalism illuminates how *To the Lighthouse* transforms an essentialized understanding of nonwhite racial identity into a template for modern English selfhood. Clive Bell, Woolf's brother-in-law and an influential London art critic, posited one of the most stringent theories of English formalism in his 1914 volume, *Art*. Breaking away from received Western ideas about the symbolic, religious, or ennobling potential of art, Bell's theory of "significant form" privileges abstraction over mimetic representation: "[I]t need only be agreed that forms arranged and combined according to certain unknown and mysterious laws do move us in a particular way, and that it is the business of an artist so to combine and arrange them that they shall move us."[1] Significant form democratizes the aesthetic experience because "we need bring nothing with us from life, no knowledge of its ideas and affairs, no familiarity with its emotions."[2] Because Bell views form as autotelic, rising above "the accidents of time and history,"[3] *Art* moves freely through chronologies and geographies and claims formal commonalities among fifth-century Wei figurines,

---

1. Clive Bell, *Art*, p. 11, and see "[Significant Form]," this edition, pp. 235–39 [*Editor*].
2. Bell, *Art*, 25.
3. Bell, *Art*, 36.

Peruvian pottery, sixth-century Byzantine mosaics, and primitivist drawings by modern European artists like Cézanne and Picasso.

Bell's formalist theories gesture toward but do not probe deeply into the art of non-Western cultures. Fry's formalism, however, centralizes the impact of racial identity on artistic potential, adding very specific cultural associations to Bell's rhetoric of formal aesthetic purity. Fry's 1920 collection of essays on formalist aesthetics, *Vision and Design,* spans an eclectic range of artistic traditions, containing essays on paintings by Giotto and Matisse, as well as on artwork by Ottoman and Mohammedan artists. The book's illustrations include a sculpted Negro head, a Persian miniature, a Sassanian miniature, and drawings by Durer, el Greco, and Rouault. Whereas Bell's *Art* posits an aesthetics of appreciation, Fry's *Vision and Design* employs racial determinism to explain why non-Western cultures create *form* and Western cultures create *concepts.* In its complex cultural dialectic between Eastern, Western, and African arts, *Vision and Design* exalts nonwhite artists whose marvelous creative facilities shame the rational, post-Enlightenment Western artist.

Two essays from *Vision and Design* are particularly relevant to my reading of *To the Lighthouse*: "The Art of the Bushmen," where Fry examines Paleolithic line drawings of animals, and "Negro Sculpture," where Fry discusses the artistic process of "nameless savages" who create exquisitely true sculptures of the human form.[4] * * *

* * * Fry promises English artists that accessing formal purity is a worthy and attainable goal. The artistic vision of the Negro or Bushman, Fry urges, should be wrested from its culturally paralyzed origins and transported to the sophisticated, civilized, white Western world. If English artists hope to jettison their own moribund artistic legacy, they will have to emulate those nonwhite artists whose perceptions remain unclouded by the trappings of modernity.

The theory that race determines one's relation to formal aesthetics manifested itself concretely in the art objects made by Fry's arts collective, the Omega Workshops. Fry founded the Omega in 1913, hoping to vivify the decorative arts in England by encouraging original and provocative designs for furniture, textiles, and pottery. To this end, he invited twenty-five young artists (including Vanessa Bell, Duncan Grant, Wyndham Lewis, Frederick Etchells, Ethel Sands, and Henri Doucet) to join the Omega Workshops at 33 Fitzroy Street in Bloomsbury. The Omega opened on July 8, 1913, and the artists displayed an astounding array of works that included beads, parasols, carpets, stained glass, tiles, vases, screens, clothing, menu cards, and

4. Fry, *Vision and Design*, pp. 56–68. For another reading of Fry's embrace of African art in relation to the Dreadnought Hoax and other Bloomsbury racial performances, see Gretchen Gerzina, "Bushmen and Blackface: Bloomsbury and 'Race'," *The South Carolina Review* 38.2 (2006): 46–64 [*Editor*].

children's toys. Ironically, what Fry dubbed the Omega's "definitively English tradition" drew its primary inspiration from decidedly non-English cultures.[5] From the Workshop's outset, the Omega artists rejected conventional representation and pledged to follow the paths of less "civilized" cultures where art is unspoiled by intellectualism and progress; their efforts to imitate non-Western, premodern perceptual modes supported Fry's view that aesthetic integrity emerged out of an unthinking, sensuous creative spirit. Fry's introduction to the Omega Workshops Catalogue reinforces a racialized formulation of artistry consistent with the writings in *Vision and Design*, opening the doors for a more fully global view of decorative art than London had seen:

> If you look at a pot or a woven cloth made by a negro savage of the Congo with the crude instruments at his disposal, you may begin by despising it for its want of finish. . . . But if you will allow the poor savage's handiwork a longer contemplation you will find something in it of greater value and significance than in the Sévres china or Lyons velvet.
>
> It will become apparent that the negro enjoyed making his pot or cloth, that he pondered delightedly over the possibilities of his craft and that his enjoyment finds expression in many ways; and as these become increasingly apparent to you, you share his joy in creation, and in that forget the roughness of the result. . . . [The Omega Workshops] try to keep the spontaneous freshness of primitive or peasant work while satisfying the needs and expressing the feelings of modern cultivated man. (qtd. in Anscombe 32)

The Omega artists capitalized on the ahistorical leanings of formalism, confidently imitating and modifying artistic forms from Africa, the Middle East, and Asia. Accordingly, the artwork produced by the Omega Workshops between 1913 and 1919 demonstrates a dizzying, dazzling cultural hybridity; the Omega artists' varied use of race anticipates Virginia Woolf's own deployment of competing racial discourses in her novels. * * * Omega art embodies the belief that non-Western art is shaped by purer, more direct vision than Western art, and that nonwhite racial otherness floats freely, infinitely interchangeable and adaptable.

Woolf's formalist literary inventions in *To the Lighthouse* reflect the ahistoric, nonmimetic aesthetic philosophy that compelled English formalist painting, sculpture, and decorative arts. In a letter to Fry written shortly after *To the Lighthouse* was published, Woolf famously

5. Fry is quoted in Spalding, *Roger Fry*, p. 176.

commits to a narrative formalism that eschews any alliance with symbolism:

> I meant *nothing* by the lighthouse. One has to have a central line down the middle of the book to hold the design together. I saw that all sorts of feelings would accrue to this, but I refused to think them out, and trusted that people would make the deposit for their own emotions—which they have done, one thinking it means one thing another another. I can't manage Symbolism except in this vague, generalised way. Whether its right or wrong I don't know, but directly I'm told what a thing means, it becomes hateful to me.[6]

Further, Woolf shares Fry's approach to achieving aesthetic purity through racial difference: in *To the Lighthouse*, Woolf's most radical revisions to a nineteenth-century literary legacy stem from the racial alterity she inscribes onto Lily Briscoe. Woolf's Orientalist depiction of Lily Briscoe catalyzes the novel's celebration of formalist aesthetics; race-based formalism in *To the Lighthouse* overturns a narrative economy traditionally structured around marriage and social stability. That Lily Briscoe uses her painting to escape the marriage-plot is, of course, a widely accepted feminist reading of *To the Lighthouse*'s breakthrough modernist ending. Less obvious is the reading that the encrypted foreignness of Lily Briscoe's "little Chinese eyes" first forces Lily's sexual devaluation and subsequently enables her artistic freedom. Racial difference, in other words, provides a meeting ground for social critique and aesthetic innovation in *To the Lighthouse*.

Lily Briscoe's tortured views of patriarchy and marriage shape her reactions to the Ramsay family in the novel's opening section, "The Window," where the narrative flits in and out of her consciousness. In "The Lighthouse," when Lily has rejected marriage and conventional femininity, Woolf makes her the novel's final center of consciousness. Lily's heightened narrative authority is a function of her implicit racial alterity: Woolf uses Lily's "Chinese eyes" to effect the transition between Lily the "skimpy old maid" and Lily the accomplished artist (131). To guarantee Lily's exclusion from marital and sexual economies, Woolf alludes to Lily's Chinese eyes whenever romantic possibilities arise. From Lily's first appearance in the novel, Woolf links her Oriental features to her sexual unavailability: "With her little Chinese eyes and her puckered-up face, she would never marry; one could not take her painting very seriously; she was an independent little creature, and Mrs. Ramsay liked her for it" (15–16). The "Chinese eyes" invite a host of reductive Orientalist associations; Woolf repeatedly characterizes Lily as inscrutable, diminutive,

6. *Letters* 3: 385; this edition, p. 182 [*Editor*].

and unsuited for the married life that awaits the newly engaged
Minta Doyle and Paul Rayley: "[Lily] faded, under Minta's glow;
became more inconspicuous than ever, in her little grey dress with
her little puckered face and her little Chinese eyes. Everything about
her was so small. . . . There was in Lily a thread of something; a flare
of something; something of her own which Mrs. Ramsay liked very
much indeed, but no man would, she feared" (79). While suggestions
of Oriental identity impose a mandatory sexual exile on Lily, they
also grant acuity to her reactions against social convention. Lily
resists sympathizing with Charles Tansley's "burning desire to break
into the conversation" during Mrs. Ramsay's dinner-party: "But, she
thought, screwing up her Chinese eyes, and remembering how he
sneered at women, 'can't paint, can't write,' why should I help him to
relieve himself?" (69). Lily perceives marriage as a "degradation" and
a "dilution" (77), willingly distancing herself from the paradigms of
English femininity trapping Mrs. Ramsay and Prue. The Chinese
eyes work to critique as well as to exclude, and Orientalizing Lily's
vision helps Woolf to write her out of Victorian patriarchal expectations. As a foreign object of the Victorian gaze *and* as a perceiver in
her own right, Lily occupies a textual space bounded and stabilized
by racial difference.

   The Chinese eyes that look mutinously on gendered social traditions also resist constraining artistic traditions. In concert with
Roger Fry's praise for the nonwhite artist's aesthetic sensibility,
Woolf constructs Lily's resistance to artistic realism as a function
of her Oriental vision. Lily's evolving artistic vision mirrors the novel's
critique of a late nineteenth-century worldview: her first painting is
a tortured attempt to express meaning in the Ramsays' world, while
the complete self-sufficiency of her final painting rejects prewar
social structures. As she recognizes that she has no place in conventionally ordered Victorian society, Lily's paintings become less
mimetic and increasingly abstract, pieces of formalist art whose self-
referentiality protects the female artist from patriarchy's demands.
Lily enters the novel at work on a portrait of Mrs. Ramsay and James,
executing this painting in a prewar moment when other artists paint
impressionistic "lemon-coloured sailing-boats, and pink women
on the beach" (13). Rejecting Impressionism's injunction to "see
everything pale, elegant, semitransparent," Lily struggles for an art
form that breaks completely free of its object (17). And although
the "triangular purple shape" she paints to represent Mrs. Ramsay
and James seems detached from conventional reverence for a mother
and child, Lily subordinates aesthetic achievement to her worry
that the painting will "never be seen; never be hung" (42, 39). Because
Lily looks beyond the canvas boundaries to determine the painting's worth, this first effort at formal purity fails to achieve what Fry

calls "the conviction of a new and definite reality."[7] The broken and devastated material world of the war's aftermath demands the creation of such a reality; it is only then that Lily's Chinese eyes envision a painting that breaks free of the patriarchal and imperialist hierarchies of the Ramsays' world.

Lily awakens to a newly broken civilization at the end of "Time Passes," when, after a stormy night, "tenderly the light fell (it seemed to come through her eyelids)" (106). Eyelids have long been used to differentiate "Oriental" peoples from "Caucasian" peoples; this image not only calls attention to Lily's race-based sexual exile, but also anticipates the fruitful connection between Lily's racial identity and her artistic potential. After returning to the Ramsay household and rediscovering her old canvas, Lily hunts for an art form that bears no correspondence to the sexual and racial belief systems of late Victorian English culture. Impressionist paintings adhere too faithfully to the objects they represent, and the material realities of prewar existence have been shattered: ultimately, Lily arrives at a formalist methodology that promises both artistic autonomy and an alternative to the suspended emotional and social expectations that torment the other characters. Anguished by the bleak, incomplete landscape of the Ramsay family, Lily turns to her easel, "screwing up her little Chinese eyes in her small puckered face" (115). Her final, triumphant painting floats free of any signifiers of imperial Victorianism:

> There it was—her picture. Yes, with all its greens and blues, its lines running up and across, its attempt at something. It would be hung up in attics, she thought; it would be destroyed. But what did that matter? She asked herself, taking up her brush again. She looked at the steps; they were empty; she looked at her canvas; it was blurred. With a sudden intensity, as if she saw it clear for a second, she drew a line there, in the center. It was done; it was finished. Yes, she thought, laying down her brush in extreme fatigue, I have had my vision. (150)

Neither the painting's impermanence nor its absence of symbolic meaning hinders Lily from a sense of completion. Her "little Chinese eyes" attain the "ultra-primitive directness of vision" that Fry attributes to East Asian cultures, and her arrangement of forms is liberating because it is finally autotelic. Privileging the completion of Lily's painting over mending broken familial structures, Woolf creates a racially differentiated model for modern English subjectivity that holds itself separate from patriarchal and imperialist hierarchies. Lily Briscoe's "vision" signals a new English femininity that, paradoxically, employs Orientalist creativity to conceive of itself apart

7. Fry, *Vision and Design*, p. 167.

from an Englishness rooted in the colonialist domination of nonwhite races.

Read in the context of Fry's ideas and the Omega Workshops, *To the Lighthouse* resonates with an Orientalism that elevates and emulates the nonwhite, non-Western other's artistry. By scripting Lily's "vision" as the solution to ideologically inadequate or unstable Victorian life-narratives, *To the Lighthouse* answers one set of racialized codes with another. The art that will grant fresh meaning to postwar modernity is as marked by cultural appropriation as the Victorian life-narratives destroyed by the war. The novel's different modes of racial appropriation, which by turn exploit, essentialize, or redeem the resources of non-Western cultures, work together in Woolf's text to create an arc of Englishness that is always racially divided. Despite the novel's wholly private English setting, we see that Woolf carves out abundant textual space for multiple negotiations of racial difference. To read *To the Lighthouse* merely as an opposition to imperialist or nationalist violence is to ignore the rich cultural texture of Woolf's writing: the several discourses operating in the novel's exploration of feminism and aesthetics rewrite Englishness as a confluence of racially differentiated perspectives.

WORKS CITED

Anscombe, Isabelle. *Omega and After: Bloomsbury and the Decorative Arts.* New York: Thames, 1981.

Battle, David, ed. *Sotheby's Concise Encyclopedia of Porcelain.* London: Conran, 1990.

Beauthéae, Nadine. "Tea Barons." *The Book of Tea.* Ed. Ghislaine Bavoillot. Trans. Deke Dusinberre. Paris: Flammarion, 1992. 57–99.

Bell, Quentin. *Virginia Woolf: A Biography.* 2 vols. New York: Harvest, 1972.

Bishop, Edward. *A Chronology of Virginia Woolf.* London: MacMillan, 1989.

Campbell, Dawn. *The Tea Book.* Louisiana: Pelican, 1995.

Chow, Kit, and Ione Kramer. *All the Tea in China.* San Francisco: China, 1990.

Forrest, Denys. *Tea for the British: The Social and Economic History of a Famous Trade.* London: Chatto, 1973.

Suleri, Sara. *The Rhetoric of English India.* Chicago: U of Chicago P, 1992.

Torgovnick, Marianna. *Gone Primitive: Savage Intellects, Modern Lives.* Chicago: U of Chicago P, 1990.

Young, Hilary. *English Porcelain, 1745–95: Its Makers, Design, Marketing and Consumption.* London: Victoria & Albert Museum, 1999.

Virginia Woolf: A Chronology

1832	Leslie Stephen born, London.
1846	Julia Prinsep Jackson born, Kolkata, India.
1867	Julia marries Herbert Duckworth (children: Stella, George, Gerald); Leslie marries Minny Thackeray (daughter: Laura).
1870	Death of Herbert Duckworth.
1875	Death of Minny Thackeray.
1878	Leslie Stephen and Julia Prinsep Duckworth marry on March 26; live at 22 Hyde Park Gate, London.
1879	Vanessa Stephen born on May 30.
1880	Thoby Stephen born on September 8.
1882	Adeline Virginia Stephen born on January 25; Leslie Stephen purchases lease on Talland House, St. Ives, Cornwall, where the family spends every summer through 1894.
1883	Adrian Stephen born on October 27.
1895	Death of Julia Stephen on May 5.
1897	Marriage followed by death of half-sister Stella Duckworth.
1899	Thoby goes to Cambridge and meets Lytton Strachey, Leonard Woolf, and Clive Bell.
1904	Death of Leslie Stephen; with her Stephen siblings, moves to Bloomsbury; first publications: two short essays for *The Guardian* in December.
1905	The Stephen siblings revisit St. Ives for the first time since 1894.
1906	The Stephen siblings travel to Greece; Thoby dies.
1907	Vanessa marries Clive Bell.
1910	Dreadnought Hoax; first Post-Impressionist Exhibition, London.
1912	Marries Leonard Woolf; second Post-Impressionist Exhibition.
1915	First novel published: *The Voyage Out,* completed 1913; Virginia and Leonard purchase Hogarth House, Richmond.

1916	Battle of the Somme, July; Vanessa, her children, and Duncan Grant move to Charleston farmhouse, Firle, Sussex.
1917	Virginia and Leonard found Hogarth Press.
1918	Votes for women over thirty; end of World War I.
1919	*Night and Day;* purchase of Monk's House, Rodmell, Sussex, as a holiday home.
1922	*Jacob's Room;* meets Vita Sackville-West.
1924	Virginia and Leonard move back to London; Hogarth begins publishing Freud's *Collected Papers.*
1925	*Mrs. Dalloway; The Common Reader;* begins *To the Lighthouse.*
1926	General Strike, May; *Victorian Photographs of Famous Men and Fair Women.*
1927	*To the Lighthouse* published, May 5; Hogarth publishes Roger Fry's *Cézanne.*
1928	*Orlando;* gives lectures that will become *A Room of One's Own.*
1929	*A Room of One's Own.*
1931	*The Waves.*
1932	*The Second Common Reader.*
1934	Death of Roger Fry.
1937	*The Years;* death of Julian Bell, Vanessa's older son, in Spanish Civil War.
1938	*Three Guineas.*
1939	World War II begins.
1939–40	Writes "A Sketch of The Past."
1940	*Roger Fry: A Biography.*
1941	Finishes revising *Between the Acts;* death by suicide, March 28.

Selected Bibliography

• Indicates work excerpted in this Norton Critical Edition

Selected Editions of *To the Lighthouse*

Caughie, Pamela L., Nick Hayward, Mark Hussey, Peter Shillingsburg, and George K. Thiruvathukal, eds. Woolf Online. Web. <www.woolfonline.com>.

Haule, James M., Virginia Woolf, and Charles Mauron, "'Le Temps Passe' and the Original Typescript: An Early Version of the 'Time Passes' Section of *To the Lighthouse*." *Twentieth Century Literature* 29:3 (Autumn 1983): 267–311.

Woolf, Virginia. *To the Lighthouse: The Original Holograph Draft*, transcribed and edited, with Woolf's notes and outlines for the novel, by Susan Dick. Toronto: U of Toronto P, 1982; London: Hogarth Press, 1983.

Woolf, Virginia. *To the Lighthouse*. Ed. Susan Dick, Shakespeare Head Edition. Oxford: Blackwell, 1992.

Woolf, Virginia. *To the Lighthouse*. Annotated and with an introduction by Mark Hussey. Orlando: Harcourt, 2005.

Other Works by Virginia Woolf

• Woolf, Virginia. A *Passionate Apprentice: The Early Journals, 1897–1909*. Ed. Mitchell A. Leaska. San Diego: Harcourt Brace Jovanovich, 1990.

———. *The Complete Shorter Fiction*. Ed. Susan Dick. New York: Harcourt Brace Jovanovich, 1980.

———. *The Diary*, 5 vols. Ed. Anne Olivier Bell. Harcourt, 1978–84.

———. *The Essays*, 6 vols. Ed. Andrew McNeillie and Stuart M. Clarke. Harcourt, 1988–2011.

———. *The Letters*, 6 vols. Ed. Nigel Nicolson and Joanne Trautmann. Harcourt, 1975–80.

• ———. *Moments of Being*, 2nd ed. Ed. Jeanne Schulkind. San Diego: Harcourt Brace Jovanovich, 1985.

———. *Roger Fry: A Biography*. New York: Harcourt Brace, 1940.

• Woolf, Virginia, Vanessa Bell, and Thoby Stephen. *Hyde Park Gate News: The Stephen Family Newspaper*. Ed. Gill Lowe. London: Hesperus, 2005.

Sources on Woolf and on *To the Lighthouse*

Abel, Elizabeth. *Virginia Woolf and the Fictions of Psychoanalysis*. Chicago: U of Chicago P, 1989.

Banfield, Ann. *The Phantom Table: Woolf, Fry, Russell and the Epistemology of Modernism*. Cambridge: Cambridge UP, 2000.

Barrett, Eileen, and Patricia Cramer, eds. *Virginia Woolf: Lesbian Readings*. New York: New York UP, 1997.

Beer, Gillian. *Virginia Woolf: The Common Ground*. Ann Arbor: U of Michigan P, 1996.

Bell, Quentin. *Virginia Woolf: A Biography*, 2 vols. New York: Harcourt Brace Jovanovich, 1972.

Berman, Jessica, ed. *A Companion to Virginia Woolf*. Oxford: Wiley-Blackwell, 2016.

• Bowlby, Rachel. *Virginia Woolf: Feminist Destinations*. Oxford: Blackwell, 1988.

Brannigan, John. *Archipelagic Modernisms: Literature in the Irish and British Isles, 1890–1970*. Edinburgh: Edinburgh UP, 2015.

Briggs, Julia. *Reading Virginia Woolf*. San Diego: Harcourt Brace Jovanovich, 2006.

———. *Virginia Woolf: An Inner Life*. San Diego: Harcourt Brace Jovanovich, 2005.

• Brown, Paul Tolliver. "Relativity, Quantum Physics, and Consciousness in Virginia Woolf's *To the Lighthouse*." *Journal of Modern Literature* 32.3 (2009): 39–62.

• Caughie, Pamela L. *Virginia Woolf and Postmodernism: Literature in Quest and Question of Itself*. Urbana: U of Illinois P, 1991.

Caughie, Pamela L., and Diana L. Swanson, eds. *Virginia Woolf: Writing the World*. Clemson U Digital P, 2015.

Daugherty, Beth Rigel, and Mary Beth Pringle, eds. *Approaches to Teaching To the Lighthouse*. New York: Modern Language Association, 2001.

Dubino, Jeanne, Gill Lowe, Vara S. Neverow, and Kathryn Simpson, eds. *Virginia Woolf: Critical and Primary Sources, 1975–2014*, 4 vols. London and New York: Bloomsbury, 2021.

Ellis, Steve. *Virginia Woolf and the Victorians*. Cambridge: Cambridge UP, 2007.

Flint, Kate. "Virginia Woolf and the General Strike." *Essays in Criticism: A Quarterly Journal of Literary Criticism* 36.4(1986): 319–34.

Friedman, Susan Stanford. "Lyric Subversion of Narrative in Women's Writing: Virginia Woolf and the Tyranny of Plot," In *Reading Narrative: Form, Ethics, Ideology*. Ed. James Phelan. Columbus: Ohio State UP, 1989, 162–85.

Froula, Christine. *Virginia Woolf and the Bloomsbury Avant-Garde: War, Civilization, Modernity*. New York: Columbia UP, 2005.

Gabler, Hans Walter. "A Tale of Two Texts: Or, How One Might Edit Virginia Woolf's *To the Lighthouse*." *Woolf Studies Annual* 10 (2004): 1–29.

Gerzina, Gretchen. "Bushmen and Blackface: Bloomsbury and 'Race.'" *South Carolina Review* 38.2 (2006): 46–64.

Gillespie, Diane. *The Sisters' Arts: The Writing and Painting of Virginia Woolf and Vanessa Bell*. Syracuse, Syracuse UP, 1988.

Goldman, Jane. *The Feminist Aesthetics of Virginia Woolf: Modernism, Post-Impressionism, and the Politics of the Visual*. Cambridge: Cambridge UP, 1998.

———. *'With You in the Hebrides': Virginia Woolf and Scotland*. London: Cecil Woolf, 2013.

———. ed. *Virginia Woolf: To the Lighthouse, The Waves*. Columbia Critical Guides. New York: Columbia UP, 1998.

Haule, James M. *"To the Lighthouse* and the Great War: Evidence of Virginia Woolf's Revisions of 'Time Passes.'" In *Virginia Woolf and War: Fiction, Reality, and Myth*. Ed. Mark Hussey. Syracuse: Syracuse UP, 1991, 164–79.

Henry, Holly. *Virginia Woolf and the Discourse of Science: The Aesthetics of Astronomy*. Cambridge: Cambridge UP, 2003.

Högberg, Elsa. *Virginia Woolf and the Ethics of Intimacy*. New York: Bloomsbury, 2020.

Humm, Maggie. *Modernist Women and Visual Cultures: Virginia Woolf, Vanessa Bell, Photography and Cinema*. New Brunswick: Rutgers UP, 2003.

Hussey, Mark. *Virginia Woolf A to Z: The Essential Reference to Her Life and Writings*. Oxford: Oxford UP, 1995.

Hussey, Mark, and Peter Shillingsburg. "The Composition, Revision, Printing and Publication of *To the Lighthouse*." Pamela L. Caughie, Nick Hayward, Mark Hussey, Peter Shillingsburg, and George K. Thiruvathukal, eds. Woolf Online.

Jacobus, Mary. "'The Third Stroke': Reading Woolf with Freud." *Grafts: Feminist Cultural Criticism*. Ed. Susan Sheridan. London: Verso, 1988, 93–110.

Kopley, Emily. *Virginia Woolf and Poetry*. Oxford: Oxford UP, 2021.

Lee, Hermione. *Virginia Woolf*. New York: Knopf, 1997.

Levenback, Karen. *Virginia Woolf and the Great War.* Syracuse: Syracuse UP, 1999.

Light, Alison. *Mrs. Woolf and the Servants: An Intimate History of Domestic Life in Bloomsbury.* New York: Bloomsbury, 2010.

Lilienfeld, Jane. "'The Deceptiveness of Beauty': Mother Love and Mother Hate in *To the Lighthouse.*" *Twentieth Century Literature* 23:3 (Oct. 1977): 345–76.

Mackin, Timothy. "Private Worlds, Public Minds: Woolf, Russell and Photographic Vision." *Journal of Modern Literature* 33.3 (2010): 112–130.

Majumdar, Robin, and Allen McLaurin, eds. *Virginia Woolf: The Critical Heritage.* London and Boston: Routledge and Kegan Paul, 1975.

Marcus, Jane. *Hearts of Darkness: White Women Write Race.* New Brunswick: Rutgers UP, 2004.

———. *Virginia Woolf and the Languages of Patriarchy.* Bloomington: Indiana UP, 1987.

Marcus, Laura, ed. *Virginia Woolf,* 2nd ed. Tavistock, Devon: Northcote, 2004.

McNees, Eleanor, ed. *Virginia Woolf: Critical Assessments,* 4 vols. Mountfield: Helm Information, 1994.

McNees, Eleanor, and Sara Veglahn, eds. *Woolf Editing/Editing Woolf: Selected Papers from the Eighteenth Annual Conference on Virginia Woolf.* Clemson: Clemson U Digital P, 2009.

Nussbaum, Martha C. "The Window: Knowledge of Other Minds in Virginia Woolf's *To the Lighthouse.*" *New Literary History* 26.4 (1995): 731–53.

Pearson, Nels. "Recovering Islands: Scotland, Ocean, and Archipelago in *To the Lighthouse.*" *Twentieth Century Literature* 64:3 (Sept. 2018): 347–70.

Pease, Alison, ed. *Cambridge Companion to* To the Lighthouse. Cambridge: Cambridge UP, 2015.

Phillips, Kathy J. *Virginia Woolf Against Empire.* Knoxville: U of Tennessee P, 1994.

Raitt, Suzanne. *Vita & Virginia: The Work and Friendship of Vita Sackville-West and Virginia Woolf.* Oxford: Oxford UP, 1993.

Randall, Bryony, and Jane Goldman, eds., *Virginia Woolf in Context.* Cambridge: Cambridge UP, 2012.

Reid, Panthea. *Art and Affection: A Life of Virginia Woolf.* Oxford: Oxford UP, 1996.

Rubenstein, Roberta. "'I meant *nothing* by The Lighthouse': Virginia Woolf's Poetics of Negation." *Journal of Modern Literature* 31.4 (2008): 36–53.

Ruotolo, Lucio P. *The Interrupted Moment: A View of Virginia Woolf's Novels.* Stanford: Stanford UP, 1986.

Scott, Bonnie Kime. *In the Hollow of the Wave: Virginia Woolf and Modernist Uses of Nature.* Charlottesville: U of Virginia P, 2012.

Sellers, Susan, ed. *The Cambridge Companion to Virginia Woolf,* 2nd ed. Cambridge: Cambridge UP, 2010.

Seshagiri, Urmila. *Race and the Modernist Imagination.* Ithaca: Cornell UP, 2010.

Spalding, Frances. *Virginia Woolf: Art, Life and Vision.* London: National Portrait Gallery, 2014.

Spivak, Gayatri C. "Unmaking and Making in *To the Lighthouse.*" In *Women and Language in Literature and Society.* Ed. Sally McConnell-Ginet, Ruth Borker, and Nelly Furman. New York: Praeger, 1980, pp. 310–27.

Tickner, Lisa. "Vanessa Bell: *Studland Beach,* Domesticity, and 'Significant Form.'" *Representations* 65 (Winter 1999): 63–92.

Winston, Janet. "'Something Out of Harmony': *To the Lighthouse* and the Subject(s) of Empire." *Woolf Studies Annual* 2 (1996): 39–70.

———. *Woolf's To the Lighthouse: A Reader's Guide.* London: Continuum, 2009.

Wurtz, James F. "'I Have Had My Vision': Empire and the Aesthetic in Woolf's *To the Lighthouse.*" *Woolf Studies Annual* 16 (2010): 95–110.

Zwerdling, Alex. *Virginia Woolf and the Real World.* Berkeley: U of California P, 1986.